CAN'T LOSE YOU

VOL. 3

WANN

D1430659

NETCOMICS

Can't Lose You Vol. 3

Story and Art by Wann

English translation rights in USA, Canada, UK, NZ,
Australia arranged by Ecomix Media Company
395-21 Seogyo-dong, Mapo-gu, Seoul, Korea 121-840
info@ecomixmedia.com

- Produced by **Ecomix Media Company**
- Translator **Jeanne**
- Editors **Nic Anders, Ernest Woo**
- Managing Editor **Soyoung Jung**
- Graphic Designer **Soohyun Park, HyeKyoung Choi**
- Pre-Press Manager **Youngsook Hwang**
- President & Publisher **Heewoon Chung**

NETCOMICS

P.O.Box 16484, Jersey City, NJ 07306
info@netcomics.com
www.NETCOMICS.com

ISBN: 1-60009-041-9

First printing: August 2006
10 9 8 7 6 5 4 3 2 1
Printed in Korea

CONTENTS

The story so far...

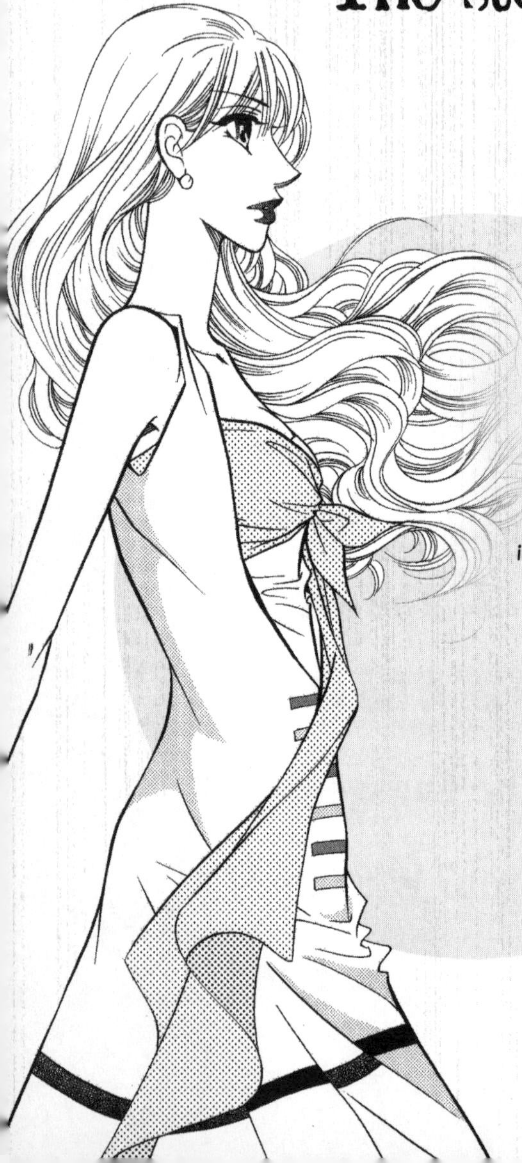

Yooi is a desperate girl working day and night to earn pennies in hopes of one day paying off her father's debts and reuniting their family. Lida comes from privilege and excess, the heiress to a huge fortune and a marriage match she cannot wait to consummate. But when the two girls meet and discover the one thing they have in common is their identical faces, their lives take an unexpected turn. As Yooi accepts the irresistible offer of becoming Lida's double, she finds herself in over her head, being chased by assassins and falling head over heels for Lida's fiancé, Gaon. Lida goes abroad to take cover from the unknown blackmailer who is after her life, leaving impoverished Yooi behind to secretly take her place.

The story so far...

To ensure Yooi's safety, she is forbidden from leaving the luxurious mansion, and is kept under the watchful eyes of Lida's faithful bodyguard, Ilya. Although she is adept at the various kinds of side jobs she held to pay off her father's debts, Yooi can't seem to get used to the challenging daily routine of a millionnairess. Tired from being cooped up all the time, Yooi sneaks out to a theme park with Gaon, where they are attacked by a sniper. Yooi is eventually saved by her bodyguard, only to be kidnapped again on her way back home! Meanwhile in a foreign land, Lida feels anxiety over her decision to leave Yooi with Gaon.

From the Author

The weather is much too hot.... It's drought season.
As for the biggest news that's happened to me...
Hahaha... I'm going to have a baby!
After getting married last year, this will be my first child.

Although it's hard to sit at a desk because of morning
sickness, I'm fervently working on the manuscript as well as
becoming a mom.

Please pray that the child in my belly will grow
uneventfully and be able to meet with the world next year.
Thank you.

Volume 3... We've arrived at the middle of this piece.
Please look forward to the climax that waits ahead.

September 2006
WANN

13. LIDA

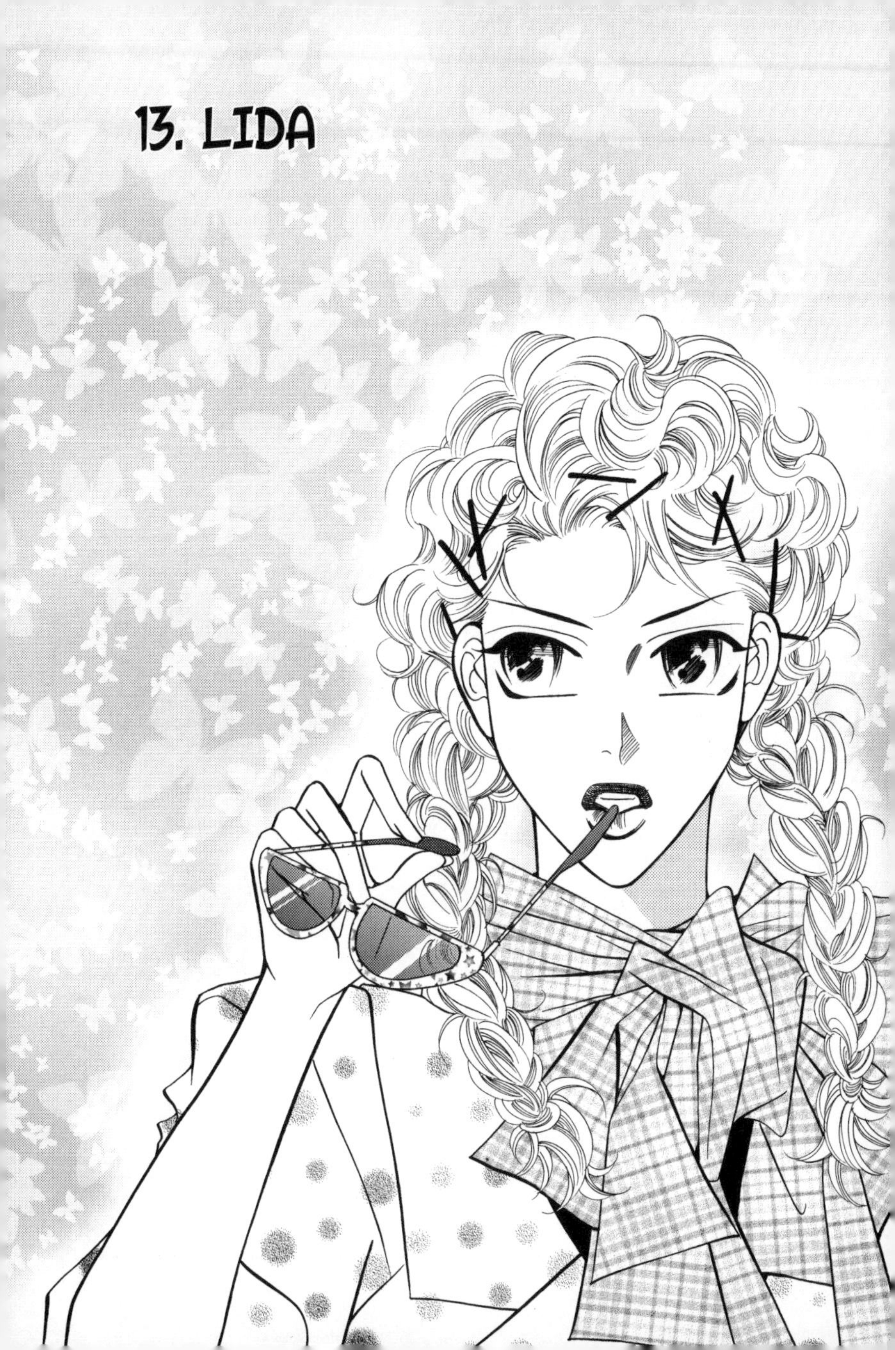

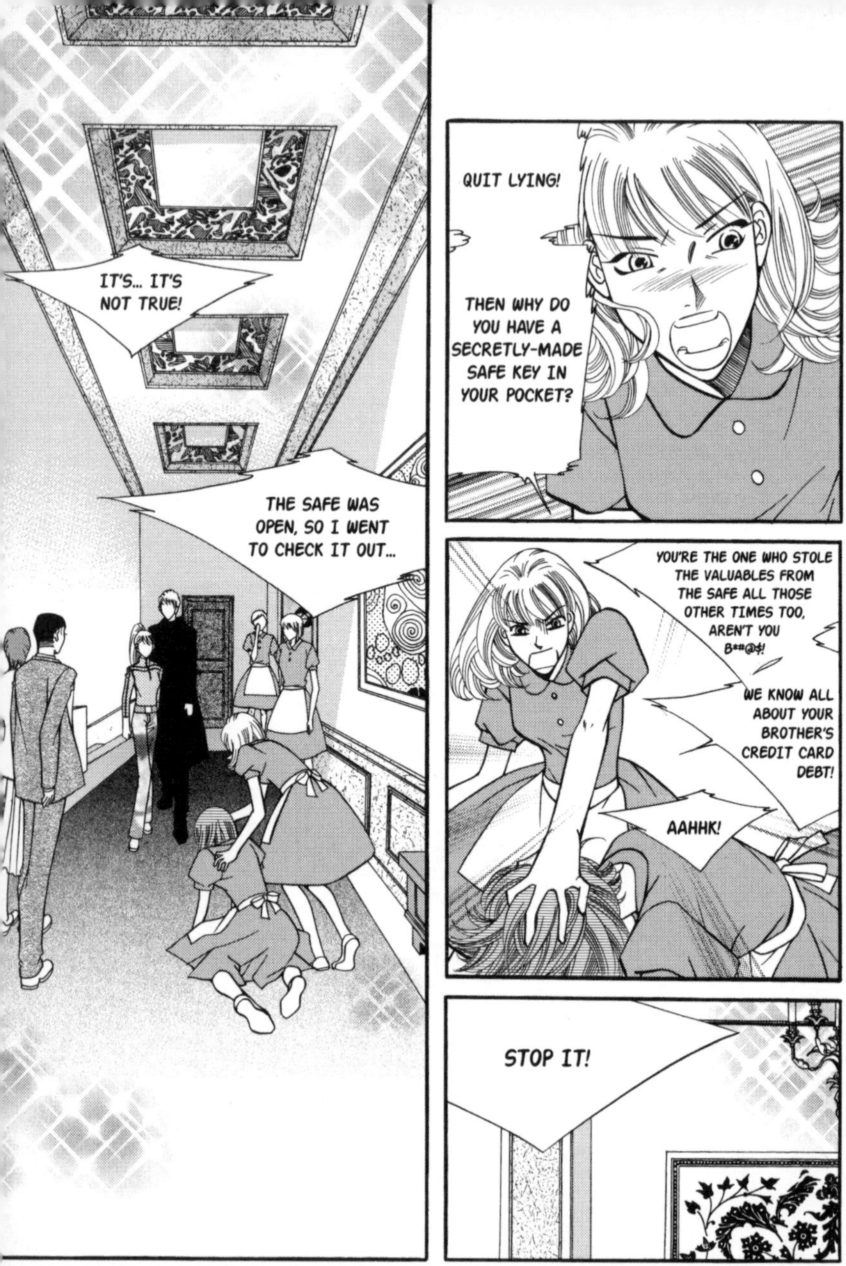
IT'S... IT'S NOT TRUE!
THE SAFE WAS OPEN, SO I WENT TO CHECK IT OUT...
QUIT LYING!
THEN WHY DO YOU HAVE A SECRETLY-MADE SAFE KEY IN YOUR POCKET?
YOU'RE THE ONE WHO STOLE THE VALUABLES FROM THE SAFE ALL THOSE OTHER TIMES TOO, AREN'T YOU B**@$!
WE KNOW ALL ABOUT YOUR BROTHER'S CREDIT CARD DEBT!
AAHHK!
STOP IT!

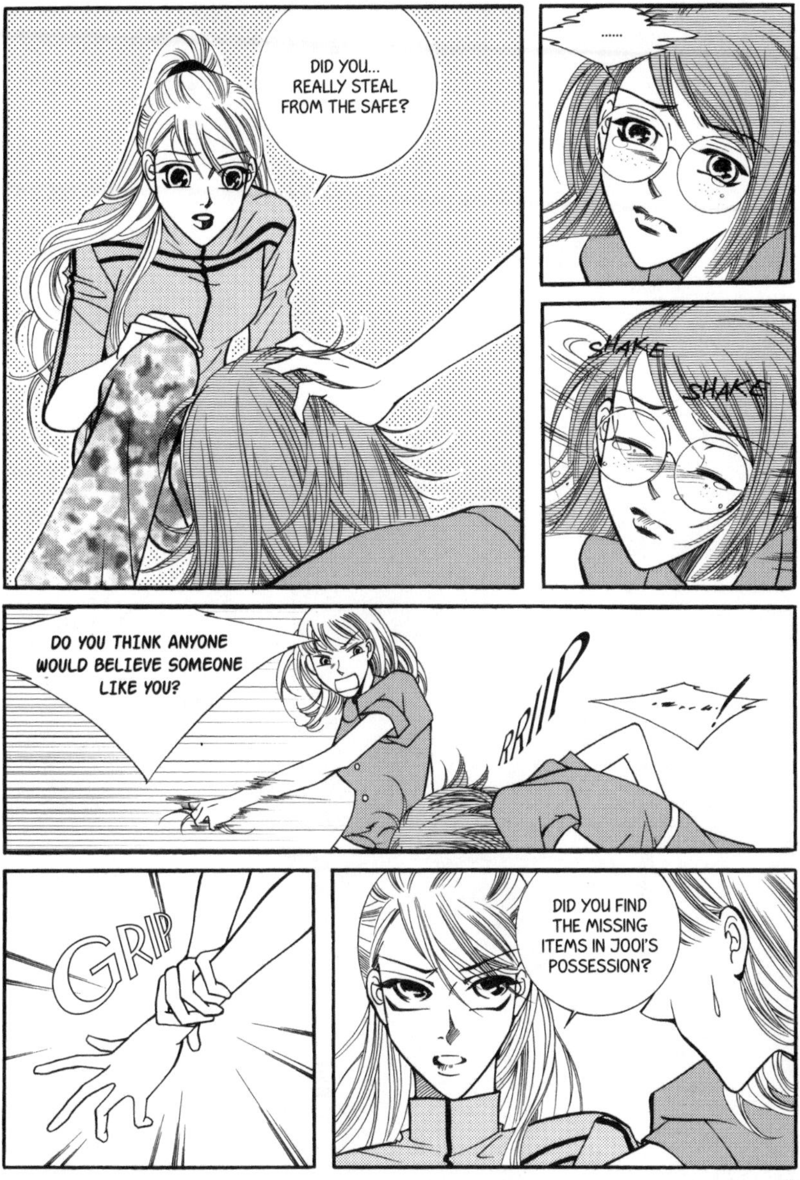

DID YOU... REALLY STEAL FROM THE SAFE?
......
SHAKE
SHAKE
DO YOU THINK ANYONE WOULD BELIEVE SOMEONE LIKE YOU?
RRIIP
......!
GRIP
DID YOU FIND THE MISSING ITEMS IN JOOI'S POSSESSION?

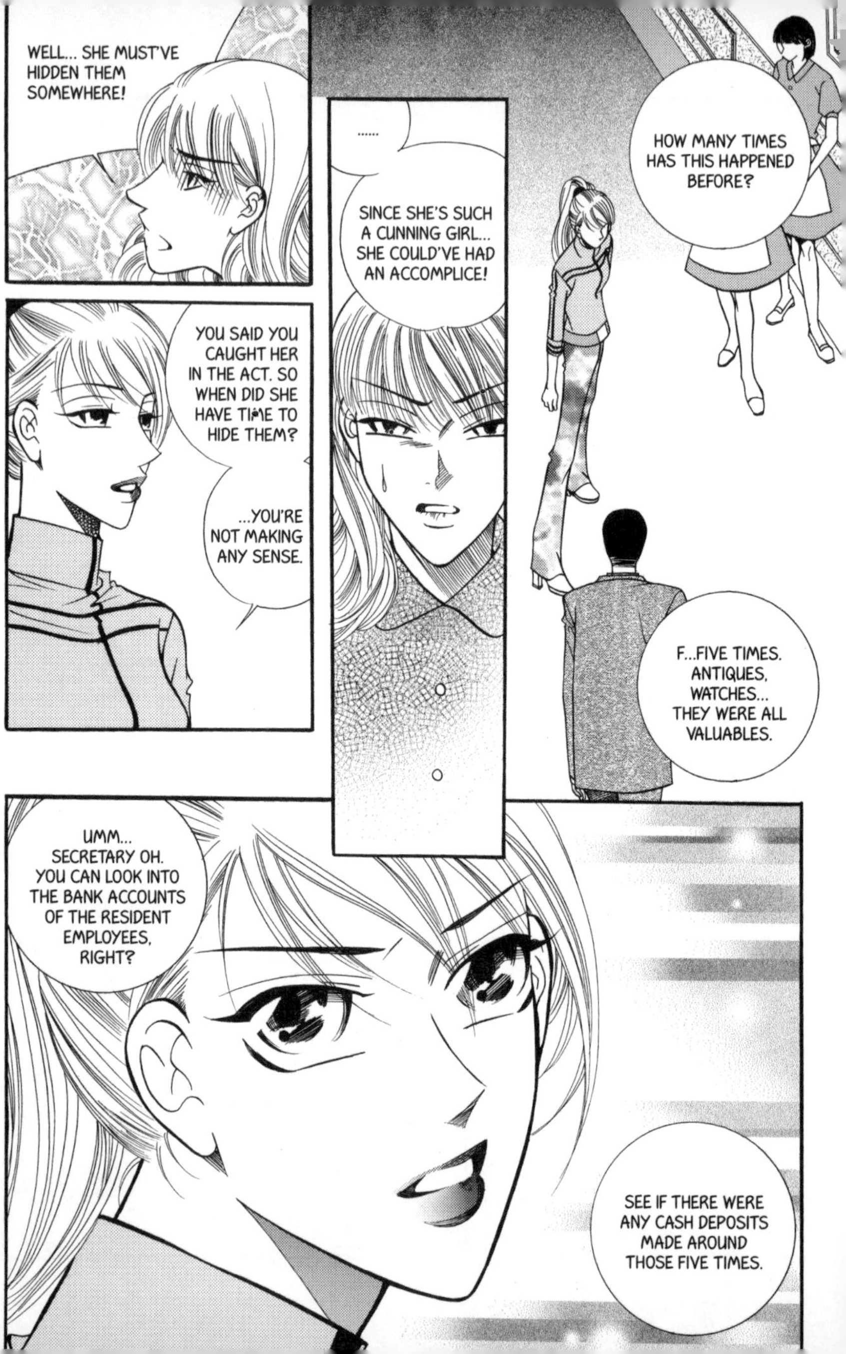
WELL... SHE MUST'VE HIDDEN THEM SOMEWHERE!
YOU SAID YOU CAUGHT HER IN THE ACT. SO WHEN DID SHE HAVE TIME TO HIDE THEM?
...YOU'RE NOT MAKING ANY SENSE.
......
SINCE SHE'S SUCH A CUNNING GIRL... SHE COULD'VE HAD AN ACCOMPLICE!
HOW MANY TIMES HAS THIS HAPPENED BEFORE?
F...FIVE TIMES. ANTIQUES, WATCHES... THEY WERE ALL VALUABLES.
UMM... SECRETARY OH. YOU CAN LOOK INTO THE BANK ACCOUNTS OF THE RESIDENT EMPLOYEES, RIGHT?
SEE IF THERE WERE ANY CASH DEPOSITS MADE AROUND THOSE FIVE TIMES.

......

THEN DO IT.

IF SOMEONE DID THIS BECAUSE SHE NEEDED THE MONEY, SHE WOULDN'T HAVE HAD TIME TO DISPOSE OF THE STOLEN VALUABLES AT HER LEISURE.

ONCE OR TWICE COULD BE A COINCIDENCE BUT NOT FIVE TIMES.

THAT WOULD BE POSSIBLE IF WE CALL THE POLICE AND ASK FOR AN INVESTIGATION, BUT...

BUT MY LADY...

YOU HATE HAVING THE POLICE IN THE HOUSE MORE THAN ANYTHING ELSE...

STOOM

WE HAVE CAUGHT THE SUSPECT, SO I WILL HANDLE THIS QUIETLY.

SQZZ...

WHY NOT LEAVE THIS TO ME.

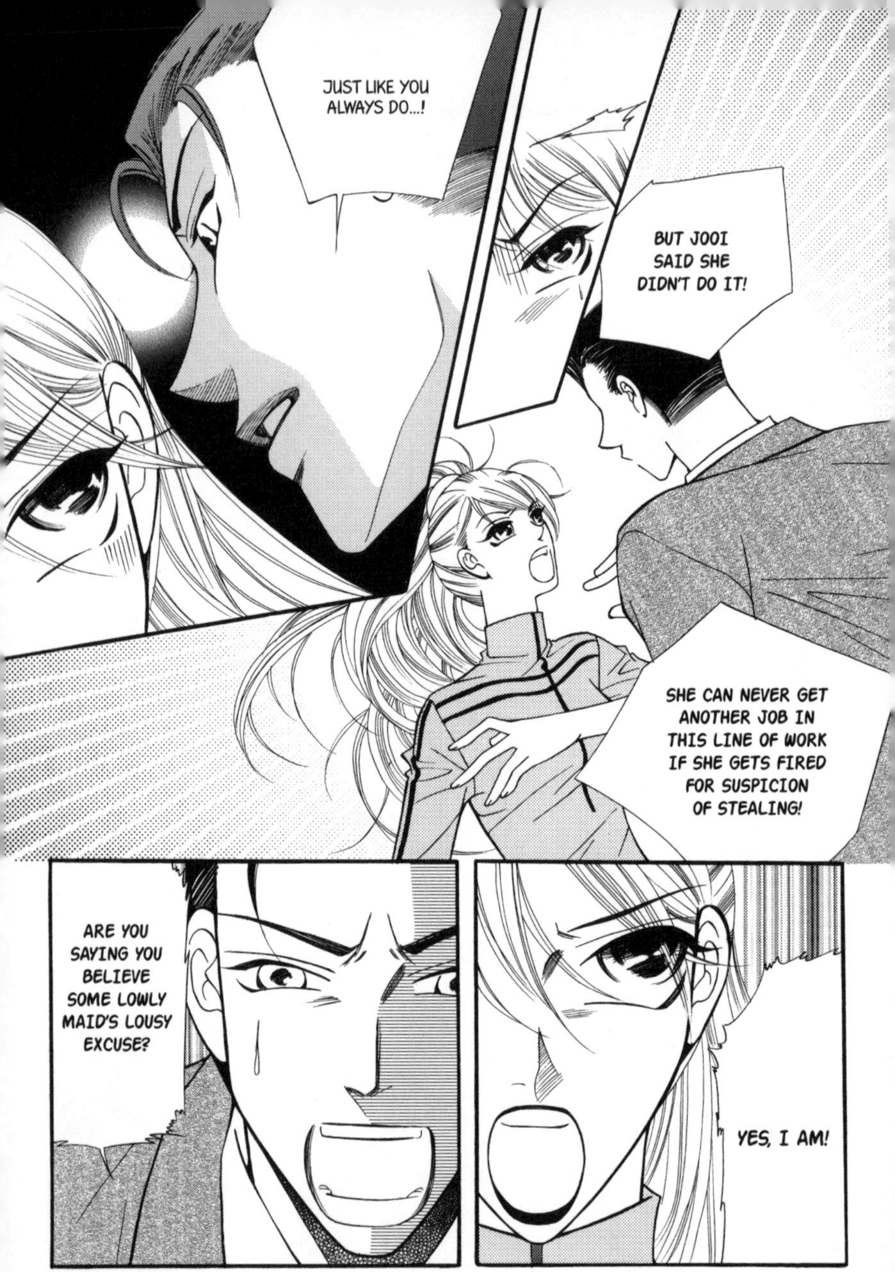
JUST LIKE YOU ALWAYS DO...!
BUT JOOI SAID SHE DIDN'T DO IT!
SHE CAN NEVER GET ANOTHER JOB IN THIS LINE OF WORK IF SHE GETS FIRED FOR SUSPICION OF STEALING!
ARE YOU SAYING YOU BELIEVE SOME LOWLY MAID'S LOUSY EXCUSE?
YES, I AM!

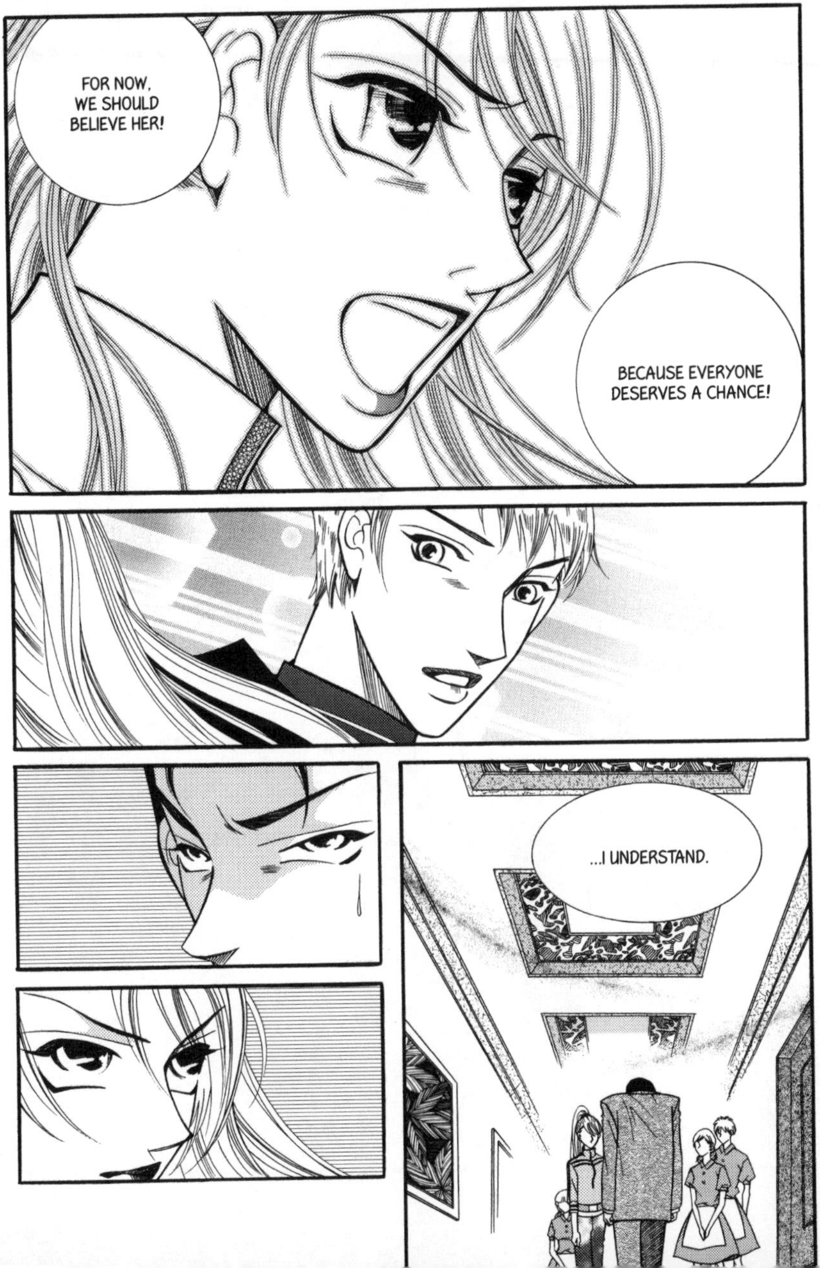
FOR NOW, WE SHOULD BELIEVE HER!
BECAUSE EVERYONE DESERVES A CHANCE!
...I UNDERSTAND.

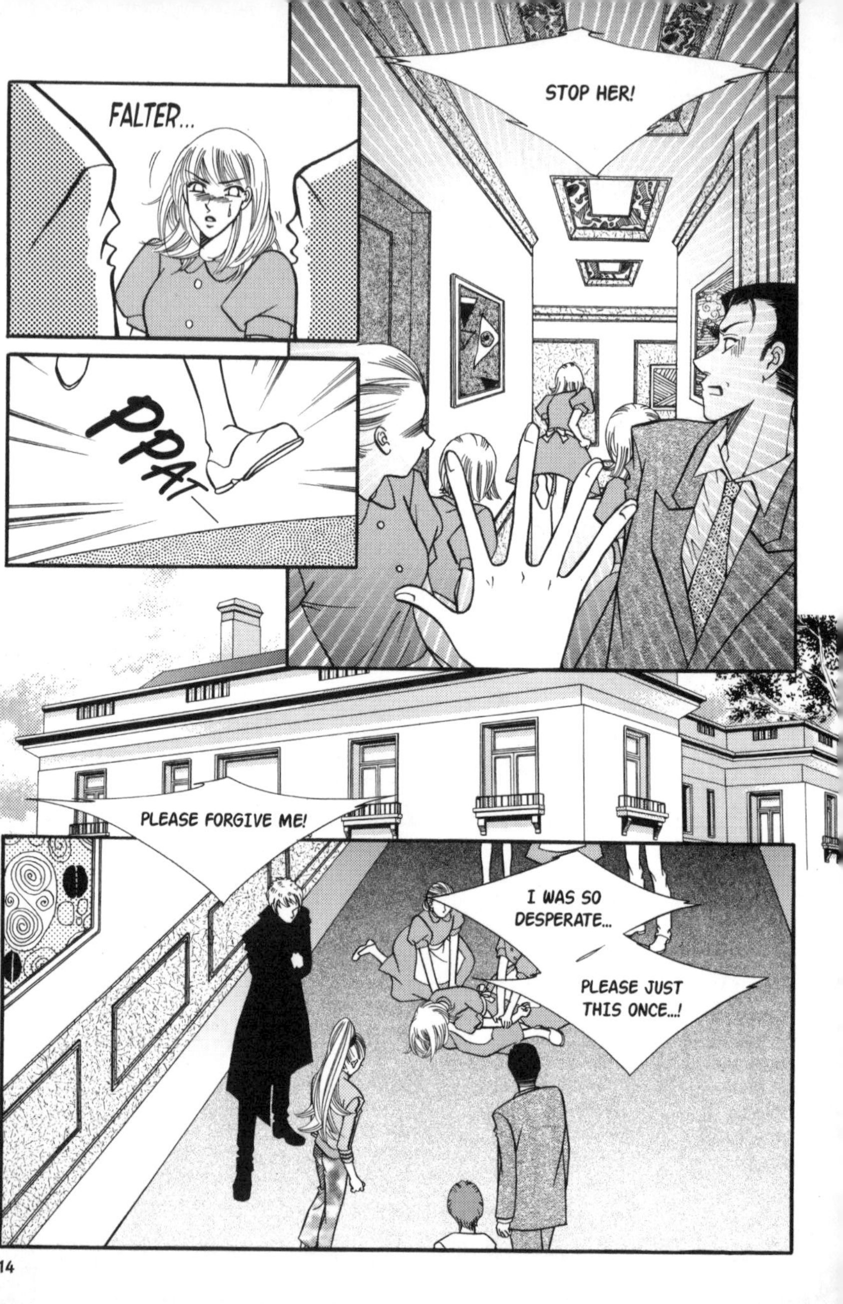
FALTER...
PPAT
STOP HER!
PLEASE FORGIVE ME!
I WAS SO DESPERATE...
PLEASE JUST THIS ONCE...!

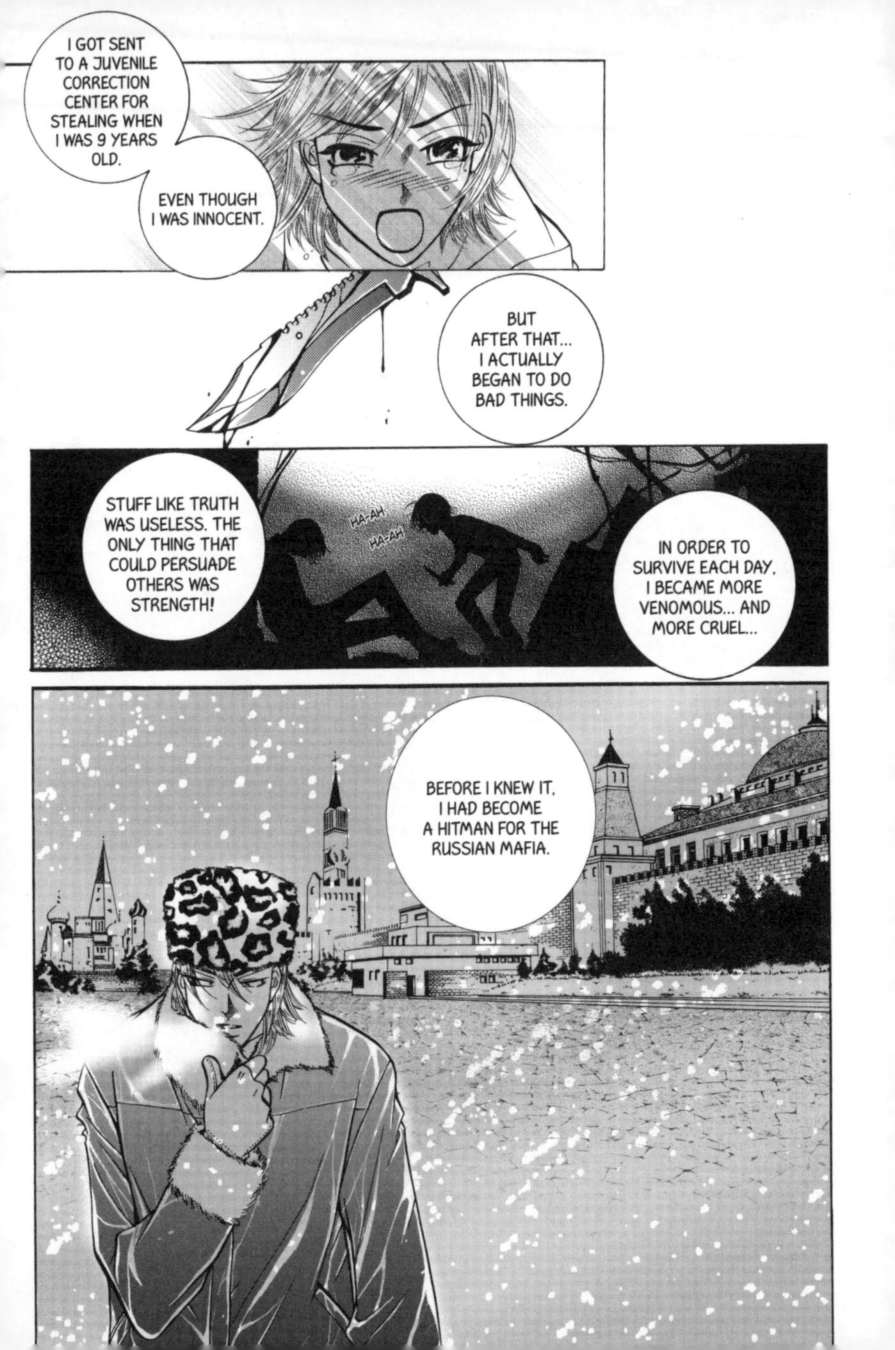

I GOT SENT TO A JUVENILE CORRECTION CENTER FOR STEALING WHEN I WAS 9 YEARS OLD.
EVEN THOUGH I WAS INNOCENT.
BUT AFTER THAT... I ACTUALLY BEGAN TO DO BAD THINGS.
STUFF LIKE TRUTH WAS USELESS. THE ONLY THING THAT COULD PERSUADE OTHERS WAS STRENGTH!
HA-AH
HA-AH
IN ORDER TO SURVIVE EACH DAY, I BECAME MORE VENOMOUS... AND MORE CRUEL...
BEFORE I KNEW IT, I HAD BECOME A HITMAN FOR THE RUSSIAN MAFIA.

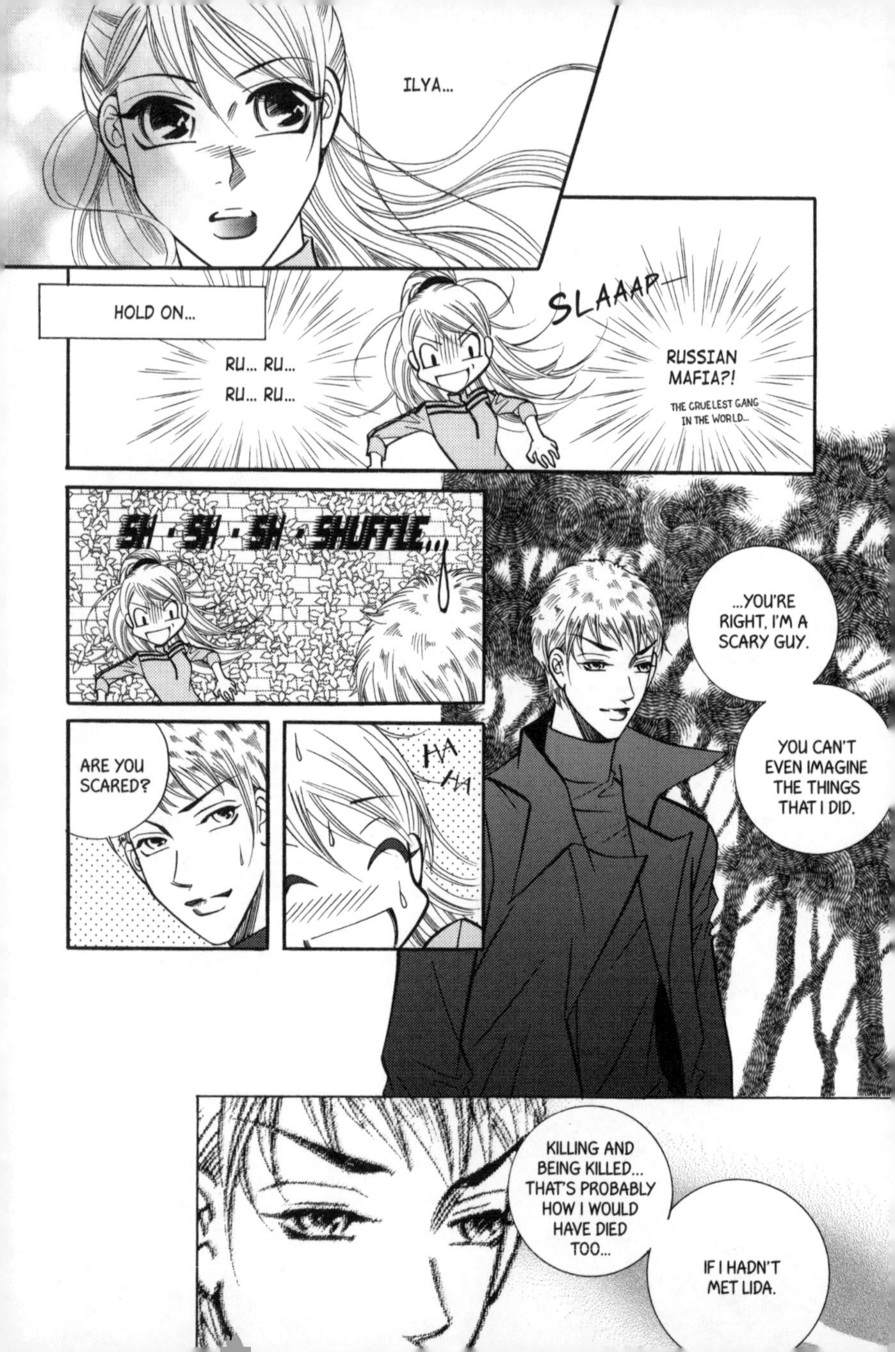
ILYA...
HOLD ON...
RU... RU...
RU... RU...
SLAAAP
RUSSIAN MAFIA?!
THE CRUELEST GANG IN THE WORLD...
SH · SH · SH · SHUFFLE...
ARE YOU SCARED?
HA HA
...YOU'RE RIGHT, I'M A SCARY GUY.
YOU CAN'T EVEN IMAGINE THE THINGS THAT I DID.
KILLING AND BEING KILLED... THAT'S PROBABLY HOW I WOULD HAVE DIED TOO...
IF I HADN'T MET LIDA.

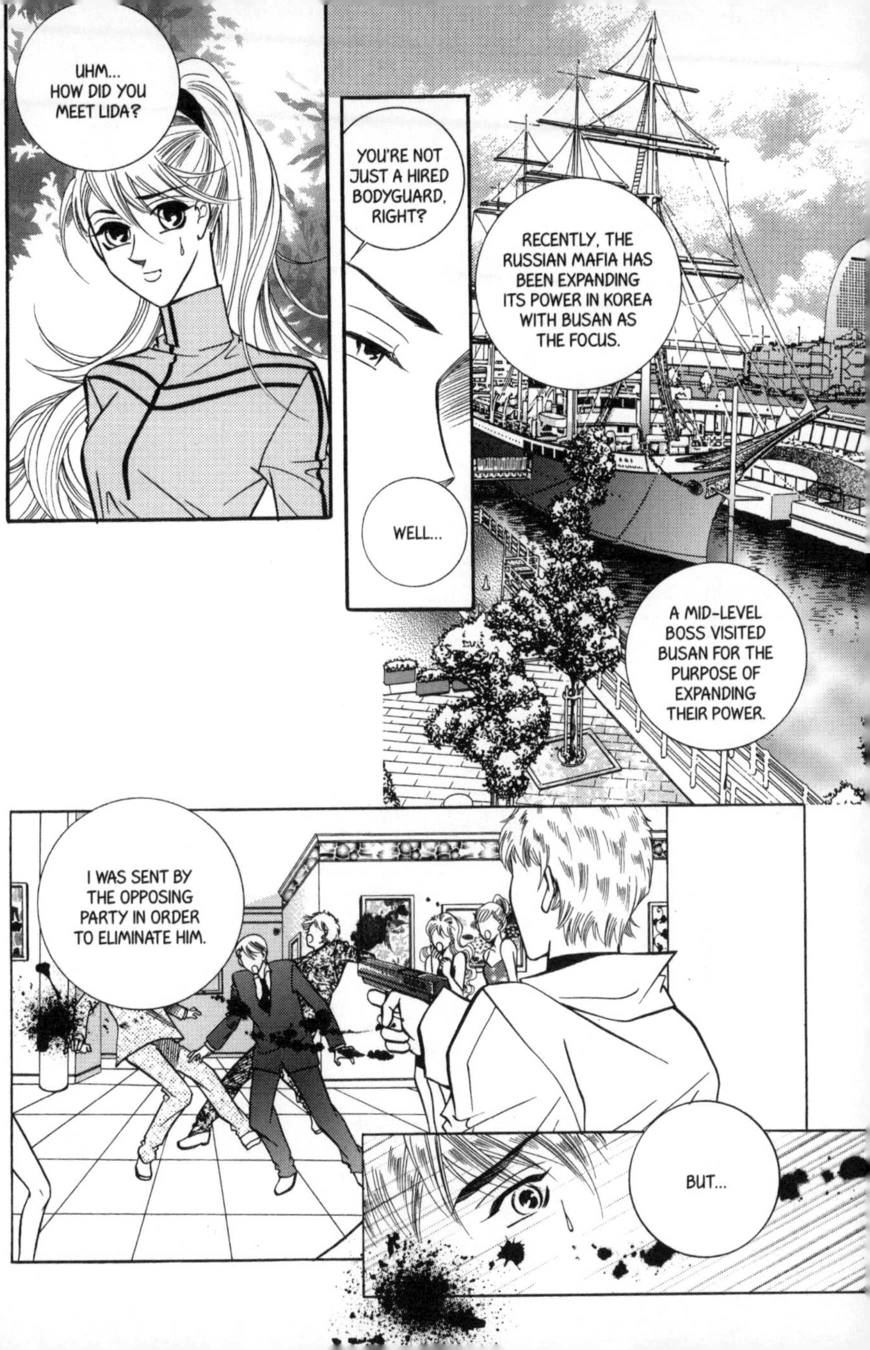
UHM... HOW DID YOU MEET LIDA?
YOU'RE NOT JUST A HIRED BODYGUARD, RIGHT?
WELL...
RECENTLY, THE RUSSIAN MAFIA HAS BEEN EXPANDING ITS POWER IN KOREA WITH BUSAN AS THE FOCUS.
A MID-LEVEL BOSS VISITED BUSAN FOR THE PURPOSE OF EXPANDING THEIR POWER.
I WAS SENT BY THE OPPOSING PARTY IN ORDER TO ELIMINATE HIM.
BUT...

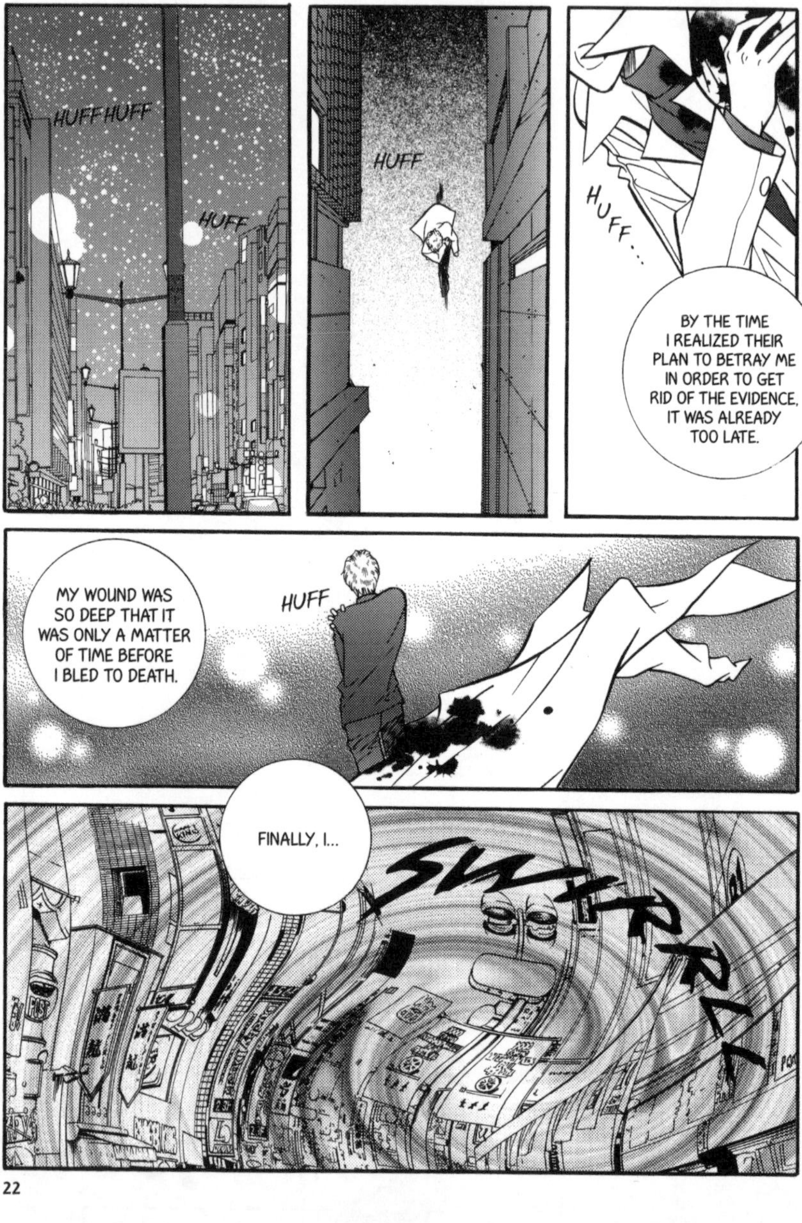

HUFF HUFF
HUFF
HUFF
HUFF...
BY THE TIME I REALIZED THEIR PLAN TO BETRAY ME IN ORDER TO GET RID OF THE EVIDENCE, IT WAS ALREADY TOO LATE.
MY WOUND WAS SO DEEP THAT IT WAS ONLY A MATTER OF TIME BEFORE I BLED TO DEATH.
HUFF
FINALLY, I...
SWIRRL

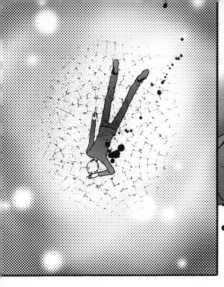

VROOOM

SQUEAL

KLIK

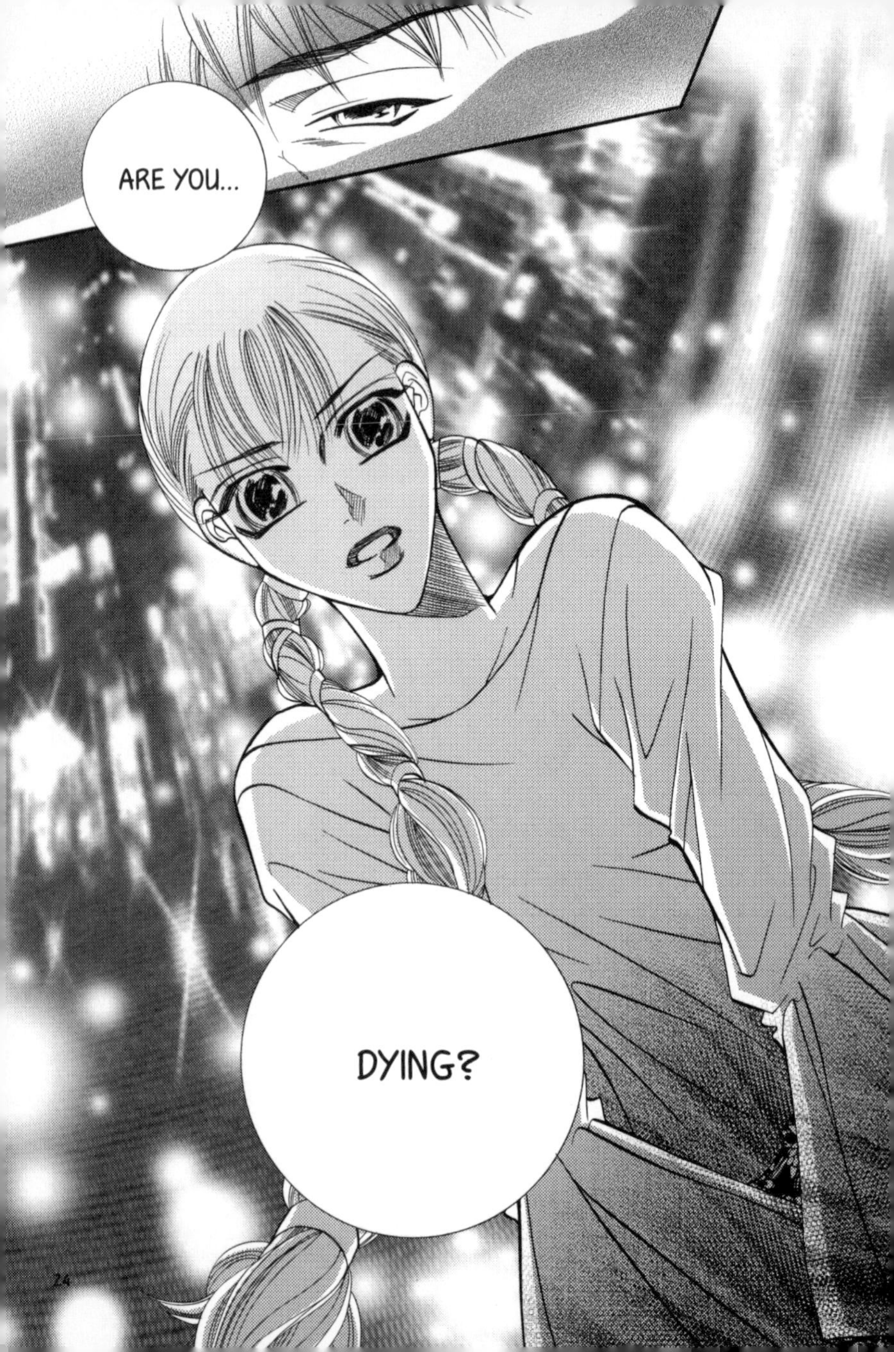
ARE YOU...
DYING?

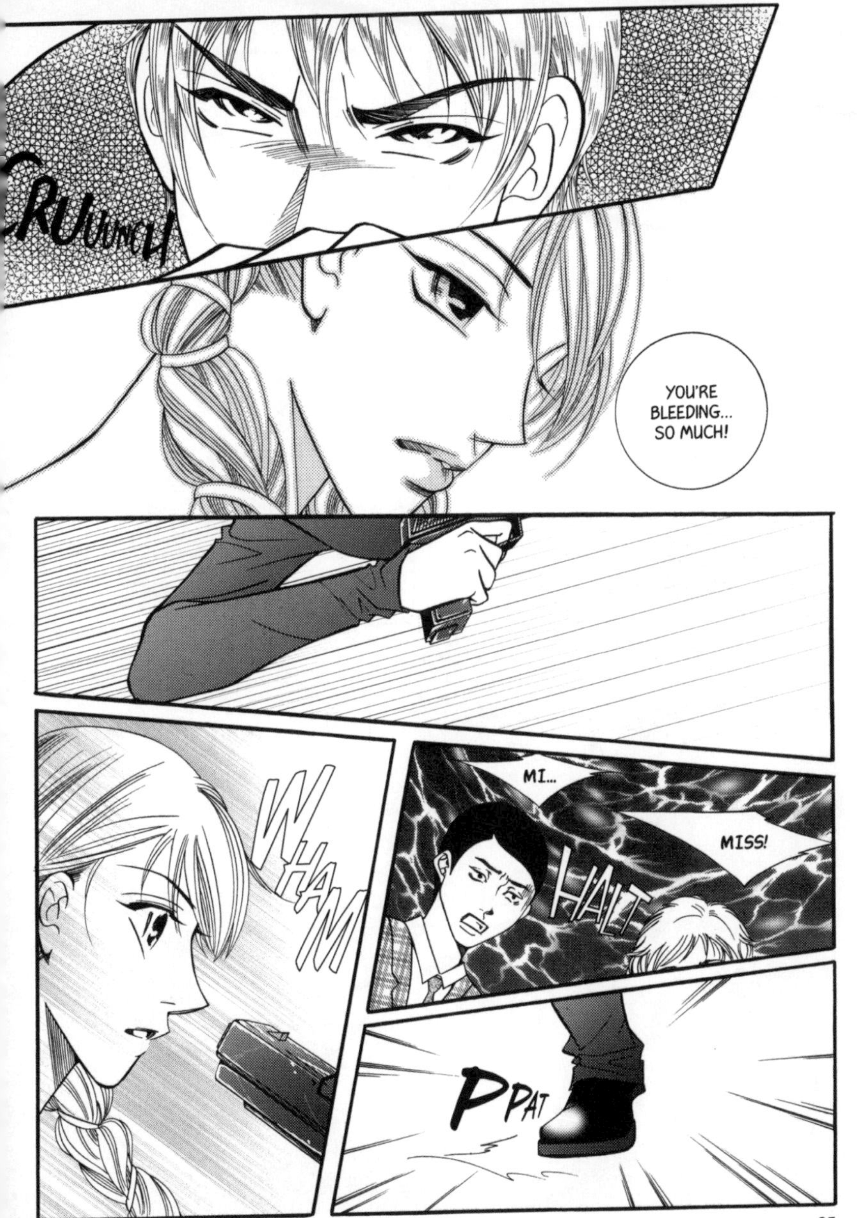
CRUUUNCH
YOU'RE BLEEDING... SO MUCH!
WHAM
MI...
MISS!
HALT
PPAT

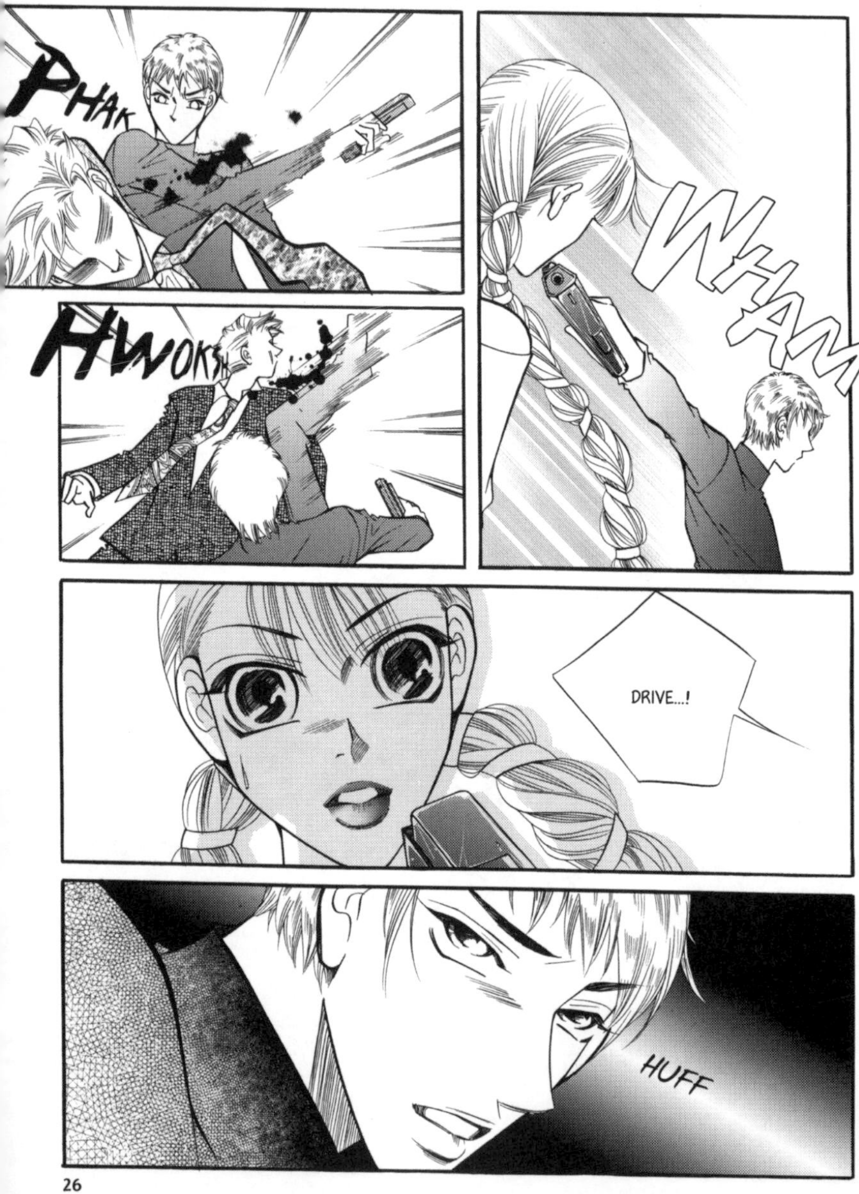
PHAK
WHAM
HWOKSH
DRIVE...!
HUFF

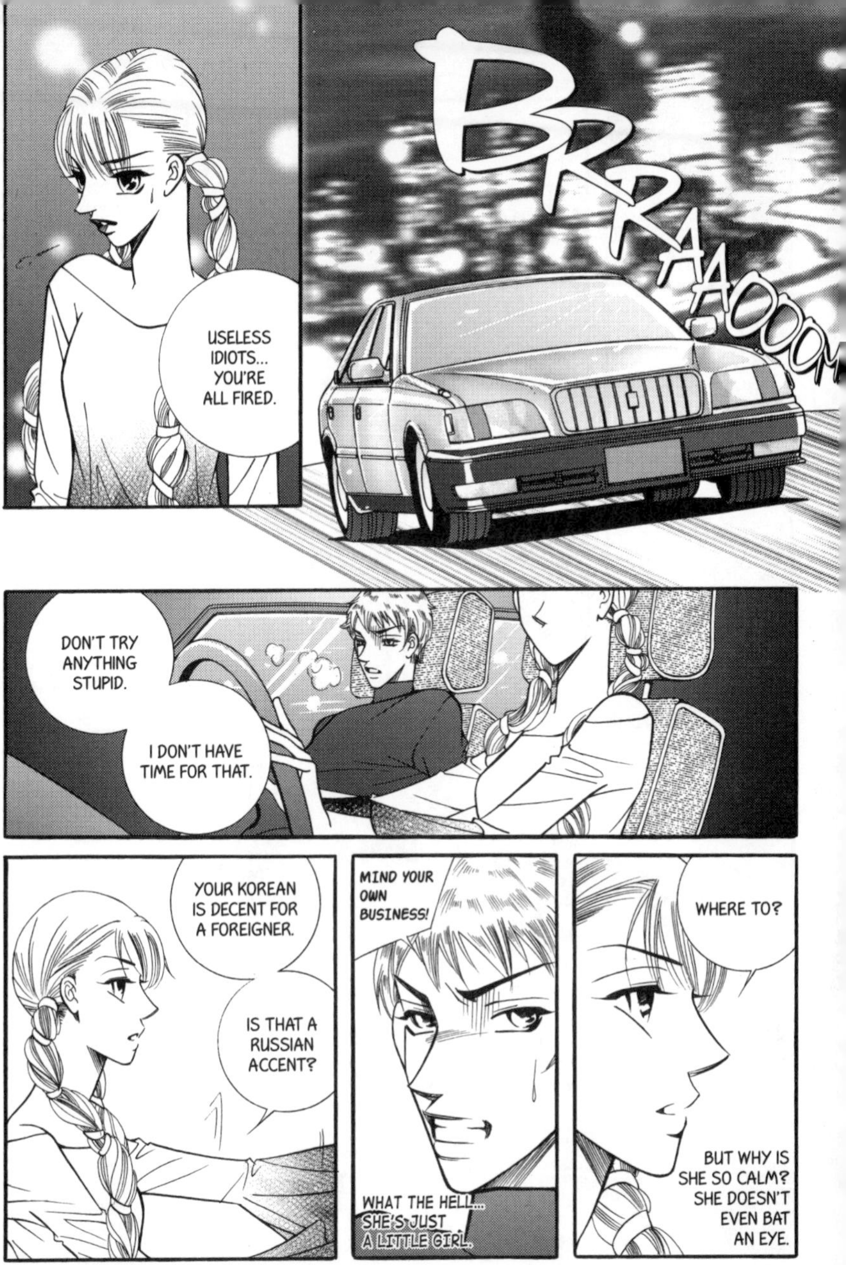
USELESS IDIOTS... YOU'RE ALL FIRED.
BRRAAOOOM
DON'T TRY ANYTHING STUPID.
I DON'T HAVE TIME FOR THAT.
YOUR KOREAN IS DECENT FOR A FOREIGNER.
IS THAT A RUSSIAN ACCENT?
MIND YOUR OWN BUSINESS!
WHAT THE HELL... SHE'S JUST A LITTLE GIRL.
WHERE TO?
BUT WHY IS SHE SO CALM? SHE DOESN'T EVEN BAT AN EYE.

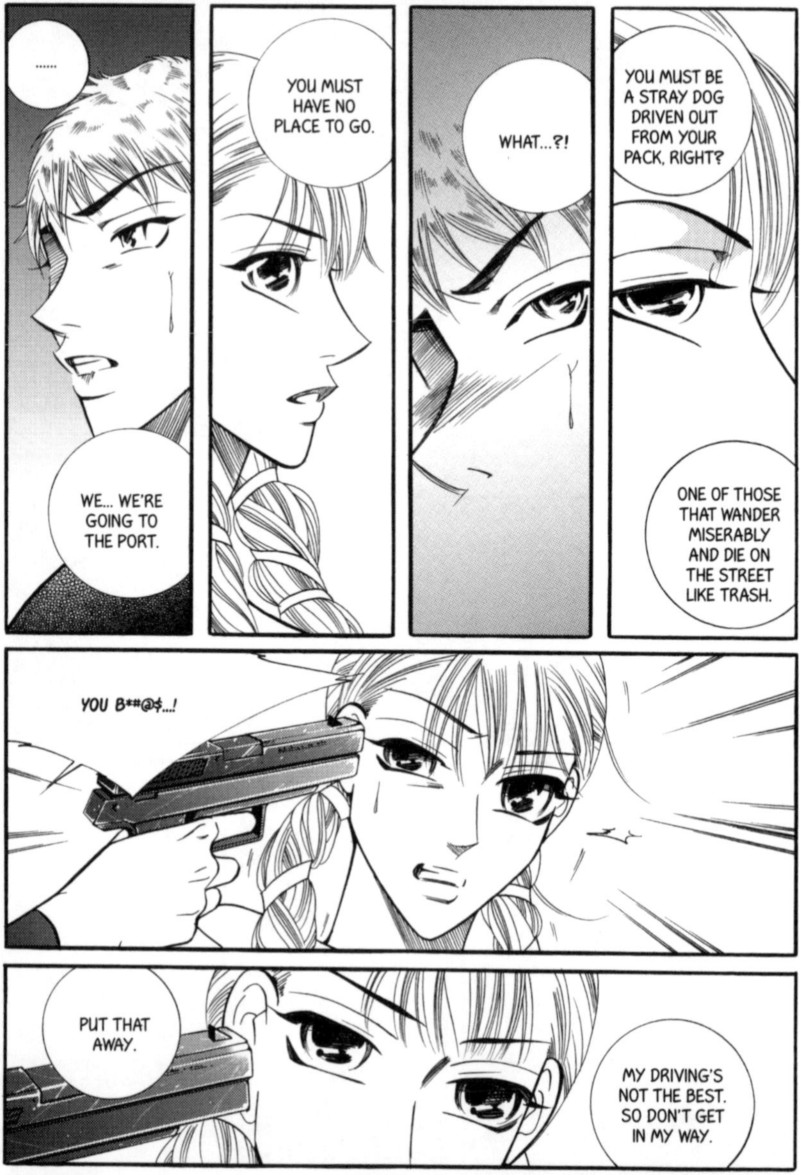
......
WE... WE'RE GOING TO THE PORT.
YOU MUST HAVE NO PLACE TO GO.
WHAT...?!
YOU MUST BE A STRAY DOG DRIVEN OUT FROM YOUR PACK, RIGHT?
ONE OF THOSE THAT WANDER MISERABLY AND DIE ON THE STREET LIKE TRASH.
YOU B*#@$...!
PUT THAT AWAY.
MY DRIVING'S NOT THE BEST. SO DON'T GET IN MY WAY.

LIDA WAS 13 YEARS OLD THEN… AND SHE WAS ALREADY DRIVING…?!
DON'T' BE SO CYNICAL… MAYBE SHE LEARNED TO DRIVE JUST IN CASE
SHE WAS KIDNAPPED… OR SOMETHING LIKE THAT.

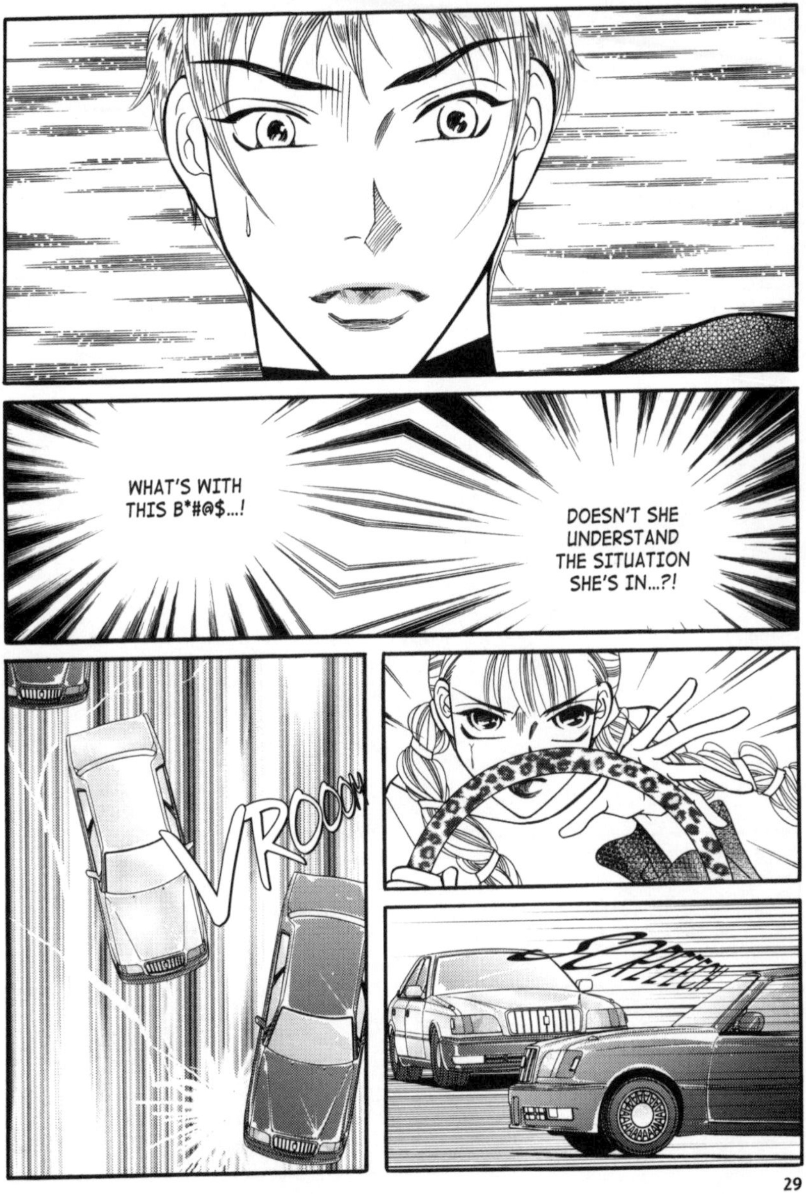
WHAT'S WITH THIS B*#@$...!
DOESN'T SHE UNDERSTAND THE SITUATION SHE'S IN...?!
VROOOM
SCREEECH

K THUNK

SON OF A B**@$!

WHY CAN'T YOU DIE QUIETLY INSTEAD OF ANNOYING US LIKE THIS...!

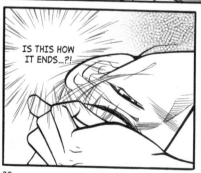

IS THIS HOW IT ENDS...?!

BOSS, WHAT SHOULD WE DO WITH THE GIRL?

IT'S NO GOOD TO LEAVE A WITNESS. BURY HER WITH HIM!

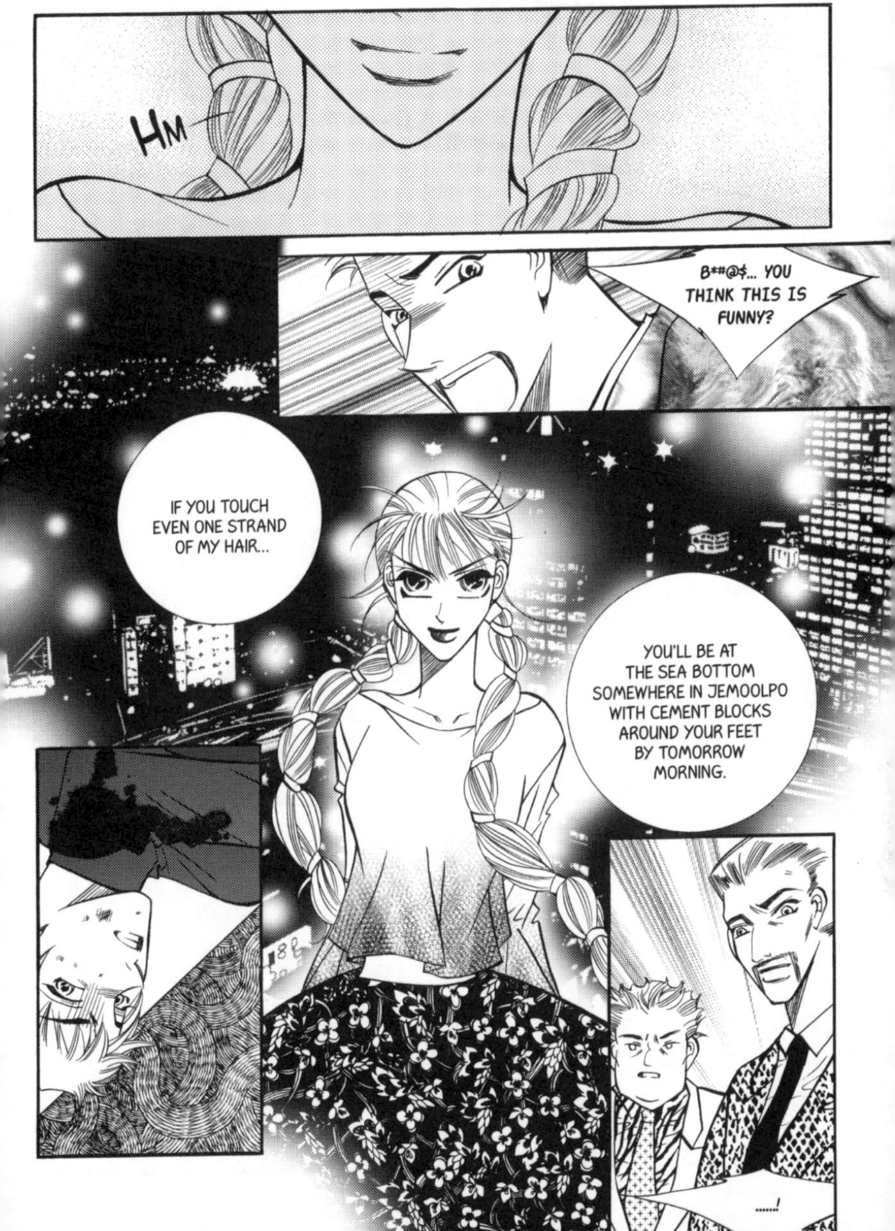
HM
B*#@$... YOU THINK THIS IS FUNNY?
IF YOU TOUCH EVEN ONE STRAND OF MY HAIR...
YOU'LL BE AT THE SEA BOTTOM SOMEWHERE IN JEMOOLPO WITH CEMENT BLOCKS AROUND YOUR FEET BY TOMORROW MORNING.
......!

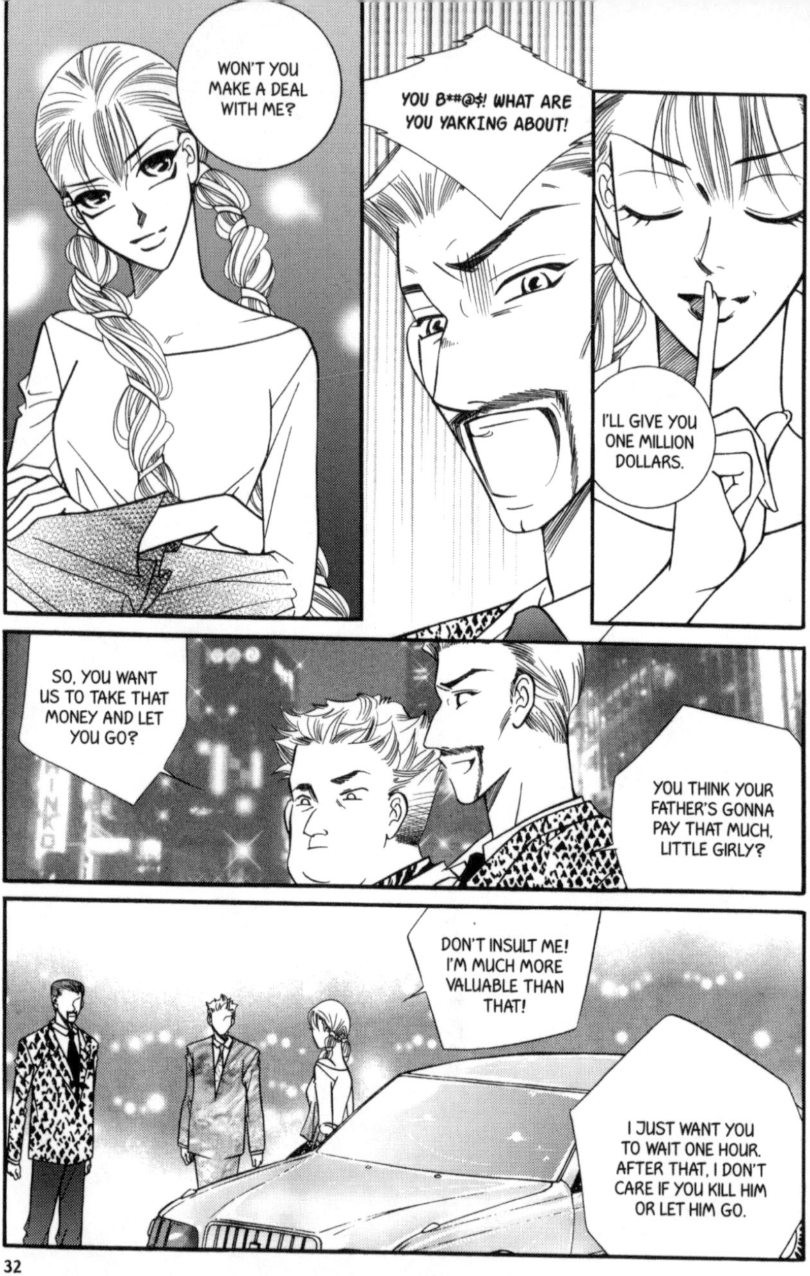
WON'T YOU MAKE A DEAL WITH ME?
YOU B**@$! WHAT ARE YOU YAKKING ABOUT!
I'LL GIVE YOU ONE MILLION DOLLARS.
SO, YOU WANT US TO TAKE THAT MONEY AND LET YOU GO?
YOU THINK YOUR FATHER'S GONNA PAY THAT MUCH, LITTLE GIRLY?
DON'T INSULT ME! I'M MUCH MORE VALUABLE THAN THAT!
I JUST WANT YOU TO WAIT ONE HOUR. AFTER THAT, I DON'T CARE IF YOU KILL HIM OR LET HIM GO.

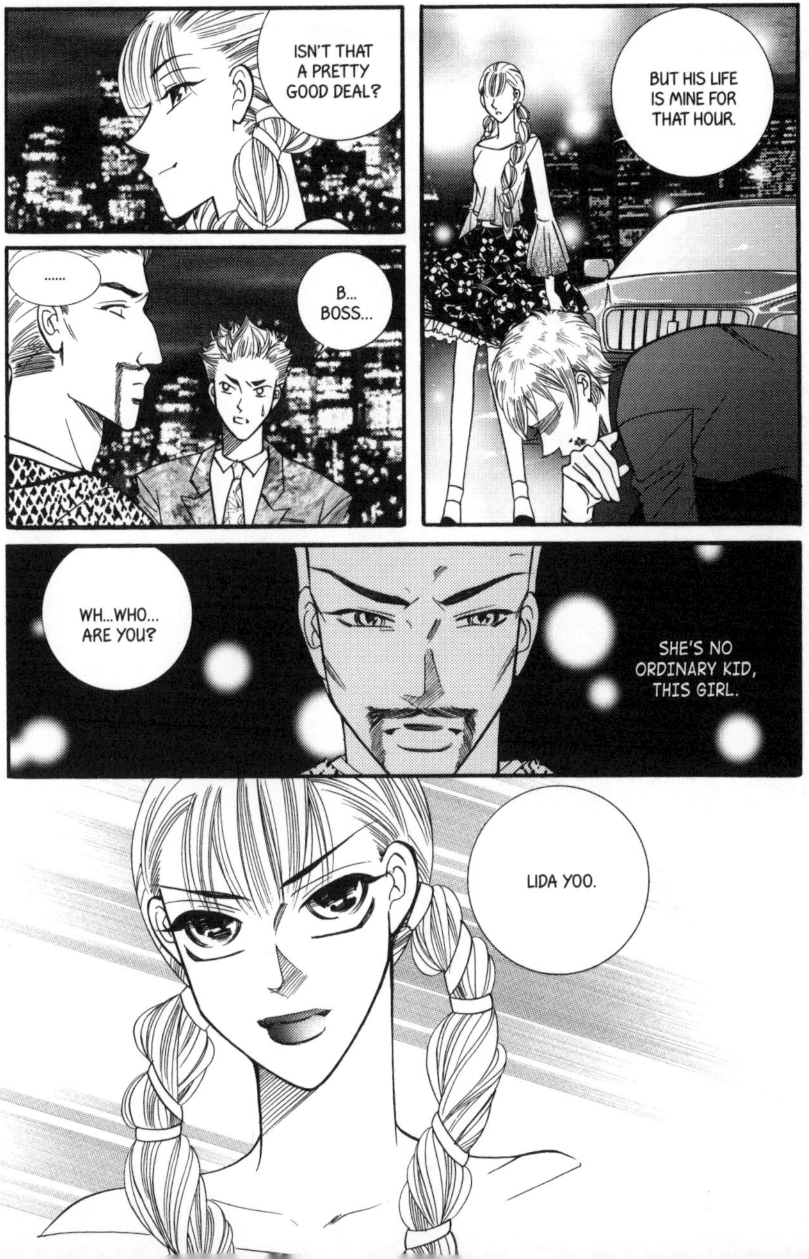
ISN'T THAT A PRETTY GOOD DEAL?
BUT HIS LIFE IS MINE FOR THAT HOUR.
......
B... BOSS...
WH...WHO... ARE YOU?
SHE'S NO ORDINARY KID, THIS GIRL.
LIDA YOO.

Wann is the Queen of Mistakes

WANN HAS ALWAYS BEEN GOOD AT SPILLING THINGS.
WOAH!
OH! TEACHER, WHAT ARE YOU DOING?
DRIIIIP
I SPILLED IT AGAIN!
BUT... THE SYMPTOMS WERE MORE SERIOUS FOR THIS DEADLINE.
REALLY... HOW MANY TIMES IS THIS!
LATER....
SNAP
SNAP
SPILL...
WIPE
WIPE
IT'S TOTALLY AUTOMATIC NOW....
IN THE END, THE STUDIO FOLKS EVEN GREW TO ENJOY IT.
DARN... I SHOULD'VE TAKEN A PICTURE.-- IT WAS SO BRILLIANT.
TEACH, VOLUME 3 MUST BE A HOT SELLER.

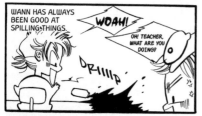

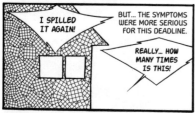

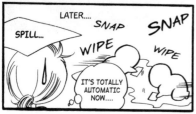

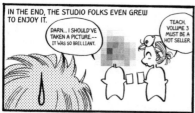

14. THE MASTER

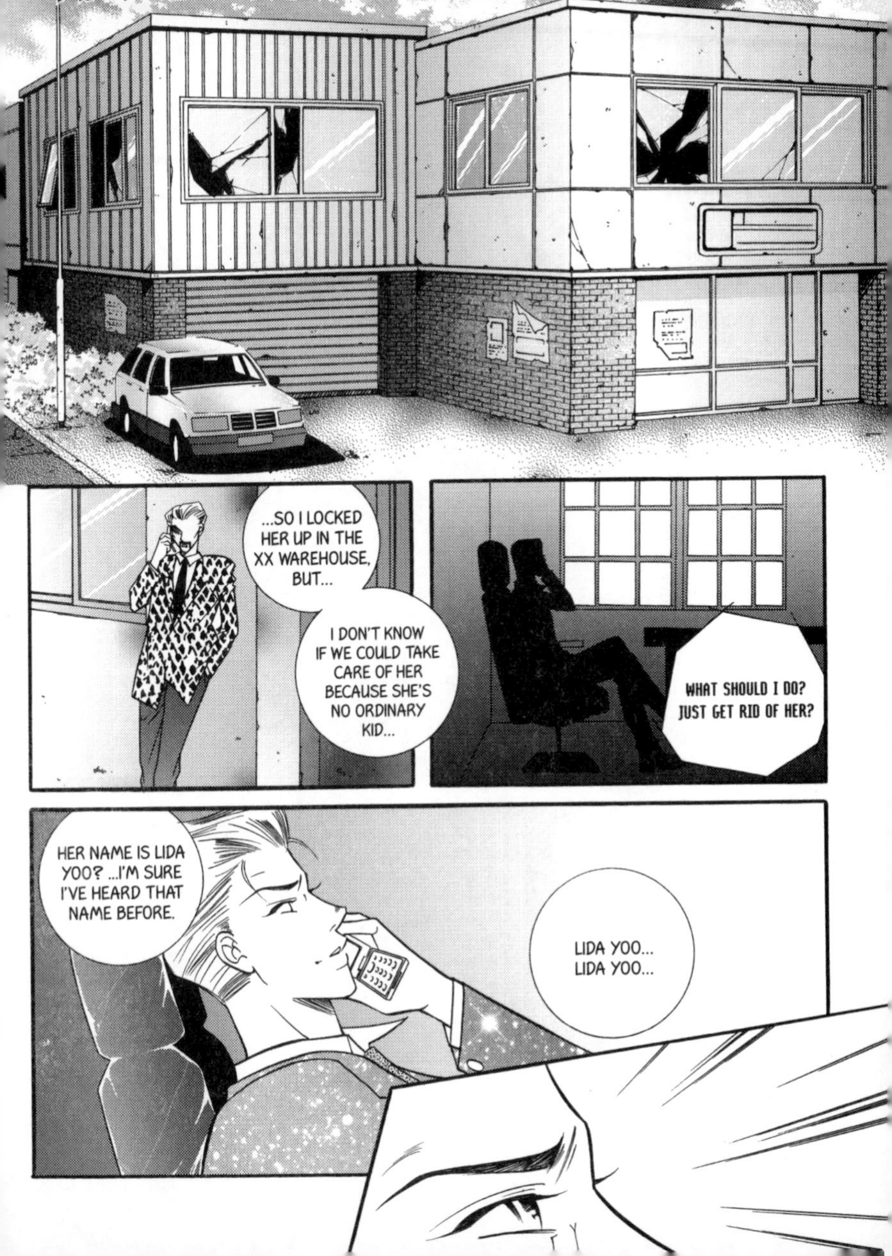
...SO I LOCKED HER UP IN THE XX WAREHOUSE, BUT...
I DON'T KNOW IF WE COULD TAKE CARE OF HER BECAUSE SHE'S NO ORDINARY KID...
WHAT SHOULD I DO? JUST GET RID OF HER?
HER NAME IS LIDA YOO? ...I'M SURE I'VE HEARD THAT NAME BEFORE.
LIDA YOO... LIDA YOO...

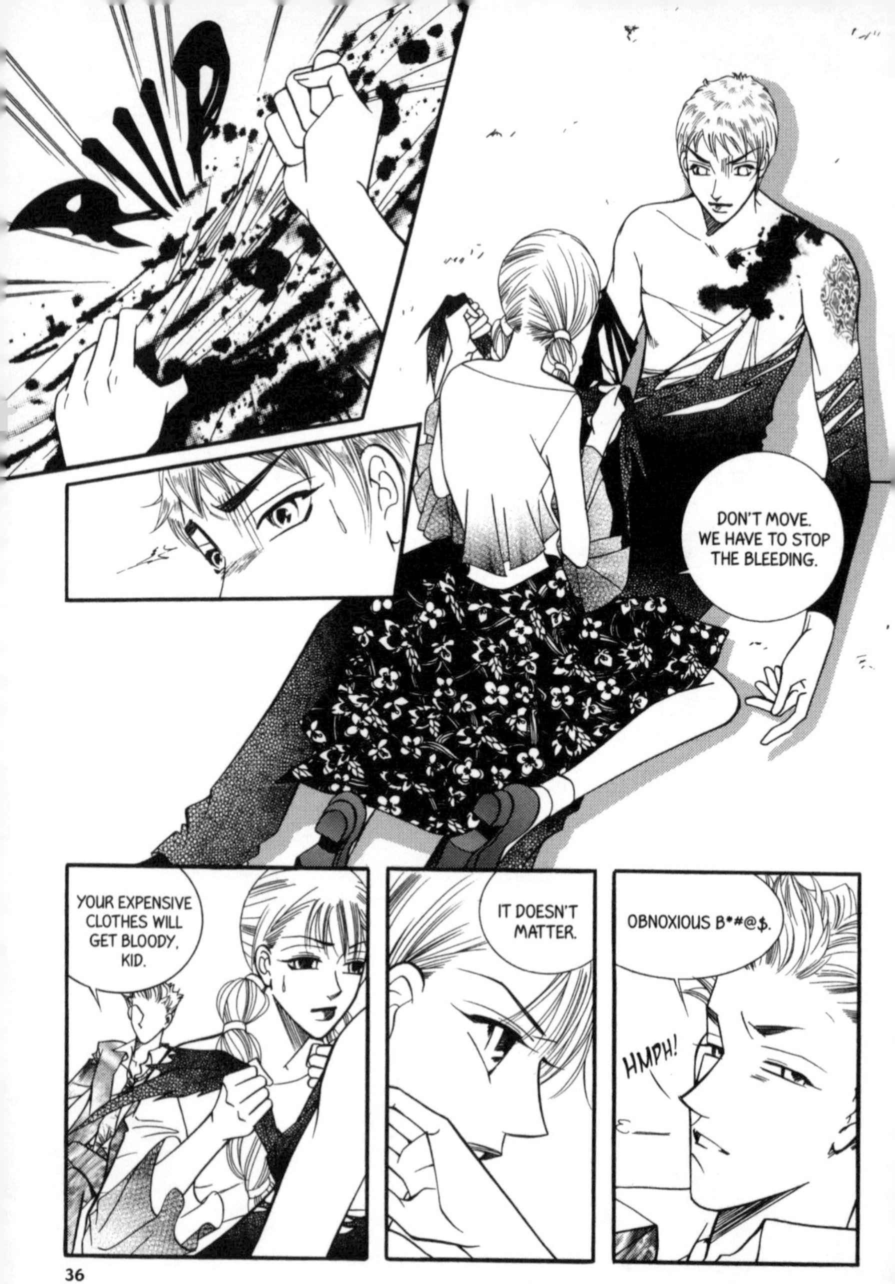
DON'T MOVE. WE HAVE TO STOP THE BLEEDING.
YOUR EXPENSIVE CLOTHES WILL GET BLOODY, KID.
IT DOESN'T MATTER.
OBNOXIOUS B*#@$.
HMPH!

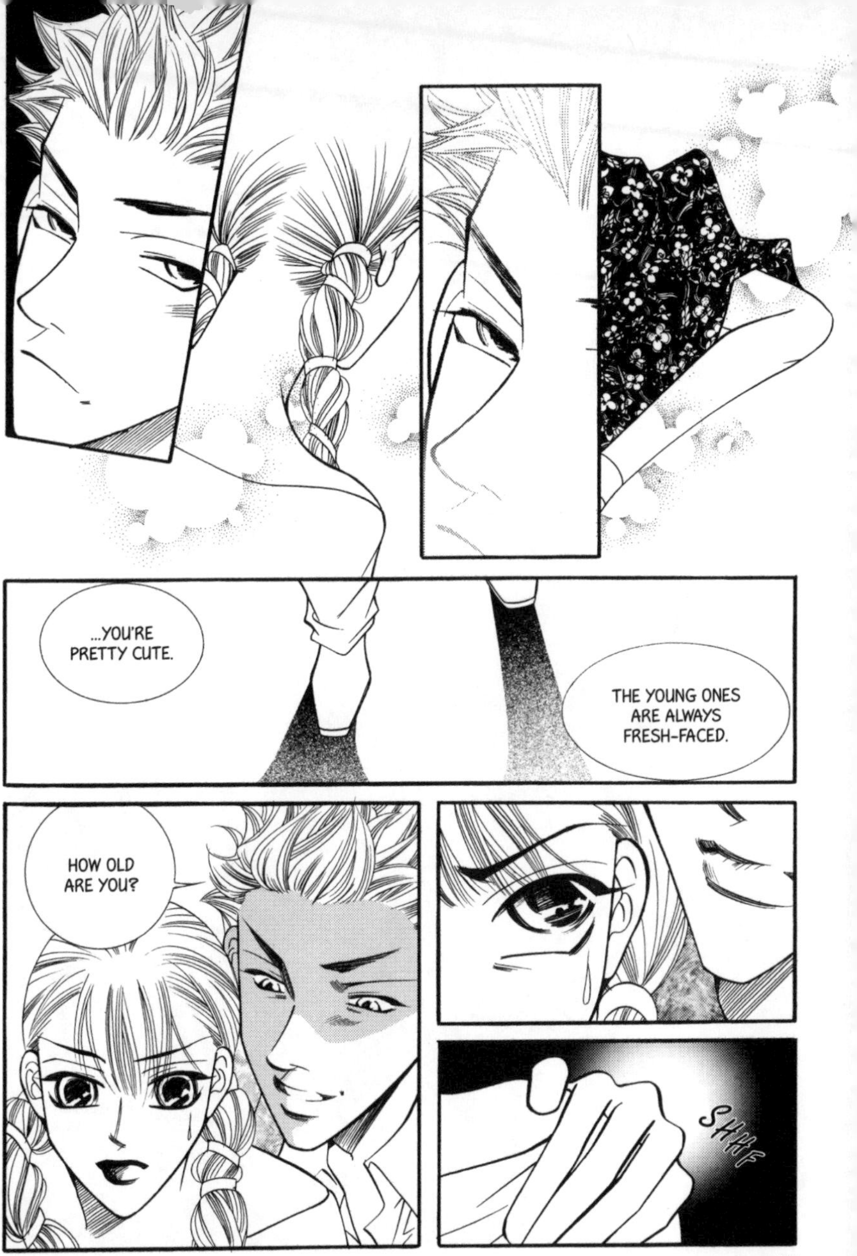
...YOU'RE PRETTY CUTE.
THE YOUNG ONES ARE ALWAYS FRESH-FACED.
HOW OLD ARE YOU?
SHHF

KA
POW!

KWAM

YOU PUNK!

YOU WANNA DIE...?!

WHAT THE HELL AM I DOING?

WHY AM I PROTECTING SOME GIRL WHEN MY LIFE'S AT STAKE...?

ALRIGHT, I'LL KILL YOU!

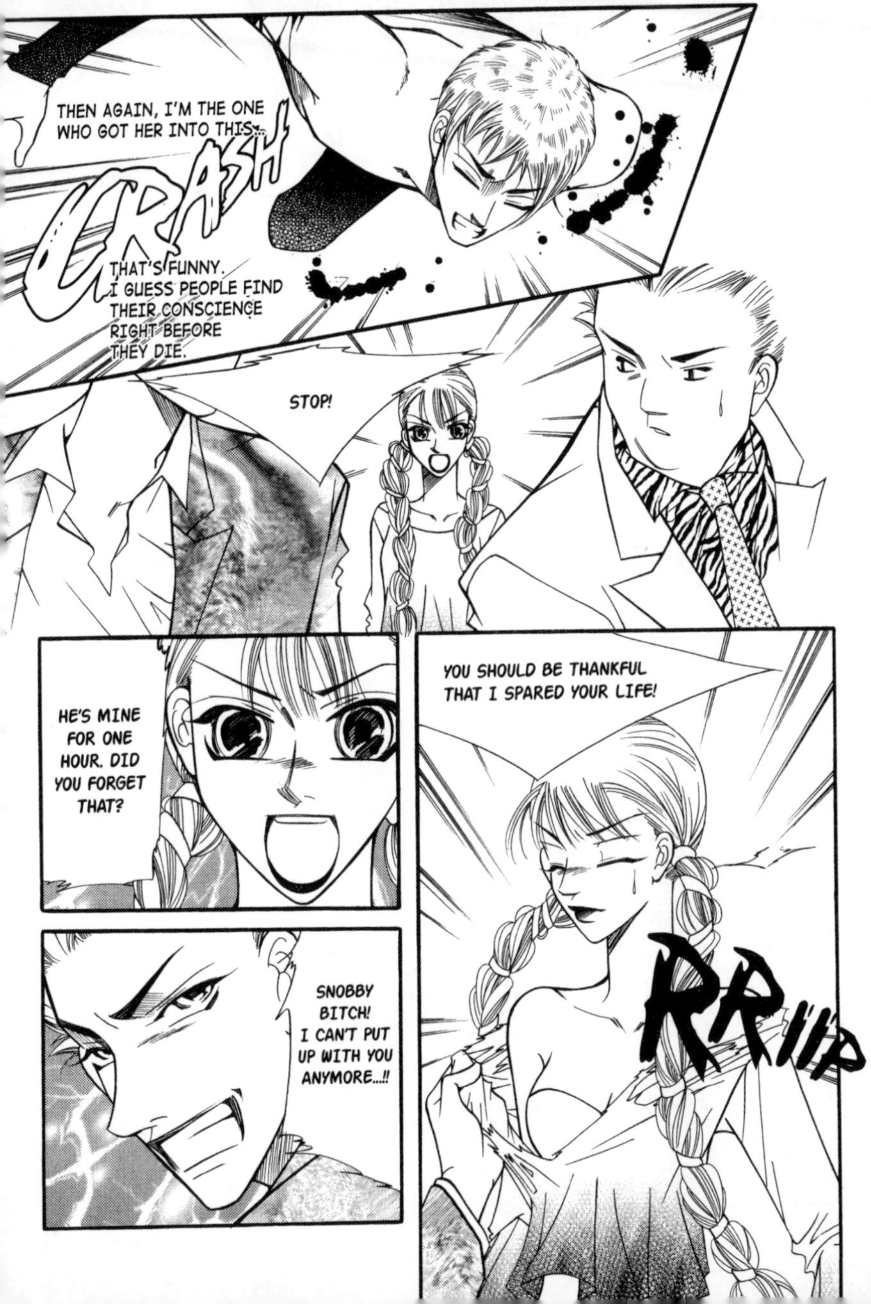
THEN AGAIN, I'M THE ONE WHO GOT HER INTO THIS...
CRASH
THAT'S FUNNY. I GUESS PEOPLE FIND THEIR CONSCIENCE RIGHT BEFORE THEY DIE.
STOP!
HE'S MINE FOR ONE HOUR. DID YOU FORGET THAT?
SNOBBY BITCH! I CAN'T PUT UP WITH YOU ANYMORE...!!
YOU SHOULD BE THANKFUL THAT I SPARED YOUR LIFE!
RRIIP

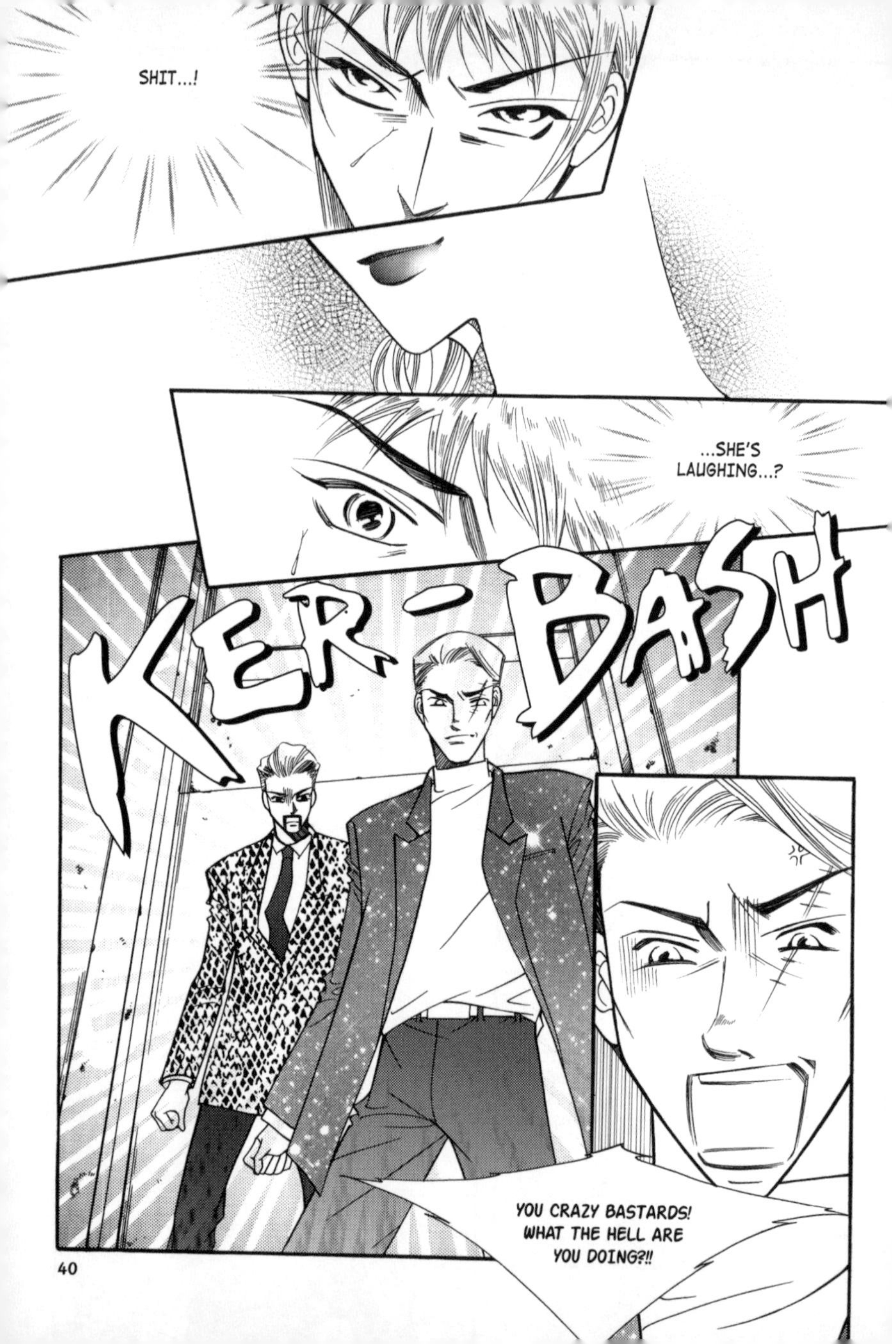
SHIT...!
...SHE'S LAUGHING...?
KER-BASH
YOU CRAZY BASTARDS! WHAT THE HELL ARE YOU DOING?!!

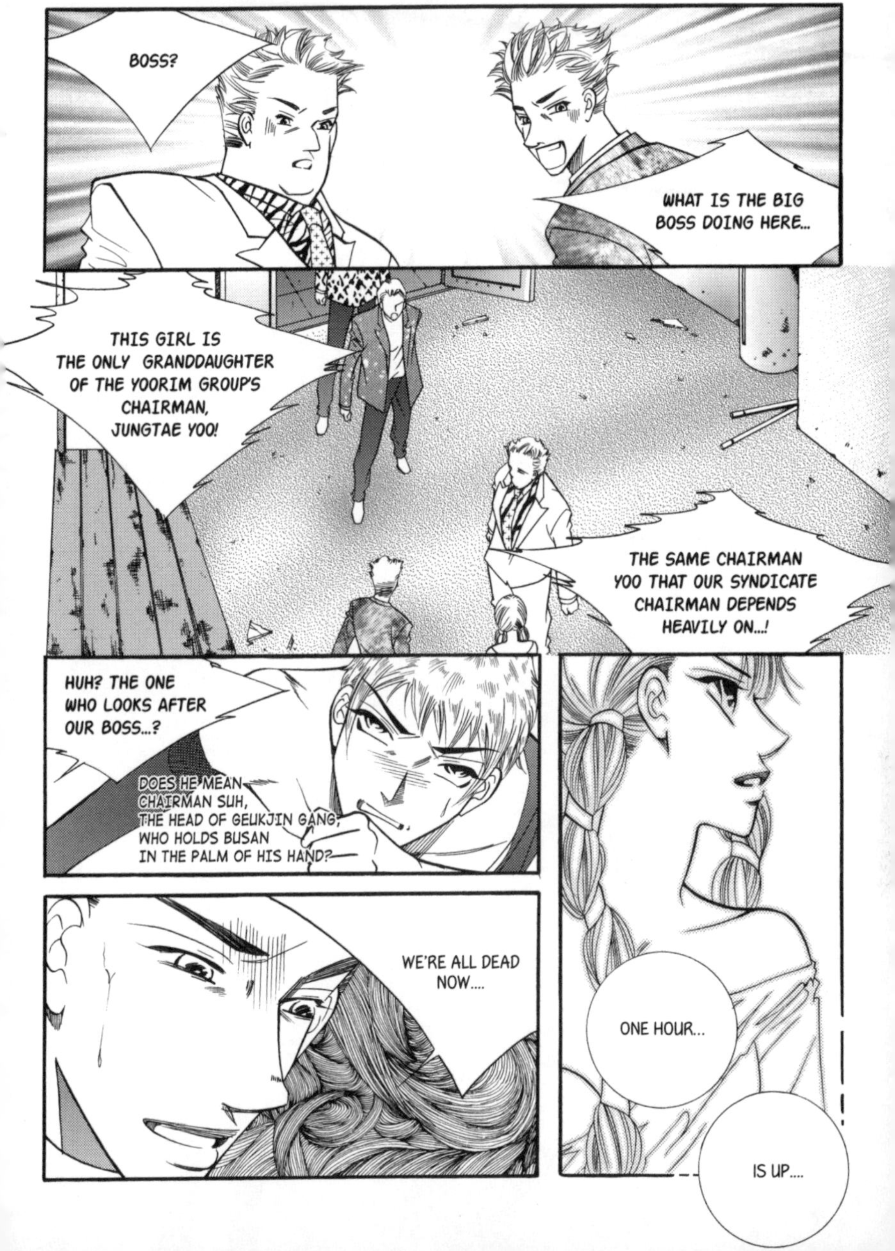
BOSS?
WHAT IS THE BIG BOSS DOING HERE...
THIS GIRL IS THE ONLY GRANDDAUGHTER OF THE YOORIM GROUP'S CHAIRMAN, JUNGTAE YOO!
THE SAME CHAIRMAN YOO THAT OUR SYNDICATE CHAIRMAN DEPENDS HEAVILY ON...!
HUH? THE ONE WHO LOOKS AFTER OUR BOSS...?
DOES HE MEAN CHAIRMAN SUH, THE HEAD OF GEUKJIN GANG, WHO HOLDS BUSAN IN THE PALM OF HIS HAND?
WE'RE ALL DEAD NOW....
ONE HOUR...
IS UP....

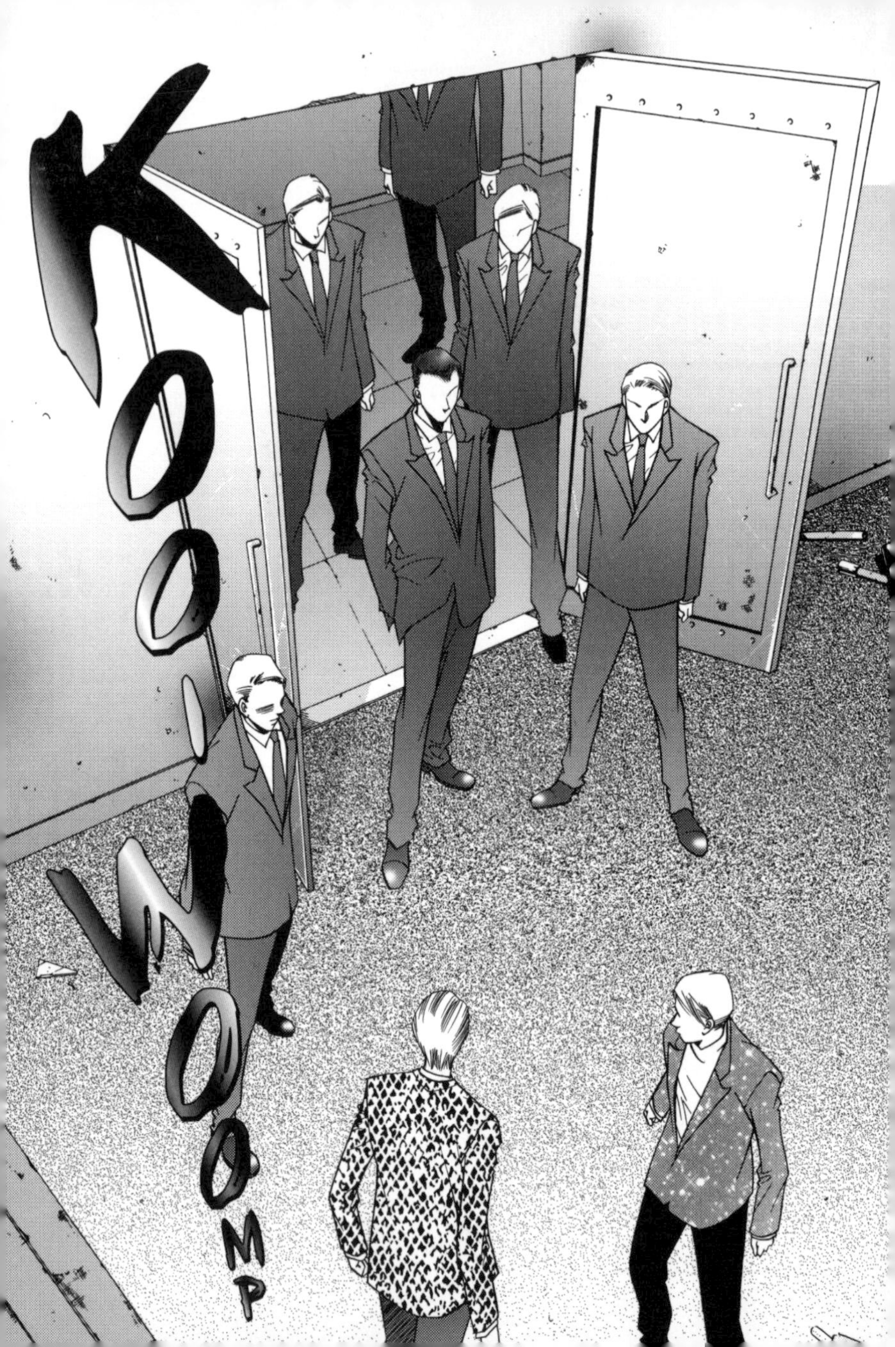
KOOOWOOMP

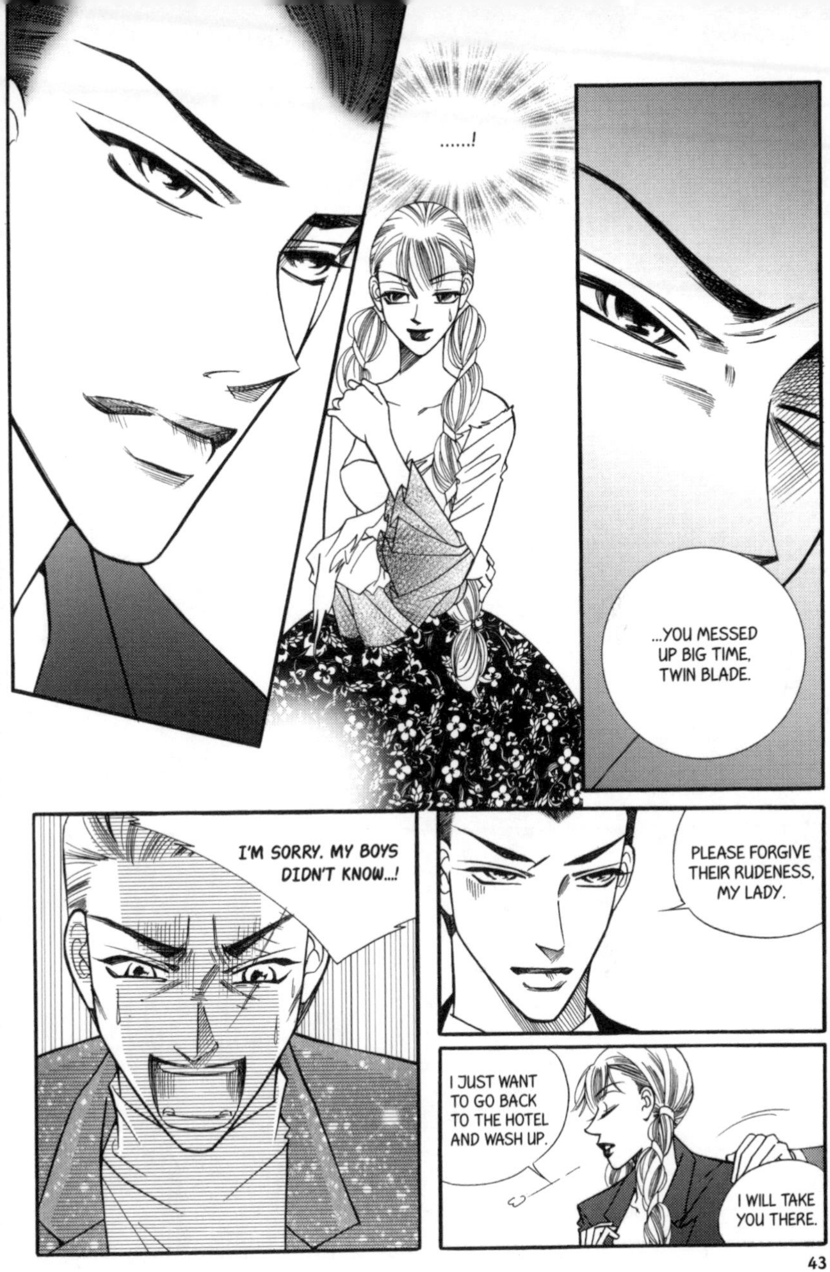
......!
...YOU MESSED UP BIG TIME, TWIN BLADE.
I'M SORRY. MY BOYS DIDN'T KNOW...!
PLEASE FORGIVE THEIR RUDENESS, MY LADY.
I JUST WANT TO GO BACK TO THE HOTEL AND WASH UP.
I WILL TAKE YOU THERE.

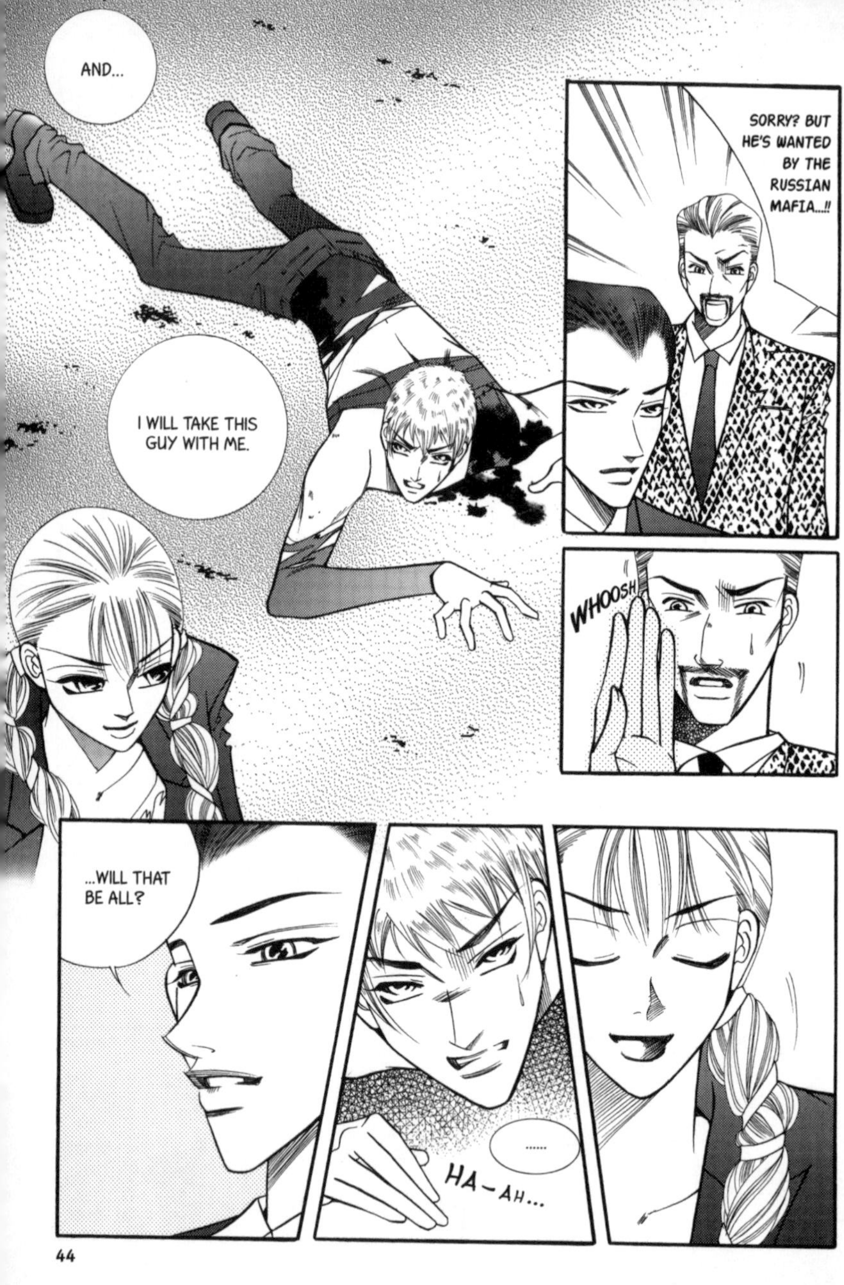
AND...
I WILL TAKE THIS GUY WITH ME.
SORRY? BUT HE'S WANTED BY THE RUSSIAN MAFIA...!!
WHOOSH
...WILL THAT BE ALL?
HA-AH...
......

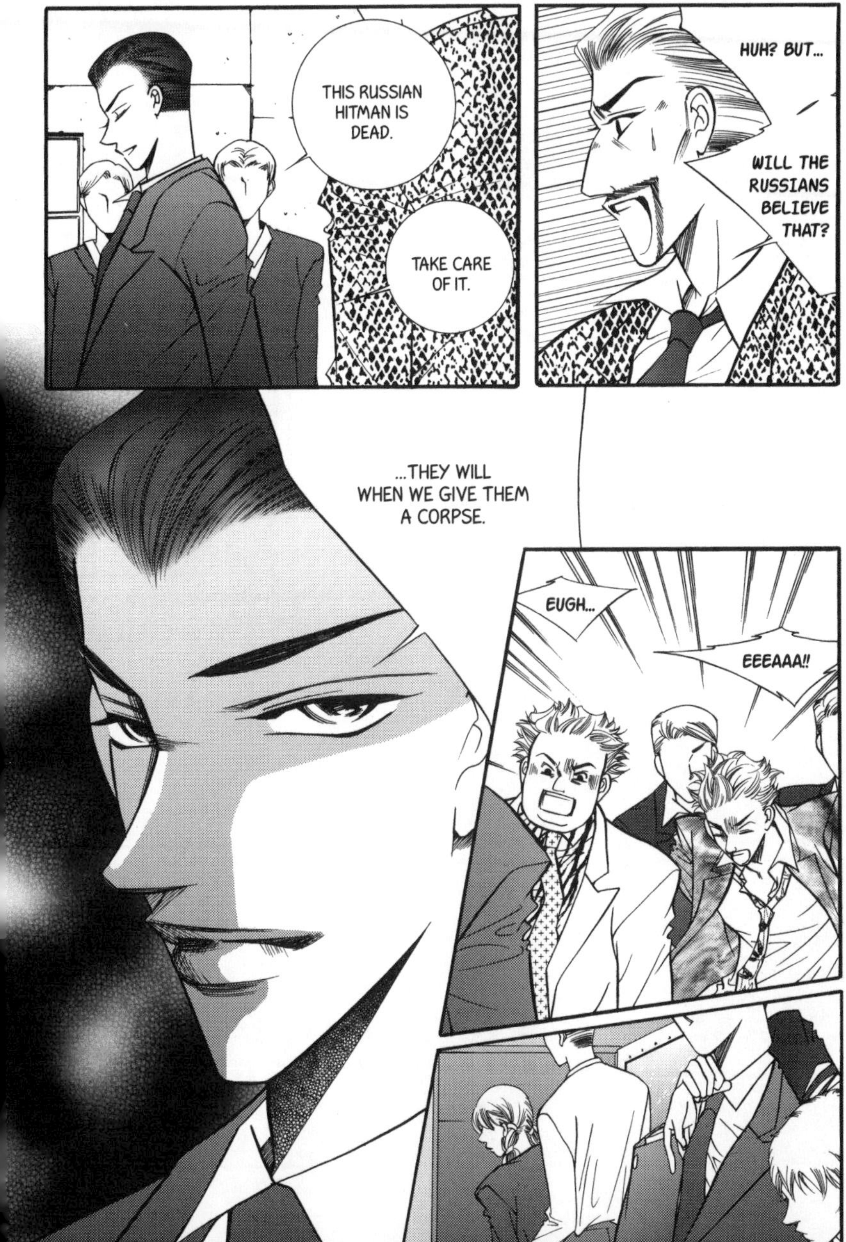
THIS RUSSIAN HITMAN IS DEAD.
TAKE CARE OF IT.
HUH? BUT...
WILL THE RUSSIANS BELIEVE THAT?
...THEY WILL WHEN WE GIVE THEM A CORPSE.
EUGH...
EEEAAA!!

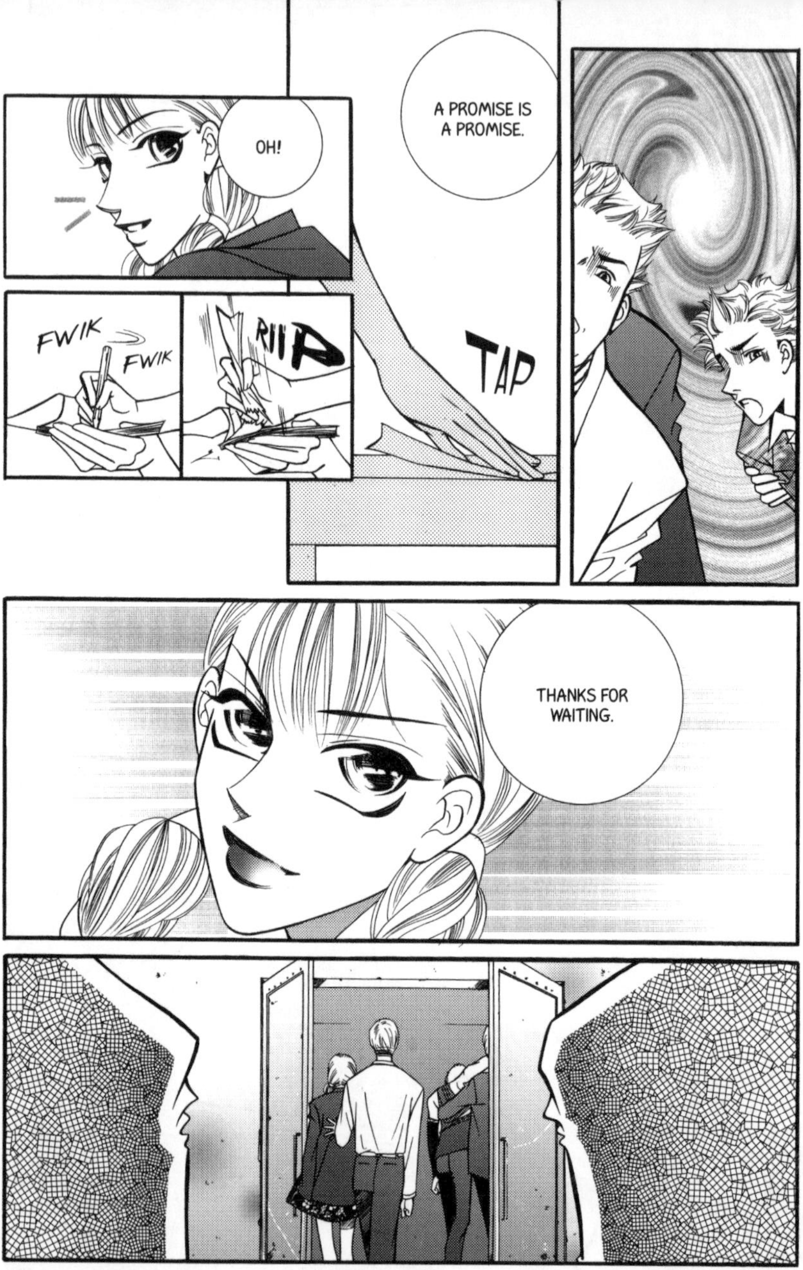
OH!
FWIK
FWIK
RIIP
A PROMISE IS A PROMISE.
TAP
THANKS FOR WAITING.

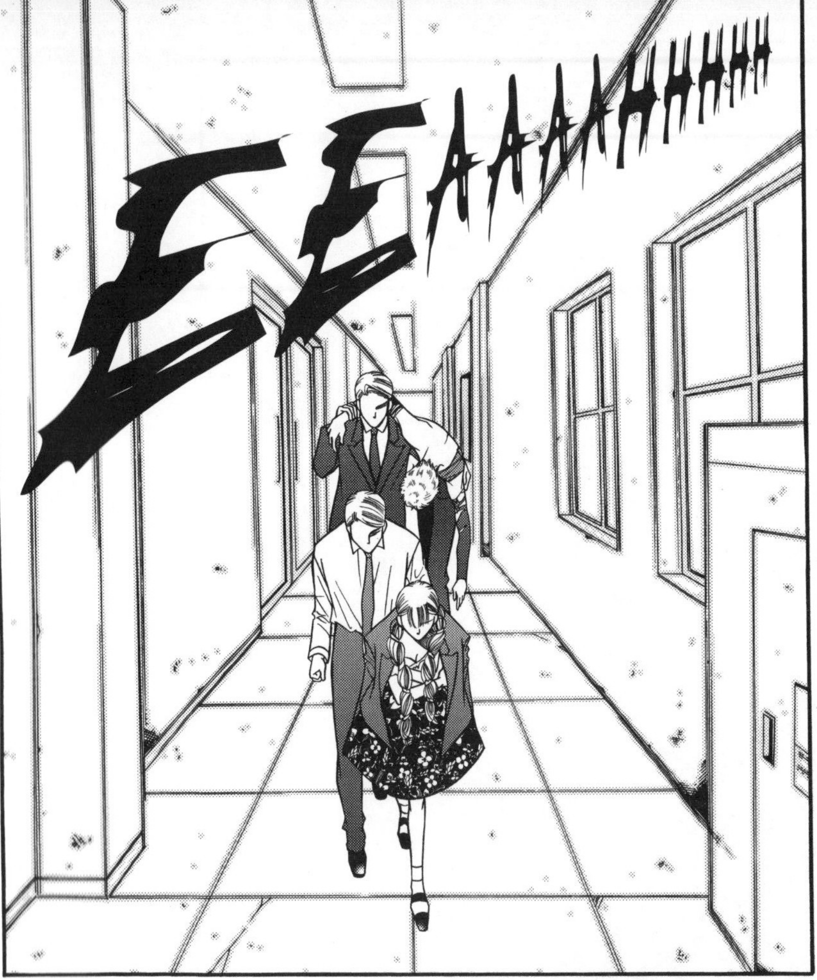
EEAAAAHHHHH
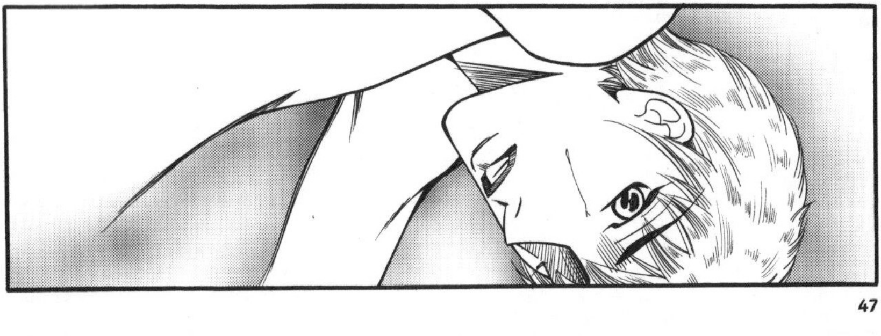

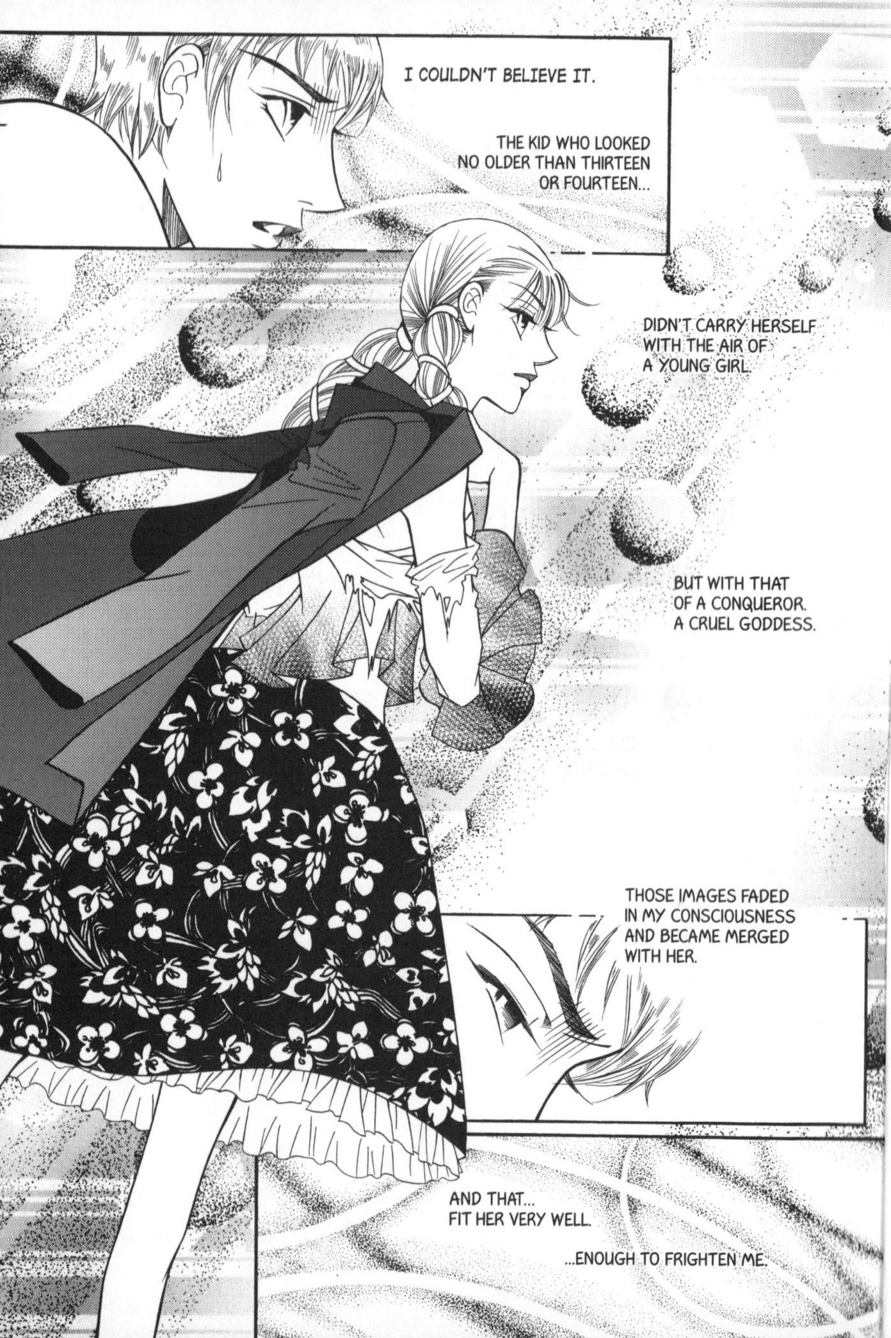
I COULDN'T BELIEVE IT.
THE KID WHO LOOKED NO OLDER THAN THIRTEEN OR FOURTEEN...
DIDN'T CARRY HERSELF WITH THE AIR OF A YOUNG GIRL.
BUT WITH THAT OF A CONQUEROR. A CRUEL GODDESS.
THOSE IMAGES FADED IN MY CONSCIOUSNESS AND BECAME MERGED WITH HER.
AND THAT... FIT HER VERY WELL.
...ENOUGH TO FRIGHTEN ME.

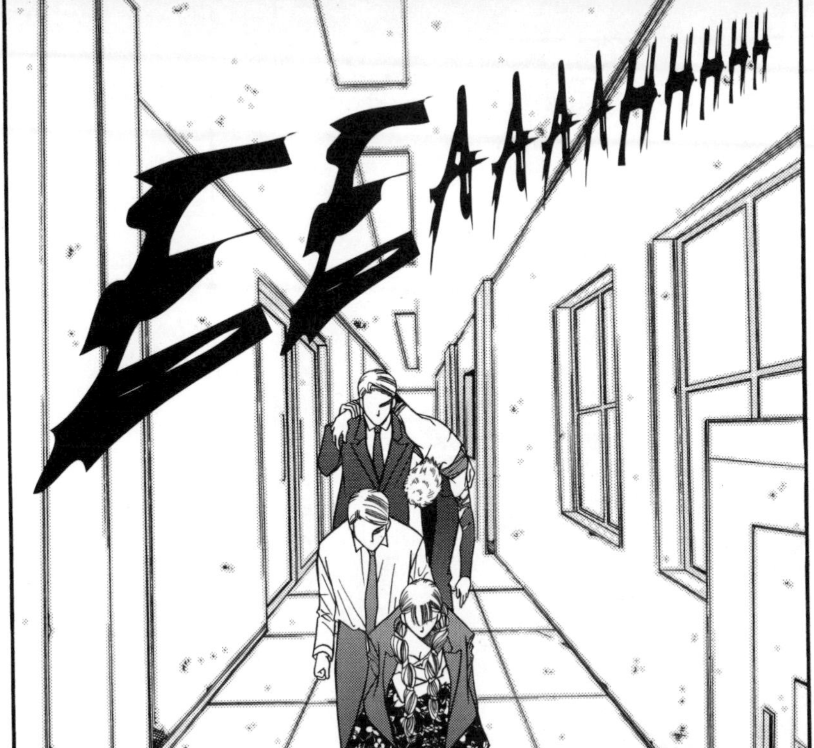
EEAAAAHHHHH
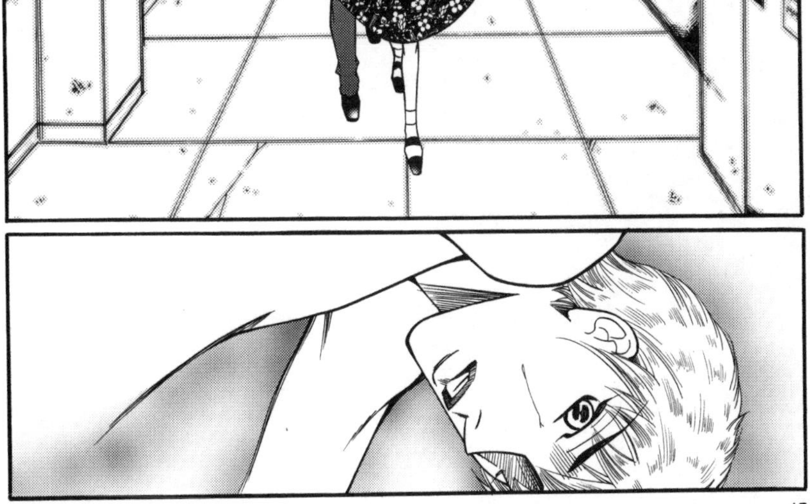

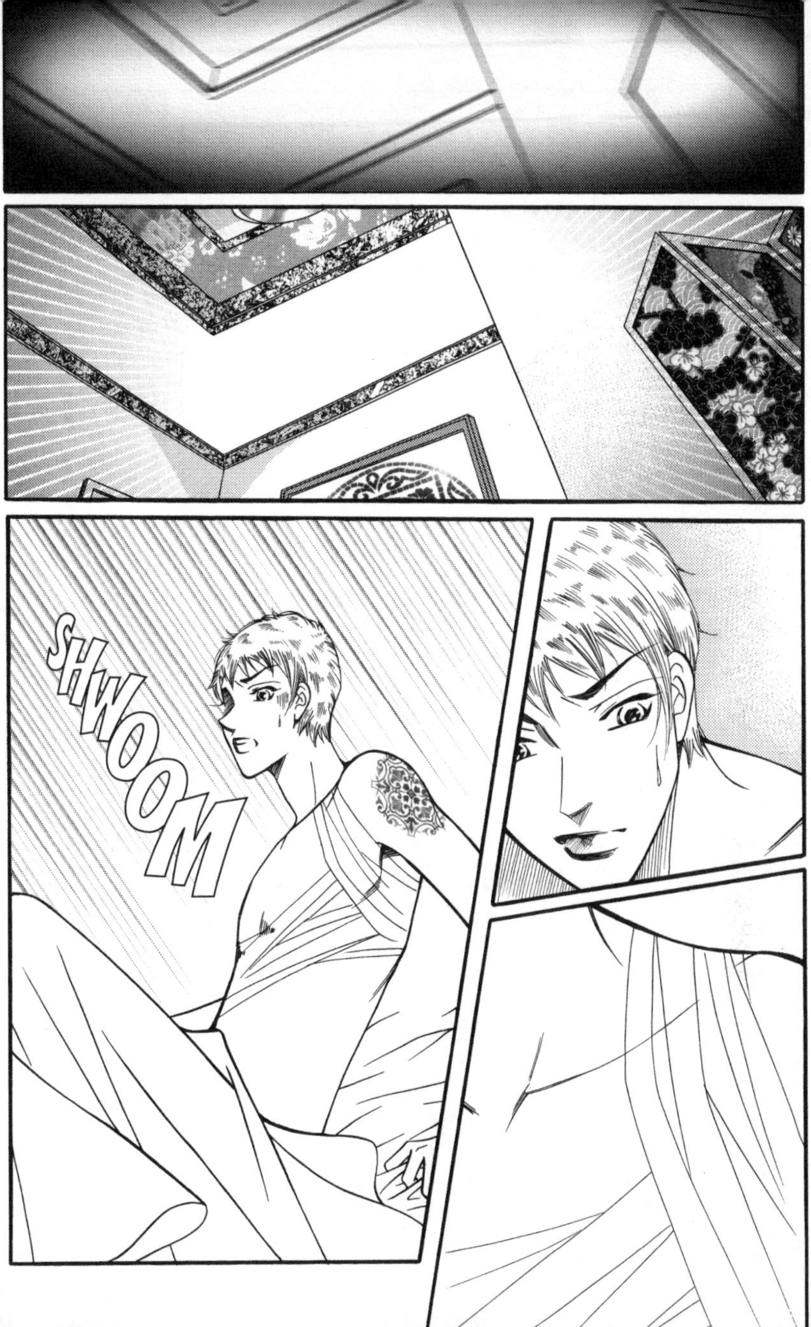
SHWOOM

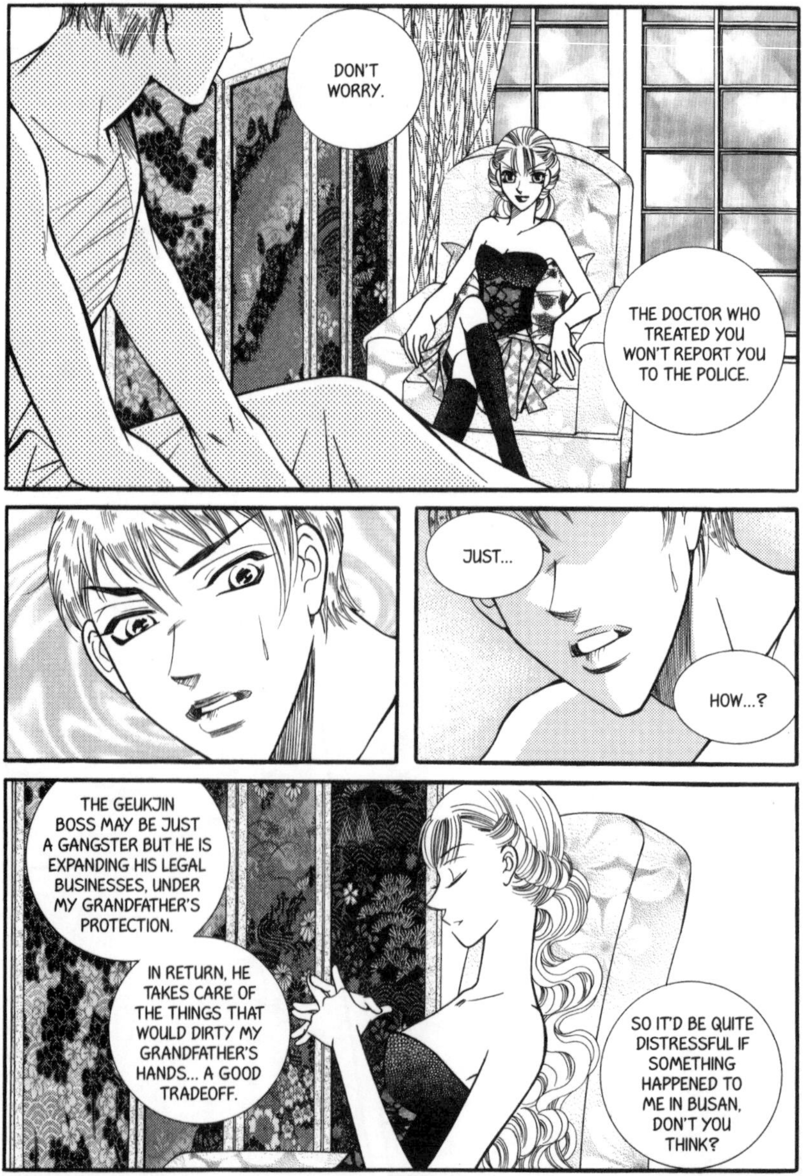
DON'T WORRY.
THE DOCTOR WHO TREATED YOU WON'T REPORT YOU TO THE POLICE.
JUST...
HOW...?
THE GEUKJIN BOSS MAY BE JUST A GANGSTER BUT HE IS EXPANDING HIS LEGAL BUSINESSES, UNDER MY GRANDFATHER'S PROTECTION.
IN RETURN, HE TAKES CARE OF THE THINGS THAT WOULD DIRTY MY GRANDFATHER'S HANDS... A GOOD TRADEOFF.
SO IT'D BE QUITE DISTRESSFUL IF SOMETHING HAPPENED TO ME IN BUSAN, DON'T YOU THINK?

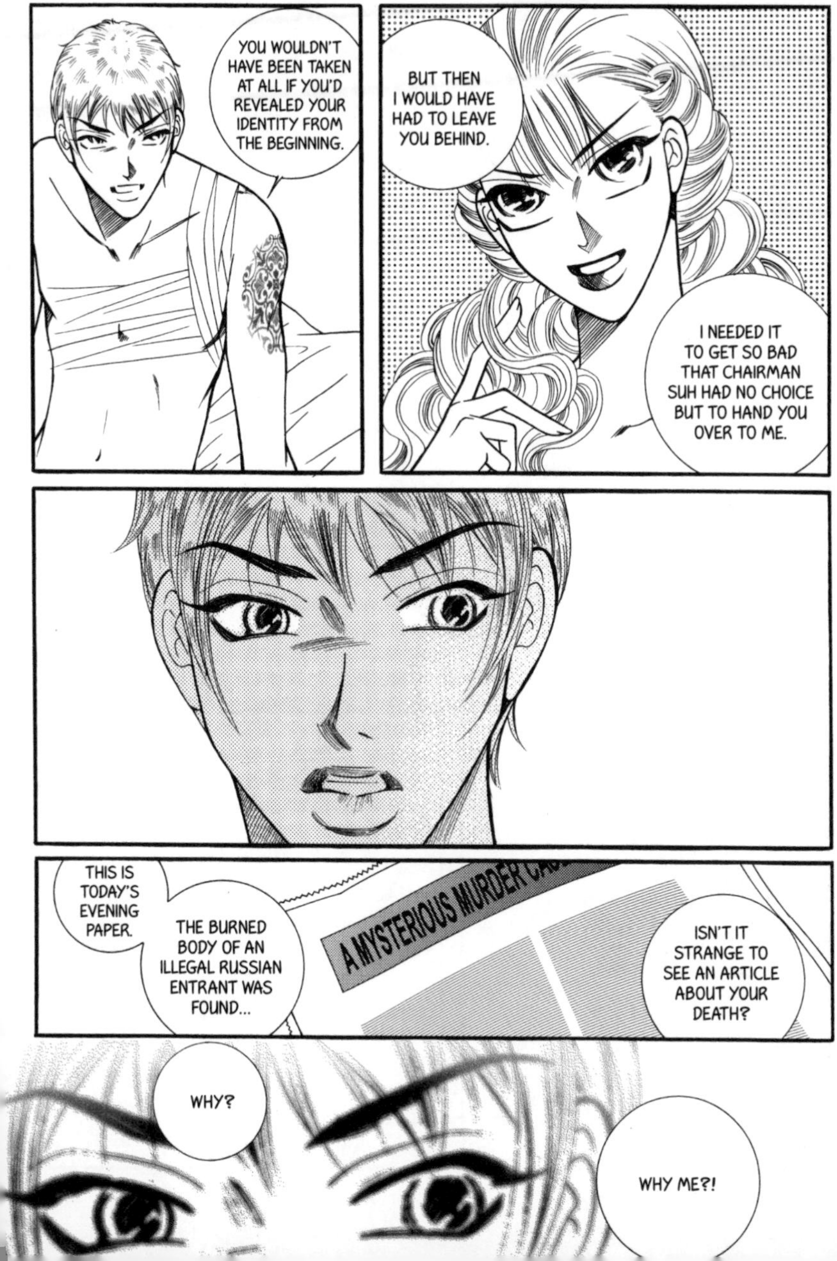
YOU WOULDN'T HAVE BEEN TAKEN AT ALL IF YOU'D REVEALED YOUR IDENTITY FROM THE BEGINNING.
BUT THEN I WOULD HAVE HAD TO LEAVE YOU BEHIND.
I NEEDED IT TO GET SO BAD THAT CHAIRMAN SUH HAD NO CHOICE BUT TO HAND YOU OVER TO ME.
THIS IS TODAY'S EVENING PAPER.
THE BURNED BODY OF AN ILLEGAL RUSSIAN ENTRANT WAS FOUND...
A MYSTERIOUS MURDER CA
ISN'T IT STRANGE TO SEE AN ARTICLE ABOUT YOUR DEATH?
WHY?
WHY ME?!

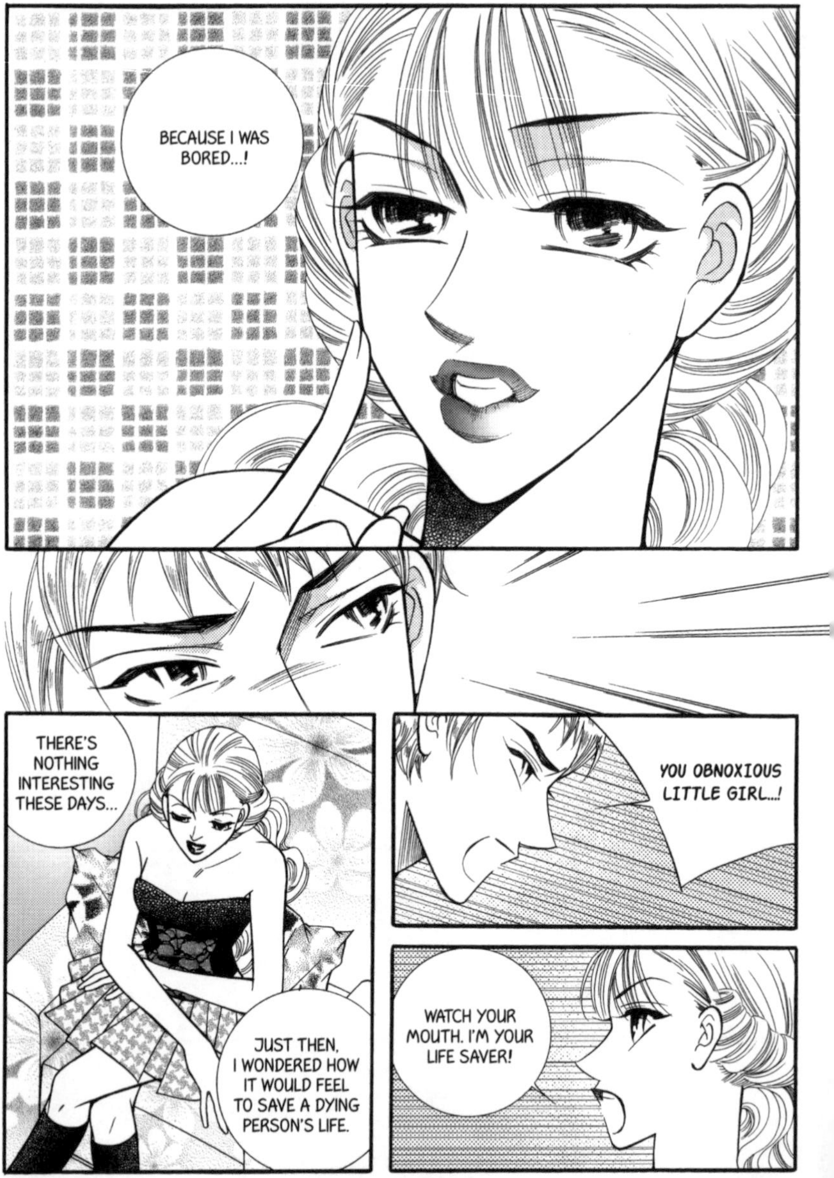
BECAUSE I WAS BORED...!
THERE'S NOTHING INTERESTING THESE DAYS...
JUST THEN, I WONDERED HOW IT WOULD FEEL TO SAVE A DYING PERSON'S LIFE.
YOU OBNOXIOUS LITTLE GIRL...!
WATCH YOUR MOUTH. I'M YOUR LIFE SAVER!

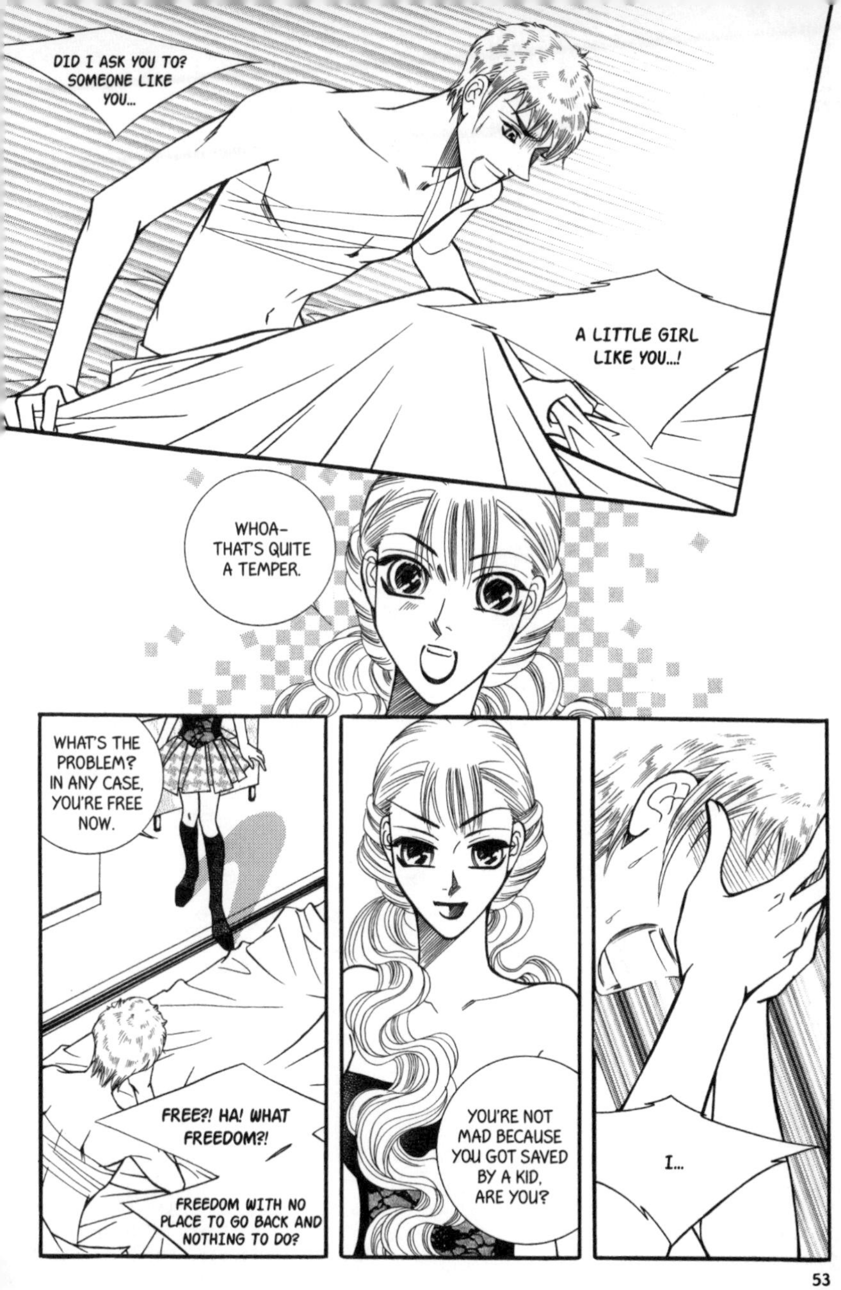
DID I ASK YOU TO? SOMEONE LIKE YOU...
A LITTLE GIRL LIKE YOU...!
WHOA- THAT'S QUITE A TEMPER.
WHAT'S THE PROBLEM? IN ANY CASE, YOU'RE FREE NOW.
FREE?! HA! WHAT FREEDOM?!
FREEDOM WITH NO PLACE TO GO BACK AND NOTHING TO DO?
YOU'RE NOT MAD BECAUSE YOU GOT SAVED BY A KID, ARE YOU?
I...

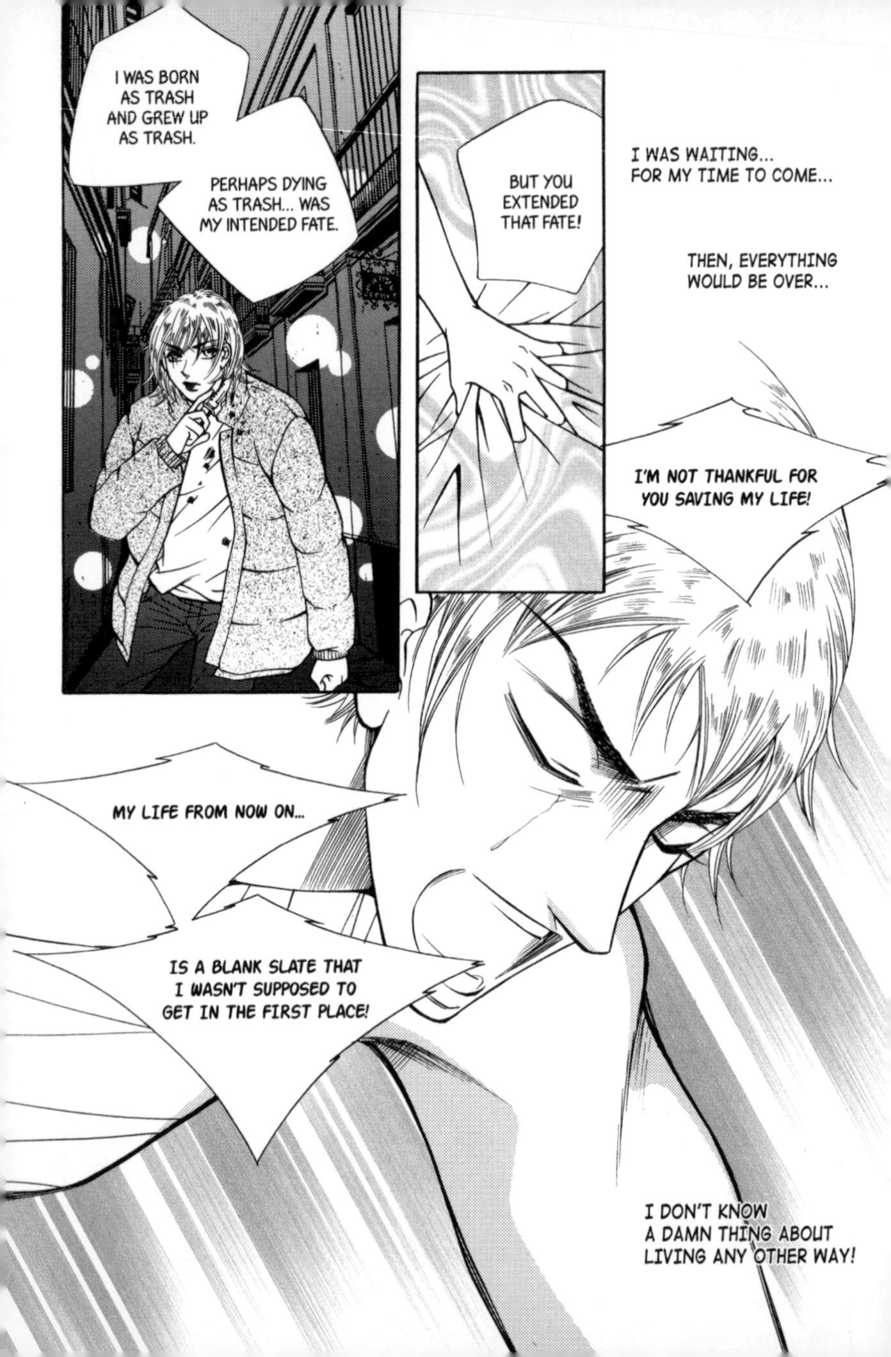

I WAS BORN AS TRASH AND GREW UP AS TRASH.
PERHAPS DYING AS TRASH... WAS MY INTENDED FATE.
BUT YOU EXTENDED THAT FATE!
I WAS WAITING... FOR MY TIME TO COME...
THEN, EVERYTHING WOULD BE OVER...
I'M NOT THANKFUL FOR YOU SAVING MY LIFE!
MY LIFE FROM NOW ON...
IS A BLANK SLATE THAT I WASN'T SUPPOSED TO GET IN THE FIRST PLACE!
I DON'T KNOW A DAMN THING ABOUT LIVING ANY OTHER WAY!

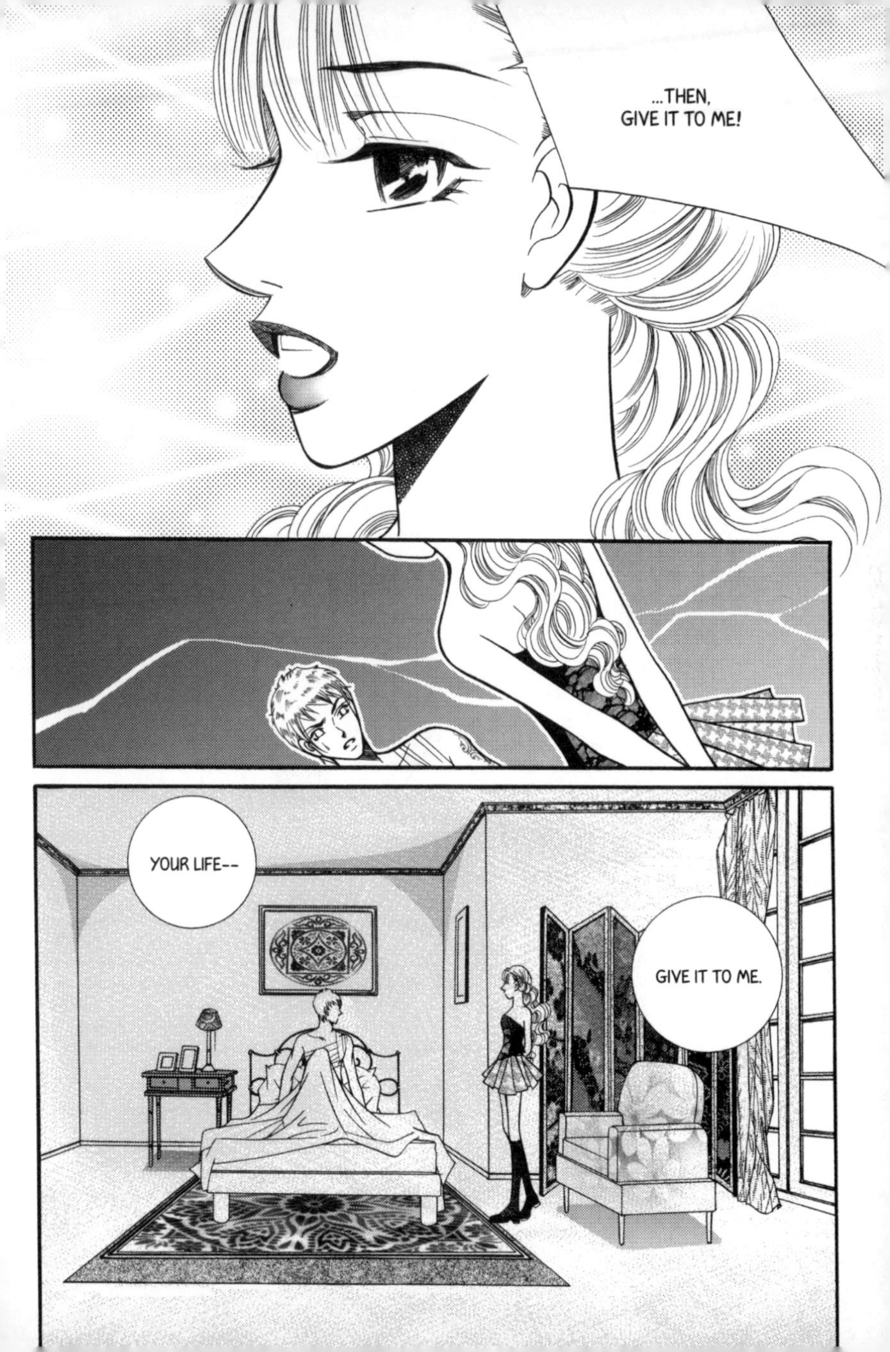
...THEN,
GIVE IT TO ME!
YOUR LIFE--
GIVE IT TO ME.

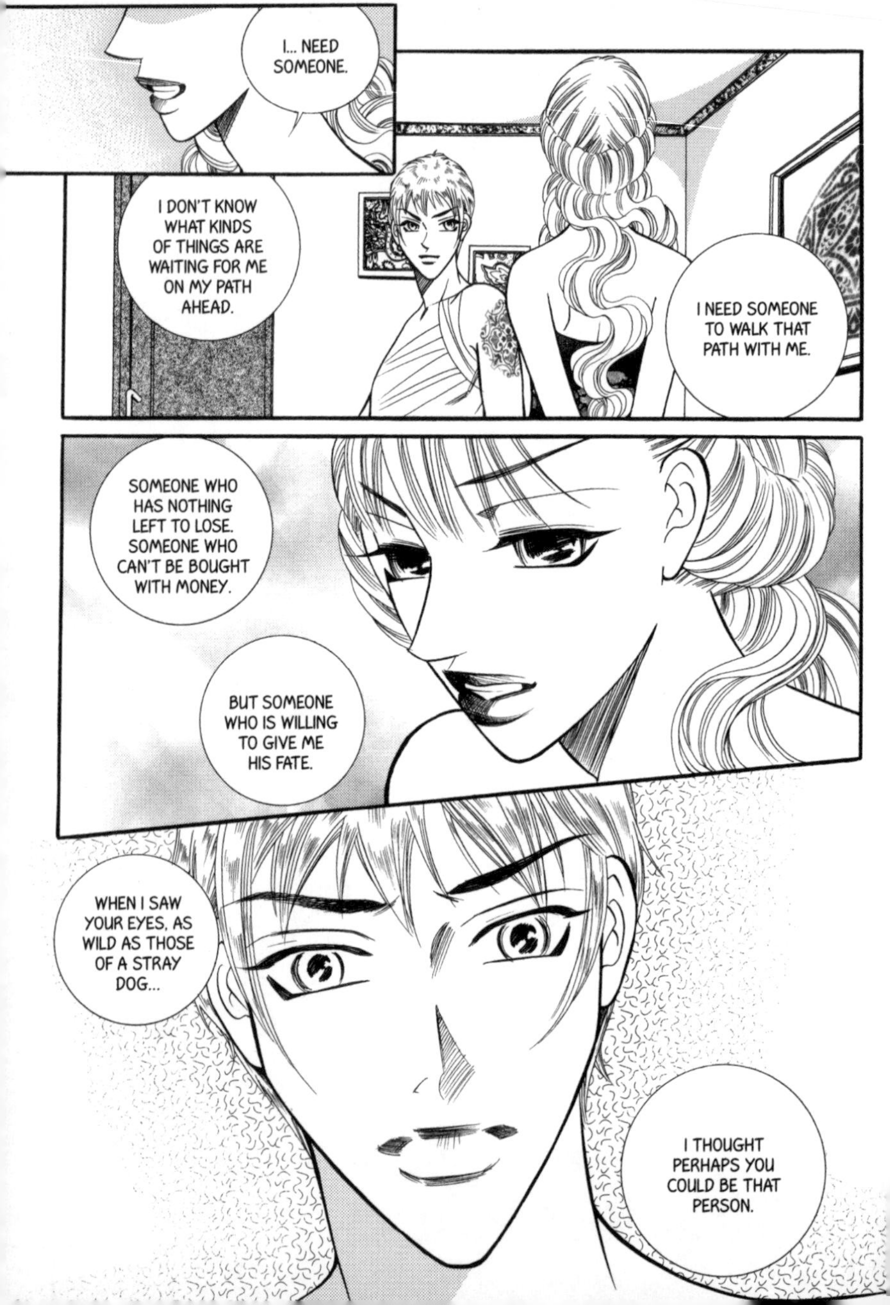
I... NEED SOMEONE.
I DON'T KNOW WHAT KINDS OF THINGS ARE WAITING FOR ME ON MY PATH AHEAD.
I NEED SOMEONE TO WALK THAT PATH WITH ME.
SOMEONE WHO HAS NOTHING LEFT TO LOSE. SOMEONE WHO CAN'T BE BOUGHT WITH MONEY.
BUT SOMEONE WHO IS WILLING TO GIVE ME HIS FATE.
WHEN I SAW YOUR EYES, AS WILD AS THOSE OF A STRAY DOG...
I THOUGHT PERHAPS YOU COULD BE THAT PERSON.

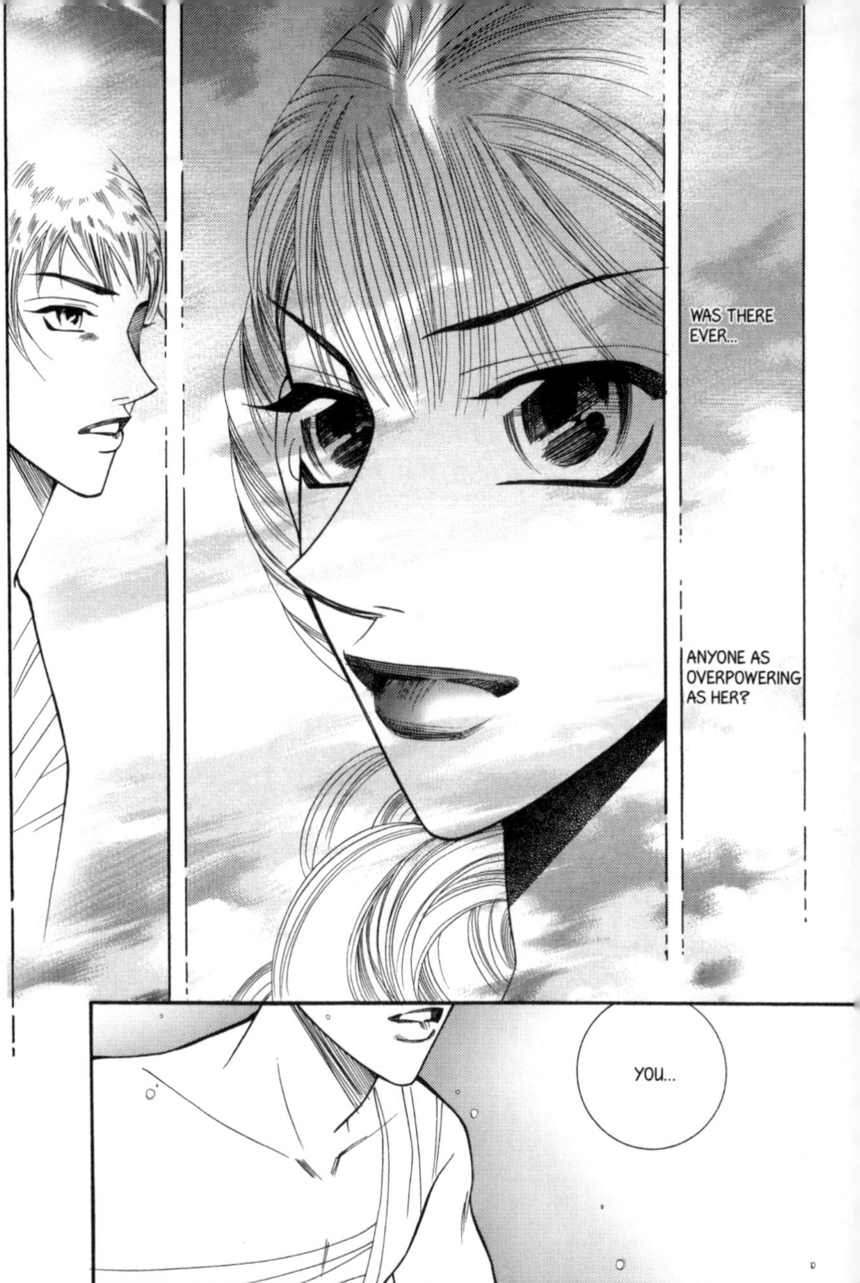
WAS THERE EVER...
ANYONE AS OVERPOWERING AS HER?
YOU...

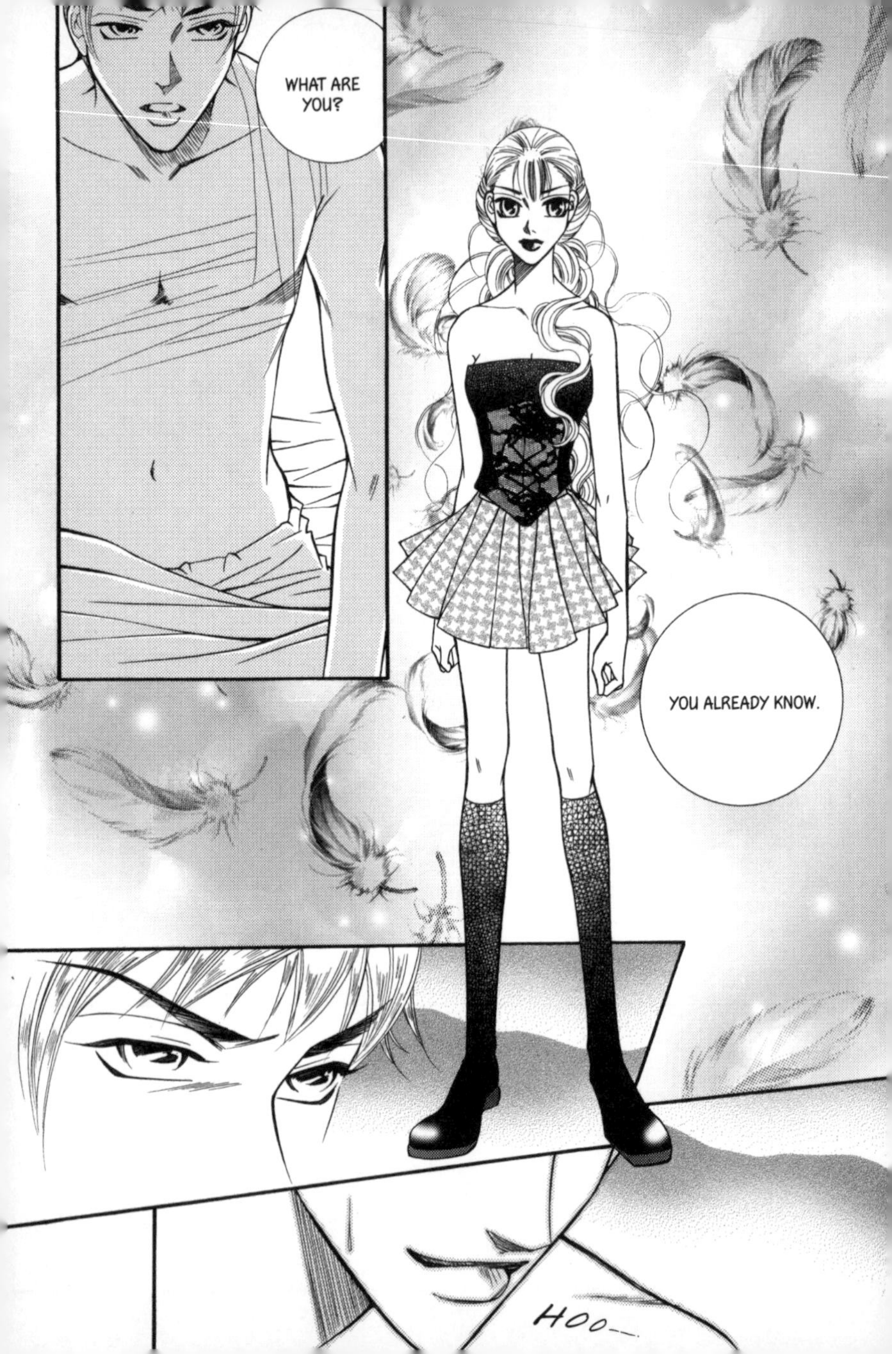
WHAT ARE YOU?
YOU ALREADY KNOW.
HOO--

HA
HA
HA

WHAT THE HELL.
THIS WAS IT
IN THE END.

BUT
WHAT
IS THIS
NOW?

THE EMPTINESS
THAT COULDN'T
EVER BE FILLED.

PROMISE ME.

WITHOUT
A THOUGHT
LIKE A BULLET
FIRED INTO
THE AIR...

I WAS FLYING
RECKLESSLY,
BUT IT WAS
ALL UNREAL,
AS IF I WAS
HAVING A
NIGHTMARE...

THIS
FEELING
AS IF I'M
ALIVE

FROM DEEP
WITHIN
MY HEART.

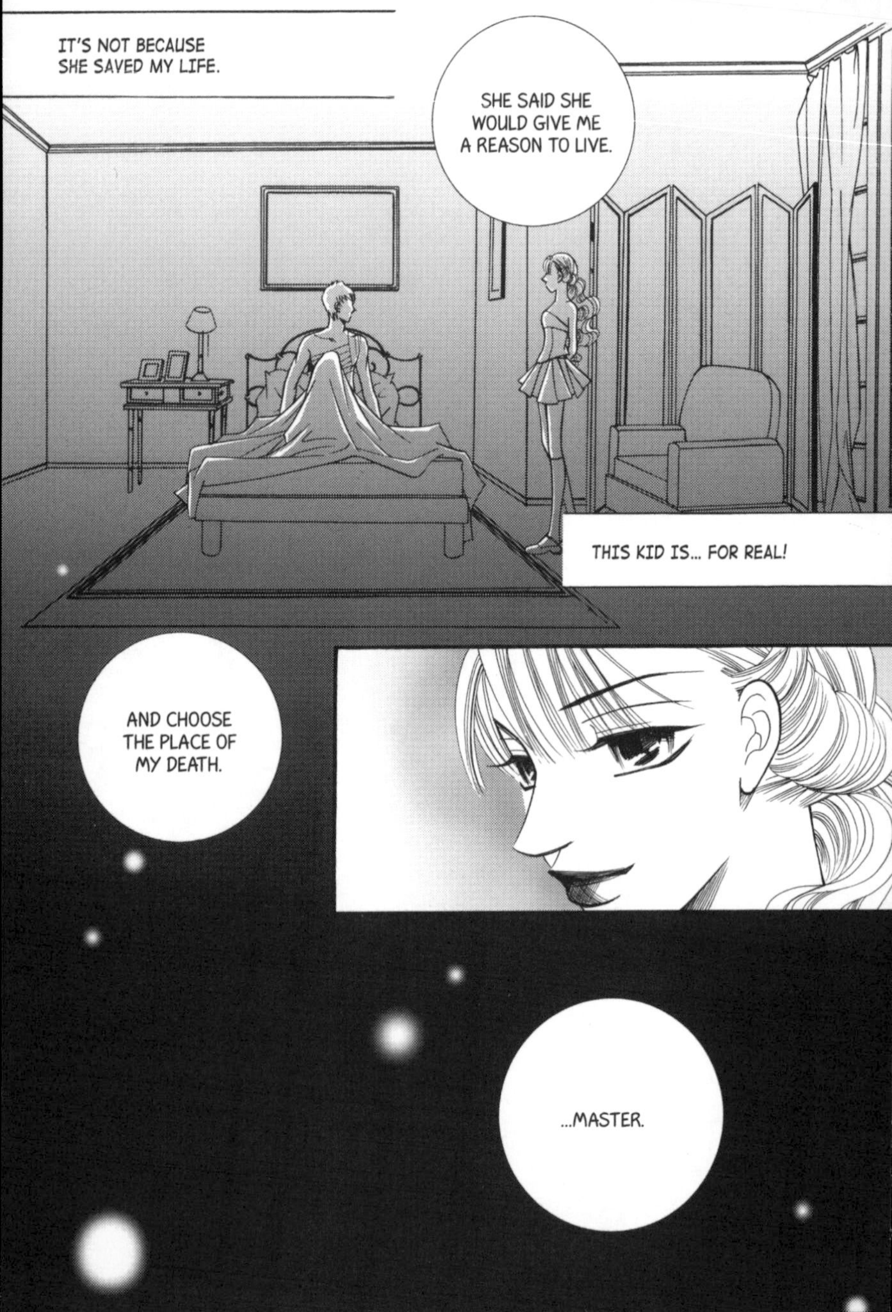
IT'S NOT BECAUSE SHE SAVED MY LIFE.
SHE SAID SHE WOULD GIVE ME A REASON TO LIVE.
THIS KID IS... FOR REAL!
AND CHOOSE THE PLACE OF MY DEATH.
...MASTER.

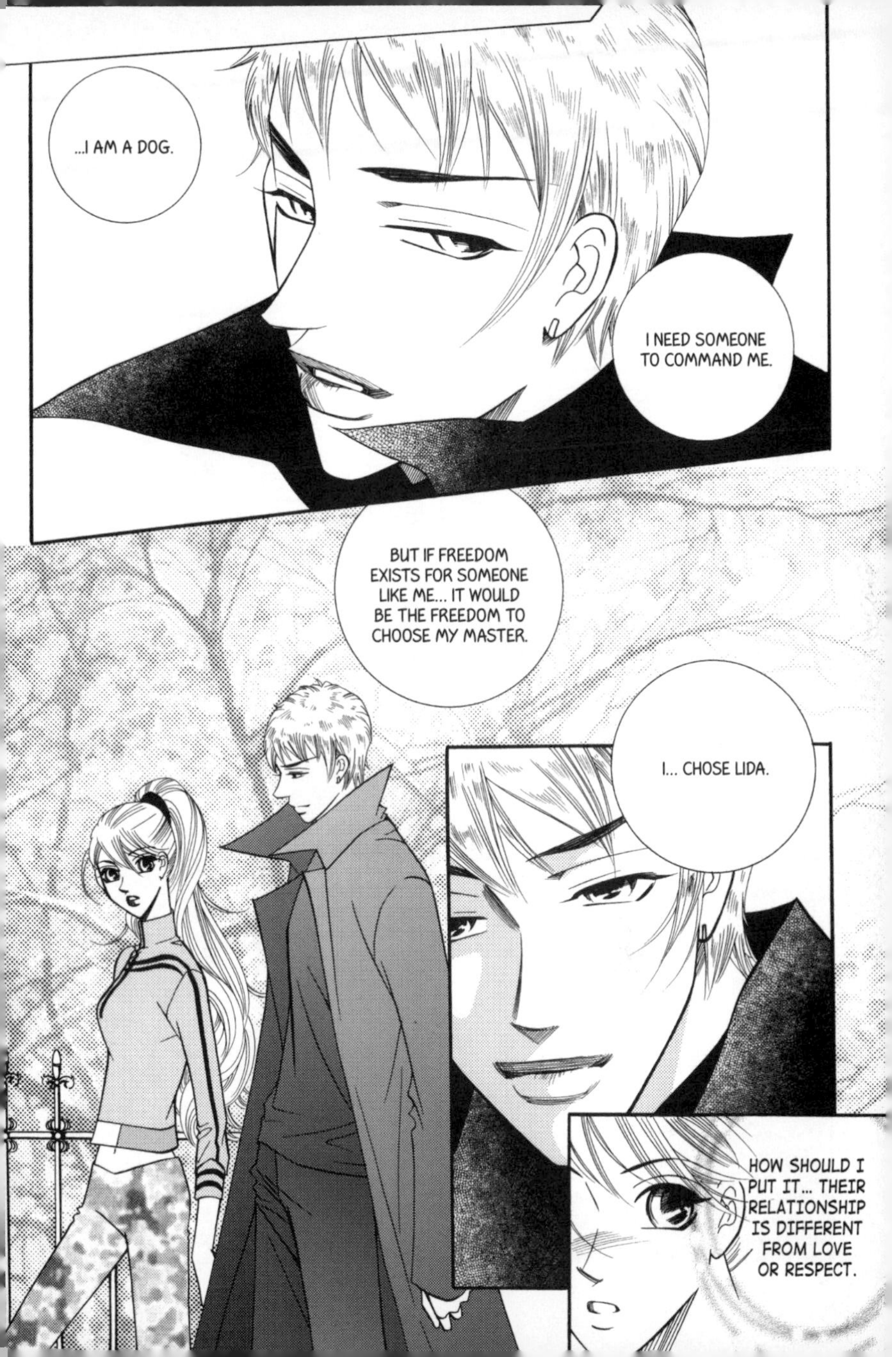
...I AM A DOG.
I NEED SOMEONE TO COMMAND ME.
BUT IF FREEDOM EXISTS FOR SOMEONE LIKE ME... IT WOULD BE THE FREEDOM TO CHOOSE MY MASTER.
I... CHOSE LIDA.
HOW SHOULD I PUT IT... THEIR RELATIONSHIP IS DIFFERENT FROM LOVE OR RESPECT.

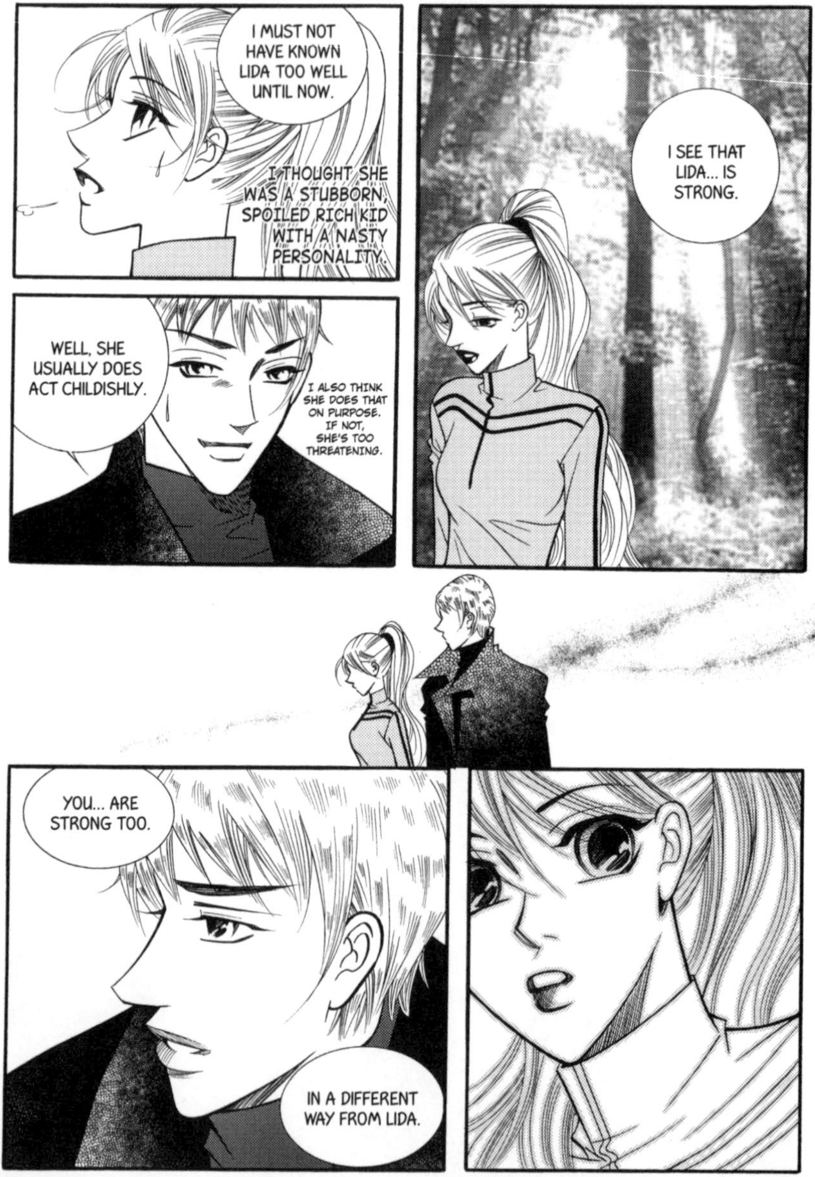
I MUST NOT HAVE KNOWN LIDA TOO WELL UNTIL NOW.
I THOUGHT SHE WAS A STUBBORN, SPOILED RICH KID WITH A NASTY PERSONALITY.
I SEE THAT LIDA... IS STRONG.
WELL, SHE USUALLY DOES ACT CHILDISHLY.
I ALSO THINK SHE DOES THAT ON PURPOSE. IF NOT, SHE'S TOO THREATENING.
YOU... ARE STRONG TOO.
IN A DIFFERENT WAY FROM LIDA.

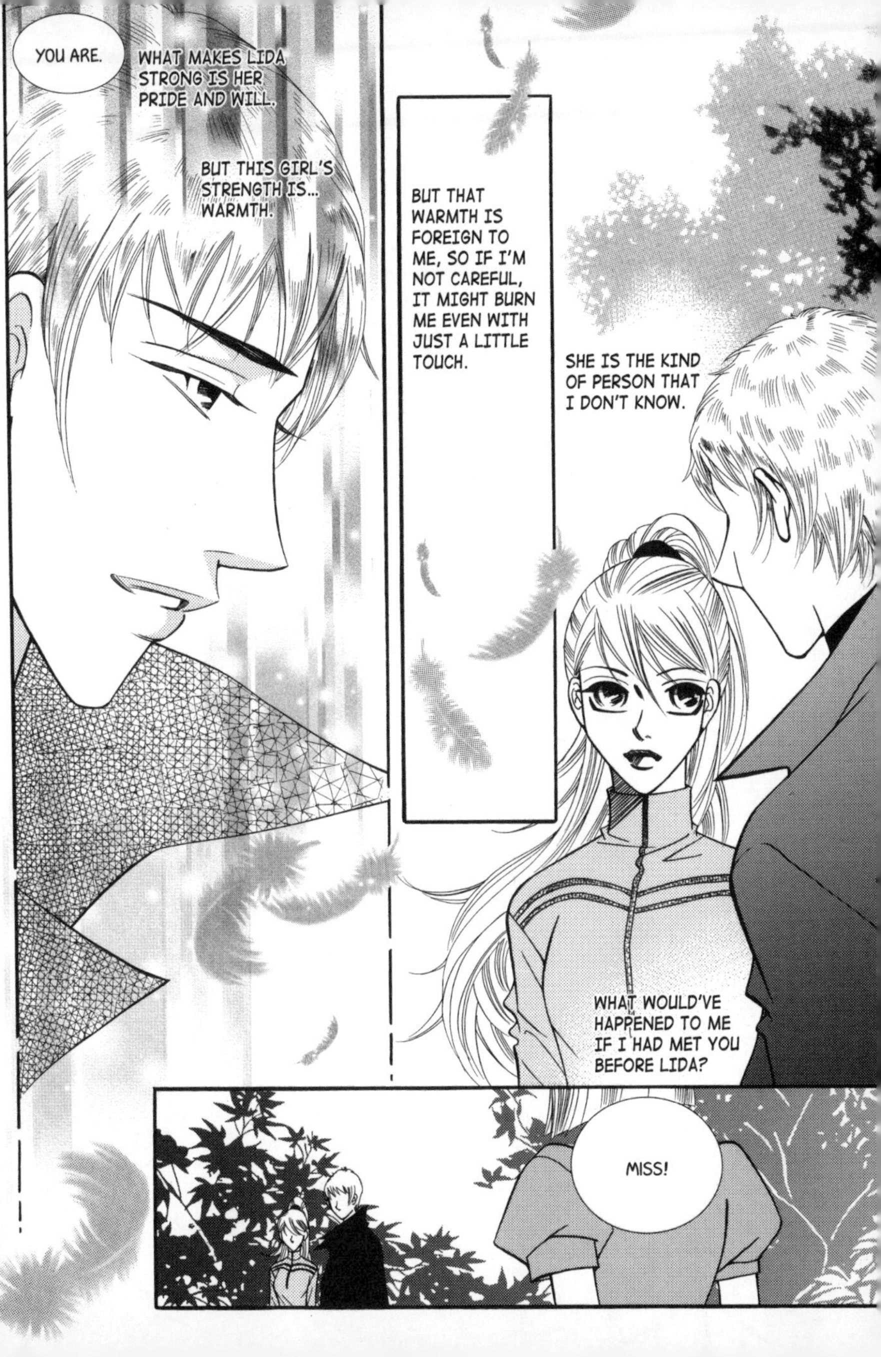
YOU ARE.
WHAT MAKES LIDA STRONG IS HER PRIDE AND WILL.
BUT THIS GIRL'S STRENGTH IS... WARMTH.
BUT THAT WARMTH IS FOREIGN TO ME, SO IF I'M NOT CAREFUL, IT MIGHT BURN ME EVEN WITH JUST A LITTLE TOUCH.
SHE IS THE KIND OF PERSON THAT I DON'T KNOW.
WHAT WOULD'VE HAPPENED TO ME IF I HAD MET YOU BEFORE LIDA?
MISS!

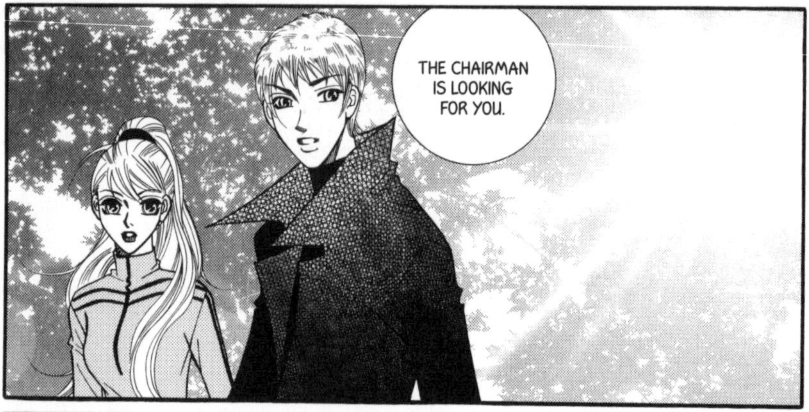
THE CHAIRMAN IS LOOKING FOR YOU.

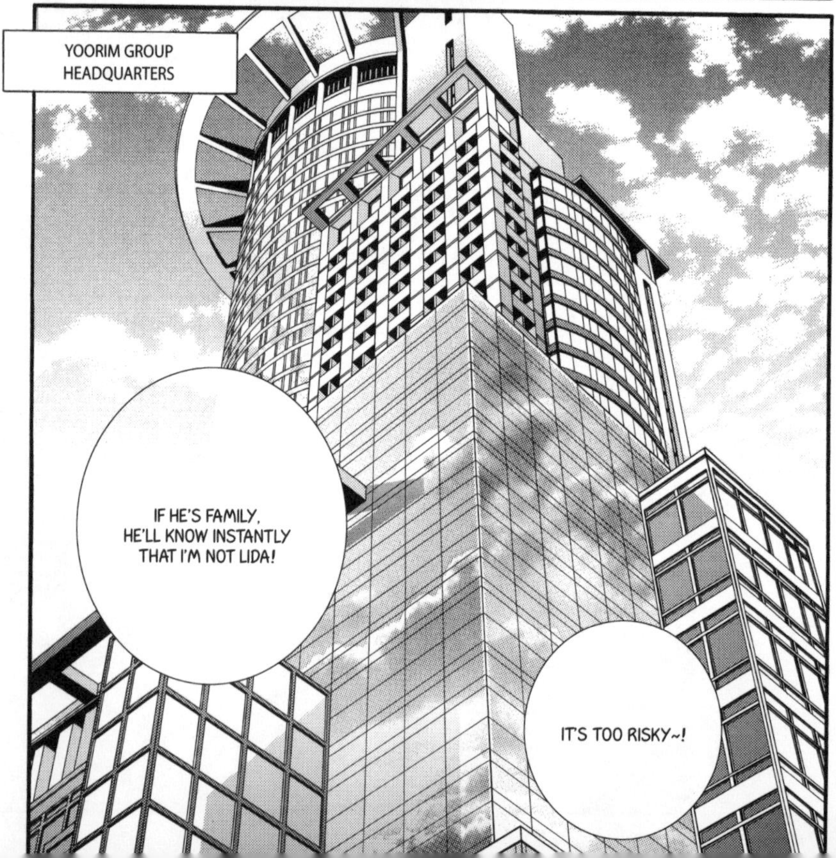
YOORIM GROUP HEADQUARTERS
IF HE'S FAMILY, HE'LL KNOW INSTANTLY THAT I'M NOT LIDA!
IT'S TOO RISKY~!

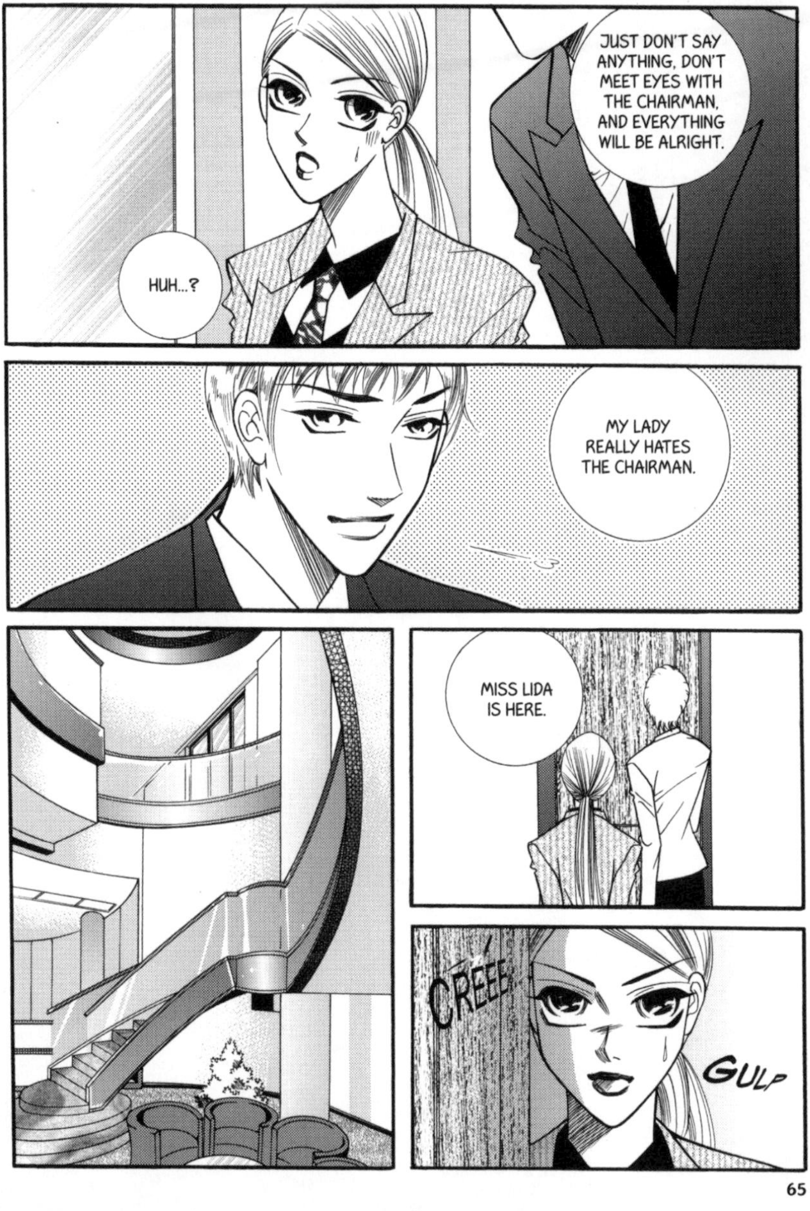
HUH...?
JUST DON'T SAY ANYTHING, DON'T MEET EYES WITH THE CHAIRMAN, AND EVERYTHING WILL BE ALRIGHT.
MY LADY REALLY HATES THE CHAIRMAN.
MISS LIDA IS HERE.
CREEE
GULP

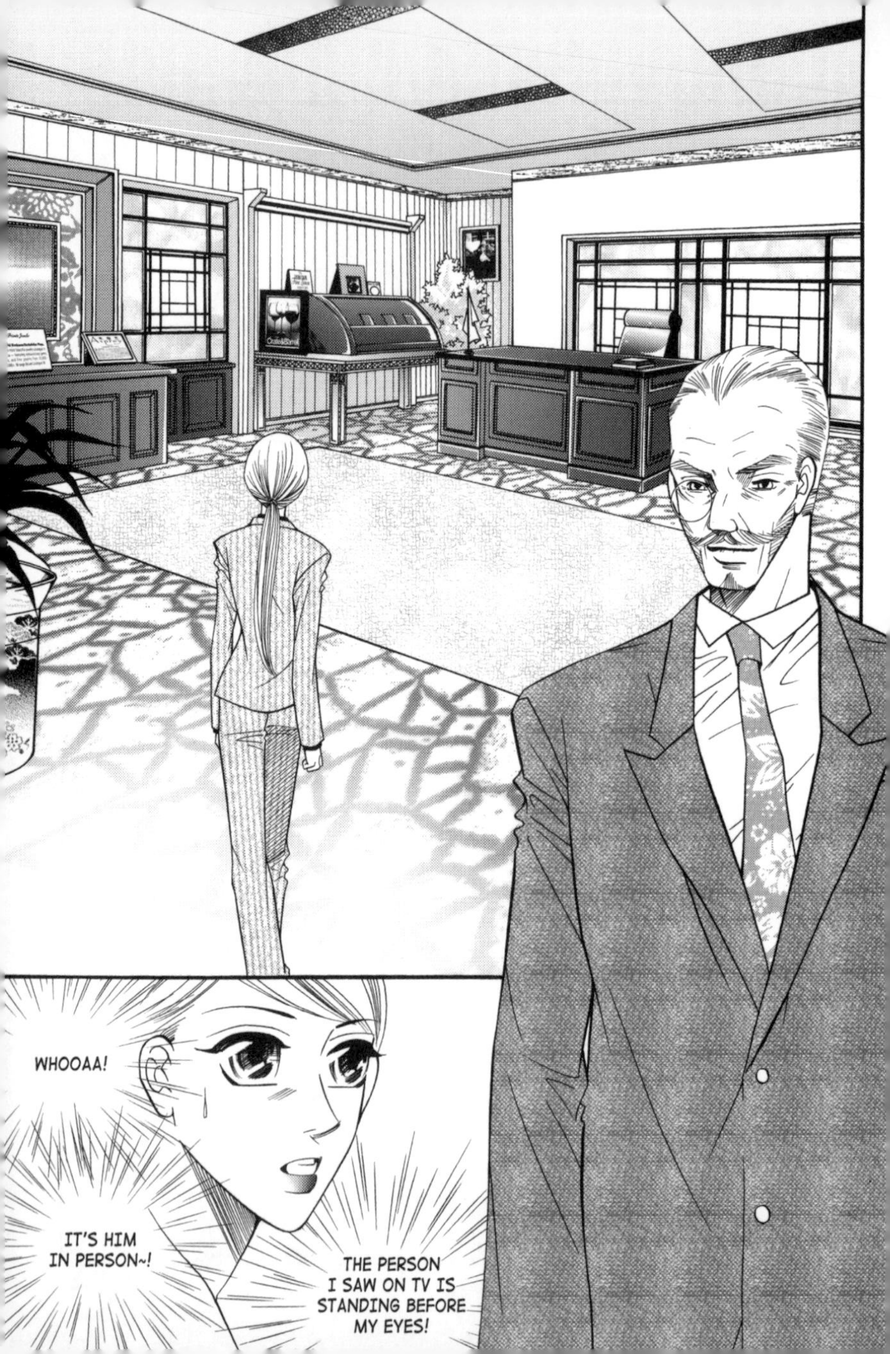
WHOOAA!
IT'S HIM IN PERSON~!
THE PERSON I SAW ON TV IS STANDING BEFORE MY EYES!

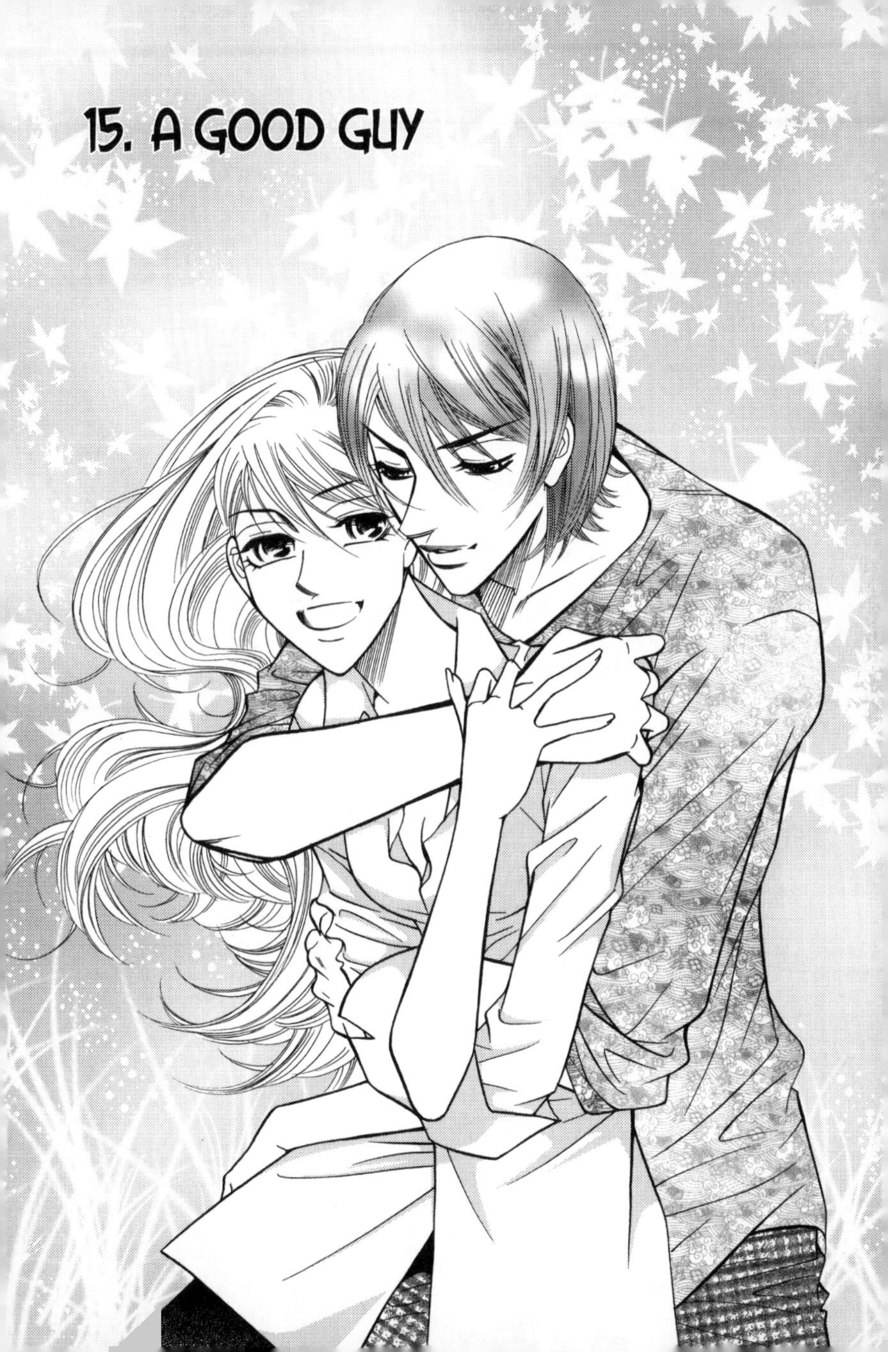
15. A GOOD GUY

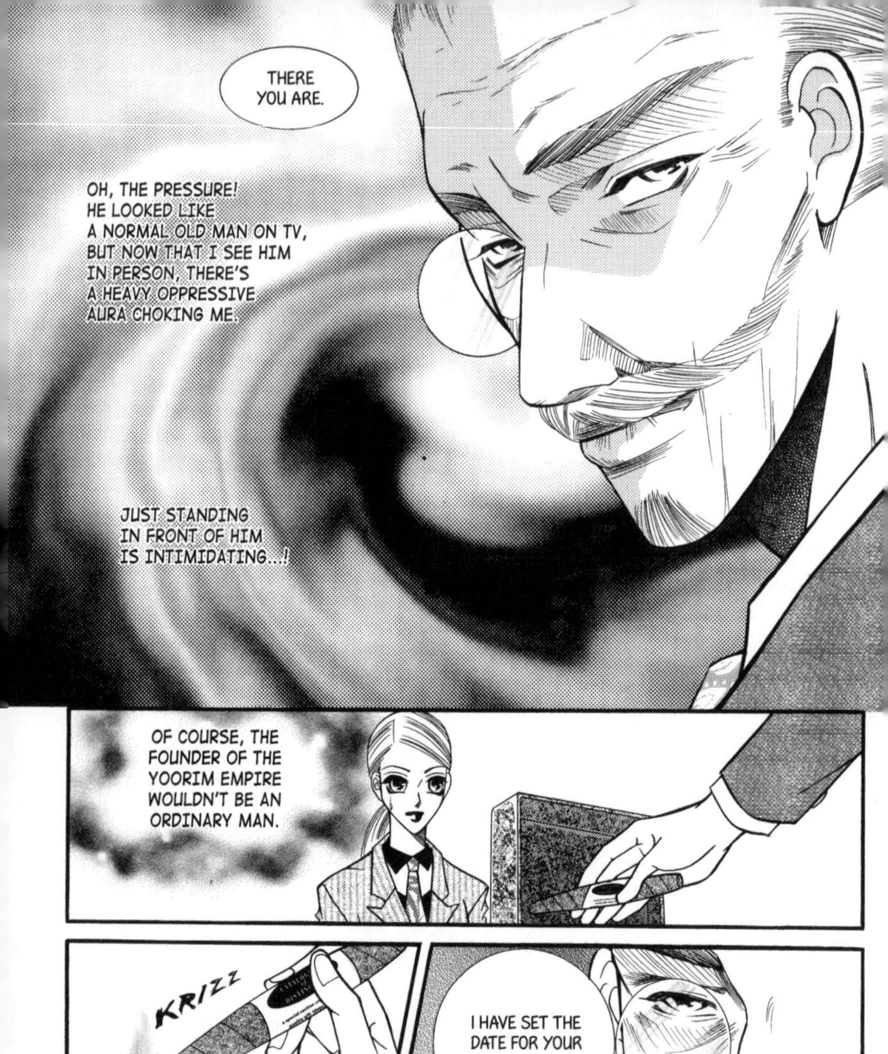
THERE YOU ARE.
OH, THE PRESSURE! HE LOOKED LIKE A NORMAL OLD MAN ON TV, BUT NOW THAT I SEE HIM IN PERSON, THERE'S A HEAVY OPPRESSIVE AURA CHOKING ME.
JUST STANDING IN FRONT OF HIM IS INTIMIDATING...!
OF COURSE, THE FOUNDER OF THE YOORIM EMPIRE WOULDN'T BE AN ORDINARY MAN.
KRIZZ
I HAVE SET THE DATE FOR YOUR ENGAGEMENT PARTY.

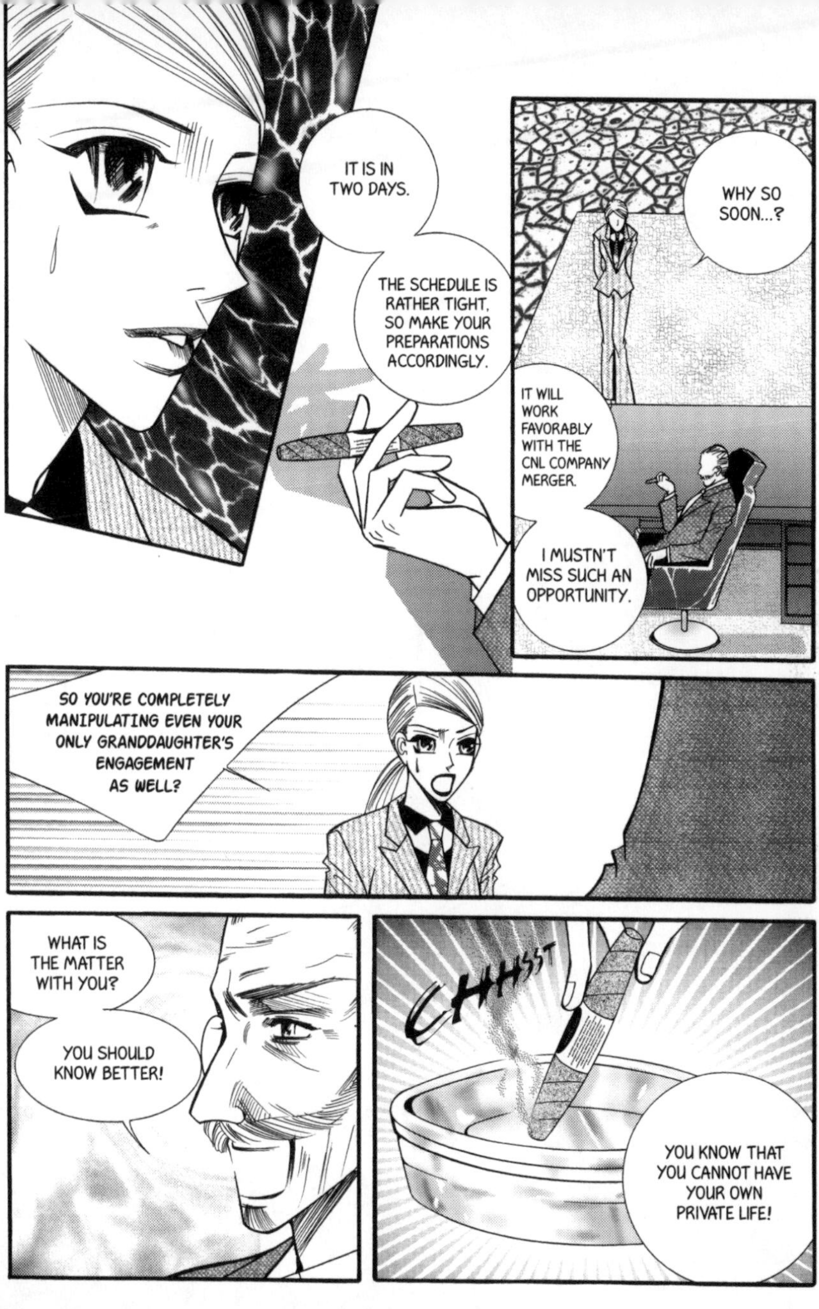
IT IS IN TWO DAYS.
THE SCHEDULE IS RATHER TIGHT, SO MAKE YOUR PREPARATIONS ACCORDINGLY.
WHY SO SOON...?
IT WILL WORK FAVORABLY WITH THE CNL COMPANY MERGER.
I MUSTN'T MISS SUCH AN OPPORTUNITY.
SO YOU'RE COMPLETELY MANIPULATING EVEN YOUR ONLY GRANDDAUGHTER'S ENGAGEMENT AS WELL?
WHAT IS THE MATTER WITH YOU?
YOU SHOULD KNOW BETTER!
CHHSST
YOU KNOW THAT YOU CANNOT HAVE YOUR OWN PRIVATE LIFE!

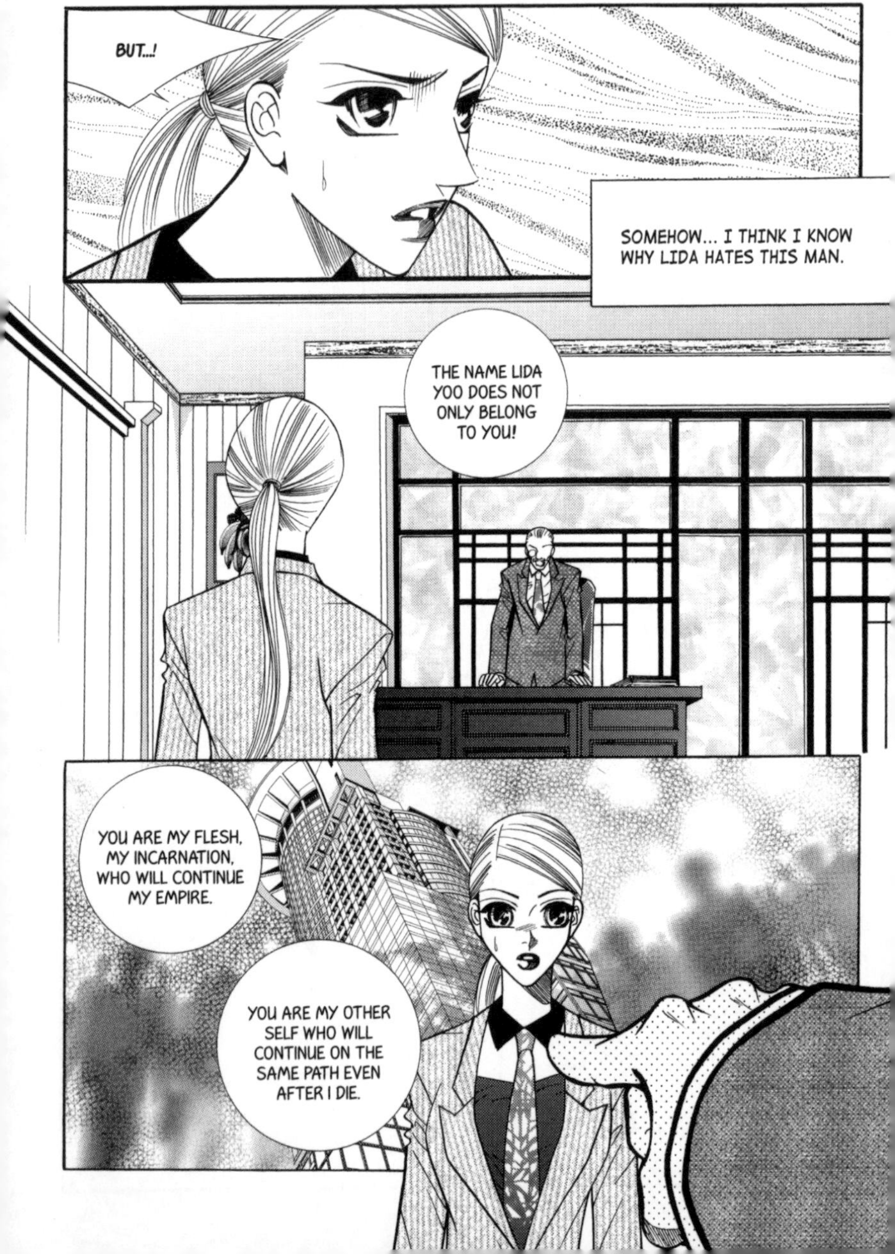
BUT...!
SOMEHOW... I THINK I KNOW WHY LIDA HATES THIS MAN.
THE NAME LIDA YOO DOES NOT ONLY BELONG TO YOU!
YOU ARE MY FLESH, MY INCARNATION, WHO WILL CONTINUE MY EMPIRE.
YOU ARE MY OTHER SELF WHO WILL CONTINUE ON THE SAME PATH EVEN AFTER I DIE.

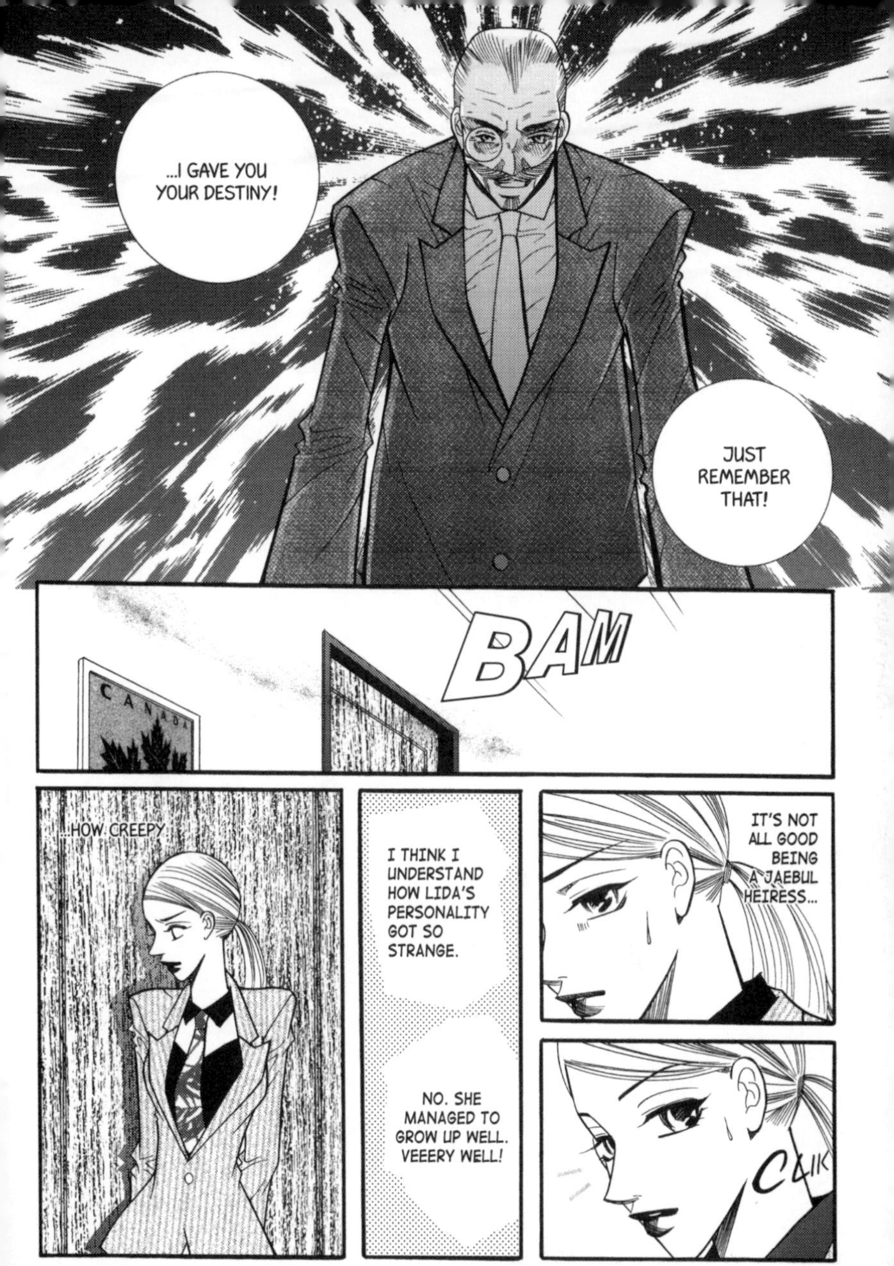
...I GAVE YOU YOUR DESTINY!
JUST REMEMBER THAT!
BAM
CANADA
...HOW CREEPY
I THINK I UNDERSTAND HOW LIDA'S PERSONALITY GOT SO STRANGE.
NO. SHE MANAGED TO GROW UP WELL. VEEERY WELL!
IT'S NOT ALL GOOD BEING A JAEBUL HEIRESS...
CLIK

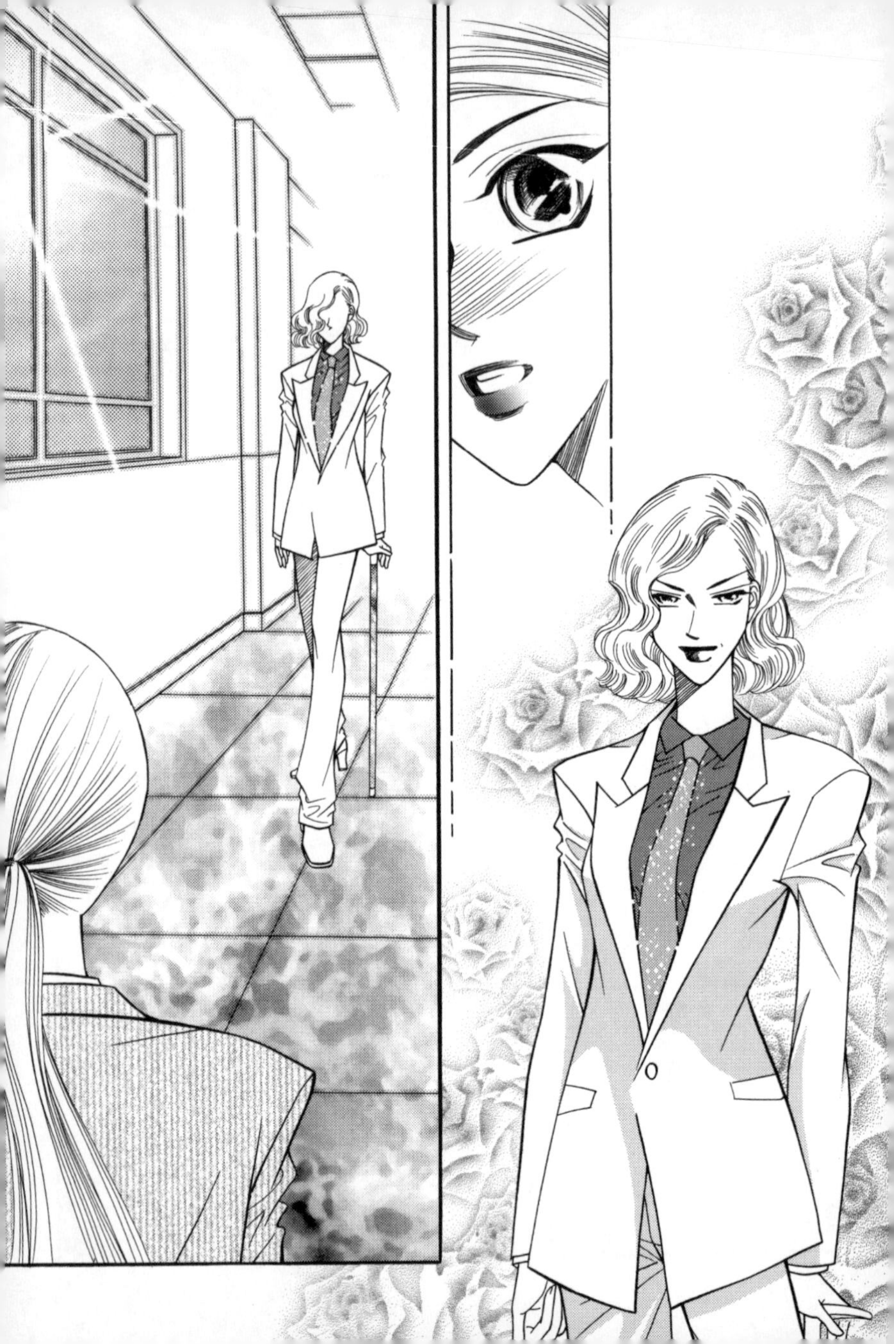

HOLY!
...A NOBLEWOMAN!

SHE'S EXACTLY A NOBLEWOMAN!

BLINDINGLY SOPHISTICATED AND ELEGANT...

CAN'T BELIEVE SUCH A PERSON REALLY EXISTS!

SO, YOU MET WITH THE CHAIRMAN.

AAHH, YES.

WHY DO YOU LOOK SO SURPRISED? DIDN'T SECRETARY OH TELL YOU OF MY ARRIVAL?

THE ENGAGEMENT WAS SCHEDULED SO SOON THAT I HAD A HARD TIME REARRANGING MY CALENDAR.

IS SHE SOMEONE THAT LIDA KNOWS?

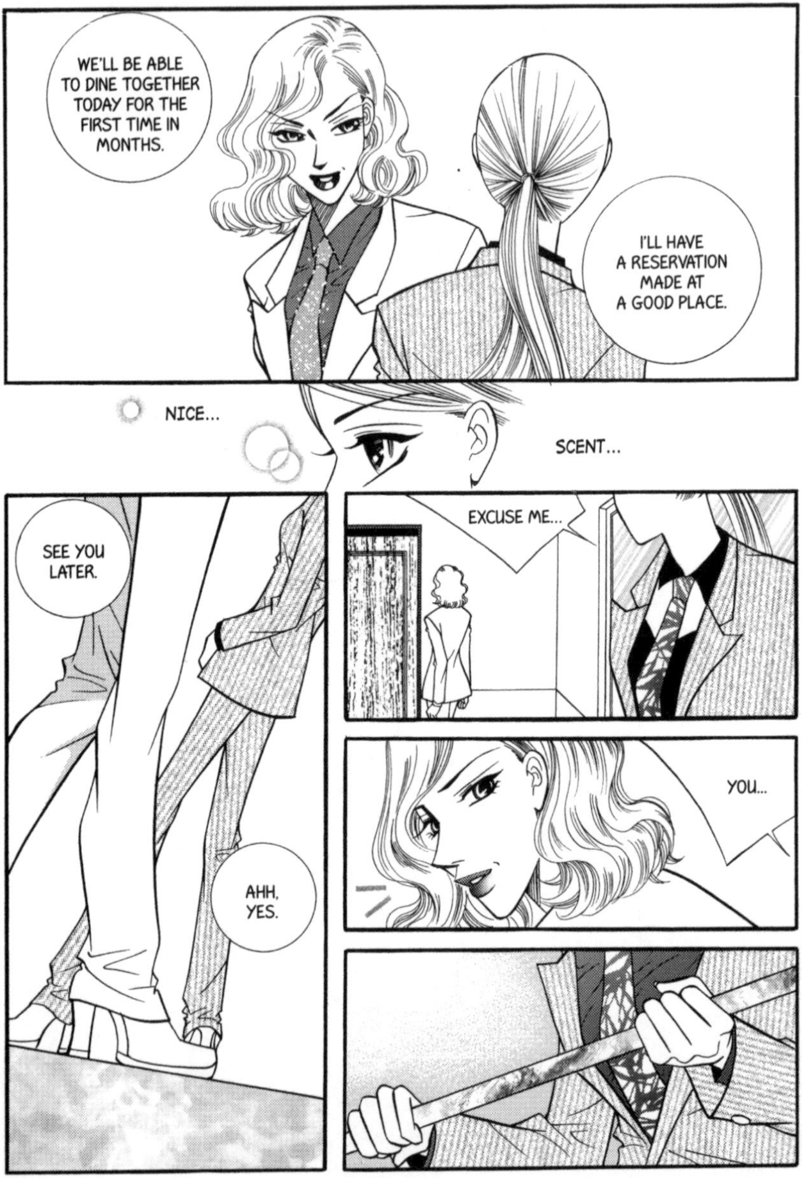
WE'LL BE ABLE TO DINE TOGETHER TODAY FOR THE FIRST TIME IN MONTHS.
I'LL HAVE A RESERVATION MADE AT A GOOD PLACE.
NICE...
SCENT...
SEE YOU LATER.
AHH, YES.
EXCUSE ME...
YOU...

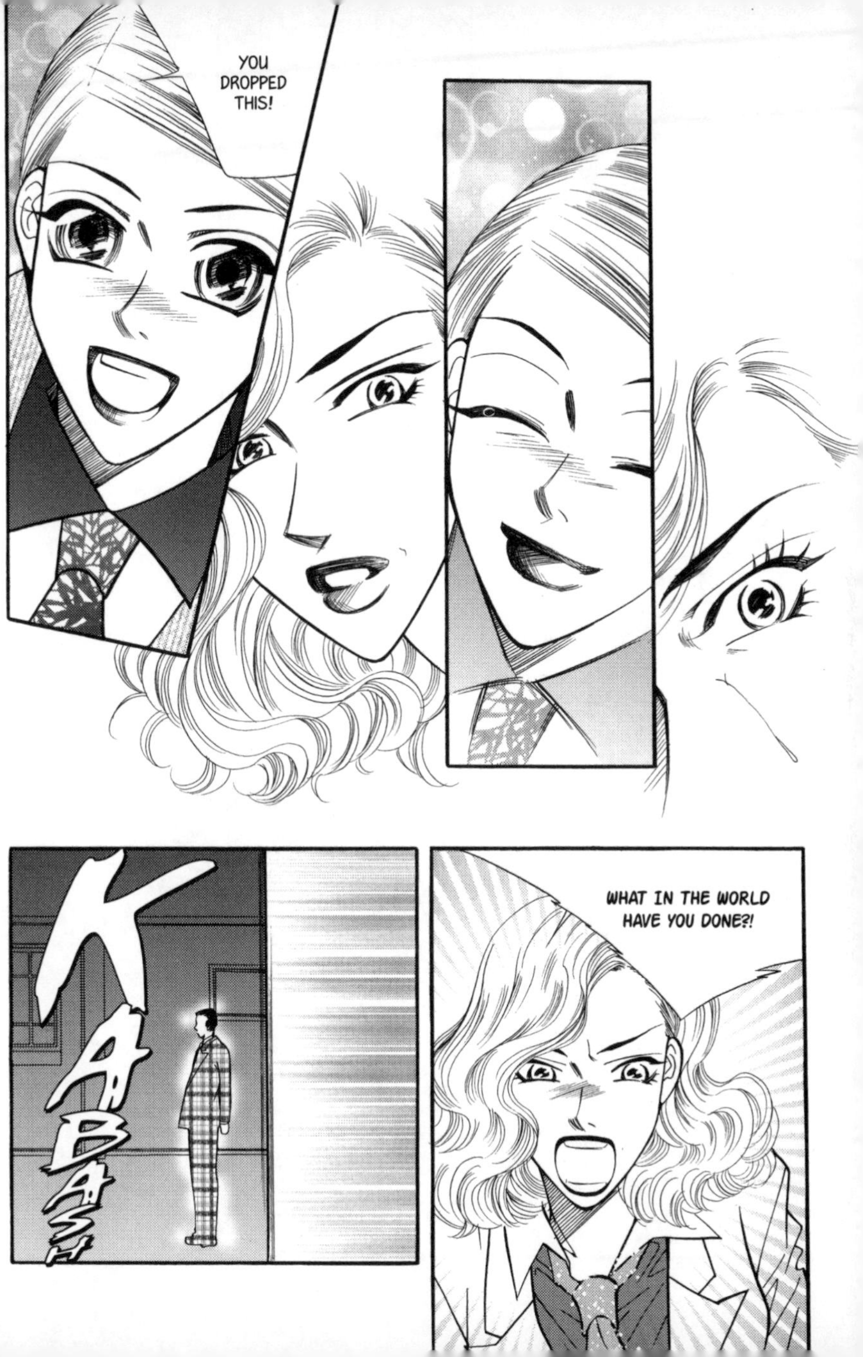
YOU DROPPED THIS!
KABASH
WHAT IN THE WORLD HAVE YOU DONE?!

MADAM....

THAT KID WHO'S PRETENDING TO BE LIDA!

PLEASE CALM DOWN.

JUST WHAT HAVE YOU DONE?

CALM DOWN?!

AT FIRST, MISS LIDA STARTED THIS AS A JOKE, BUT...

THE THREATS TURNED OUT TO BE REAL, SO I CONTINUED IT ON MY OWN.

BUT THIS ACT WILL END IN TWO DAYS!

THE BLACKMAILERS SENT A MESSAGE THAT THEY WOULD KILL HER AT THE ENGAGEMENT.

WE ARE DEFINITELY GOING TO CATCH THEM THIS TIME AND REVEAL THEIR IDENTITY!

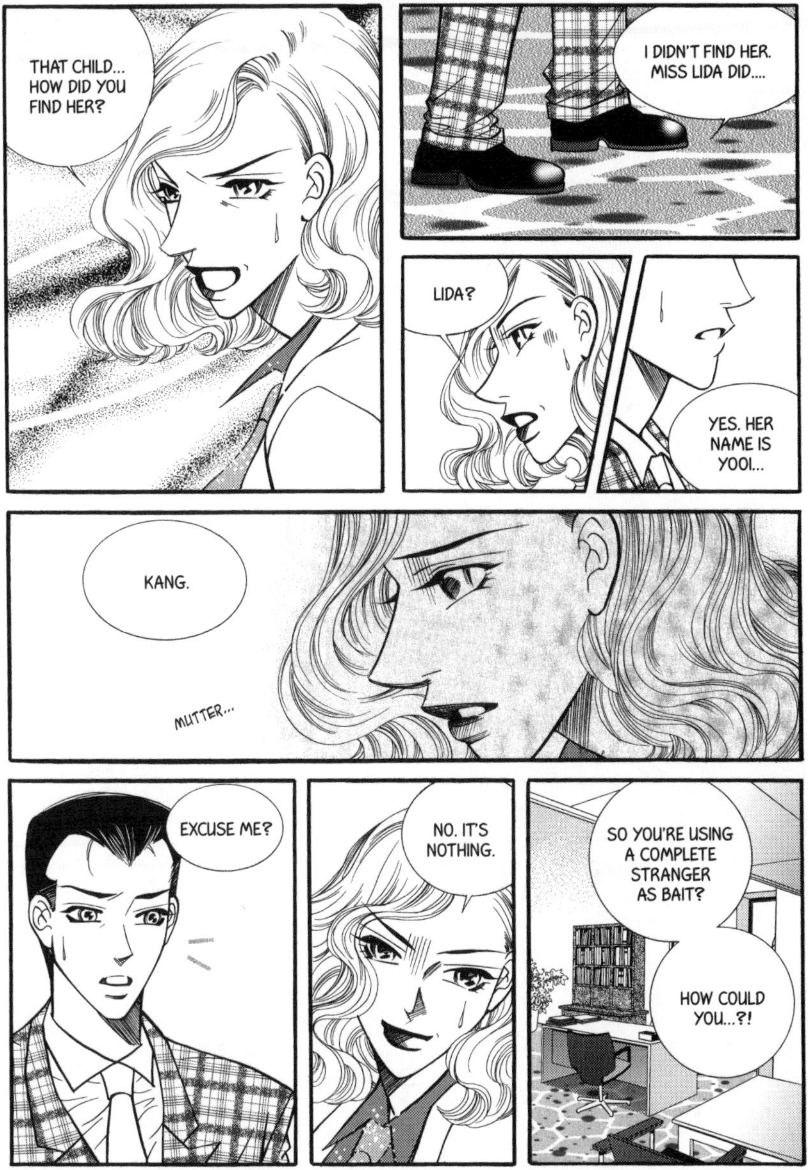
THAT CHILD... HOW DID YOU FIND HER?
I DIDN'T FIND HER. MISS LIDA DID....
LIDA?
YES. HER NAME IS YOOI...
KANG.
MUTTER...
EXCUSE ME?
NO. IT'S NOTHING.
SO YOU'RE USING A COMPLETE STRANGER AS BAIT?
HOW COULD YOU...?!

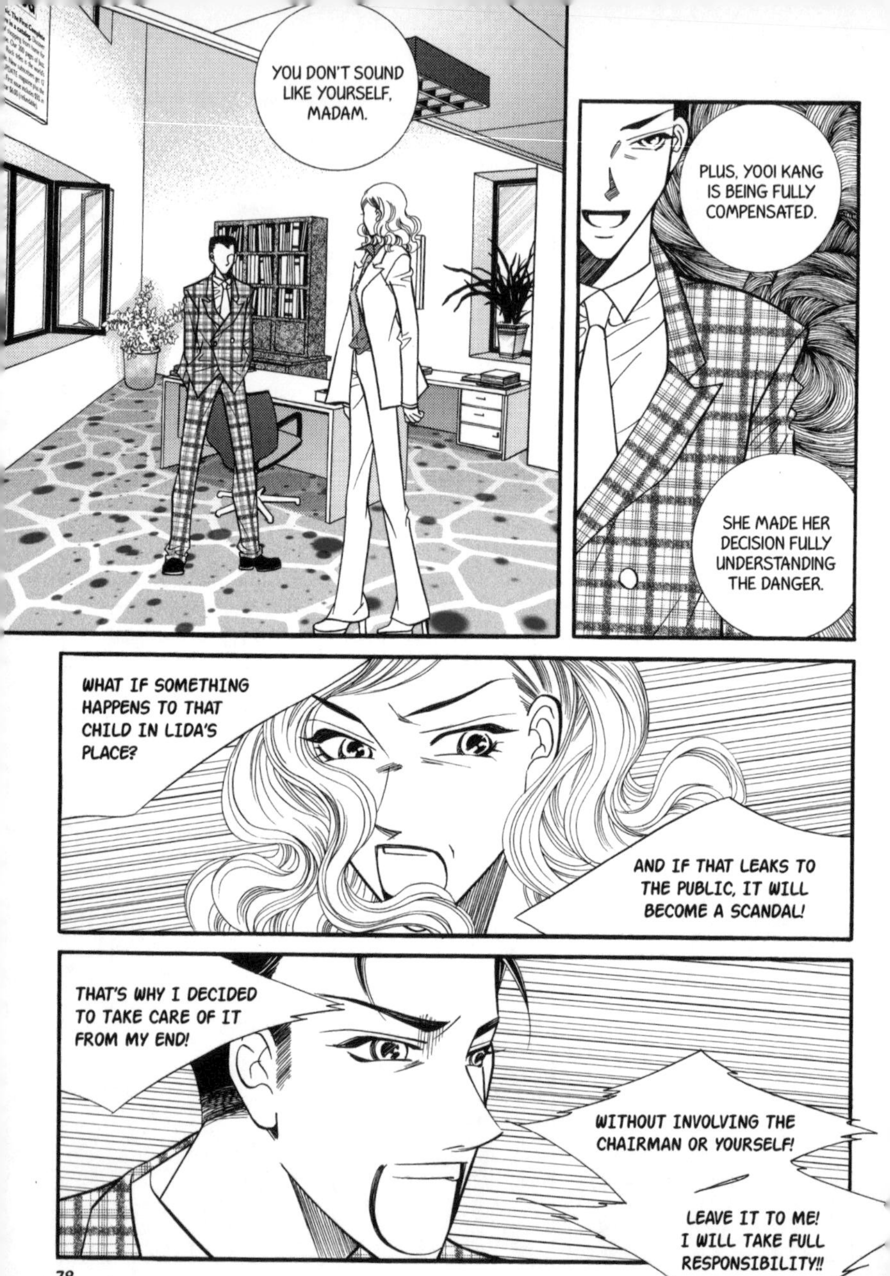
YOU DON'T SOUND LIKE YOURSELF, MADAM.
PLUS, YOOI KANG IS BEING FULLY COMPENSATED.
SHE MADE HER DECISION FULLY UNDERSTANDING THE DANGER.
WHAT IF SOMETHING HAPPENS TO THAT CHILD IN LIDA'S PLACE?
AND IF THAT LEAKS TO THE PUBLIC, IT WILL BECOME A SCANDAL!
THAT'S WHY I DECIDED TO TAKE CARE OF IT FROM MY END!
WITHOUT INVOLVING THE CHAIRMAN OR YOURSELF!
LEAVE IT TO ME! I WILL TAKE FULL RESPONSIBILITY!!

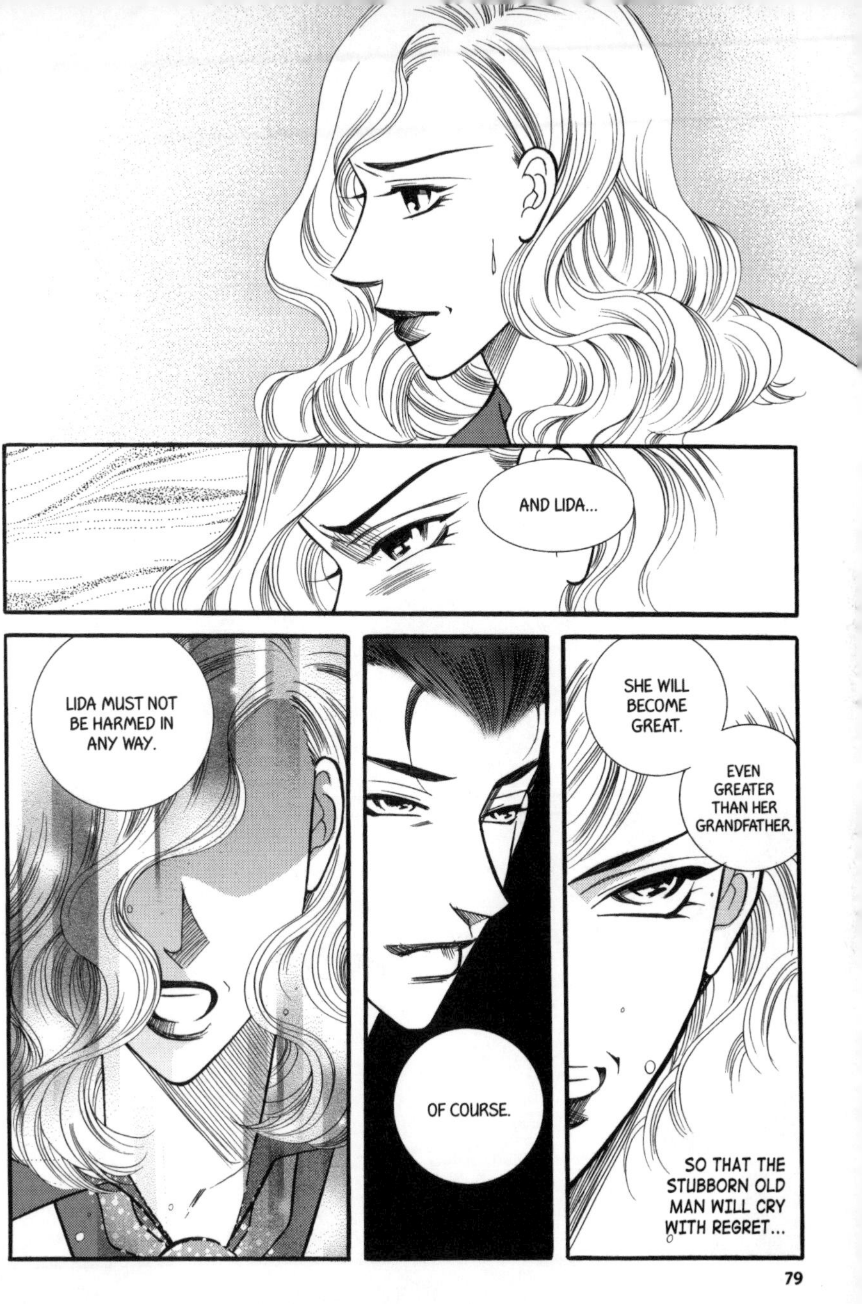
AND LIDA...
LIDA MUST NOT BE HARMED IN ANY WAY.
OF COURSE.
SHE WILL BECOME GREAT.
EVEN GREATER THAN HER GRANDFATHER.
SO THAT THE STUBBORN OLD MAN WILL CRY WITH REGRET...

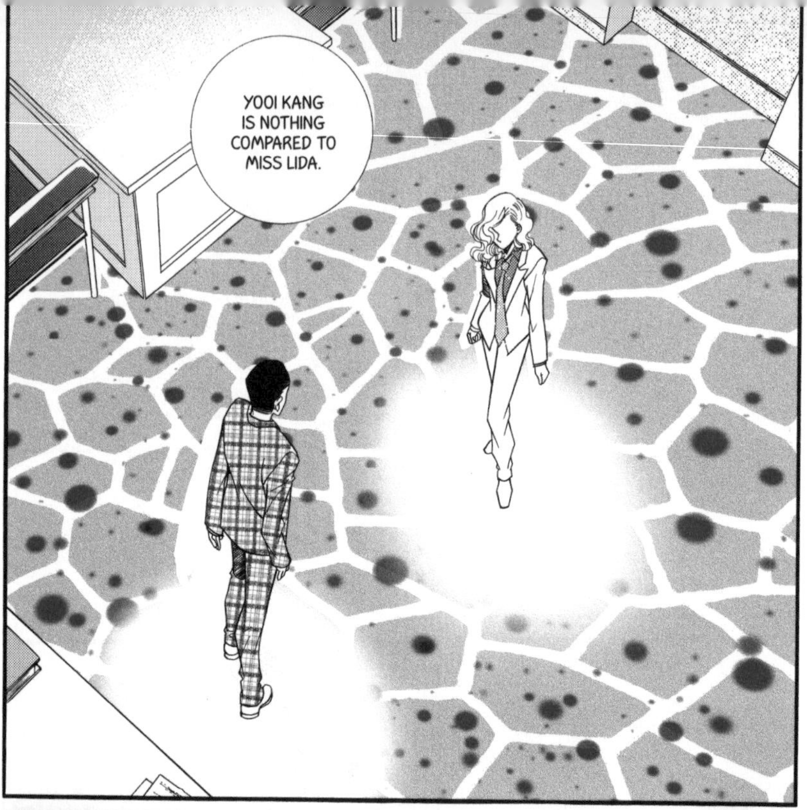
YOOI KANG IS NOTHING COMPARED TO MISS LIDA.

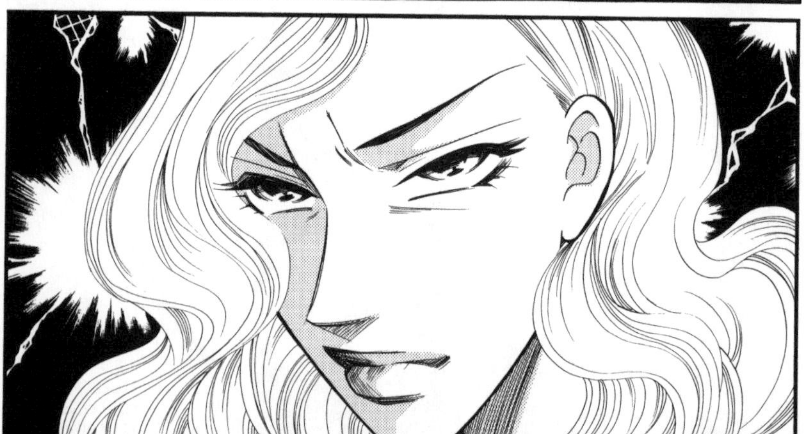

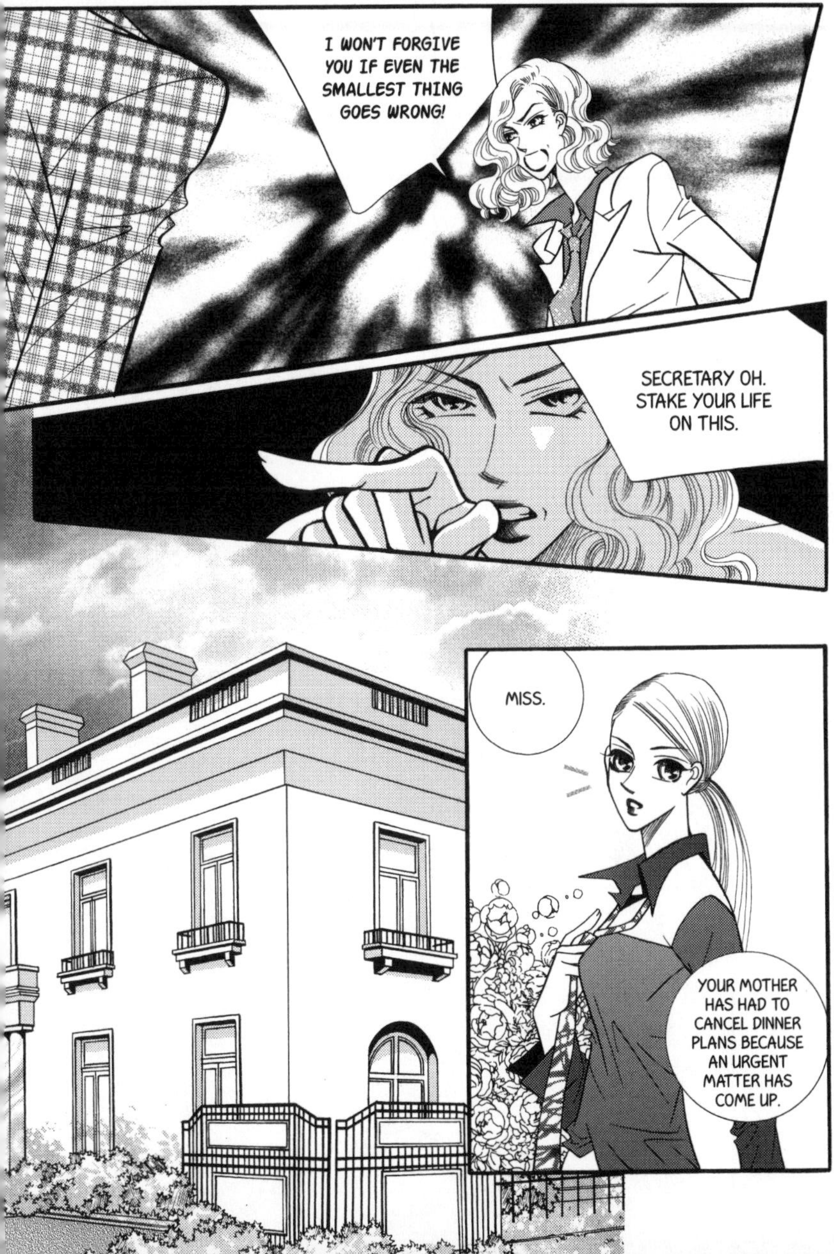
I WON'T FORGIVE YOU IF EVEN THE SMALLEST THING GOES WRONG!
SECRETARY OH. STAKE YOUR LIFE ON THIS.
MISS.
YOUR MOTHER HAS HAD TO CANCEL DINNER PLANS BECAUSE AN URGENT MATTER HAS COME UP.

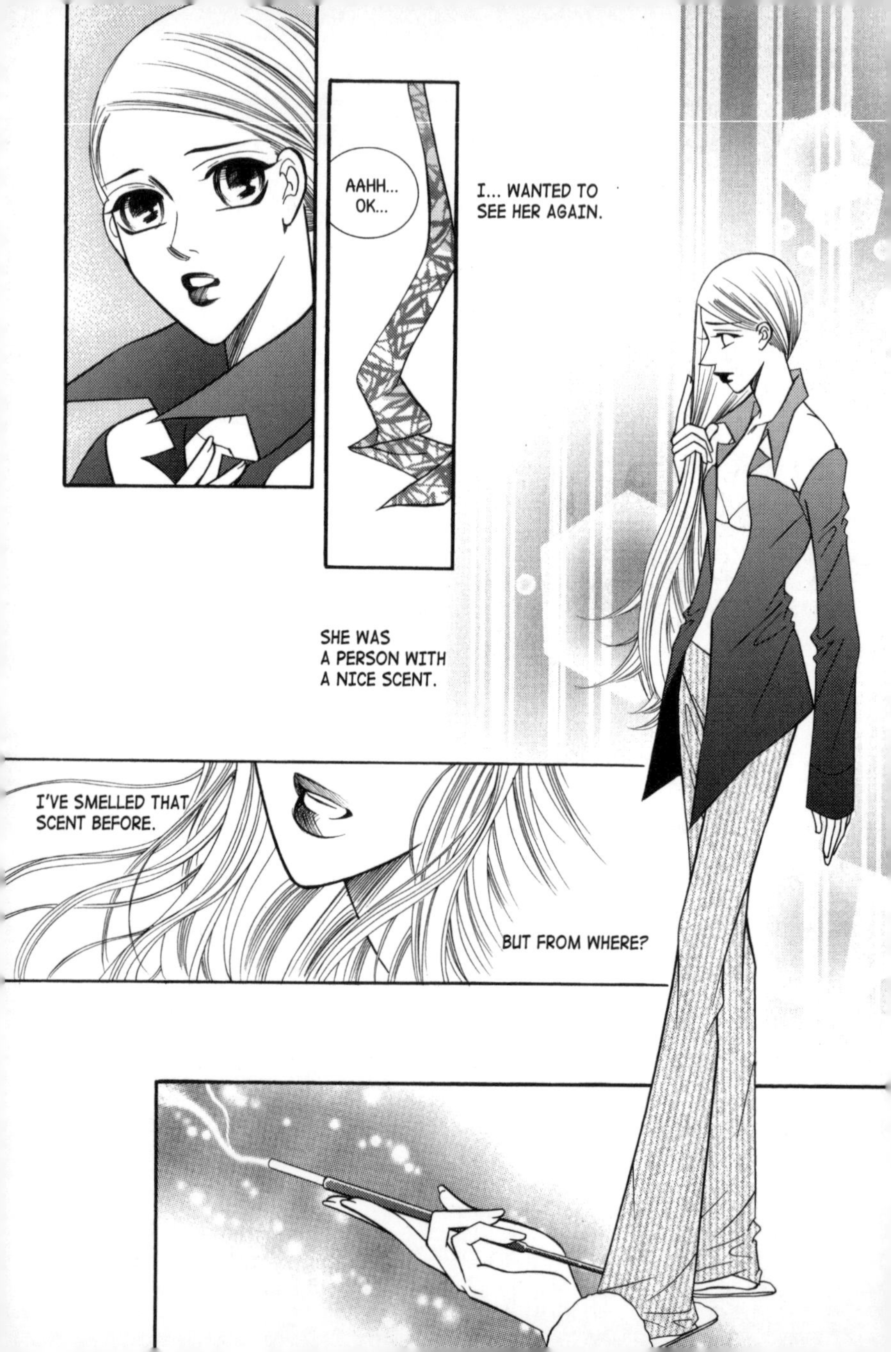

AAHH... OK...
I... WANTED TO SEE HER AGAIN.
SHE WAS A PERSON WITH A NICE SCENT.
I'VE SMELLED THAT SCENT BEFORE.
BUT FROM WHERE?

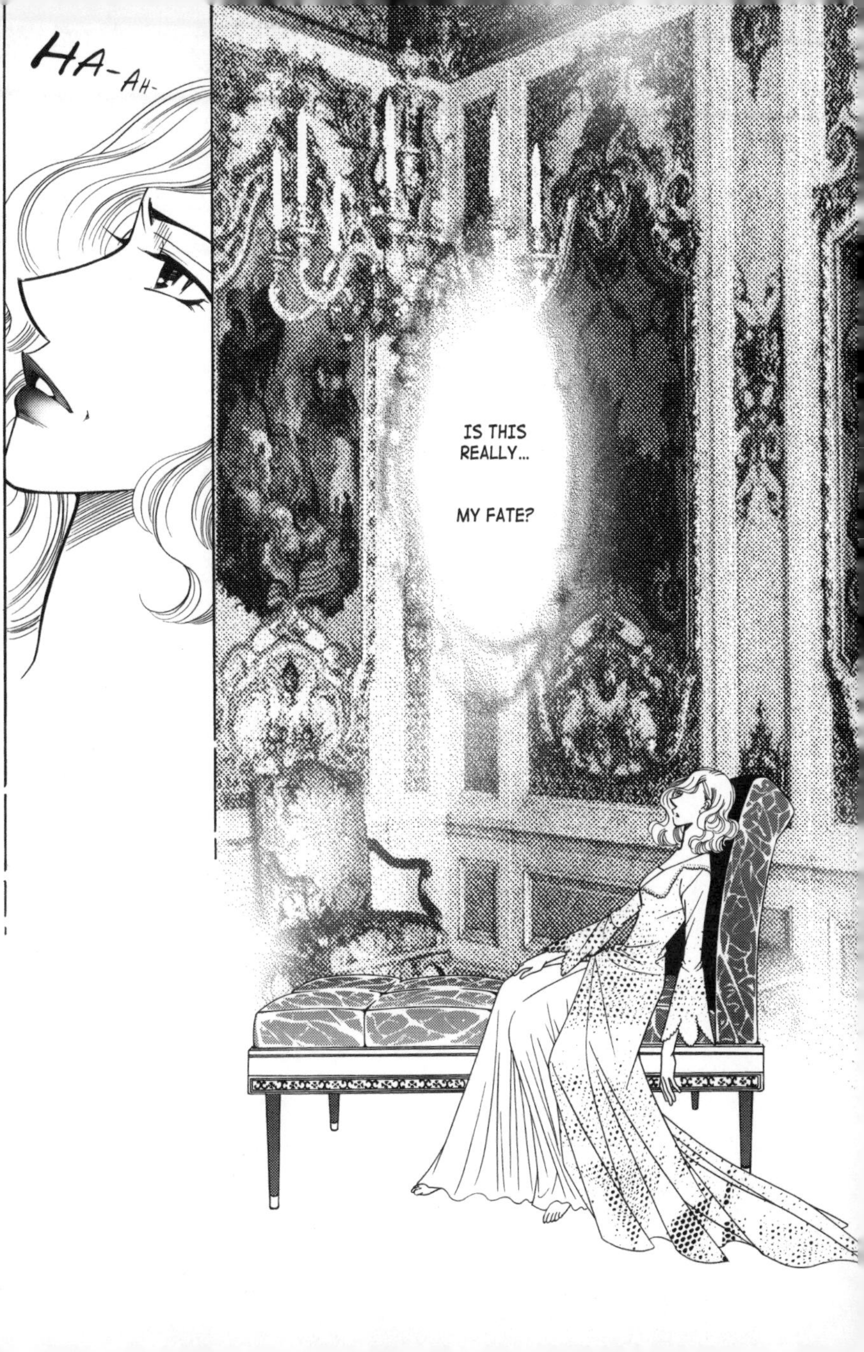

HA-AH-
IS THIS REALLY...
MY FATE?

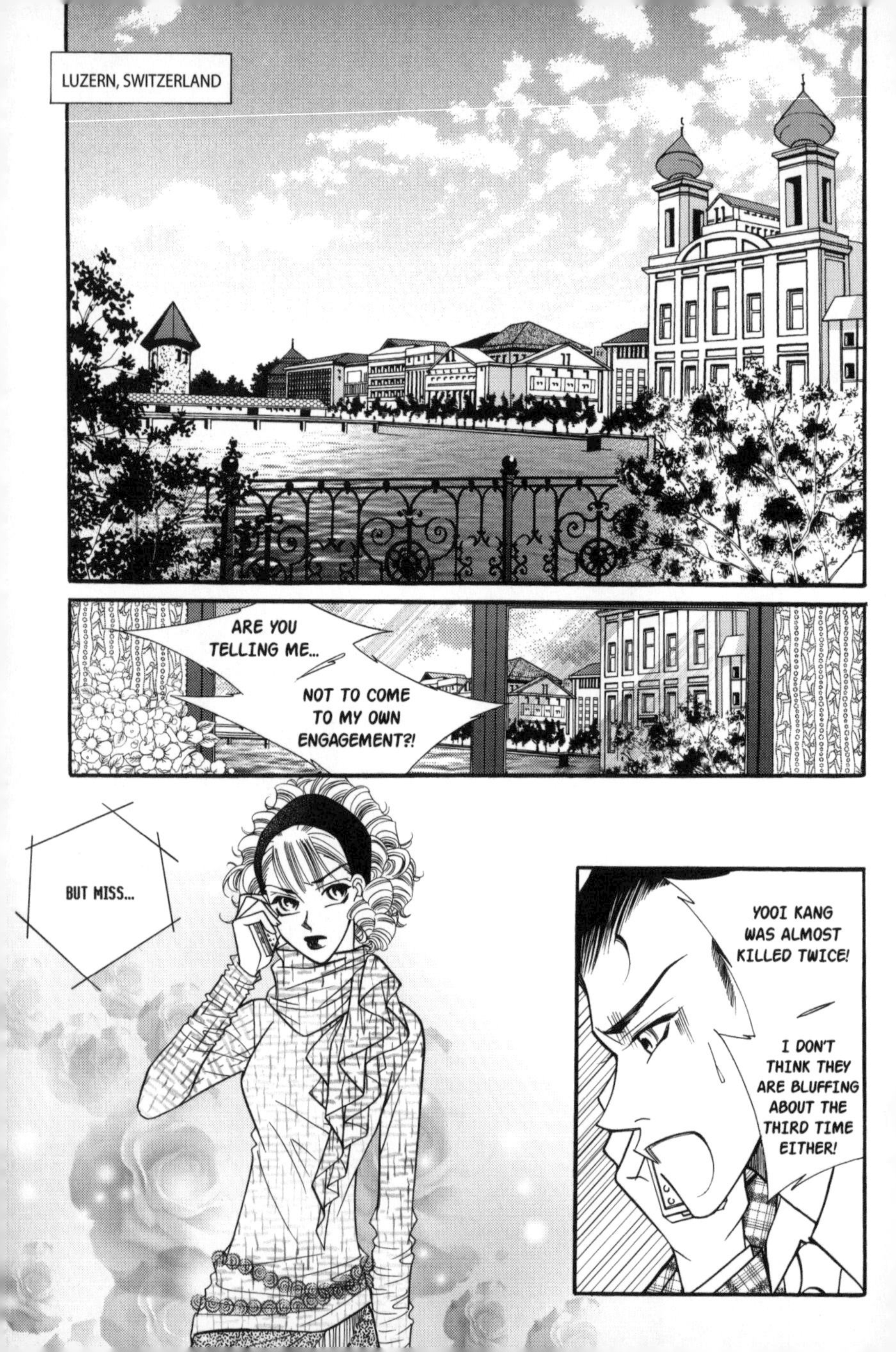
LUZERN, SWITZERLAND
ARE YOU TELLING ME...
NOT TO COME TO MY OWN ENGAGEMENT?!
BUT MISS...
YOOI KANG WAS ALMOST KILLED TWICE!
I DON'T THINK THEY ARE BLUFFING ABOUT THE THIRD TIME EITHER!

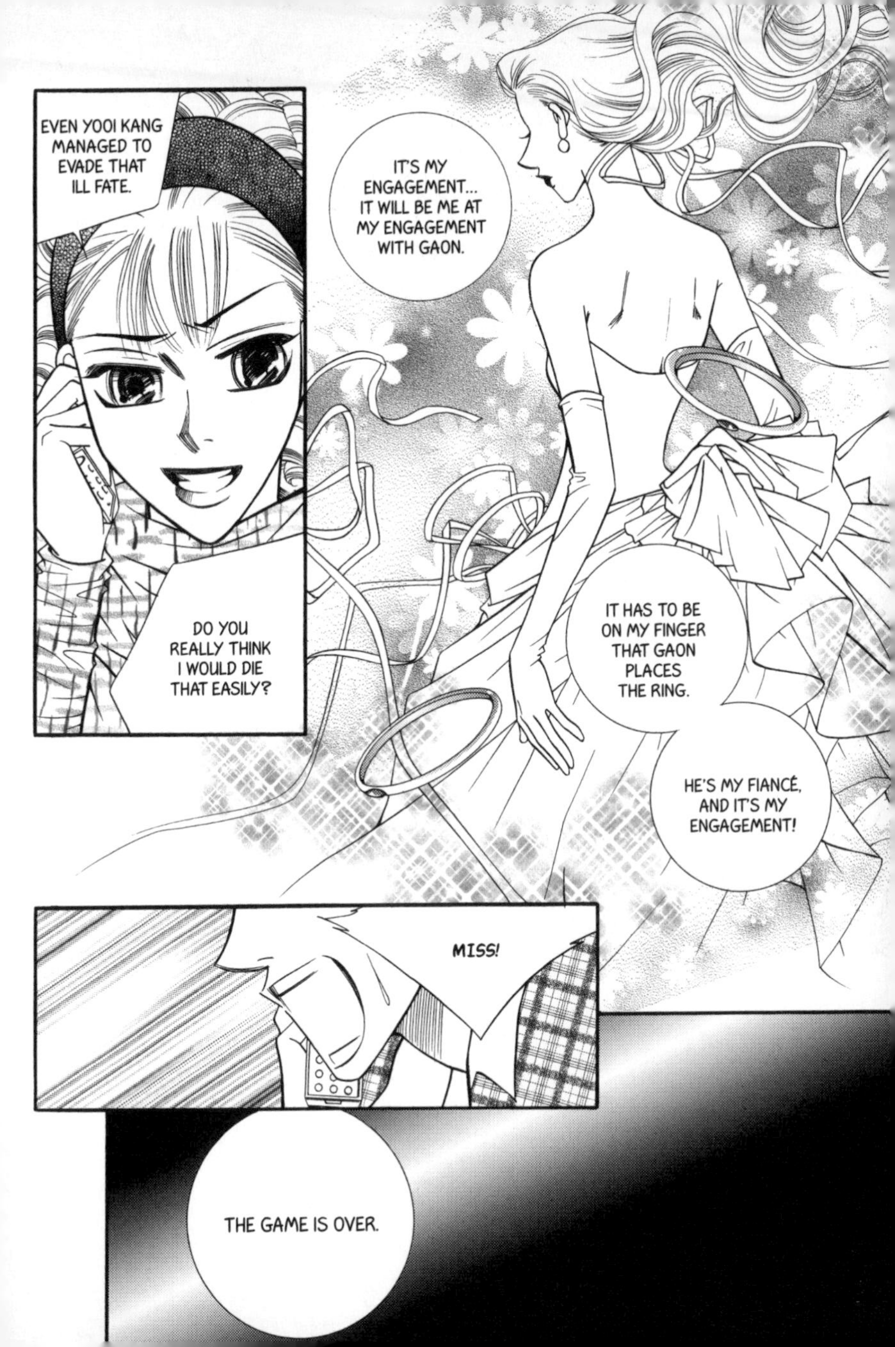
EVEN YOOI KANG MANAGED TO EVADE THAT ILL FATE.
DO YOU REALLY THINK I WOULD DIE THAT EASILY?
IT'S MY ENGAGEMENT... IT WILL BE ME AT MY ENGAGEMENT WITH GAON.
IT HAS TO BE ON MY FINGER THAT GAON PLACES THE RING.
HE'S MY FIANCÉ, AND IT'S MY ENGAGEMENT!
MISS!
THE GAME IS OVER.

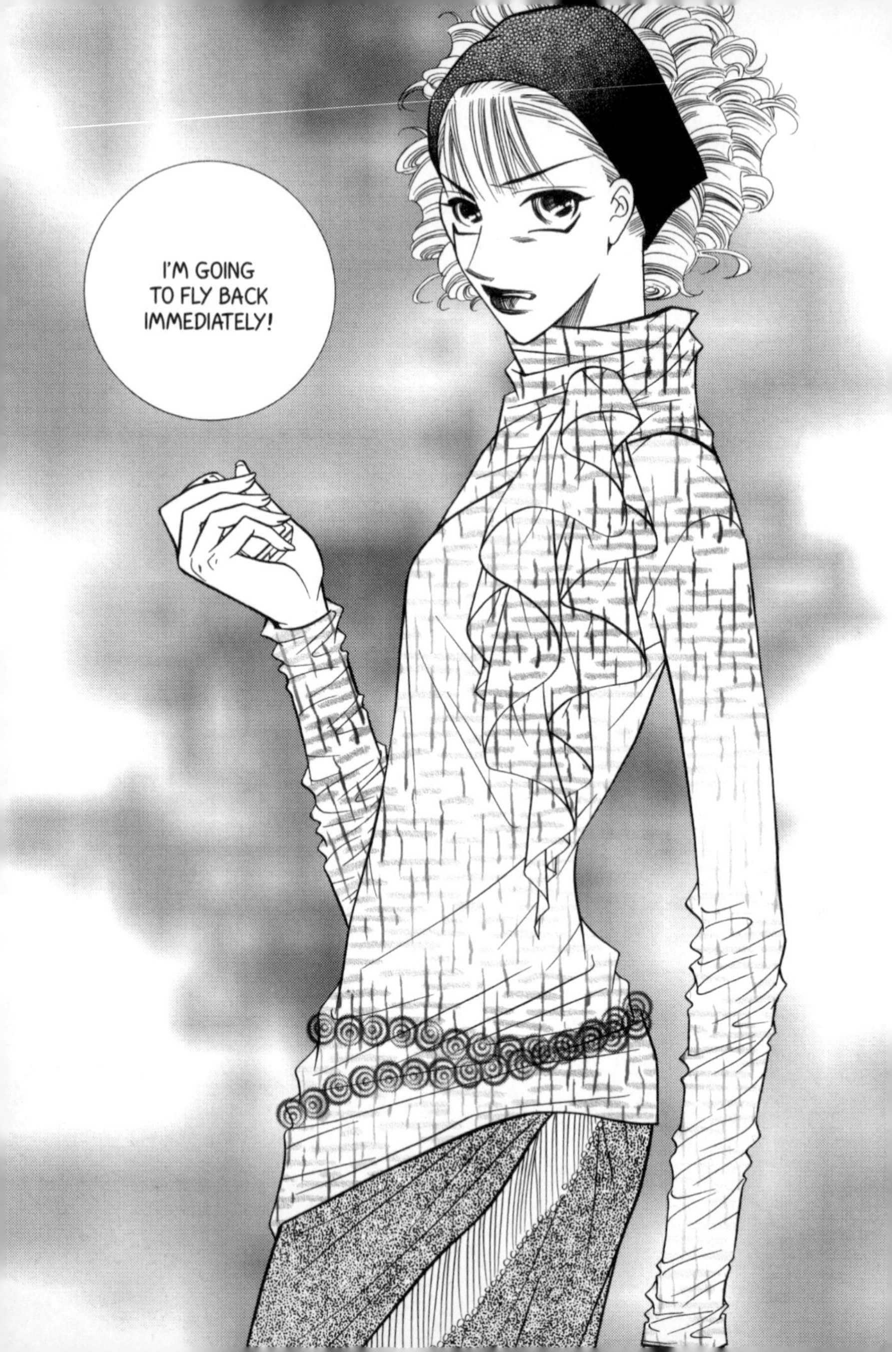
I'M GOING TO FLY BACK IMMEDIATELY!

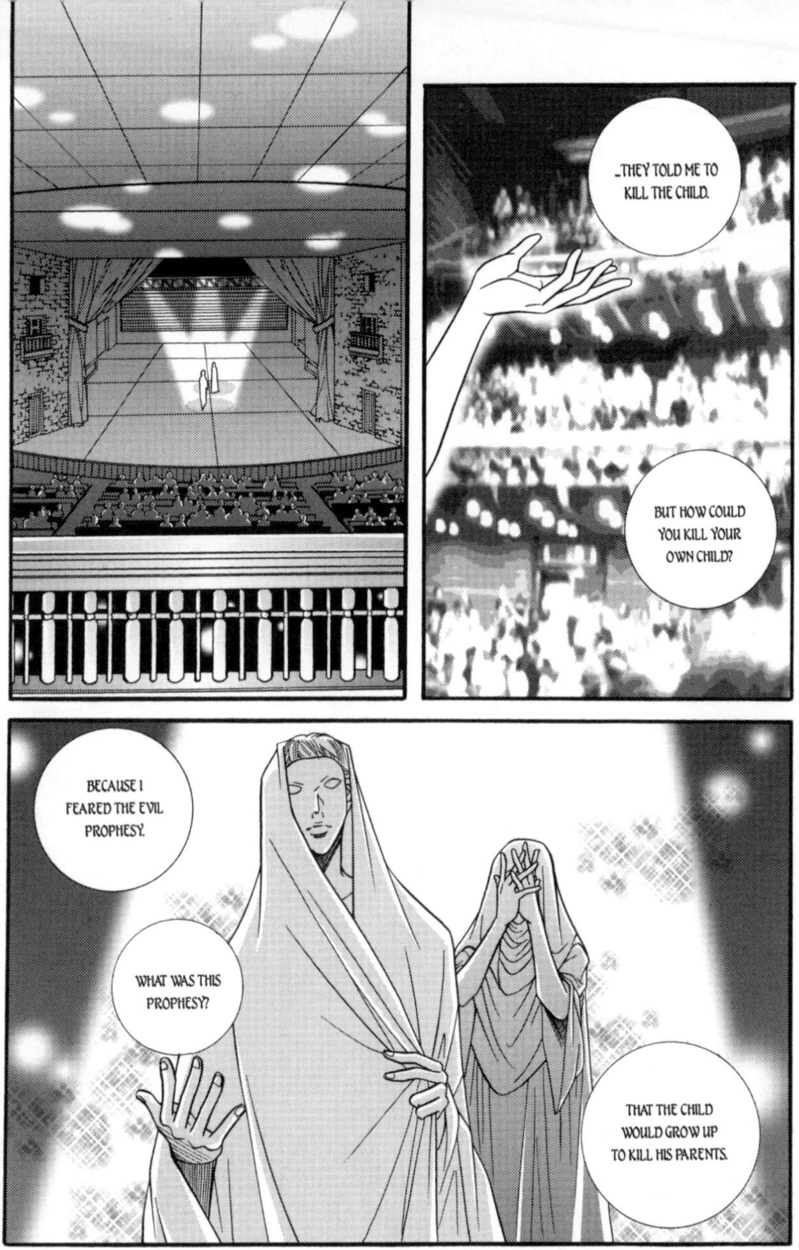
...THEY TOLD ME TO KILL THE CHILD.
BUT HOW COULD YOU KILL YOUR OWN CHILD?
BECAUSE I FEARED THE EVIL PROPHESY.
WHAT WAS THIS PROPHESY?
THAT THE CHILD WOULD GROW UP TO KILL HIS PARENTS.

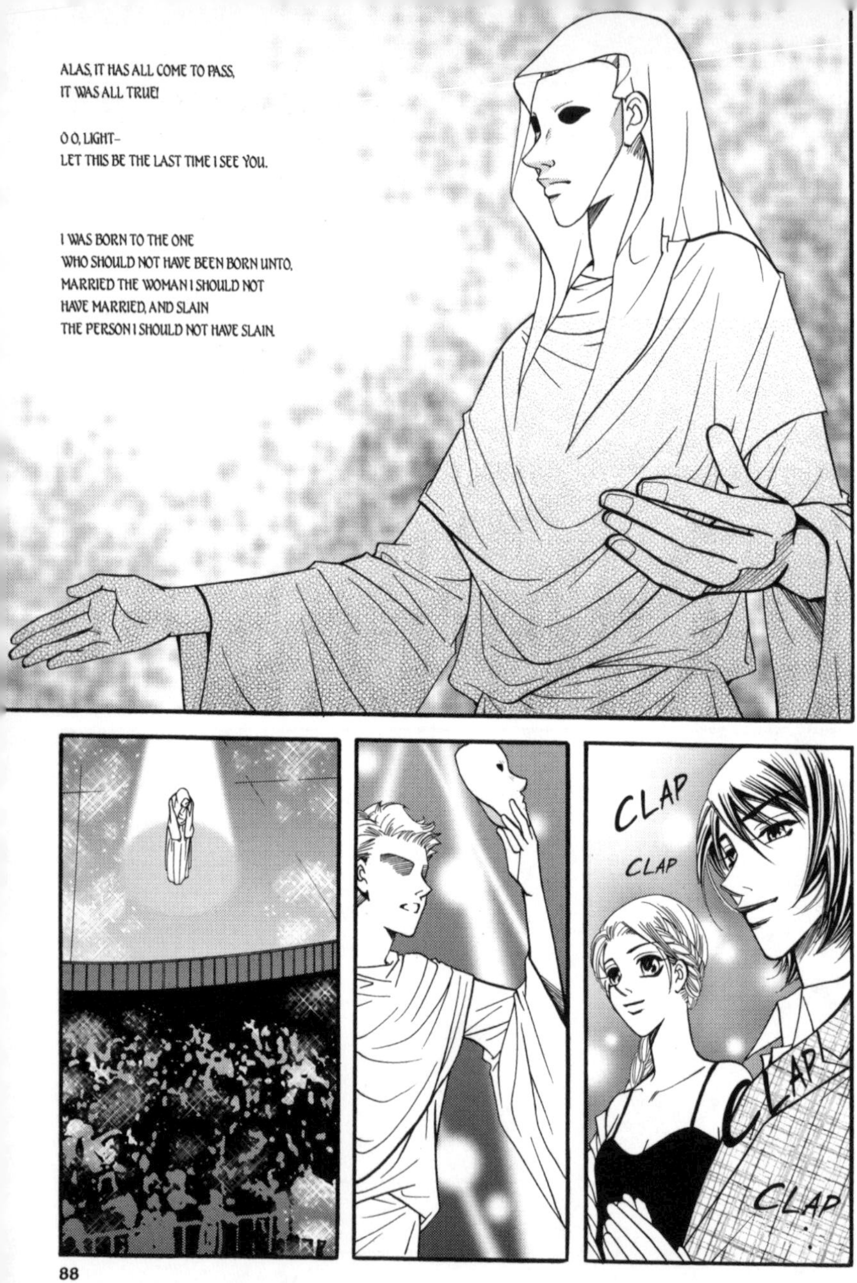
ALAS, IT HAS ALL COME TO PASS,
IT WAS ALL TRUE!
O O, LIGHT–
LET THIS BE THE LAST TIME I SEE YOU.
I WAS BORN TO THE ONE
WHO SHOULD NOT HAVE BEEN BORN UNTO,
MARRIED THE WOMAN I SHOULD NOT
HAVE MARRIED, AND SLAIN
THE PERSON I SHOULD NOT HAVE SLAIN.
CLAP
CLAP
CLAP
CLAP

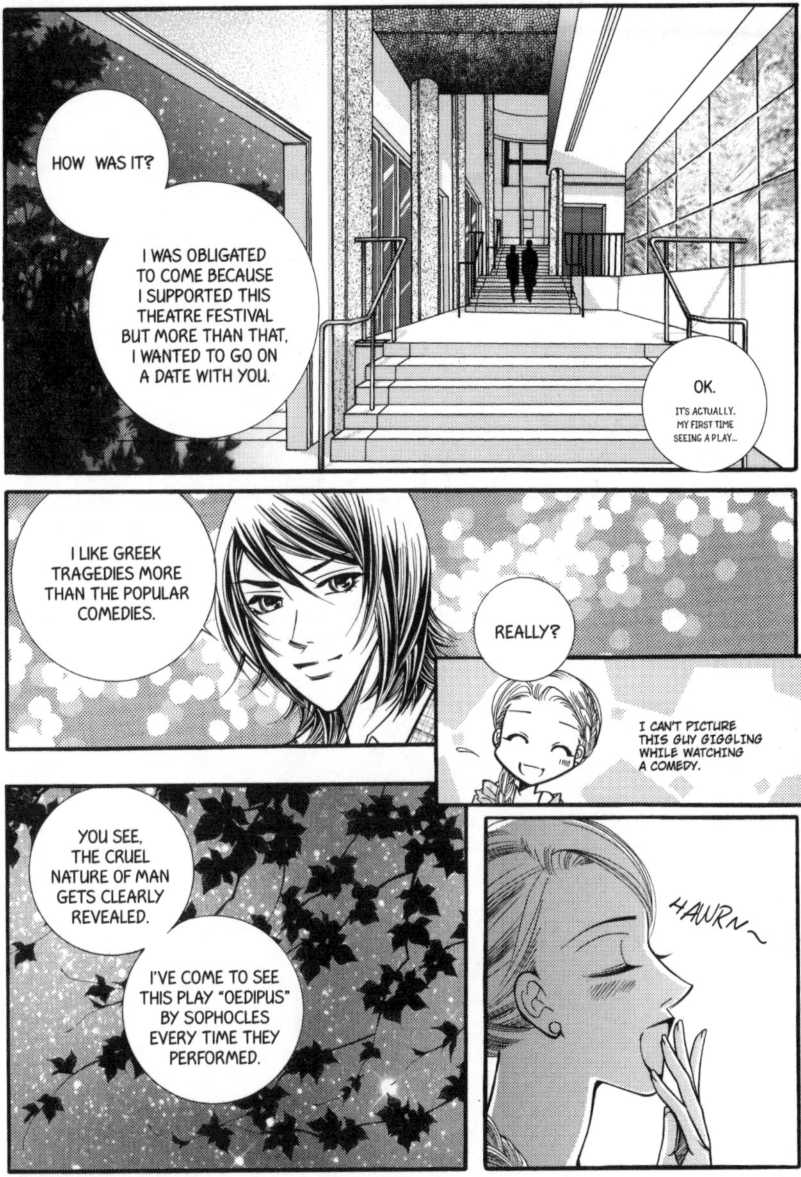
HOW WAS IT?
I WAS OBLIGATED TO COME BECAUSE I SUPPORTED THIS THEATRE FESTIVAL BUT MORE THAN THAT, I WANTED TO GO ON A DATE WITH YOU.
OK.
IT'S ACTUALLY, MY FIRST TIME SEEING A PLAY...
I LIKE GREEK TRAGEDIES MORE THAN THE POPULAR COMEDIES.
REALLY?
I CAN'T PICTURE THIS GUY GIGGLING WHILE WATCHING A COMEDY.
YOU SEE, THE CRUEL NATURE OF MAN GETS CLEARLY REVEALED.
I'VE COME TO SEE THIS PLAY "OEDIPUS" BY SOPHOCLES EVERY TIME THEY PERFORMED.
HAURN~

OH, SORRY. ARE YOU SLEEPY?

GREEK TRAGEDIES CAN BE SOMEWHAT BORING.

AH, NO, NO...

I'M JUST SHORT OF ATT

I'LL PICK SOMETHING LIGHTER NEXT TIME.

THAT'S ALRIGHT. A REFINED GENTLEMAN SHOULDN'T LOWER HIMSELF TO THE LEVEL OF A LOWER PERSON.

EEP! SORRY, SORRY!

I CAN GO ANYWHERE YOU WANT. I CAN DO COMEDY PLAYS, DAEHAKRO, STANDUP COMEDIES...

I CAN ALSO GO TO THE CONCERT OF THE LATEST IDOL GROUP THAT GIRLS LOVE... EVEN TO A LINGERIE SHOP IF NECESSARY!!!

IDOL GROUP?

LINGERIE SHOP?

ISN'T HE OVERREACTING?

YOU AREN'T MAD...?

GAON IN YOOI'S EYES

PSSS

?

TEE HEE

OH MAN, THIS GUY~!

IT'S SO NOT LIKE HIM, BUT HE'S SO CUTE SOMETIMES~!

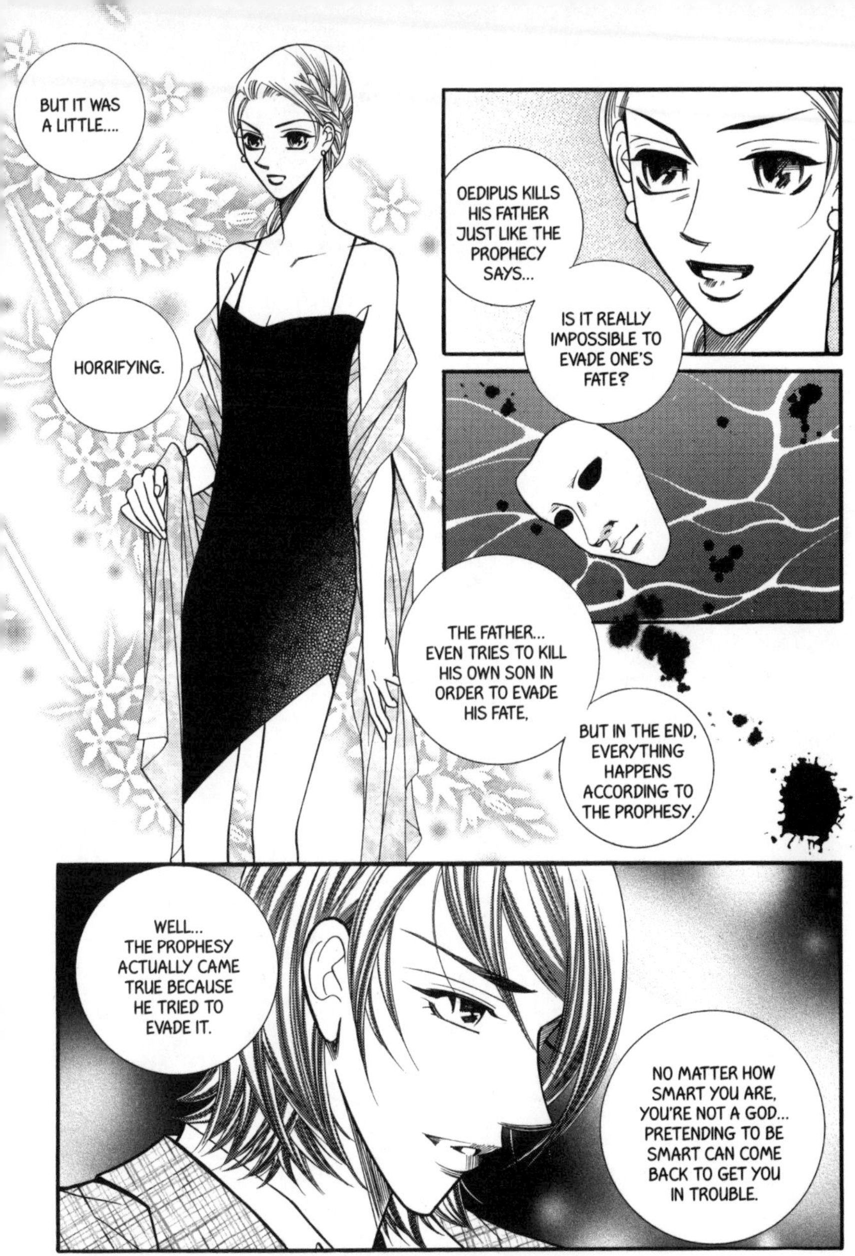
BUT IT WAS A LITTLE....
HORRIFYING.
OEDIPUS KILLS HIS FATHER JUST LIKE THE PROPHECY SAYS...
IS IT REALLY IMPOSSIBLE TO EVADE ONE'S FATE?
THE FATHER... EVEN TRIES TO KILL HIS OWN SON IN ORDER TO EVADE HIS FATE,
BUT IN THE END, EVERYTHING HAPPENS ACCORDING TO THE PROPHESY.
WELL... THE PROPHESY ACTUALLY CAME TRUE BECAUSE HE TRIED TO EVADE IT.
NO MATTER HOW SMART YOU ARE, YOU'RE NOT A GOD... PRETENDING TO BE SMART CAN COME BACK TO GET YOU IN TROUBLE.

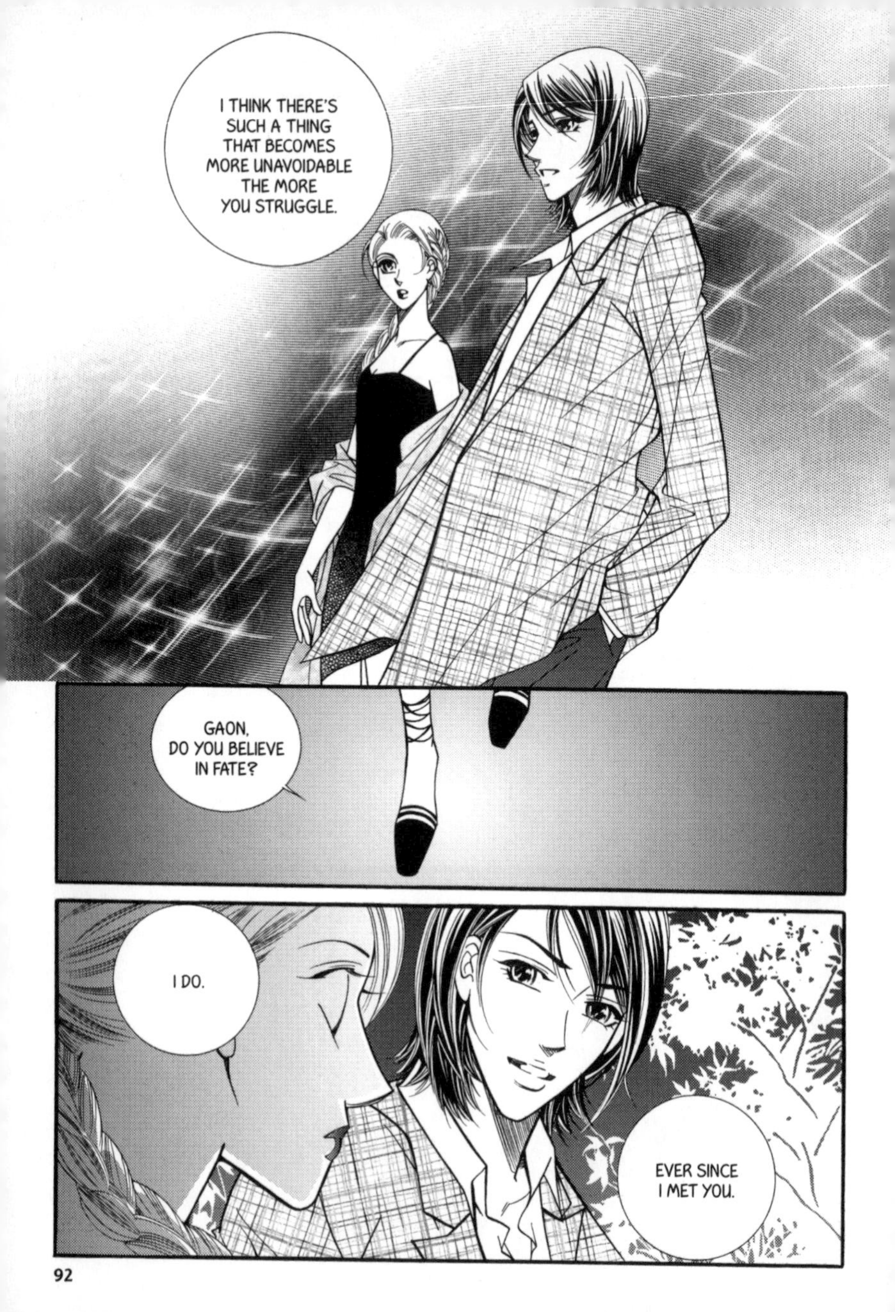
I THINK THERE'S SUCH A THING THAT BECOMES MORE UNAVOIDABLE THE MORE YOU STRUGGLE.
GAON, DO YOU BELIEVE IN FATE?
I DO.
EVER SINCE I MET YOU.

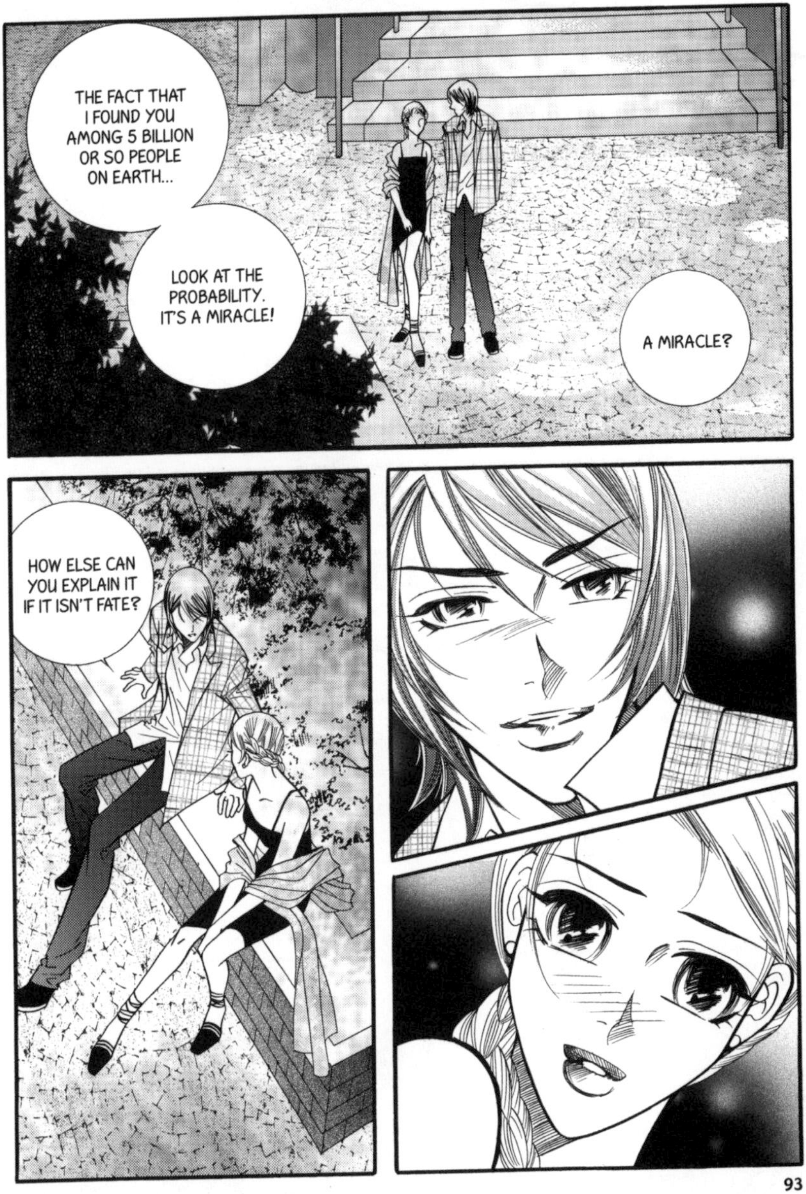
THE FACT THAT I FOUND YOU AMONG 5 BILLION OR SO PEOPLE ON EARTH...
LOOK AT THE PROBABILITY. IT'S A MIRACLE!
A MIRACLE?
HOW ELSE CAN YOU EXPLAIN IT IF IT ISN'T FATE?

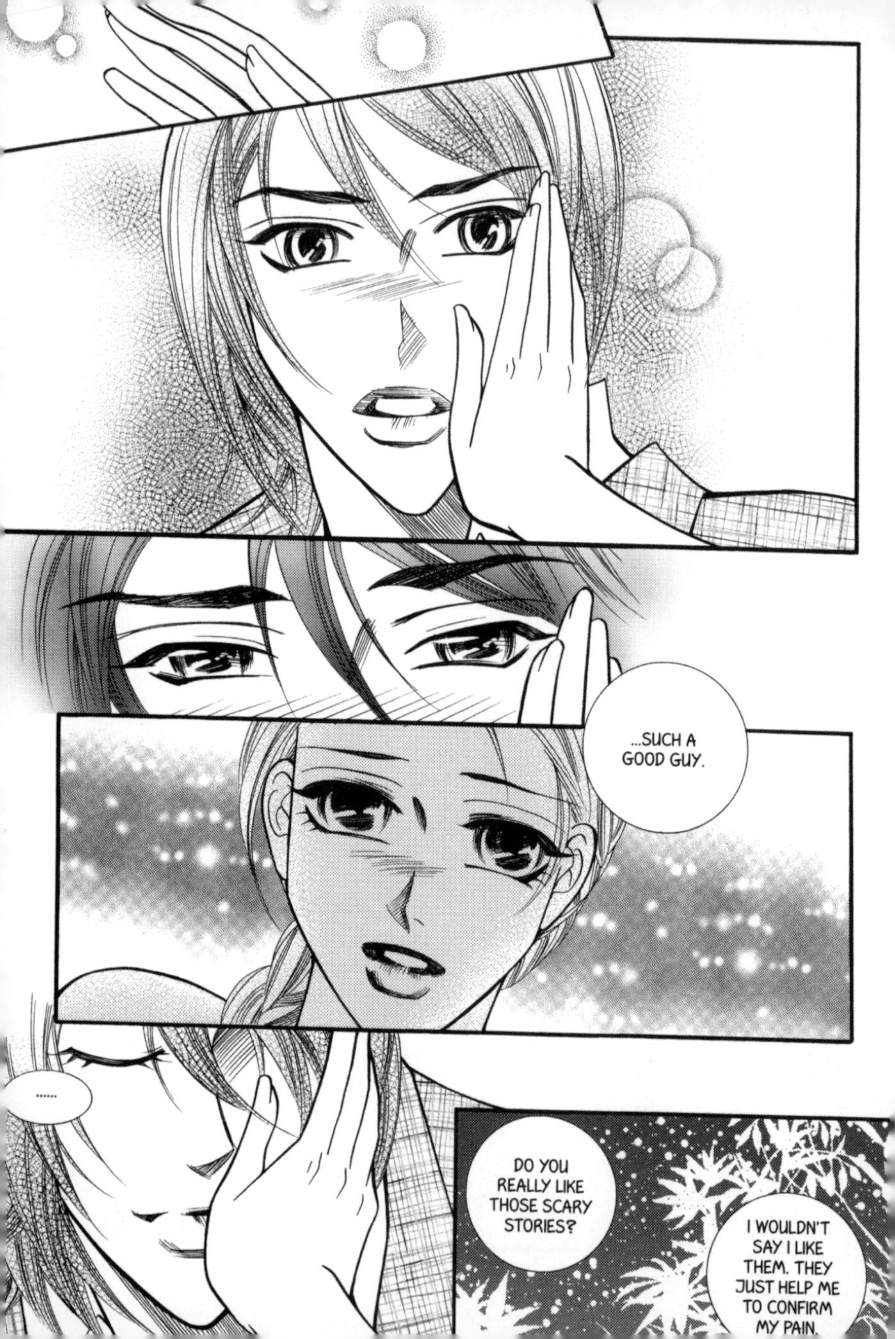
...SUCH A
GOOD GUY.
......
DO YOU
REALLY LIKE
THOSE SCARY
STORIES?
I WOULDN'T
SAY I LIKE
THEM. THEY
JUST HELP ME
TO CONFIRM
MY PAIN.

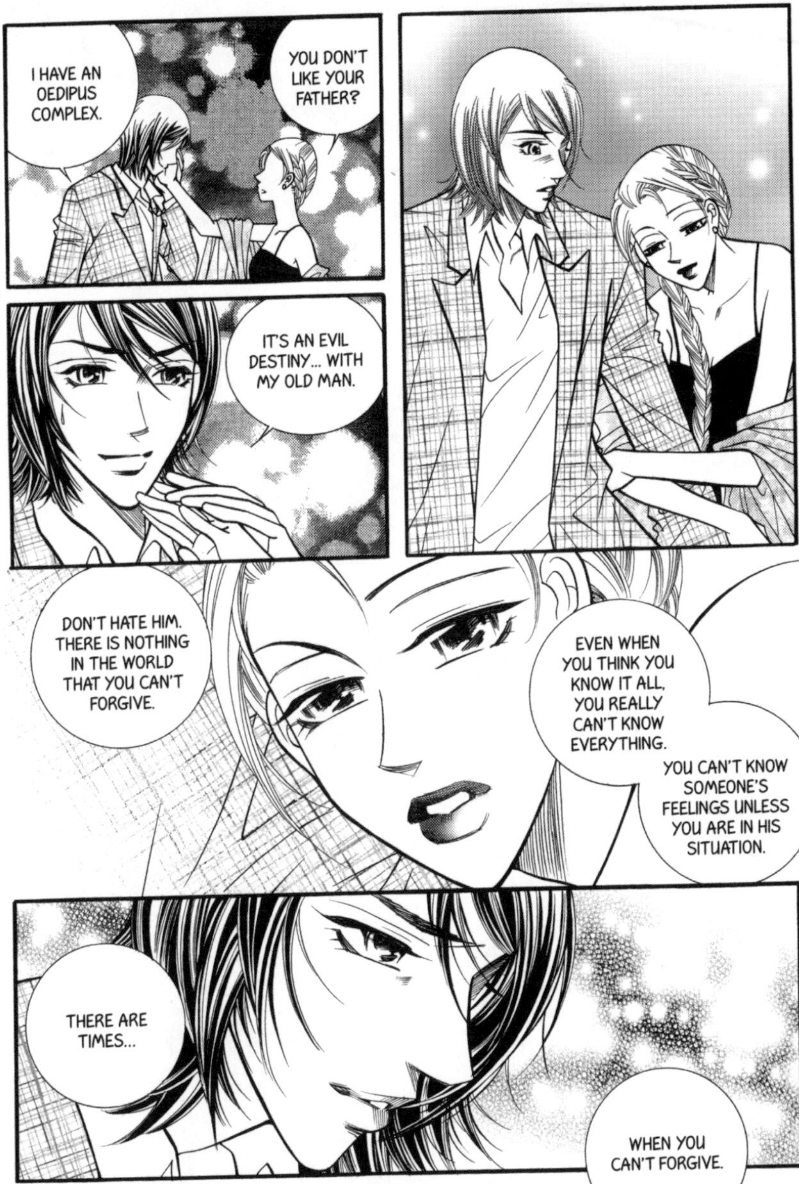
I HAVE AN OEDIPUS COMPLEX.
YOU DON'T LIKE YOUR FATHER?
IT'S AN EVIL DESTINY... WITH MY OLD MAN.
DON'T HATE HIM. THERE IS NOTHING IN THE WORLD THAT YOU CAN'T FORGIVE.
EVEN WHEN YOU THINK YOU KNOW IT ALL, YOU REALLY CAN'T KNOW EVERYTHING.
YOU CAN'T KNOW SOMEONE'S FEELINGS UNLESS YOU ARE IN HIS SITUATION.
THERE ARE TIMES...
WHEN YOU CAN'T FORGIVE.

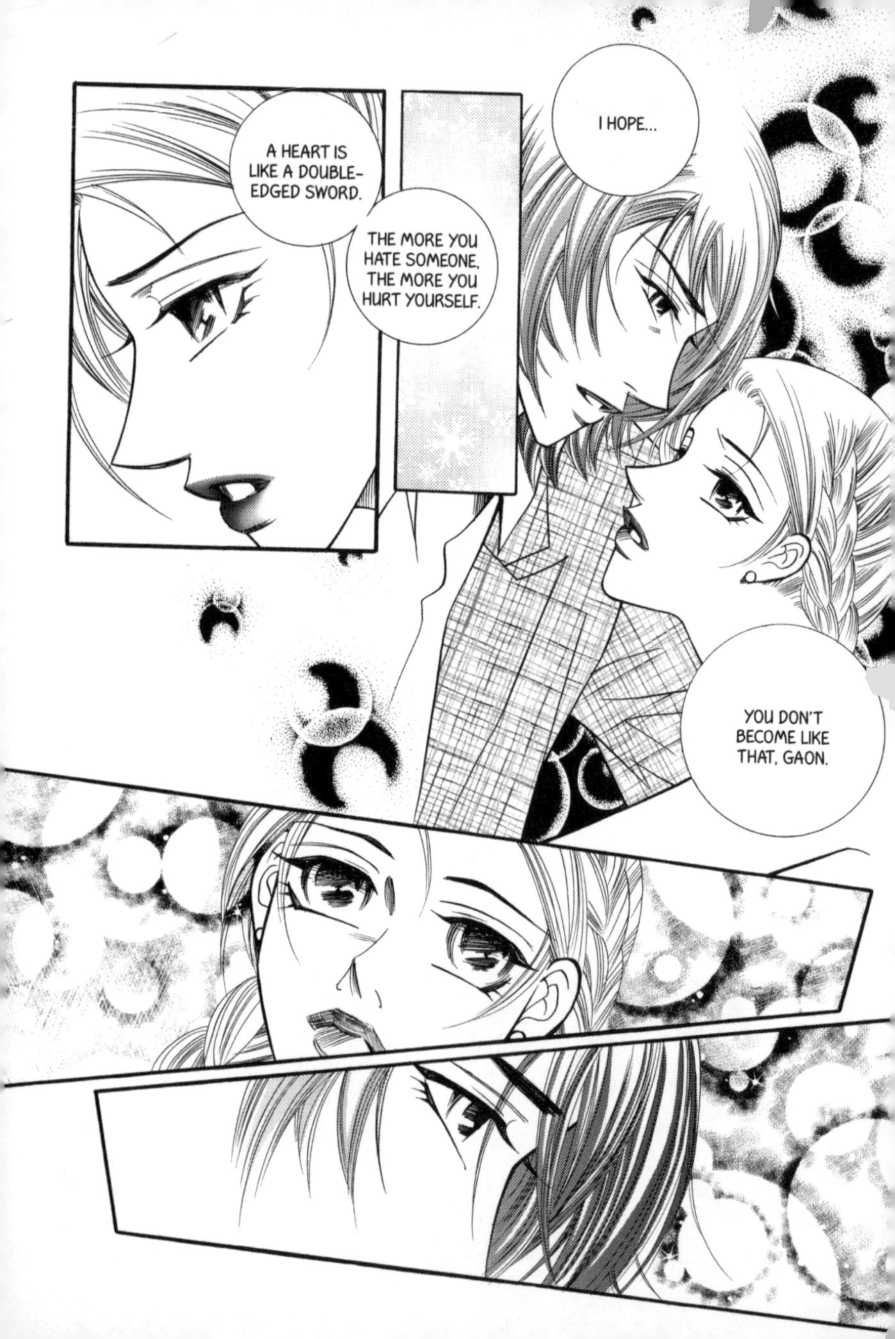
I HOPE...
A HEART IS LIKE A DOUBLE-EDGED SWORD.
THE MORE YOU HATE SOMEONE, THE MORE YOU HURT YOURSELF.
YOU DON'T BECOME LIKE THAT, GAON.

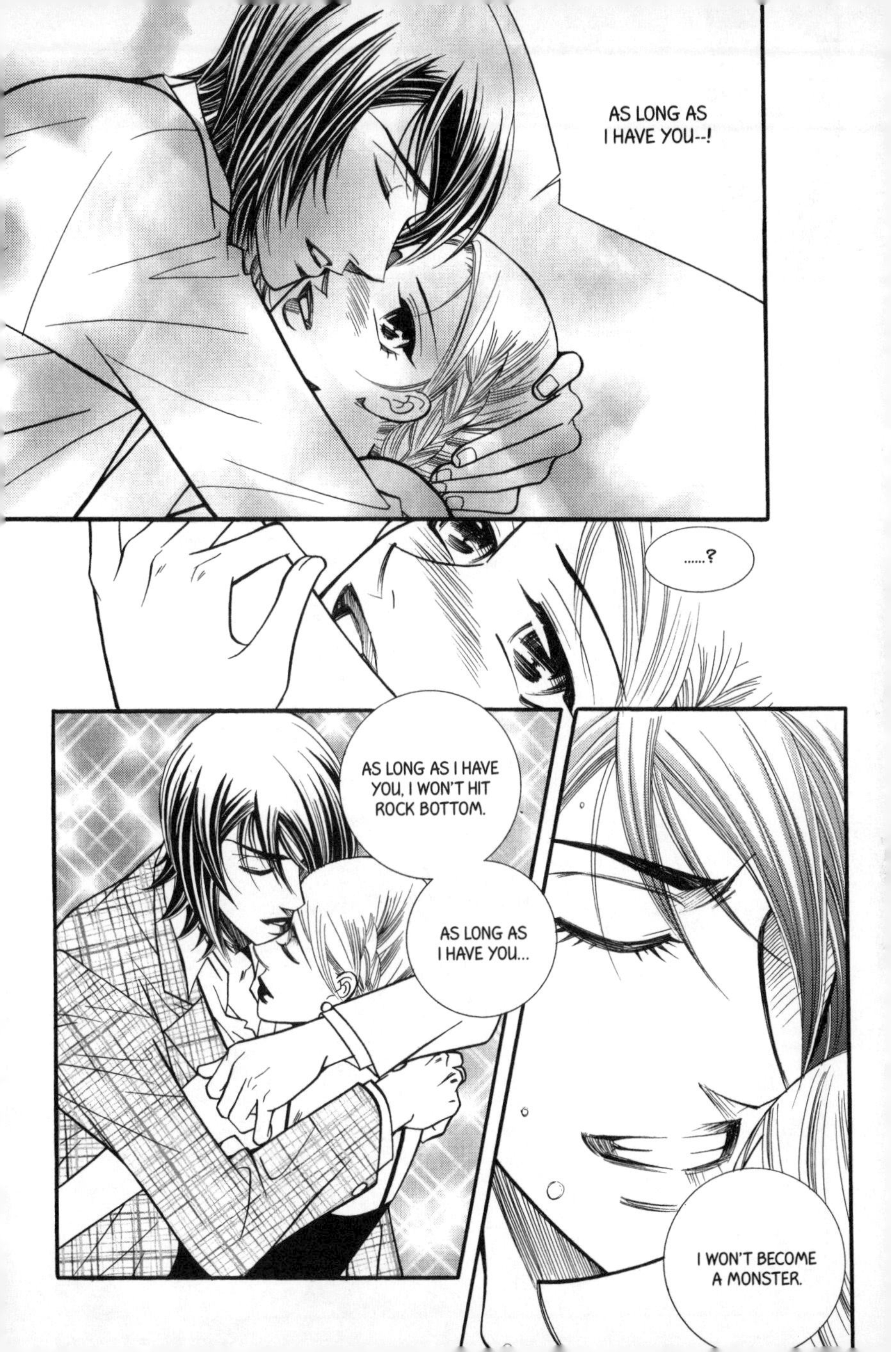
AS LONG AS I HAVE YOU--!
......?
AS LONG AS I HAVE YOU, I WON'T HIT ROCK BOTTOM.
AS LONG AS I HAVE YOU...
I WON'T BECOME A MONSTER.

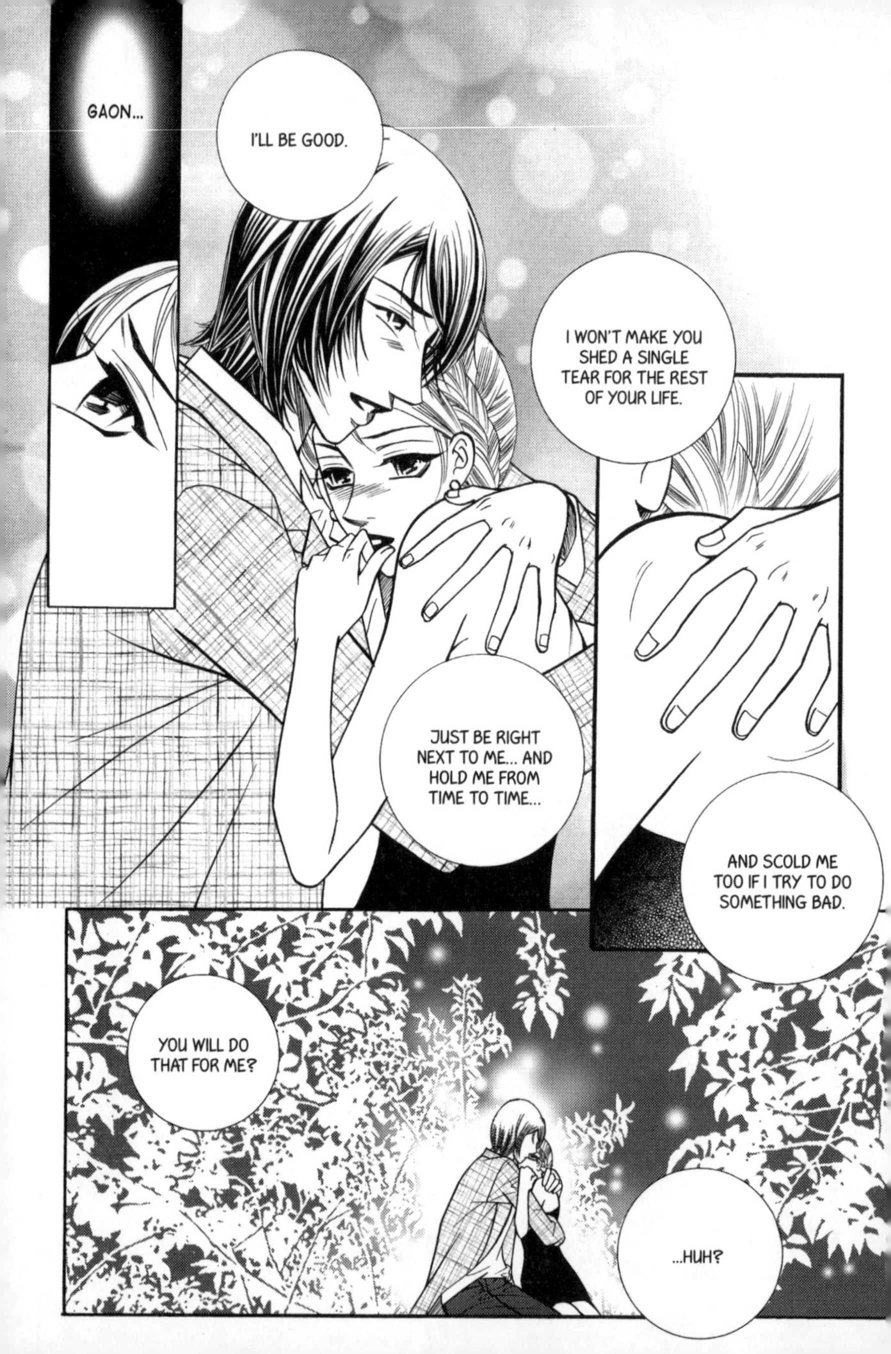
GAON...
I'LL BE GOOD.
I WON'T MAKE YOU SHED A SINGLE TEAR FOR THE REST OF YOUR LIFE.
JUST BE RIGHT NEXT TO ME... AND HOLD ME FROM TIME TO TIME...
AND SCOLD ME TOO IF I TRY TO DO SOMETHING BAD.
YOU WILL DO THAT FOR ME?
...HUH?

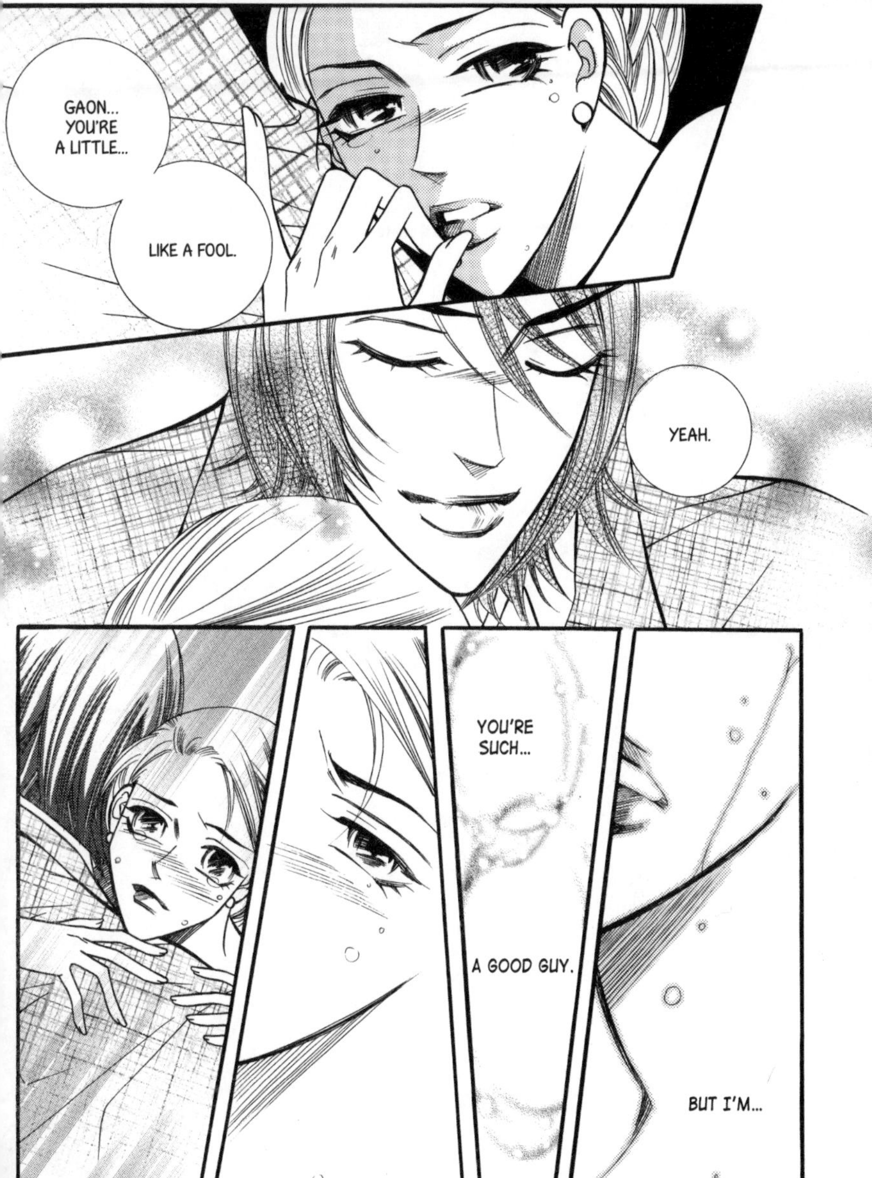
GAON... YOU'RE A LITTLE...
LIKE A FOOL.
YEAH.
YOU'RE SUCH...
A GOOD GUY.
BUT I'M...

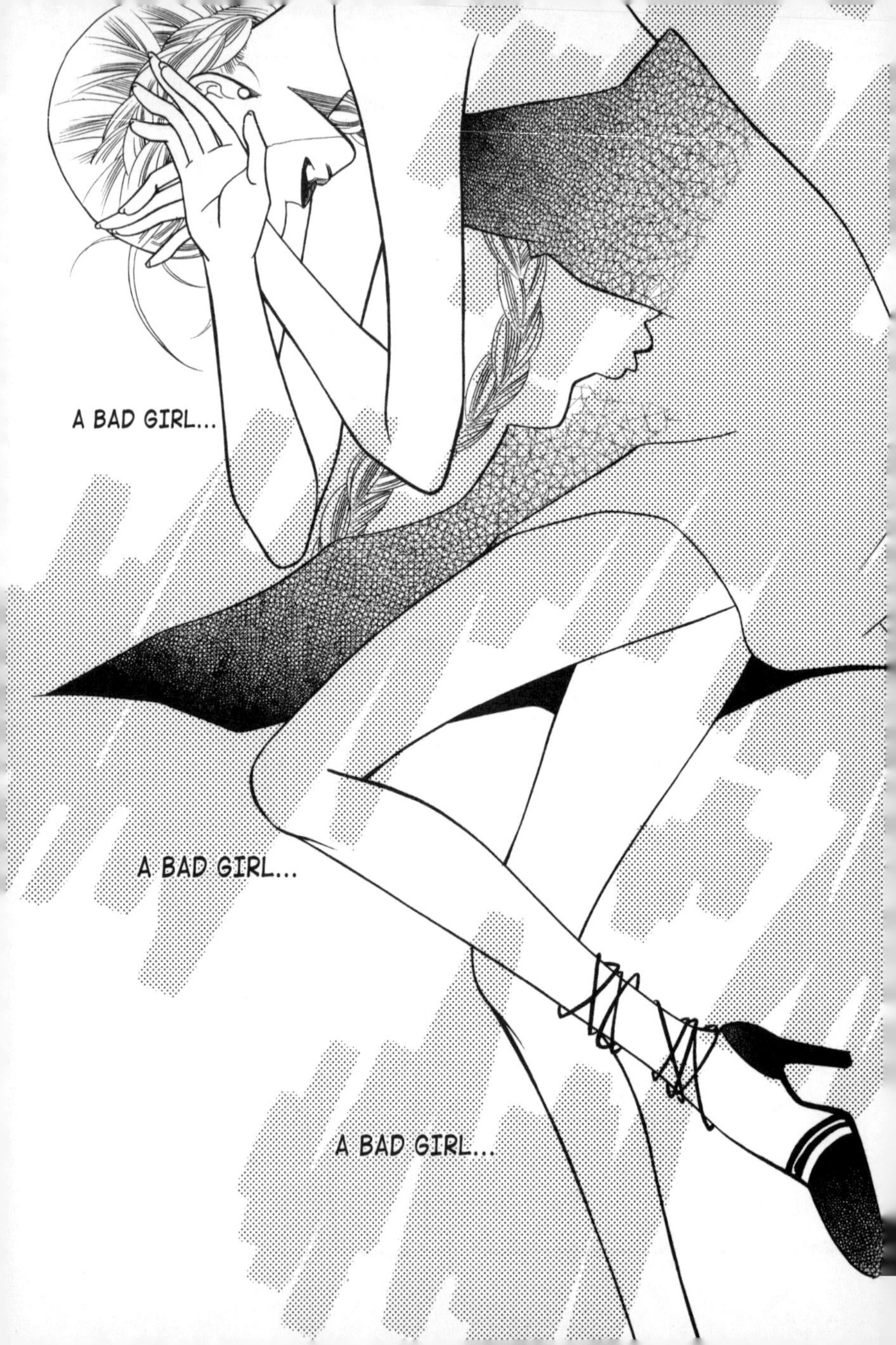
A BAD GIRL...
A BAD GIRL...
A BAD GIRL...

16. THE ENGAGEMENT

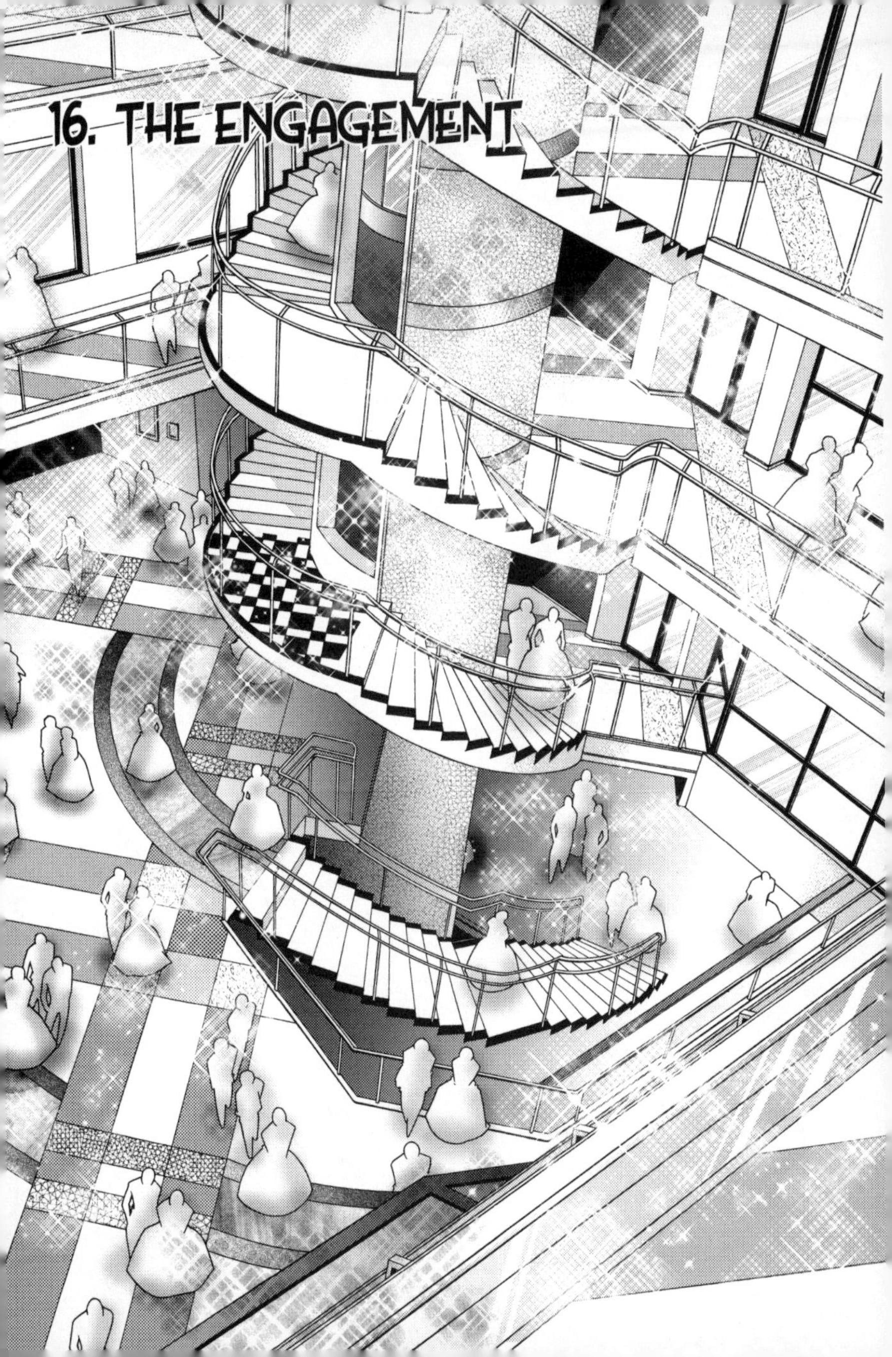

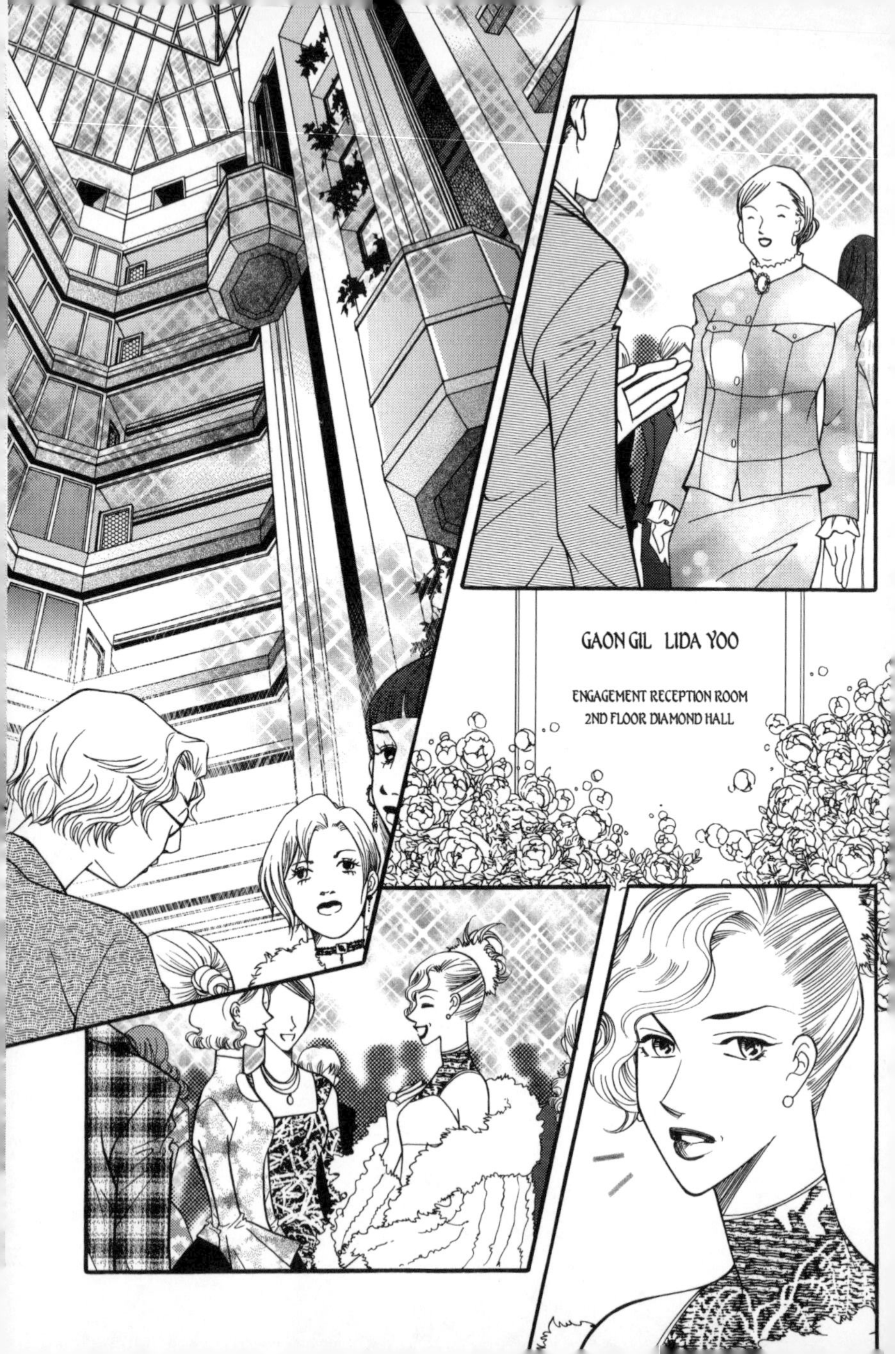
GAON GIL LIDA YOO
ENGAGEMENT RECEPTION ROOM
2ND FLOOR DIAMOND HALL

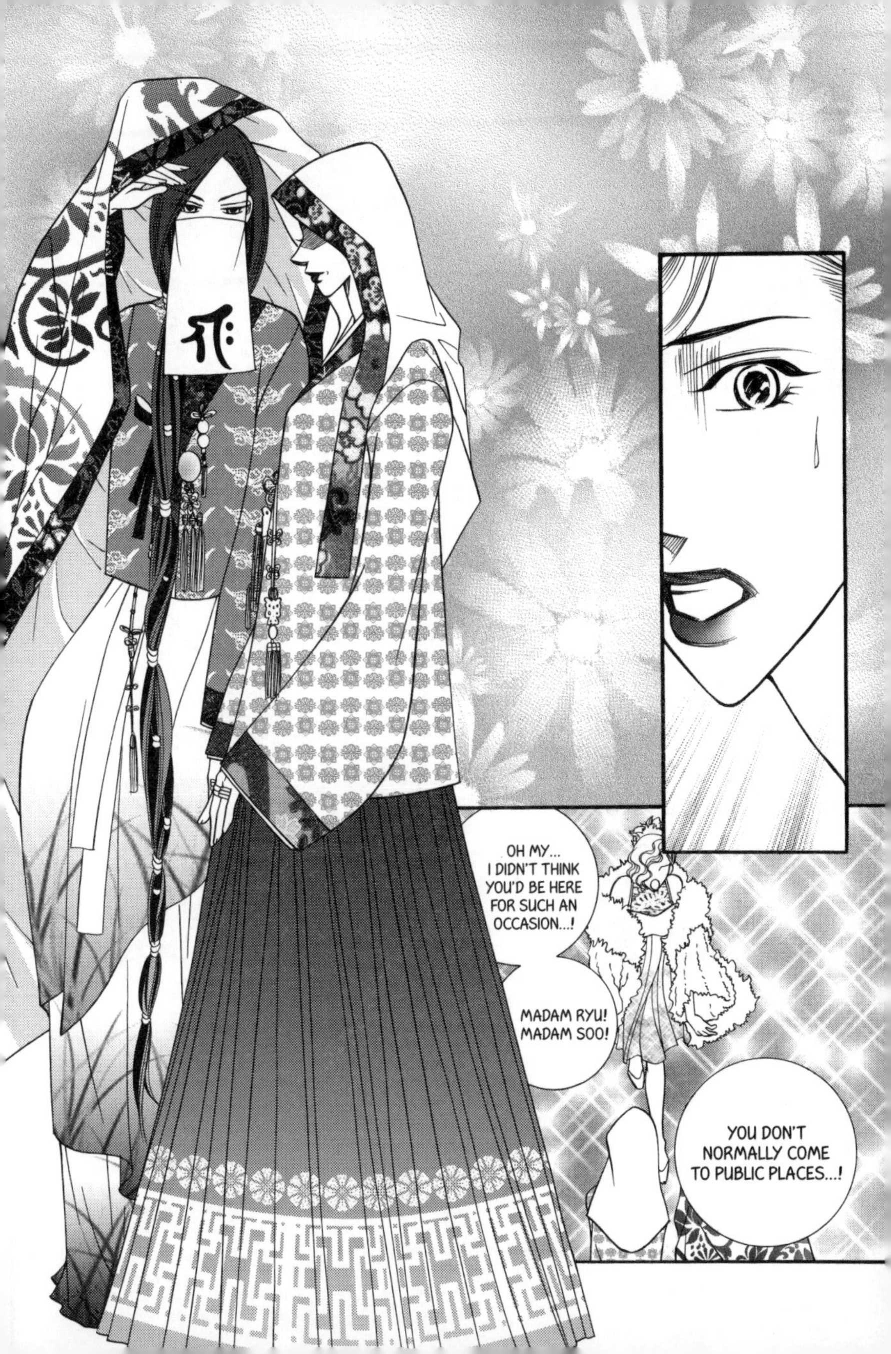
OH MY... I DIDN'T THINK YOU'D BE HERE FOR SUCH AN OCCASION...!
MADAM RYU! MADAM SOO!
YOU DON'T NORMALLY COME TO PUBLIC PLACES...!

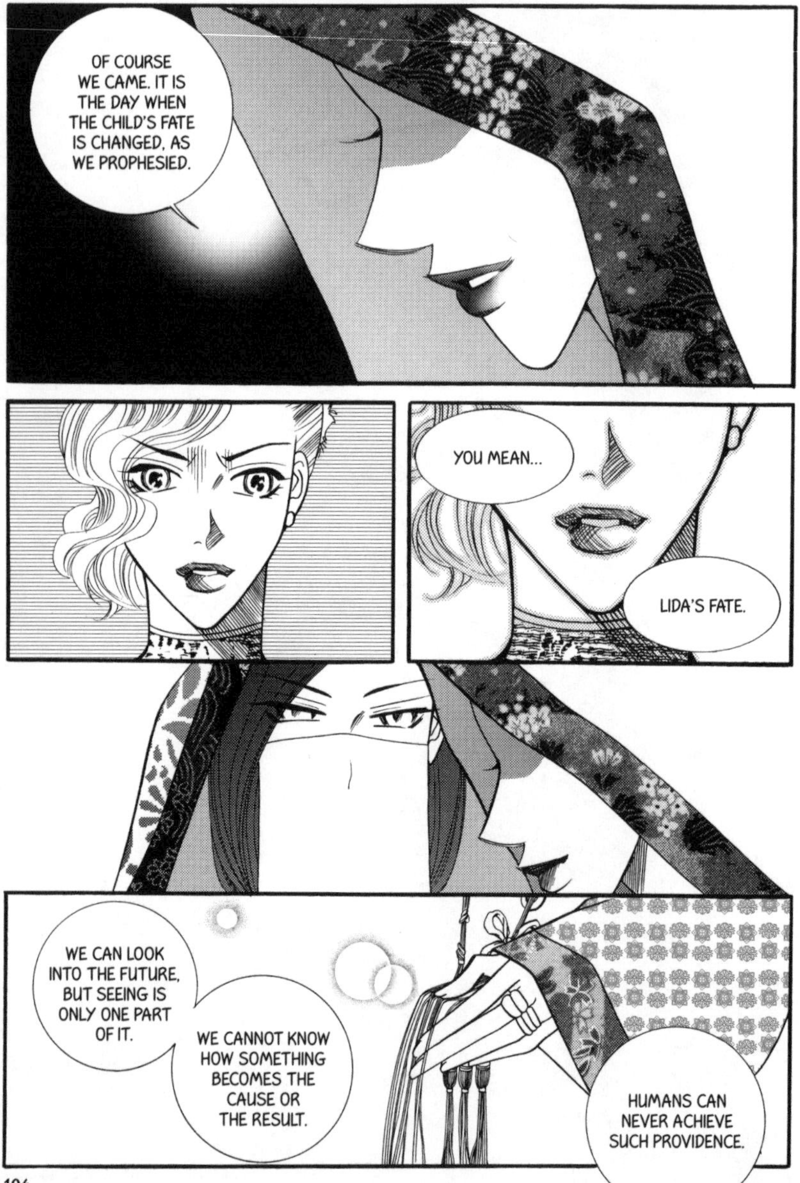
OF COURSE WE CAME. IT IS THE DAY WHEN THE CHILD'S FATE IS CHANGED, AS WE PROPHESIED.
YOU MEAN...
LIDA'S FATE.
WE CAN LOOK INTO THE FUTURE, BUT SEEING IS ONLY ONE PART OF IT.
WE CANNOT KNOW HOW SOMETHING BECOMES THE CAUSE OR THE RESULT.
HUMANS CAN NEVER ACHIEVE SUCH PROVIDENCE.

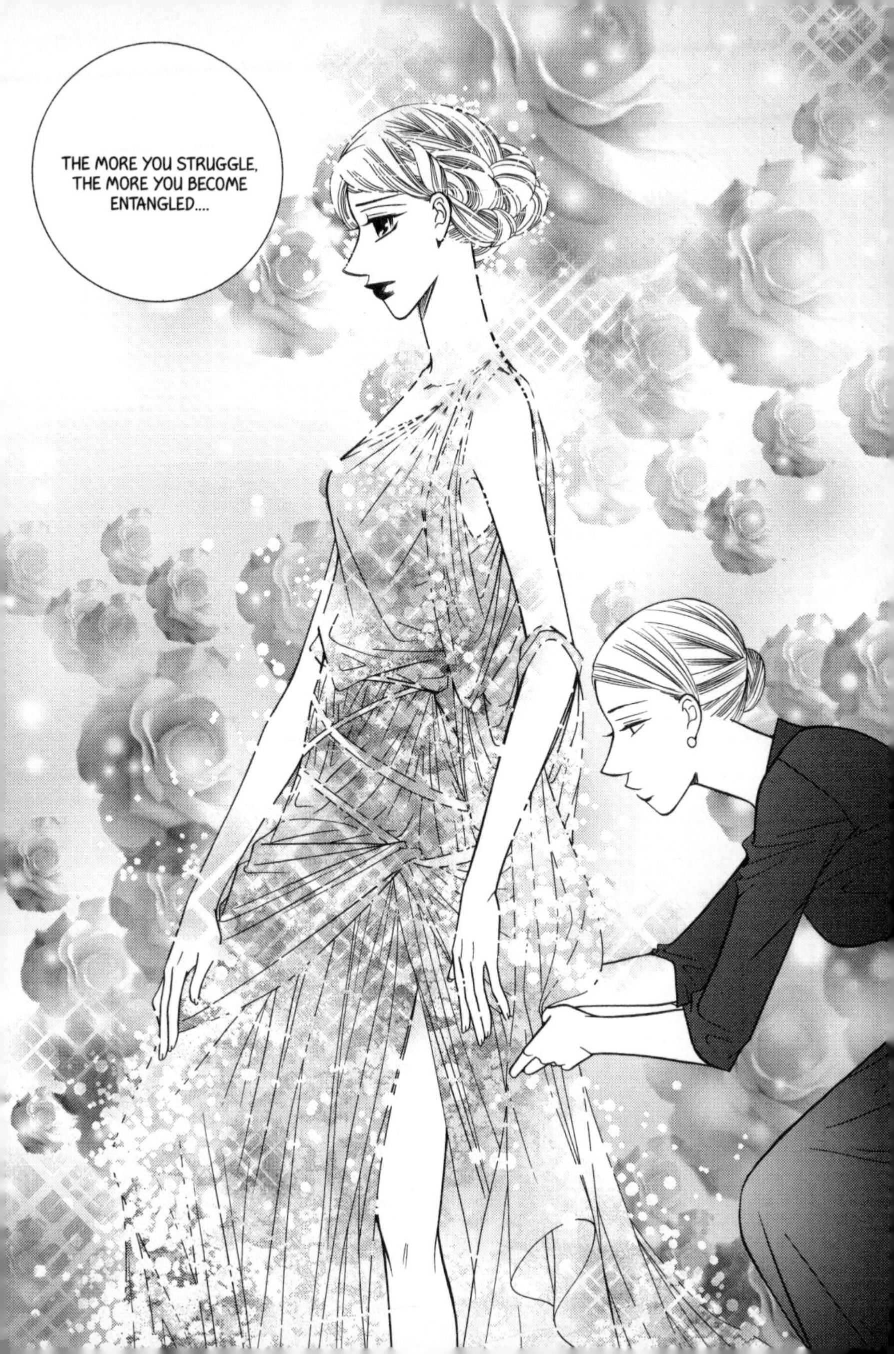
THE MORE YOU STRUGGLE,
THE MORE YOU BECOME
ENTANGLED....

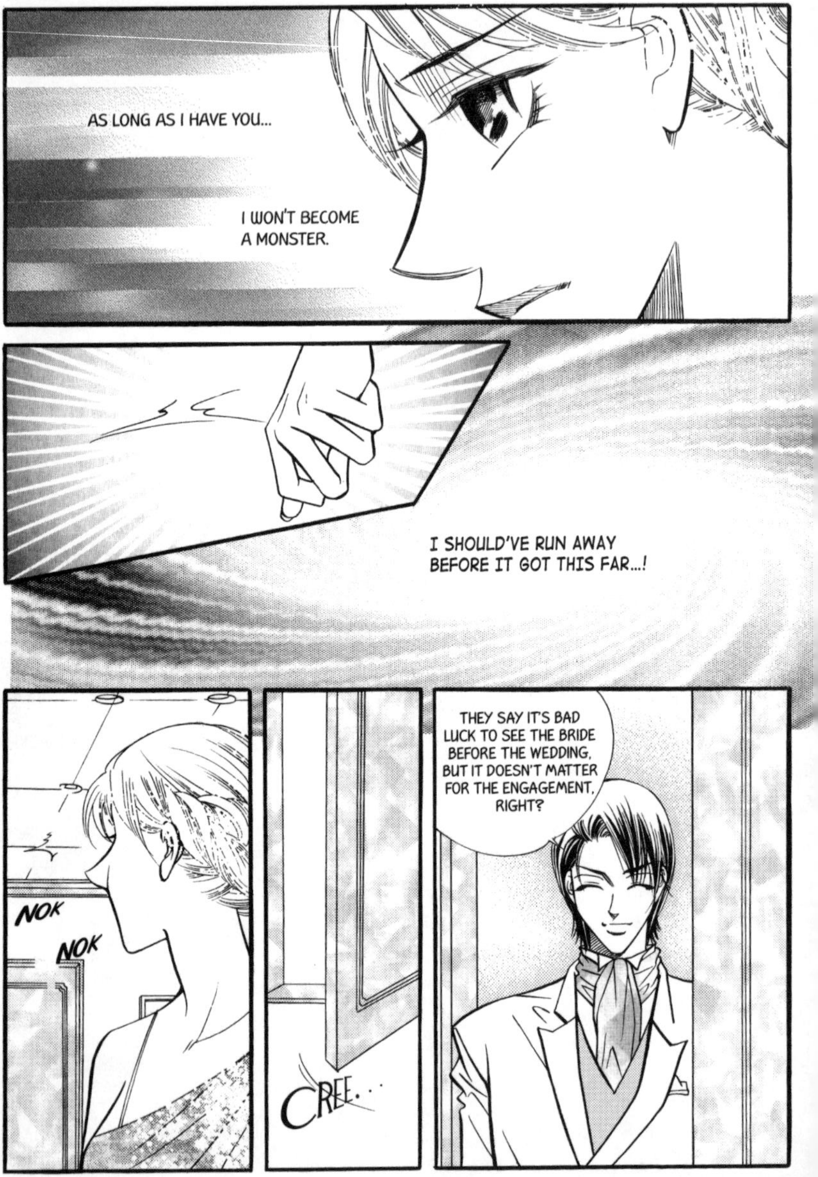
AS LONG AS I HAVE YOU...
I WON'T BECOME A MONSTER.
I SHOULD'VE RUN AWAY BEFORE IT GOT THIS FAR...!
THEY SAY IT'S BAD LUCK TO SEE THE BRIDE BEFORE THE WEDDING, BUT IT DOESN'T MATTER FOR THE ENGAGEMENT, RIGHT?
CREE...
NOK
NOK

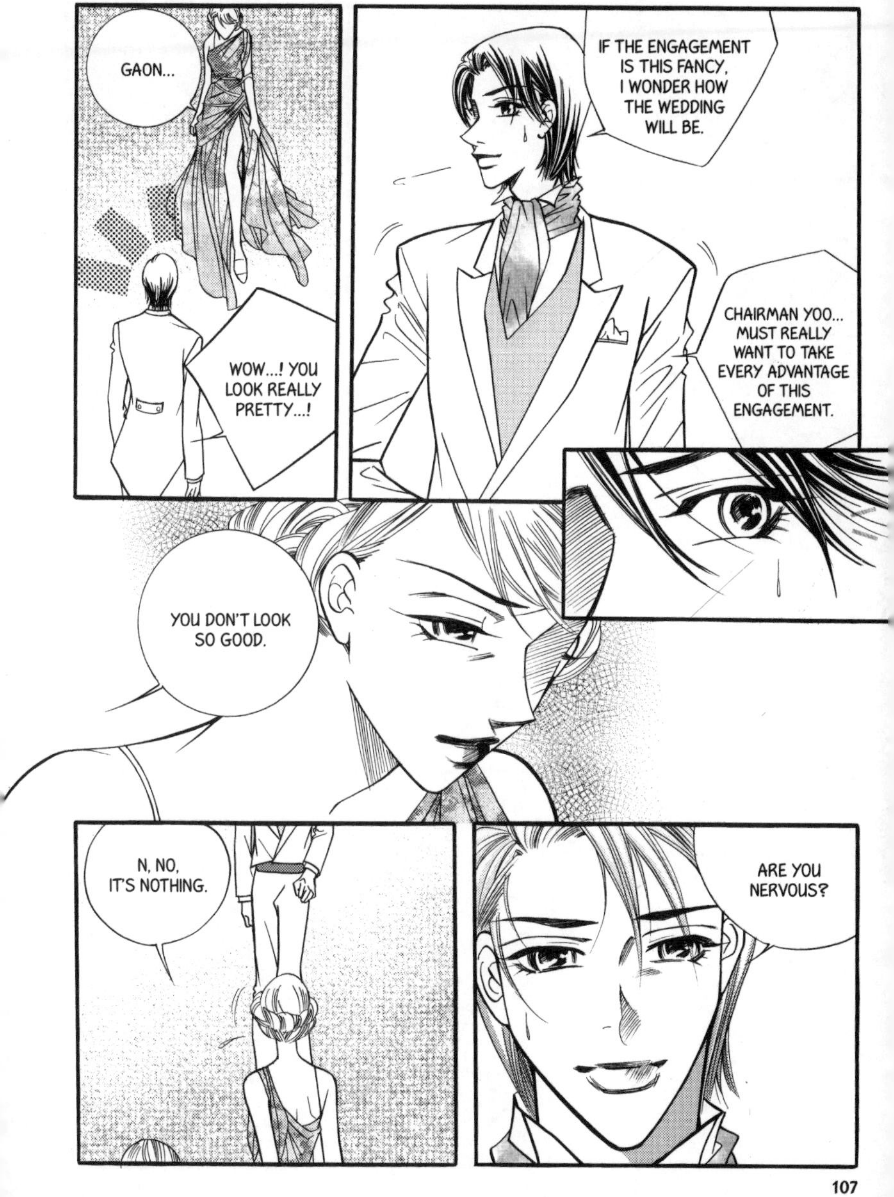
GAON...
WOW...! YOU LOOK REALLY PRETTY...!
IF THE ENGAGEMENT IS THIS FANCY, I WONDER HOW THE WEDDING WILL BE.
CHAIRMAN YOO... MUST REALLY WANT TO TAKE EVERY ADVANTAGE OF THIS ENGAGEMENT.
YOU DON'T LOOK SO GOOD.
N, NO, IT'S NOTHING.
ARE YOU NERVOUS?

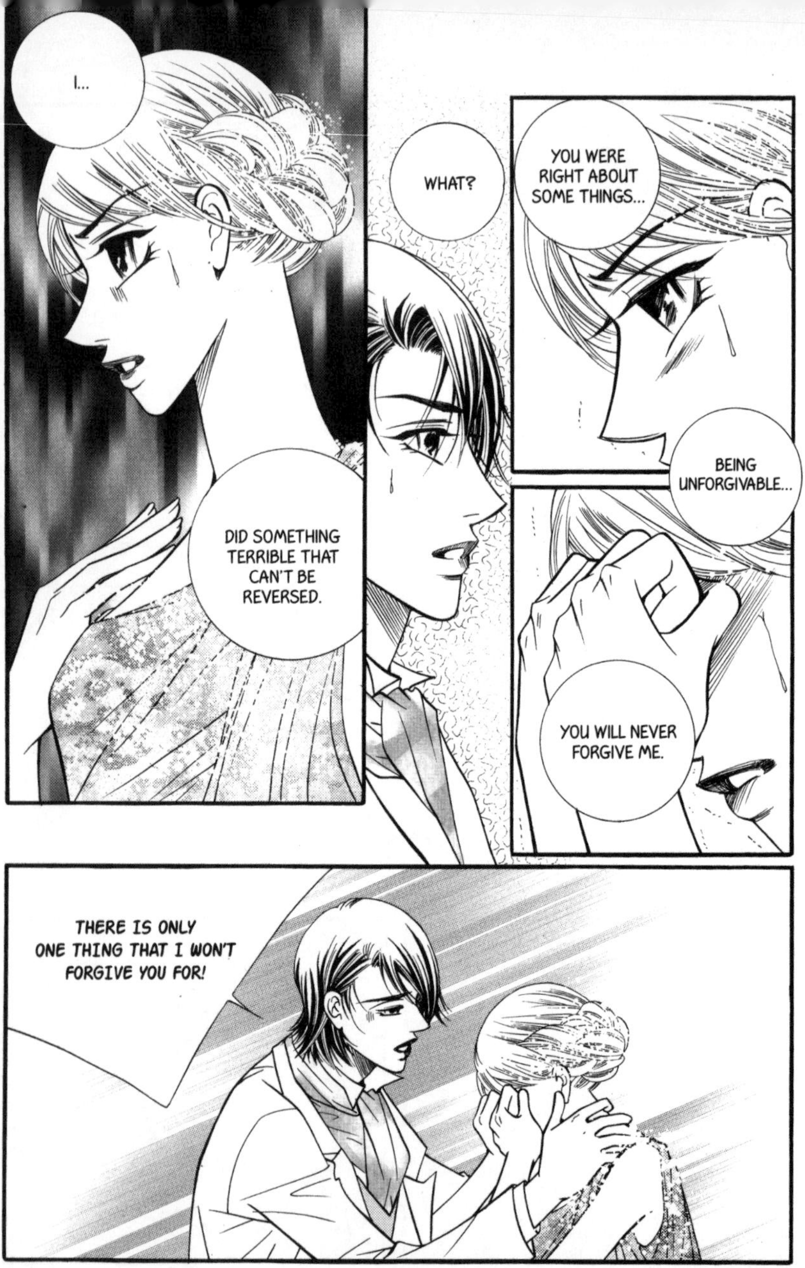
I...
DID SOMETHING TERRIBLE THAT CAN'T BE REVERSED.
WHAT?
YOU WERE RIGHT ABOUT SOME THINGS...
BEING UNFORGIVABLE...
YOU WILL NEVER FORGIVE ME.
THERE IS ONLY ONE THING THAT I WON'T FORGIVE YOU FOR!

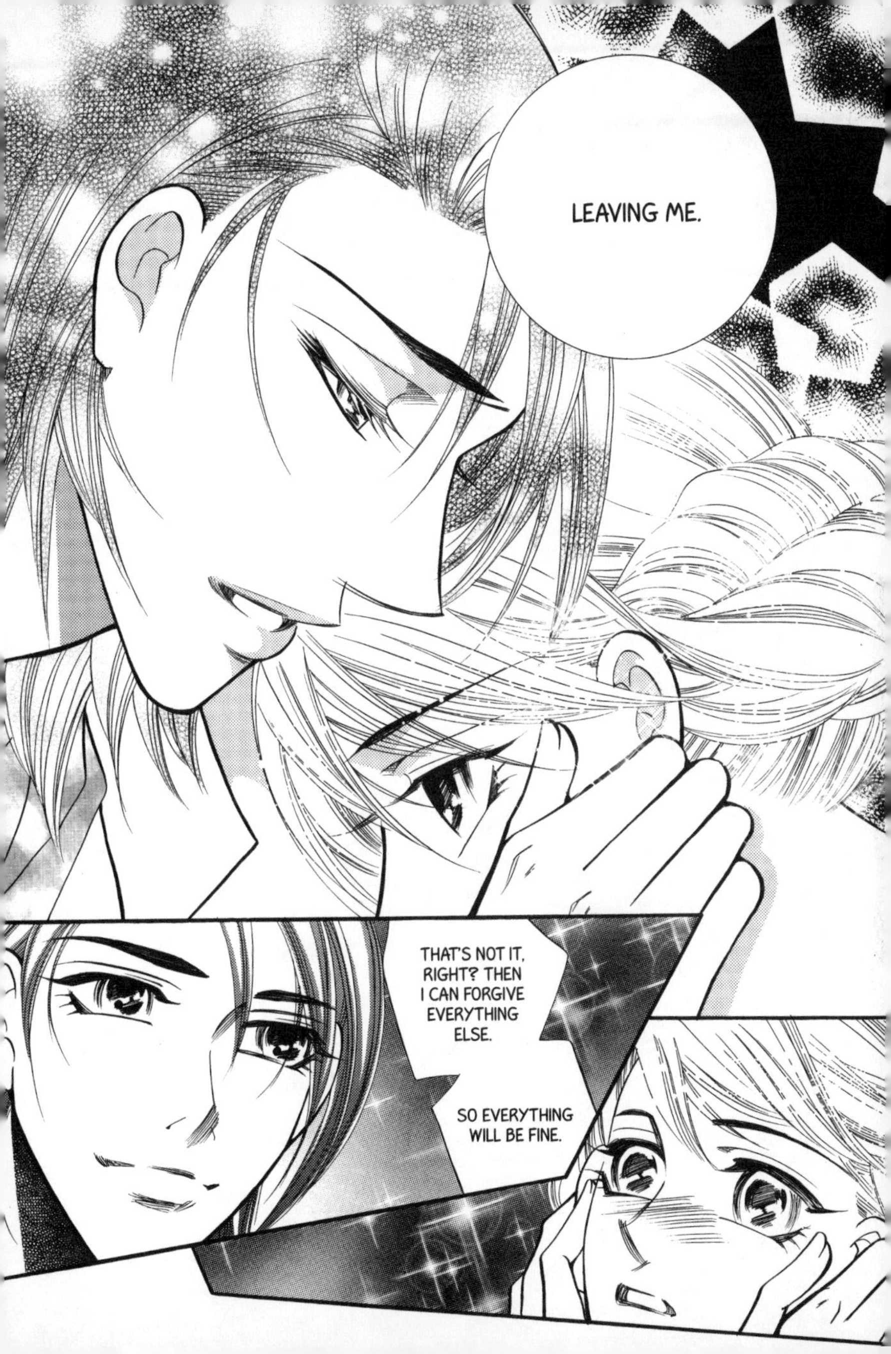
LEAVING ME.
THAT'S NOT IT, RIGHT? THEN I CAN FORGIVE EVERYTHING ELSE.
SO EVERYTHING WILL BE FINE.

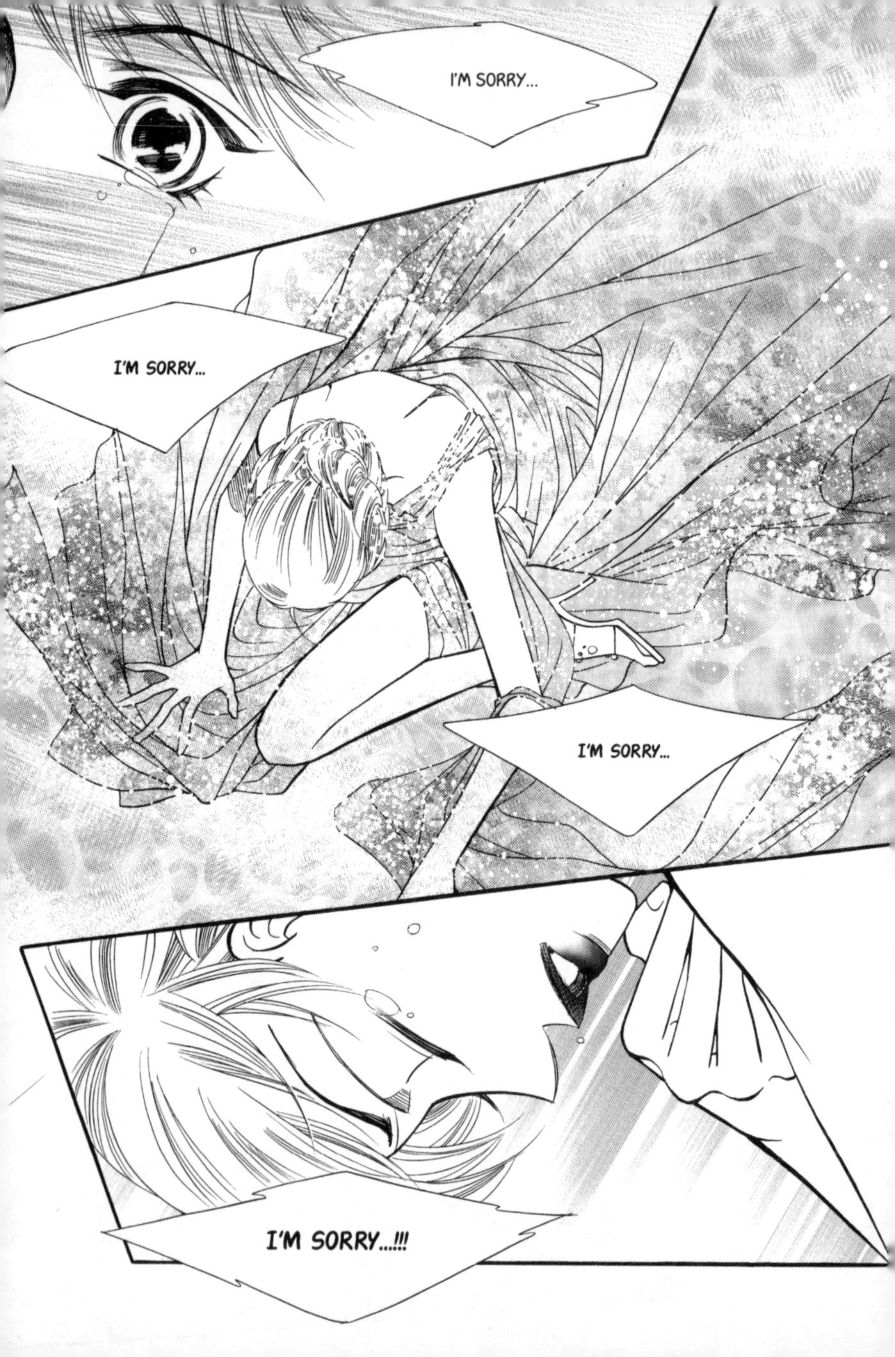
I'M SORRY...
I'M SORRY...
I'M SORRY...
I'M SORRY...!!!

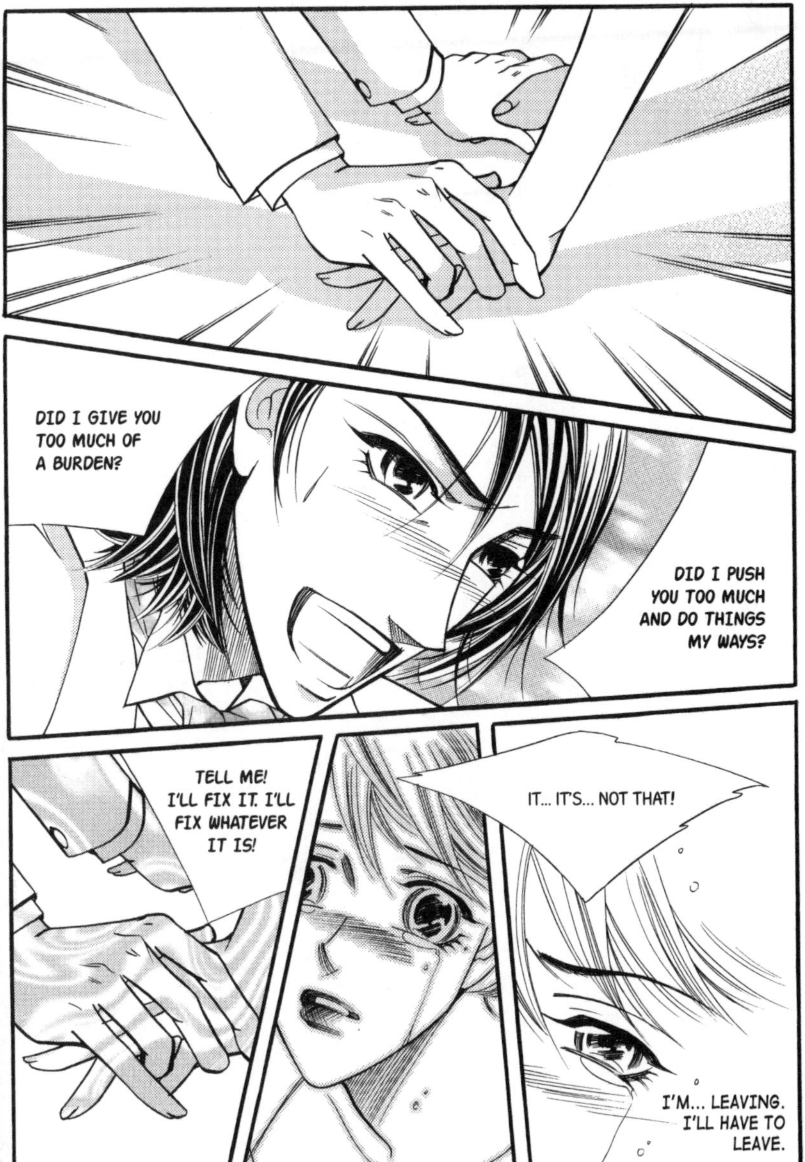
DID I GIVE YOU TOO MUCH OF A BURDEN?
DID I PUSH YOU TOO MUCH AND DO THINGS MY WAYS?
TELL ME! I'LL FIX IT. I'LL FIX WHATEVER IT IS!
IT... IT'S... NOT THAT!
I'M... LEAVING. I'LL HAVE TO LEAVE.

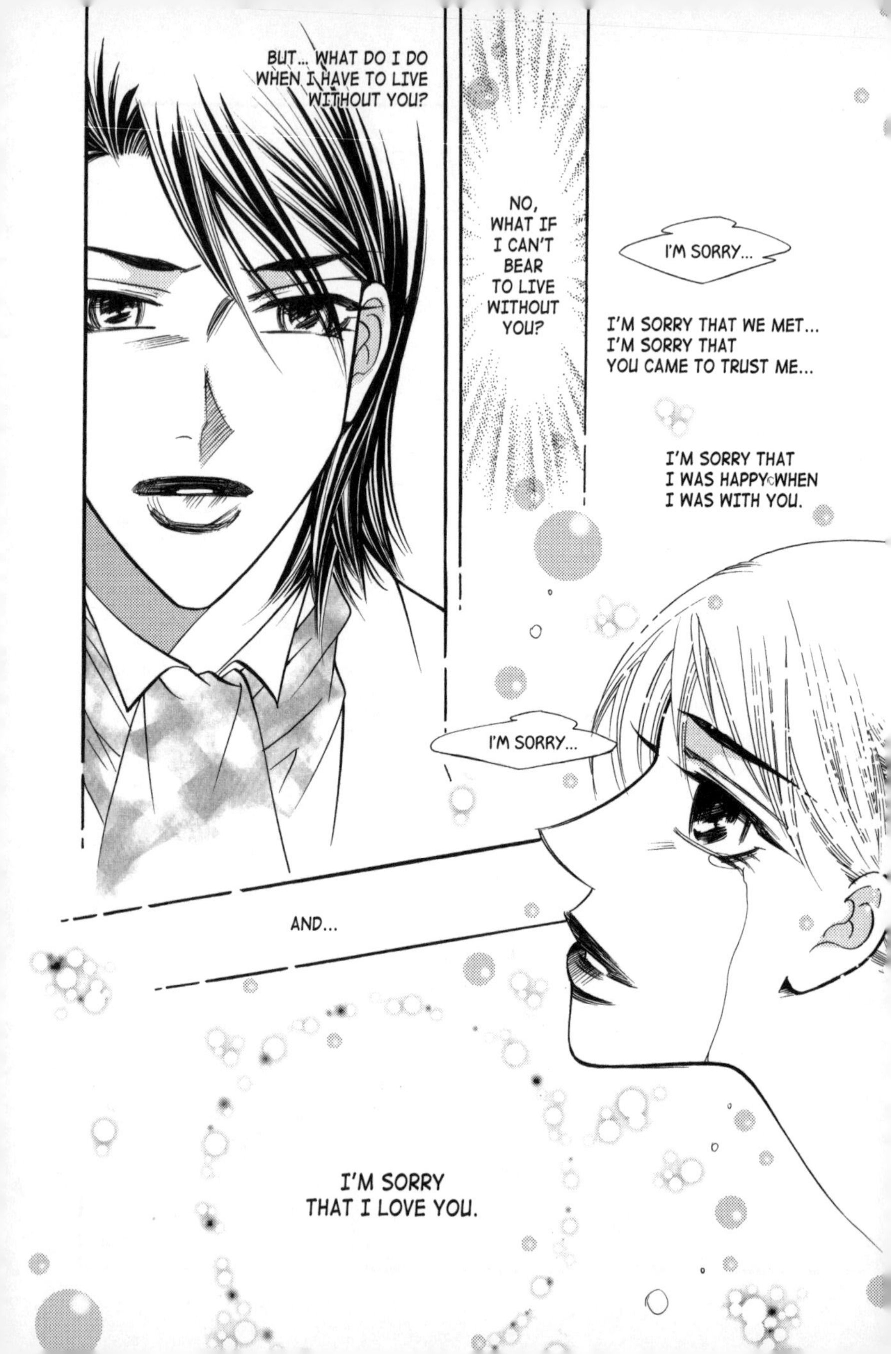
BUT... WHAT DO I DO WHEN I HAVE TO LIVE WITHOUT YOU?
NO, WHAT IF I CAN'T BEAR TO LIVE WITHOUT YOU?
I'M SORRY...
I'M SORRY THAT WE MET... I'M SORRY THAT YOU CAME TO TRUST ME...
I'M SORRY THAT I WAS HAPPY WHEN I WAS WITH YOU.
I'M SORRY...
AND...
I'M SORRY THAT I LOVE YOU.

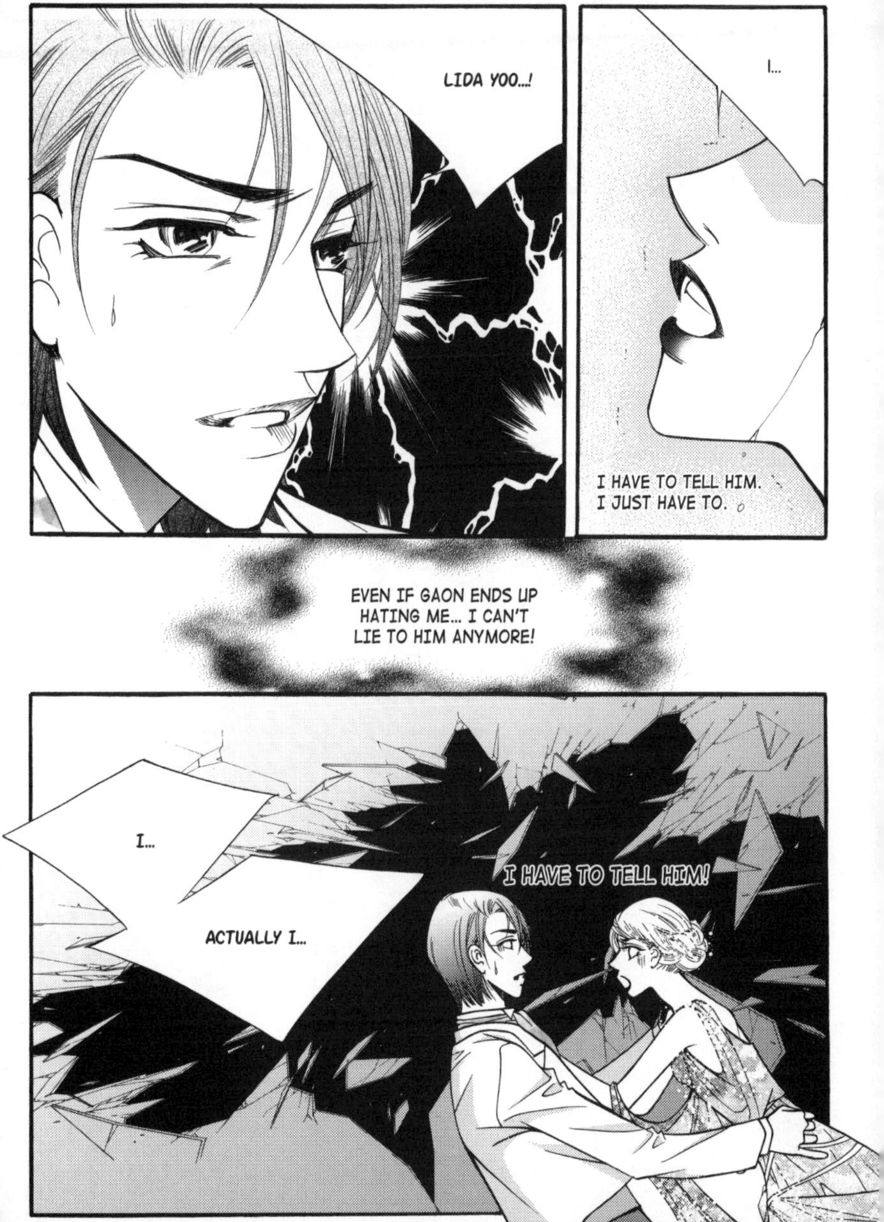
LIDA YOO...!
I...
I HAVE TO TELL HIM.
I JUST HAVE TO.
EVEN IF GAON ENDS UP HATING ME... I CAN'T LIE TO HIM ANYMORE!
I...
ACTUALLY I...
I HAVE TO TELL HIM!

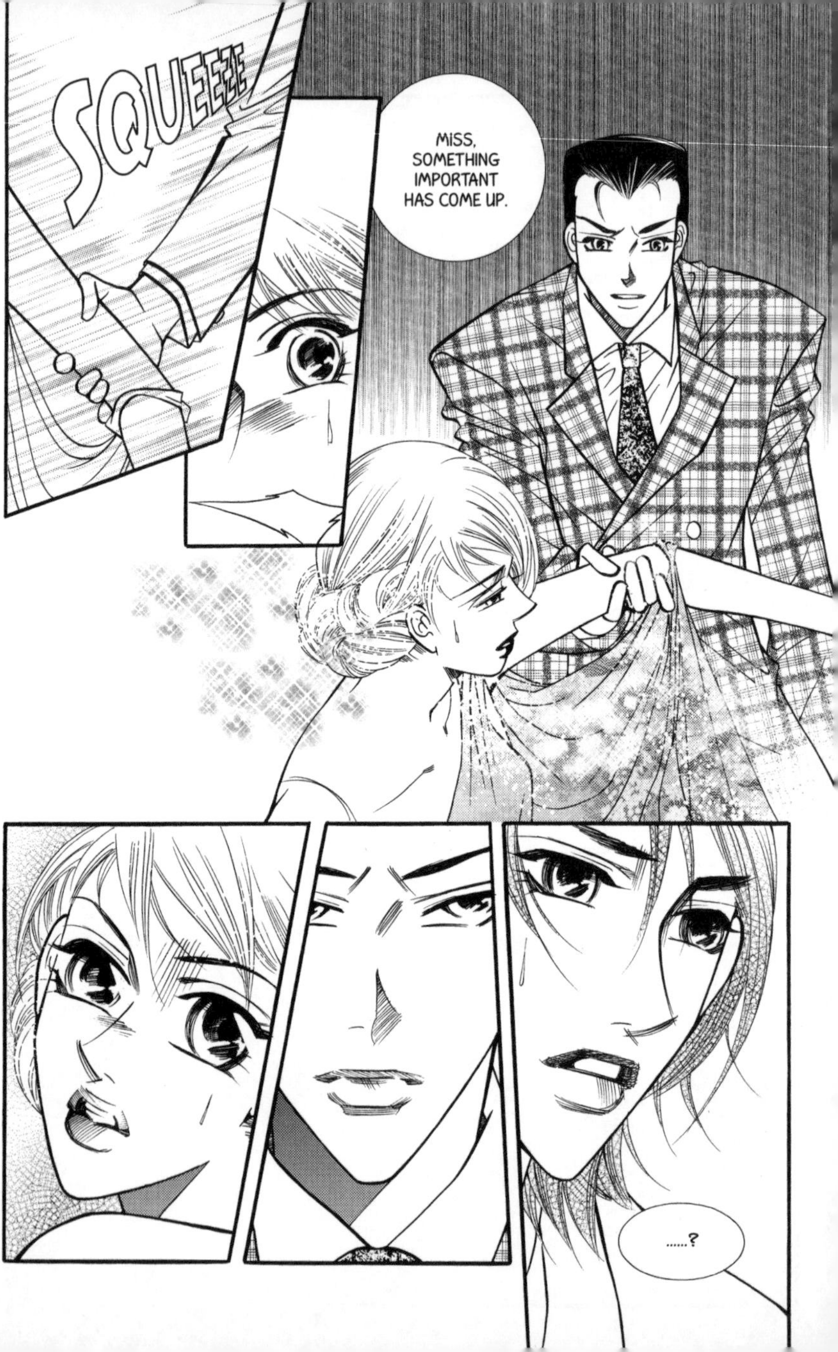
MISS, SOMETHING IMPORTANT HAS COME UP.
SQUEEZE
......?

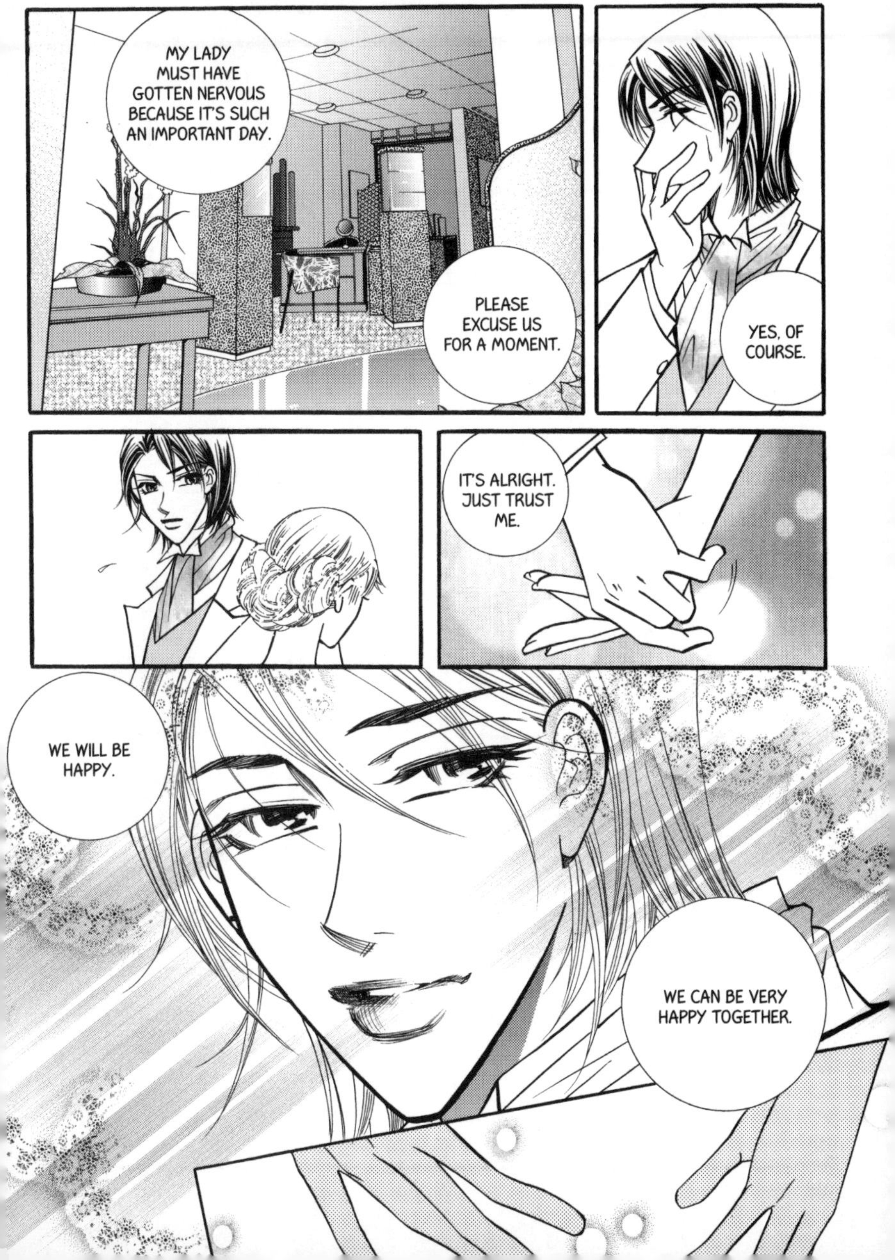
MY LADY MUST HAVE GOTTEN NERVOUS BECAUSE IT'S SUCH AN IMPORTANT DAY.
PLEASE EXCUSE US FOR A MOMENT.
YES, OF COURSE.
IT'S ALRIGHT. JUST TRUST ME.
WE WILL BE HAPPY.
WE CAN BE VERY HAPPY TOGETHER.

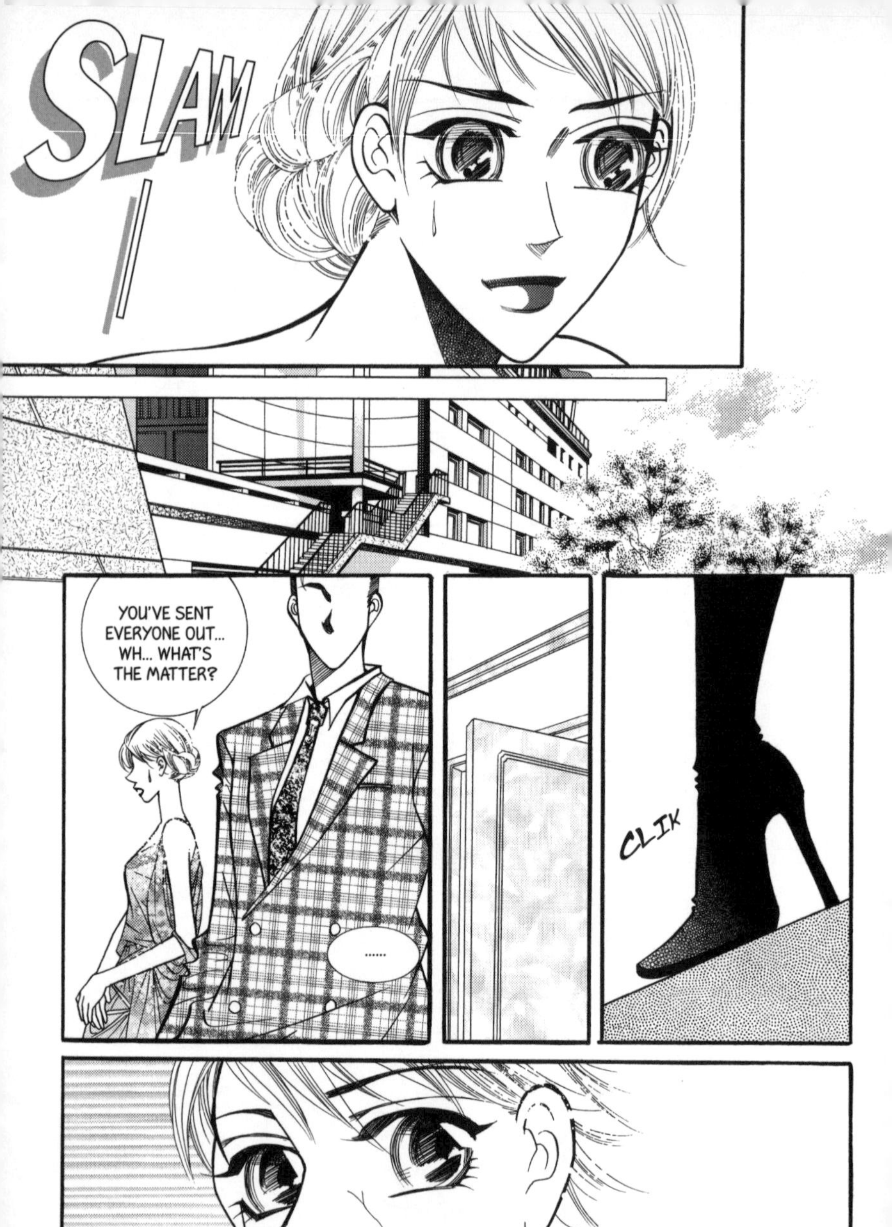
SLAM
YOU'VE SENT EVERYONE OUT... WH... WHAT'S THE MATTER?
......
CLIK

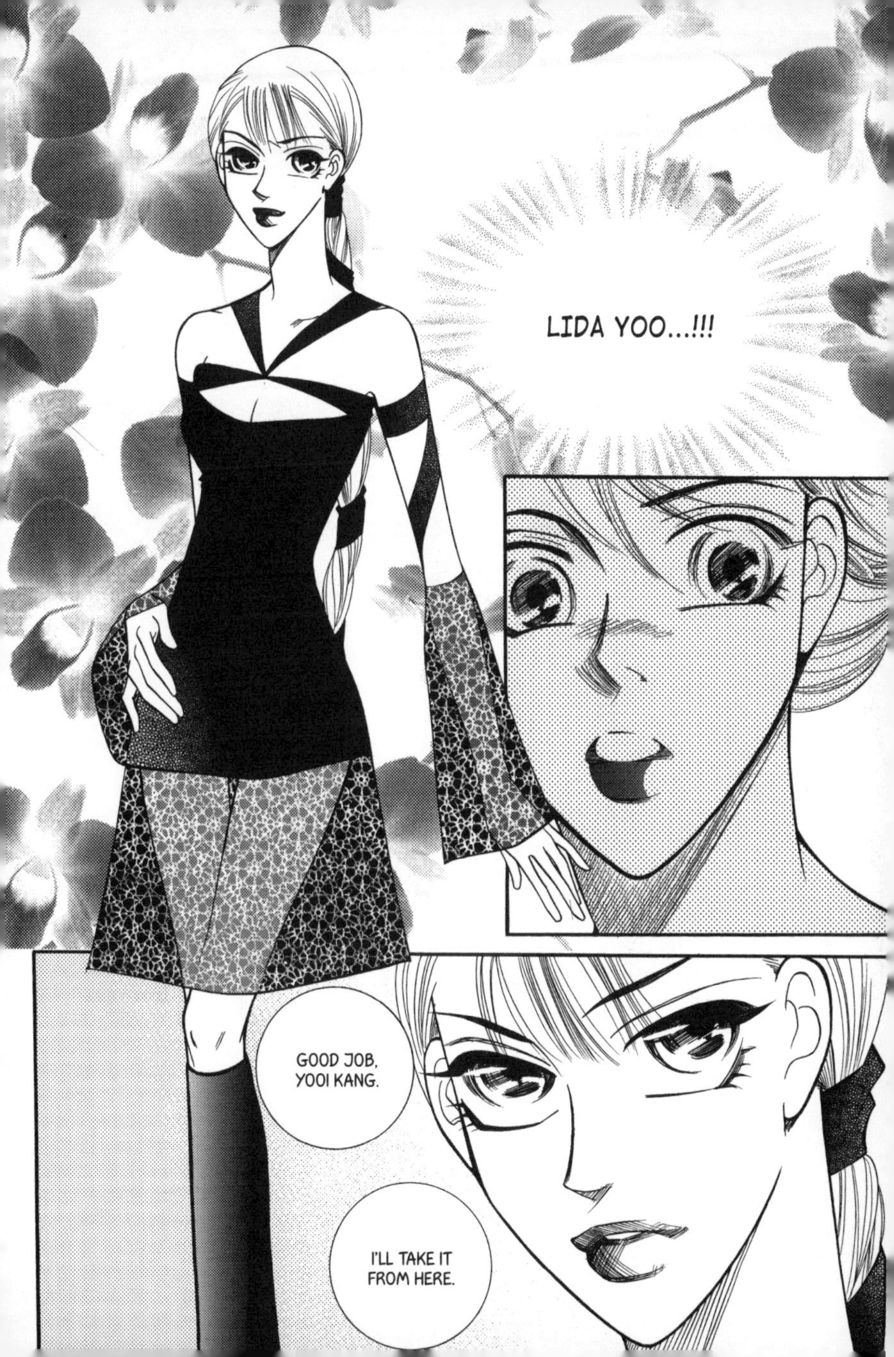
LIDA YOO...!!!
GOOD JOB, YOOI KANG.
I'LL TAKE IT FROM HERE.

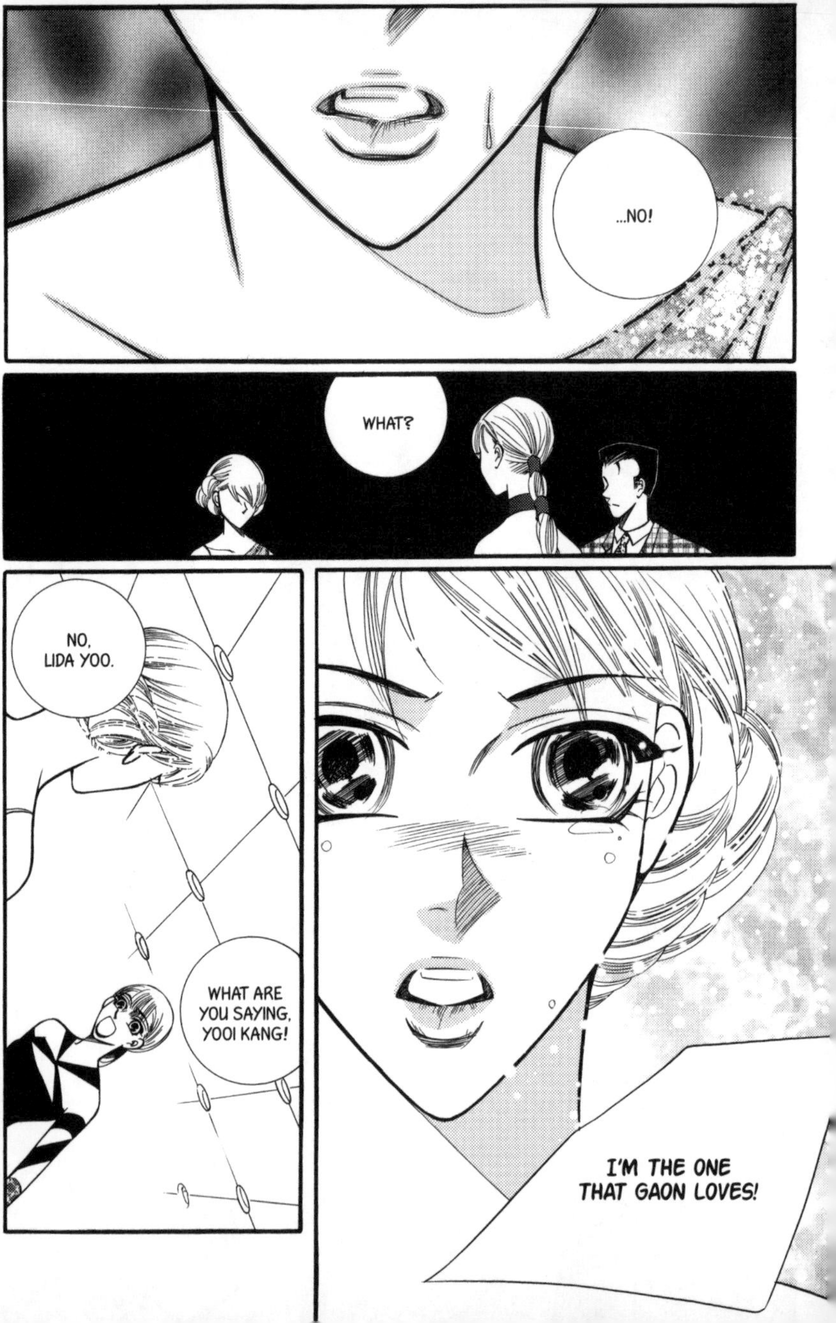
...NO!
WHAT?
NO, LIDA YOO.
WHAT ARE YOU SAYING, YOOI KANG!
I'M THE ONE THAT GAON LOVES!

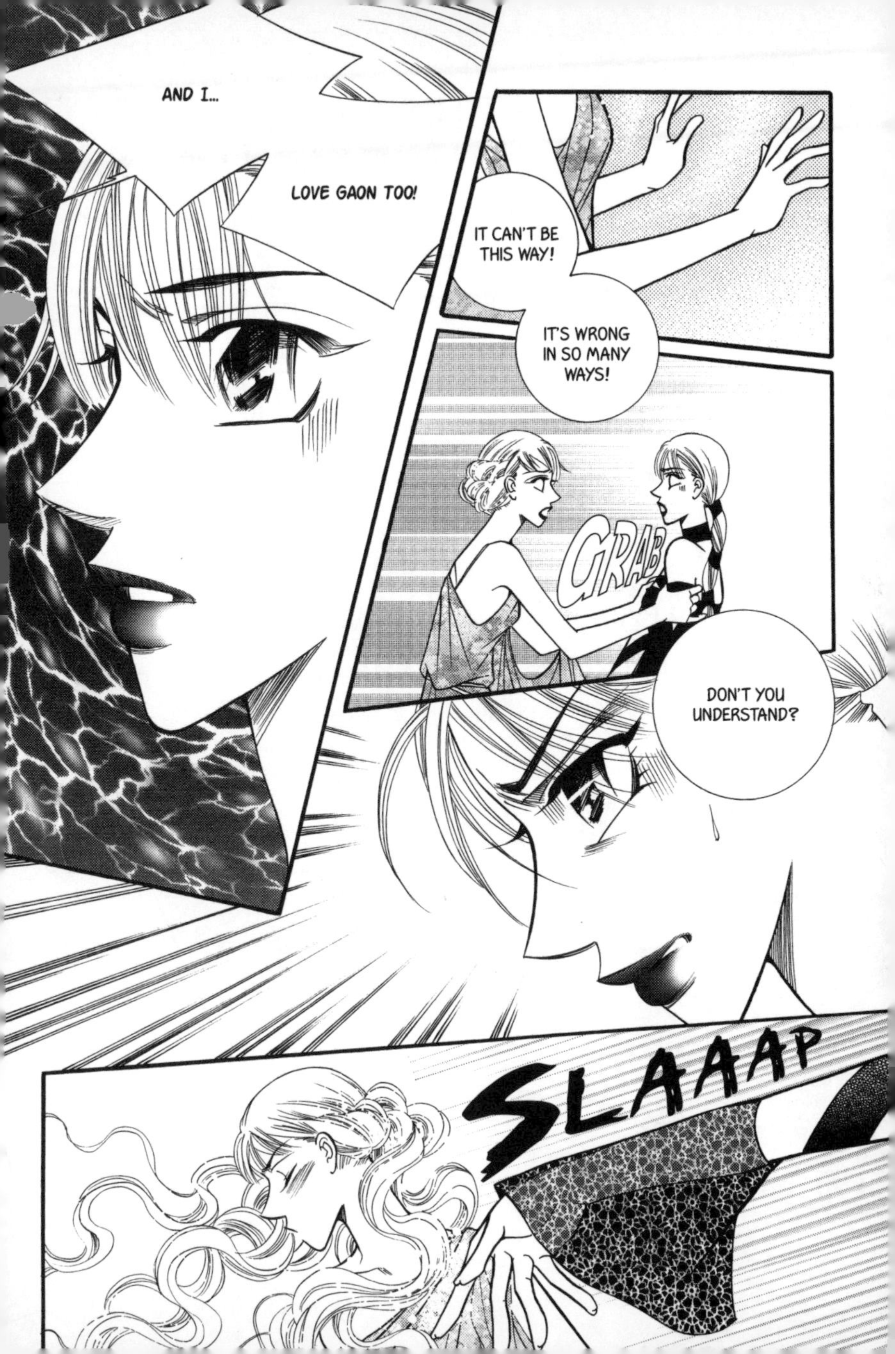
AND I...
LOVE GAON TOO!
IT CAN'T BE THIS WAY!
IT'S WRONG IN SO MANY WAYS!
GRAB
DON'T YOU UNDERSTAND?
SLAAAP

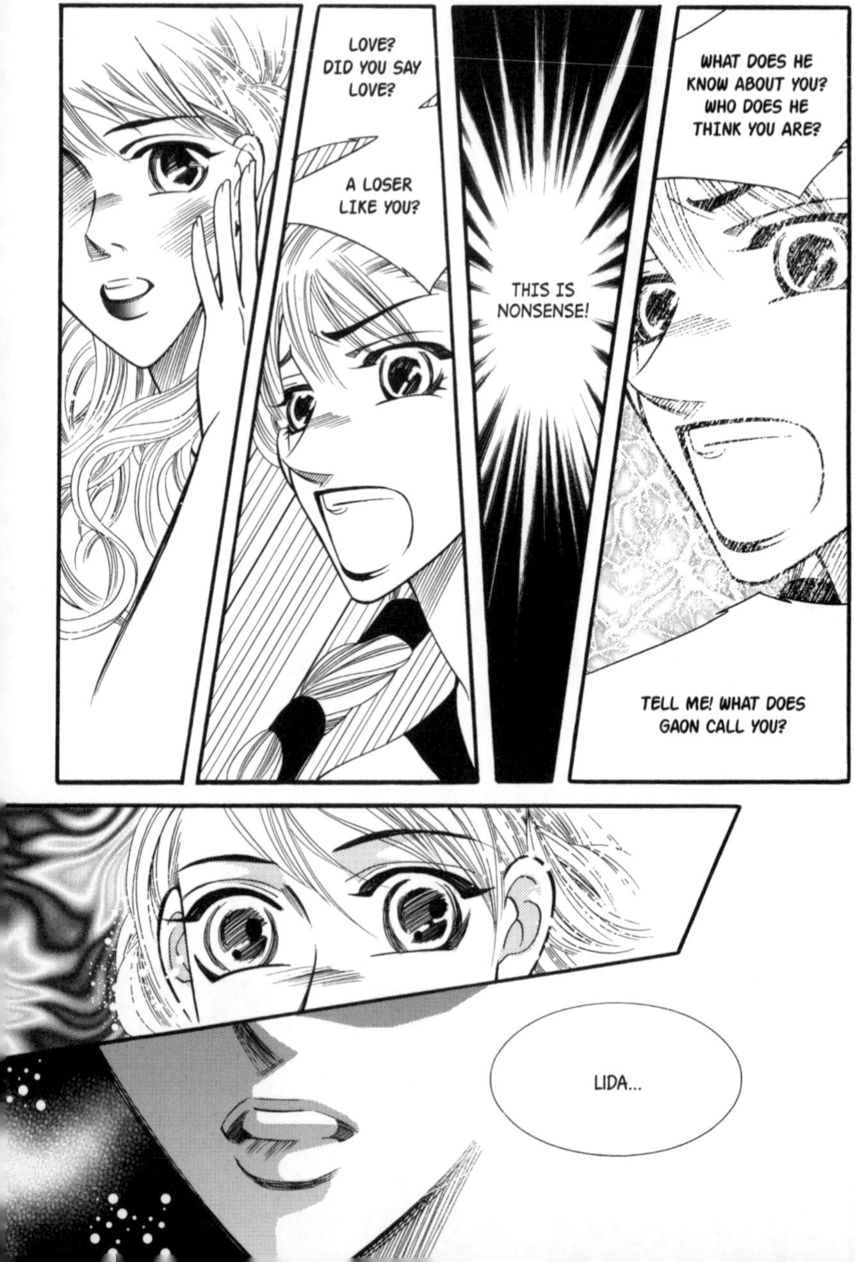
LOVE? DID YOU SAY LOVE?
A LOSER LIKE YOU?
THIS IS NONSENSE!
WHAT DOES HE KNOW ABOUT YOU? WHO DOES HE THINK YOU ARE?
TELL ME! WHAT DOES GAON CALL YOU?
LIDA...

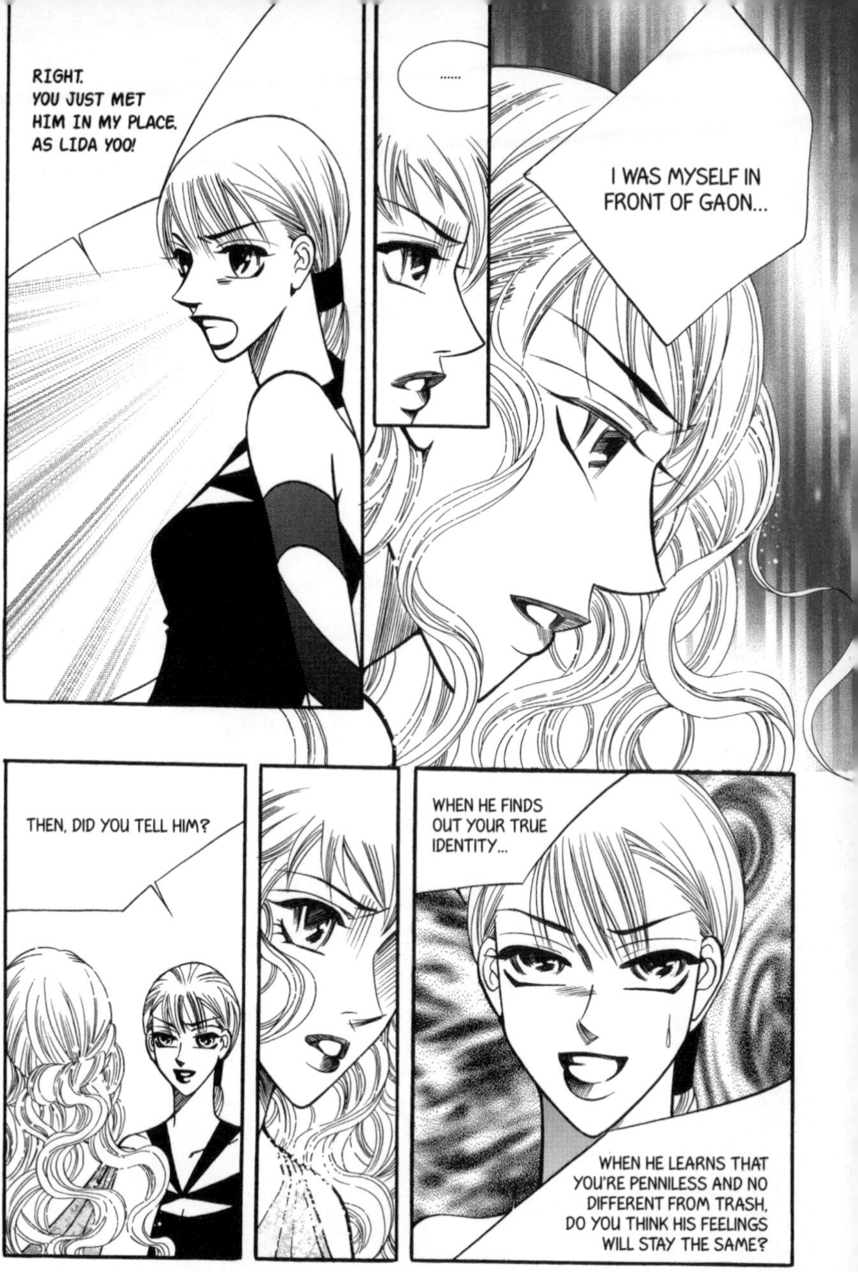
RIGHT. YOU JUST MET HIM IN MY PLACE. AS LIDA YOO!
......
I WAS MYSELF IN FRONT OF GAON...
THEN, DID YOU TELL HIM?
WHEN HE FINDS OUT YOUR TRUE IDENTITY...
WHEN HE LEARNS THAT YOU'RE PENNILESS AND NO DIFFERENT FROM TRASH, DO YOU THINK HIS FEELINGS WILL STAY THE SAME?

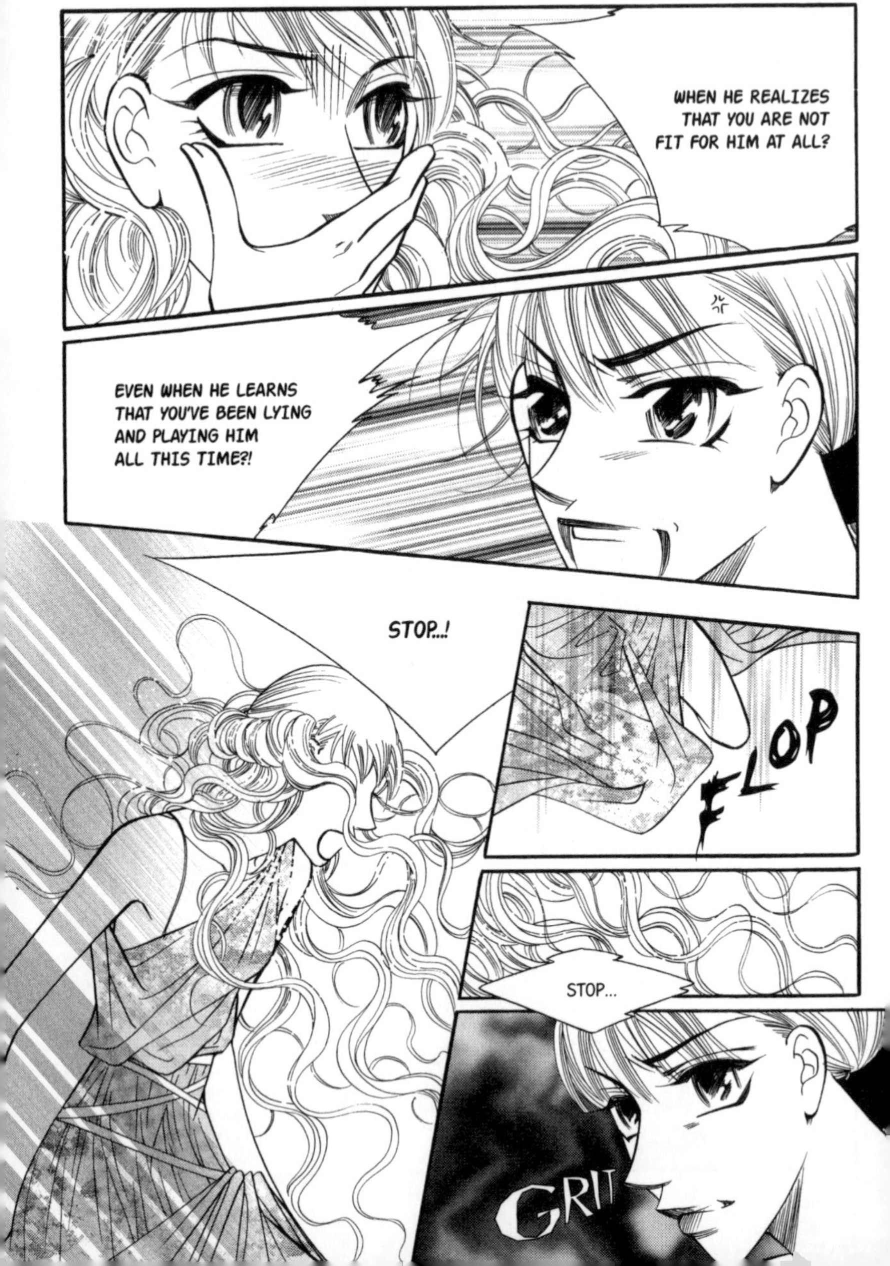
WHEN HE REALIZES THAT YOU ARE NOT FIT FOR HIM AT ALL?
EVEN WHEN HE LEARNS THAT YOU'VE BEEN LYING AND PLAYING HIM ALL THIS TIME?!
FLOP
STOP...
GRIT
STOP...!

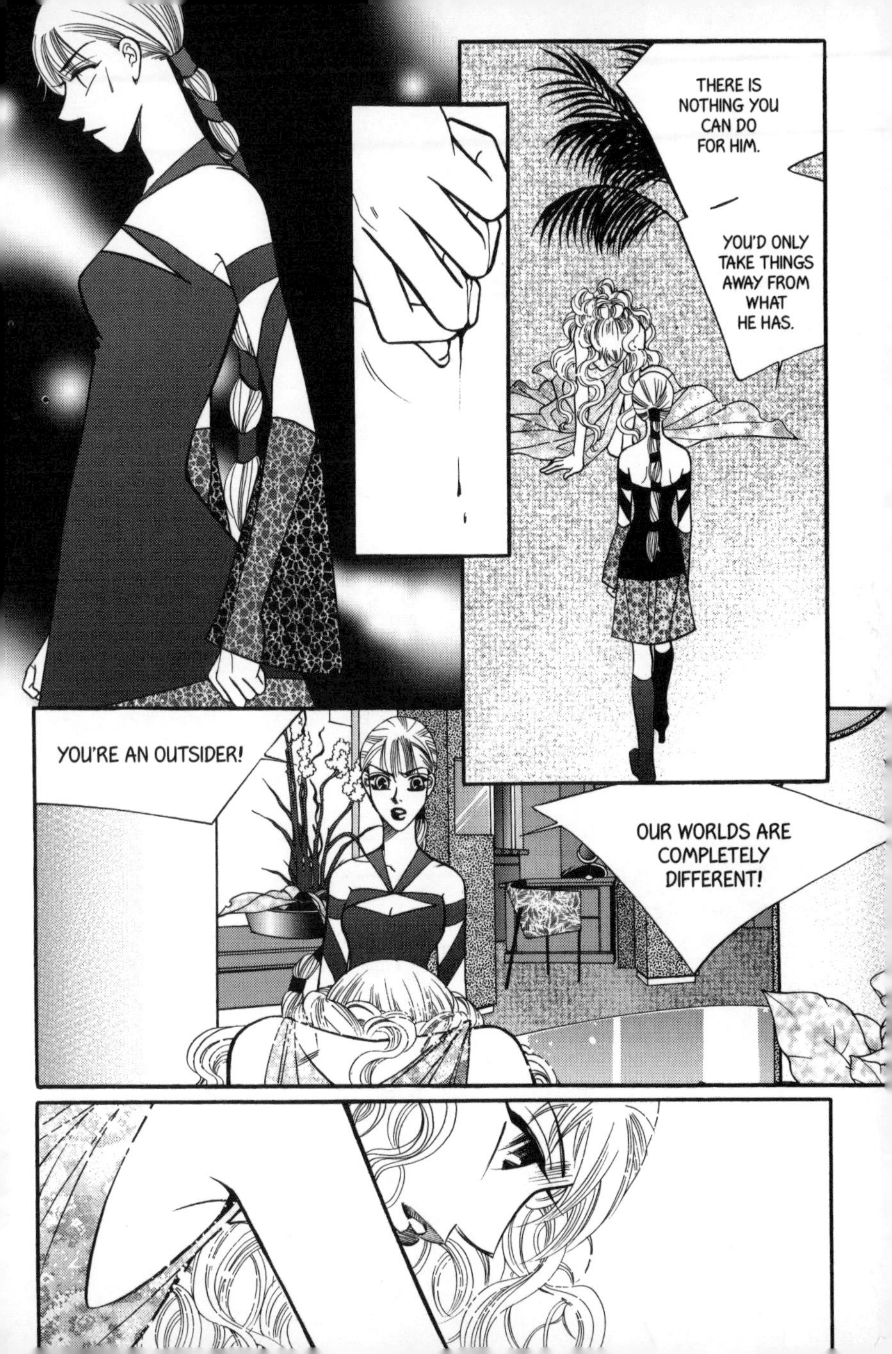

THERE IS NOTHING YOU CAN DO FOR HIM.
YOU'D ONLY TAKE THINGS AWAY FROM WHAT HE HAS.
YOU'RE AN OUTSIDER!
OUR WORLDS ARE COMPLETELY DIFFERENT!

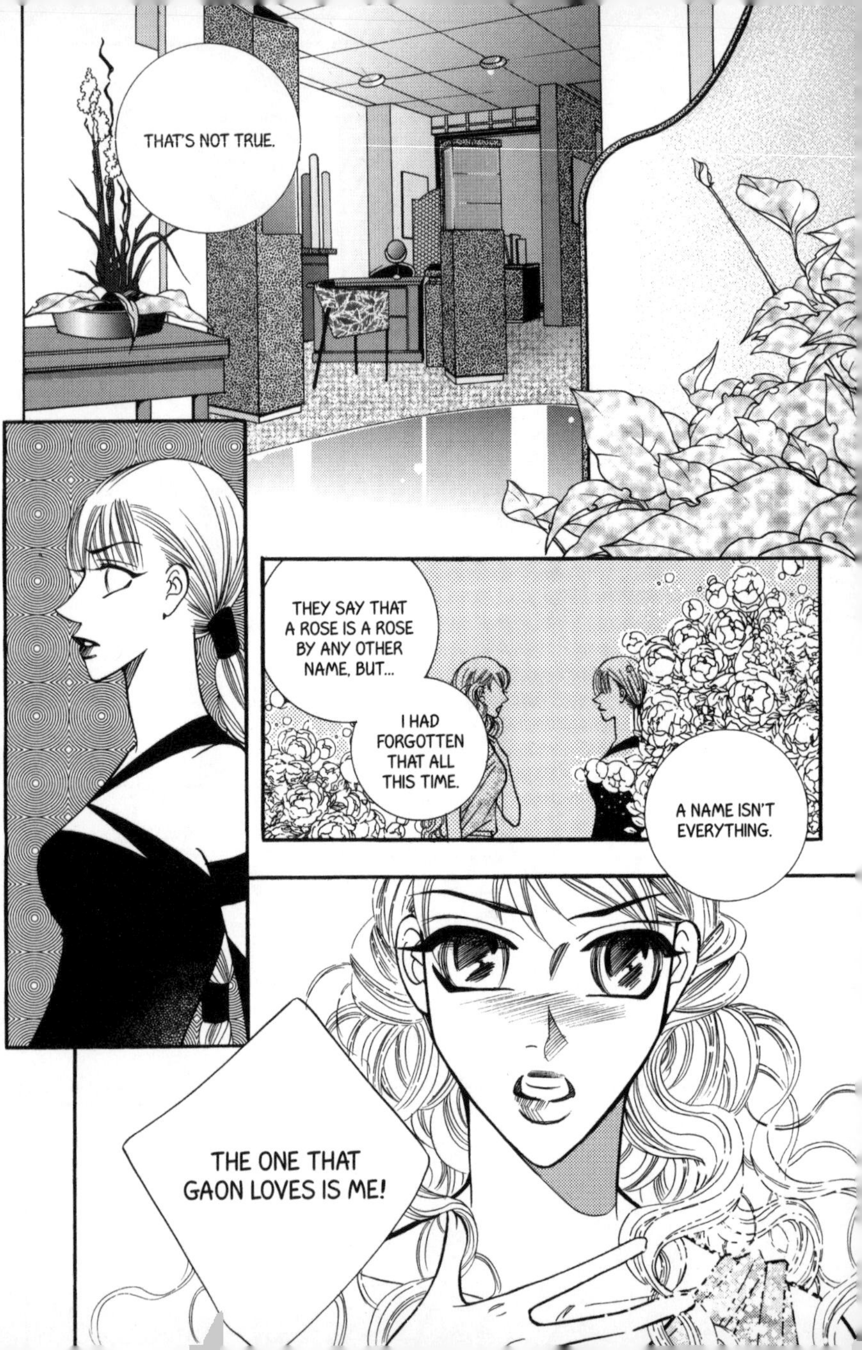
THAT'S NOT TRUE.
THEY SAY THAT A ROSE IS A ROSE BY ANY OTHER NAME, BUT...
I HAD FORGOTTEN THAT ALL THIS TIME.
A NAME ISN'T EVERYTHING.
THE ONE THAT GAON LOVES IS ME!

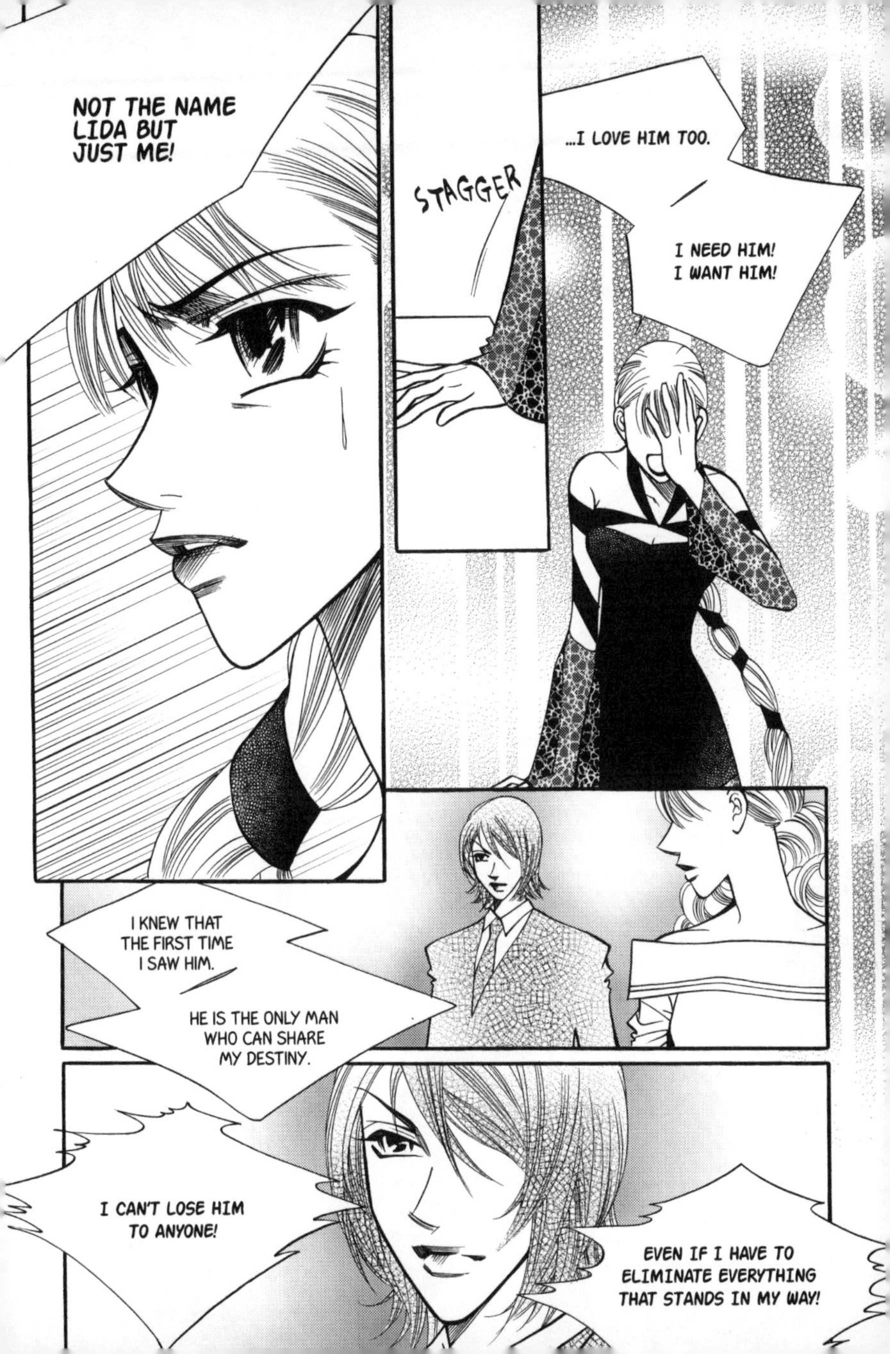
NOT THE NAME LIDA BUT JUST ME!
STAGGER
...I LOVE HIM TOO.
I NEED HIM! I WANT HIM!
I KNEW THAT THE FIRST TIME I SAW HIM.
HE IS THE ONLY MAN WHO CAN SHARE MY DESTINY.
I CAN'T LOSE HIM TO ANYONE!
EVEN IF I HAVE TO ELIMINATE EVERYTHING THAT STANDS IN MY WAY!

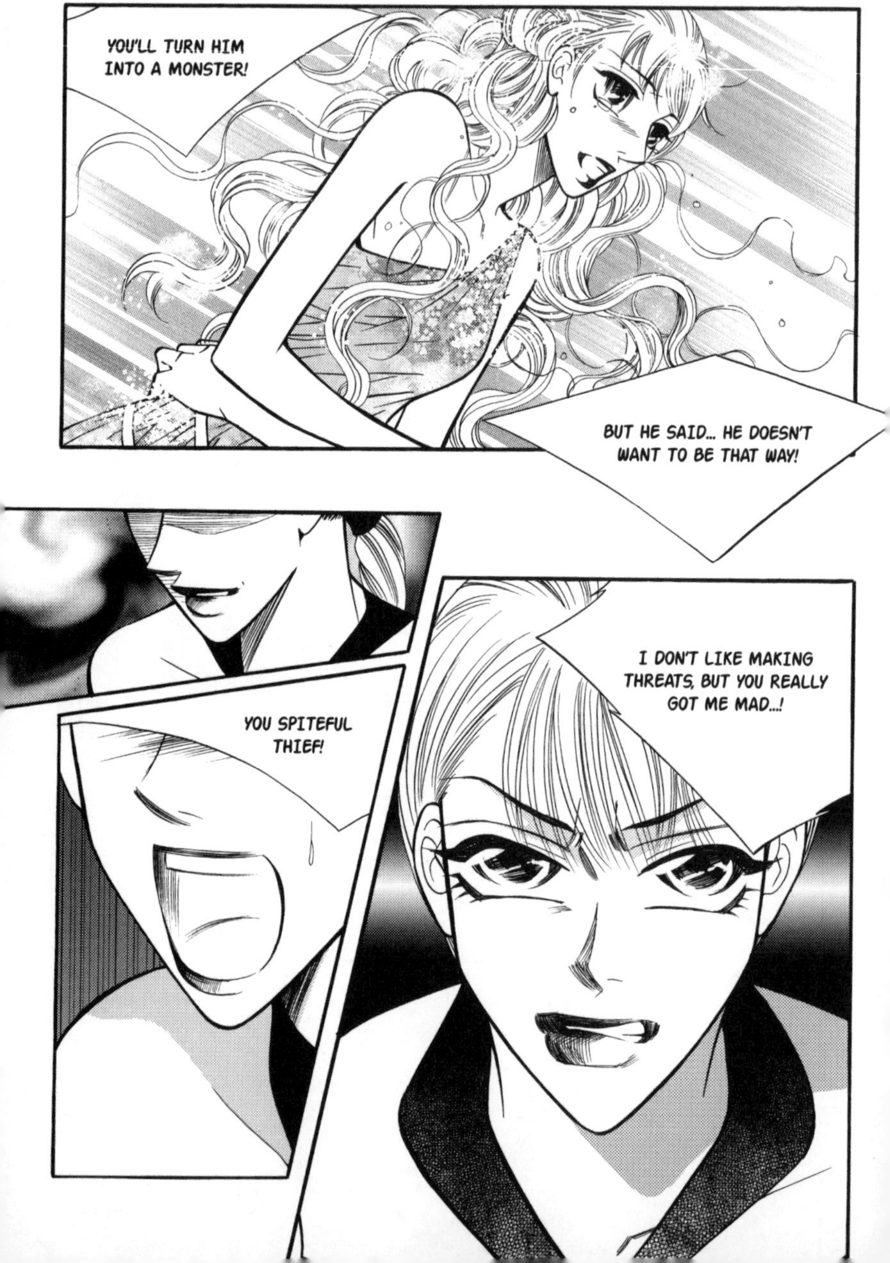
YOU'LL TURN HIM INTO A MONSTER!
BUT HE SAID... HE DOESN'T WANT TO BE THAT WAY!
YOU SPITEFUL THIEF!
I DON'T LIKE MAKING THREATS, BUT YOU REALLY GOT ME MAD...!

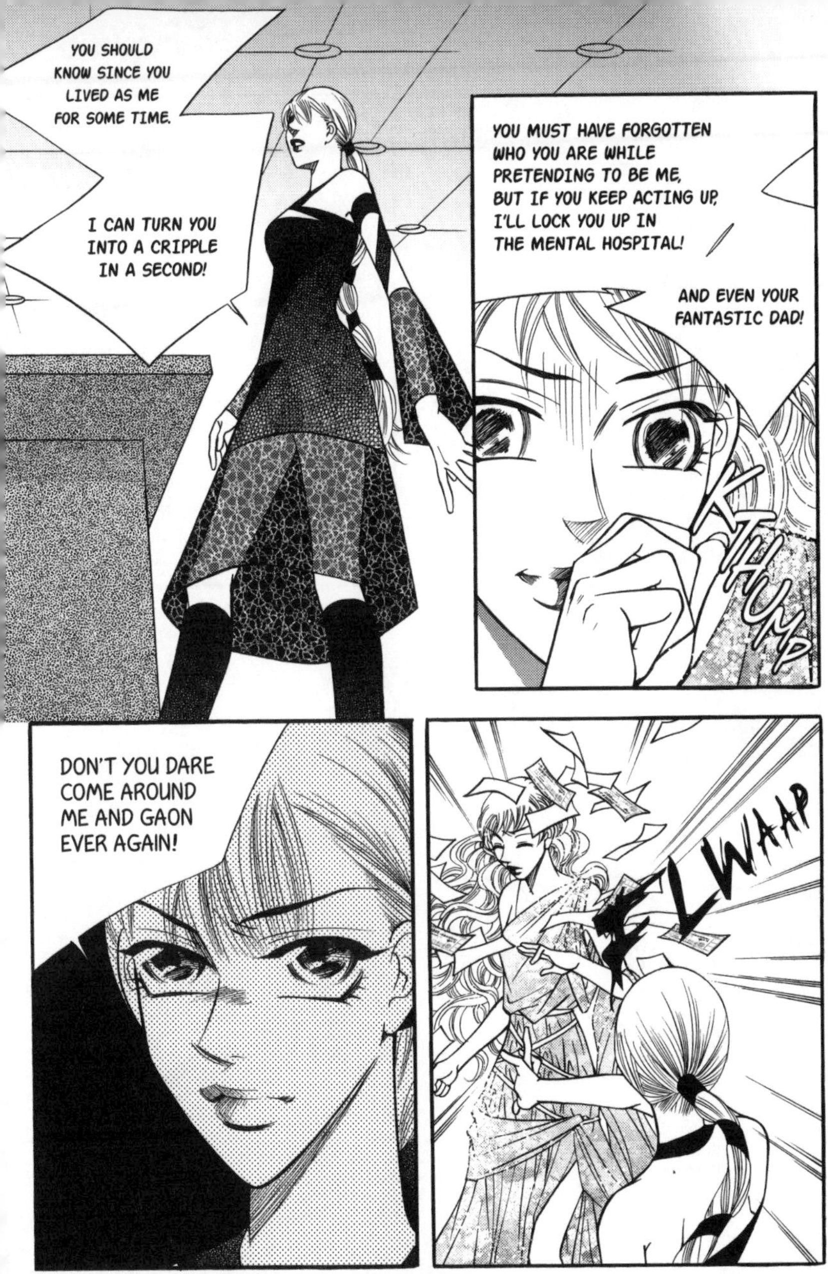
YOU SHOULD KNOW SINCE YOU LIVED AS ME FOR SOME TIME.
I CAN TURN YOU INTO A CRIPPLE IN A SECOND!
YOU MUST HAVE FORGOTTEN WHO YOU ARE WHILE PRETENDING TO BE ME, BUT IF YOU KEEP ACTING UP, I'LL LOCK YOU UP IN THE MENTAL HOSPITAL!
AND EVEN YOUR FANTASTIC DAD!
KTHUMP
DON'T YOU DARE COME AROUND ME AND GAON EVER AGAIN!
FLWAAP

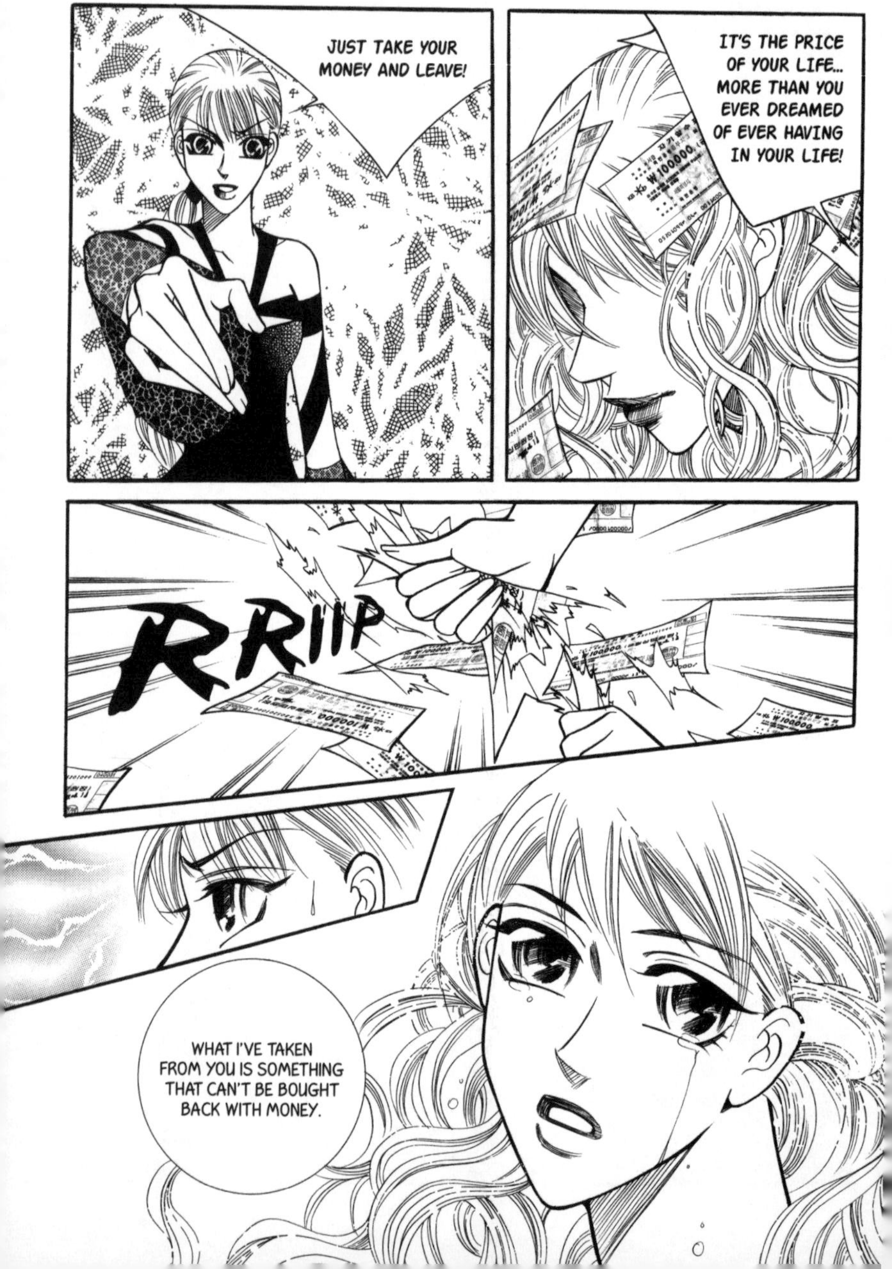
JUST TAKE YOUR MONEY AND LEAVE!
IT'S THE PRICE OF YOUR LIFE... MORE THAN YOU EVER DREAMED OF EVER HAVING IN YOUR LIFE!
RRIIP
WHAT I'VE TAKEN FROM YOU IS SOMETHING THAT CAN'T BE BOUGHT BACK WITH MONEY.

17. WHO ARE YOU, WHO AM I?

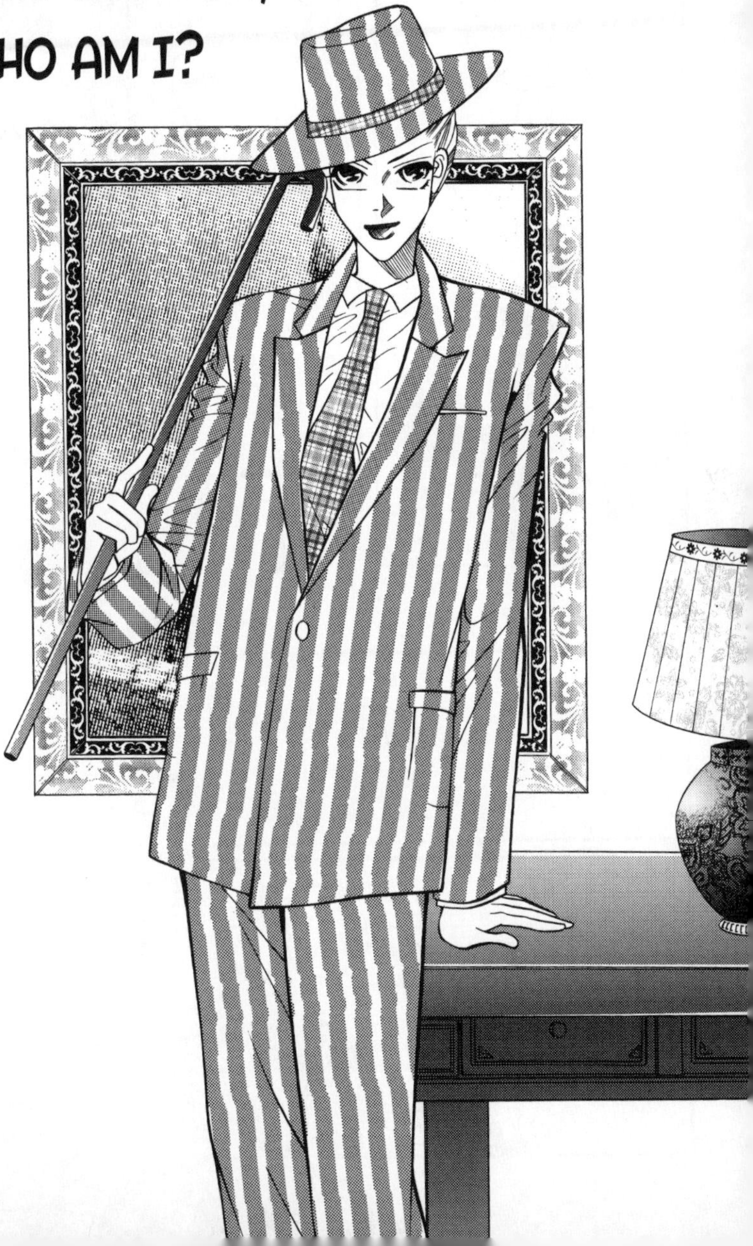

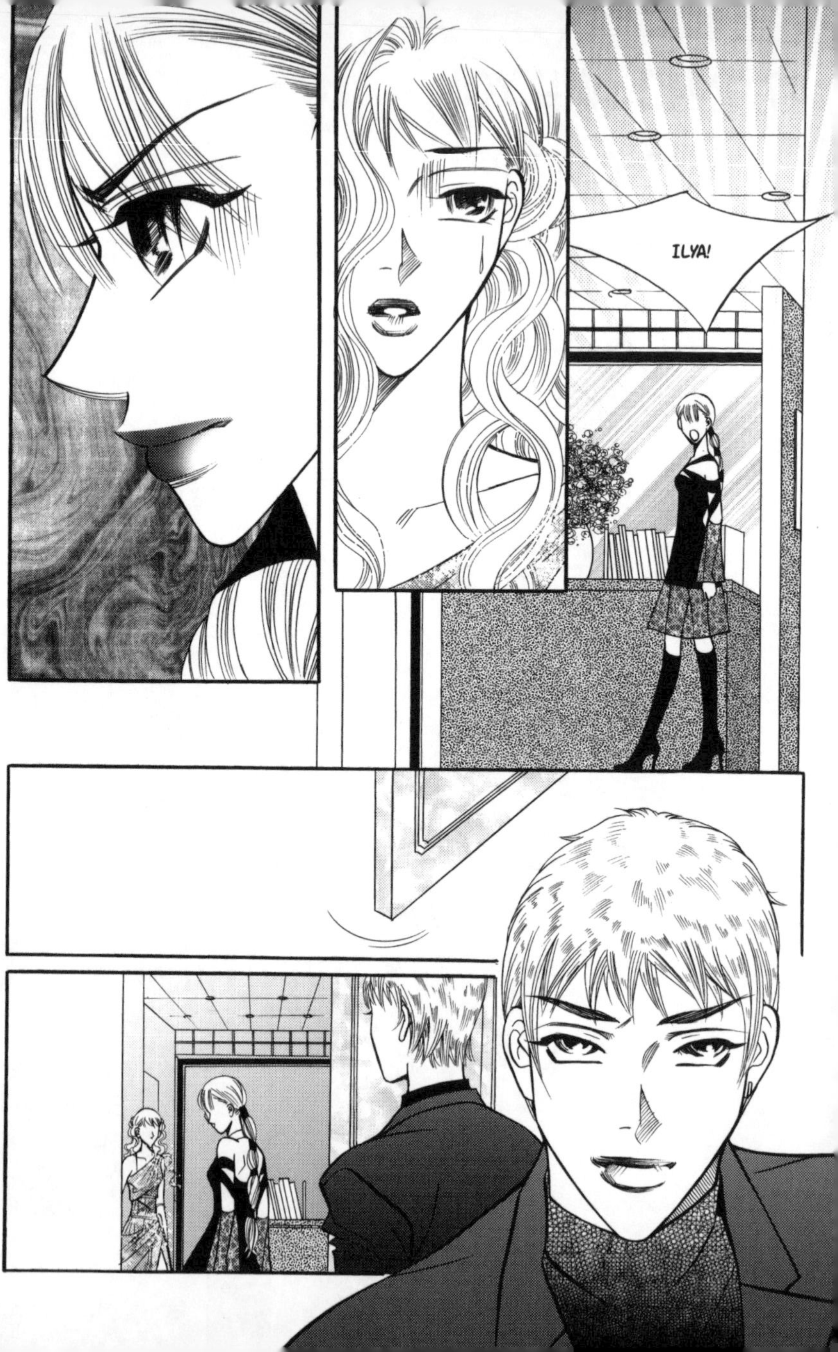
ILYA!

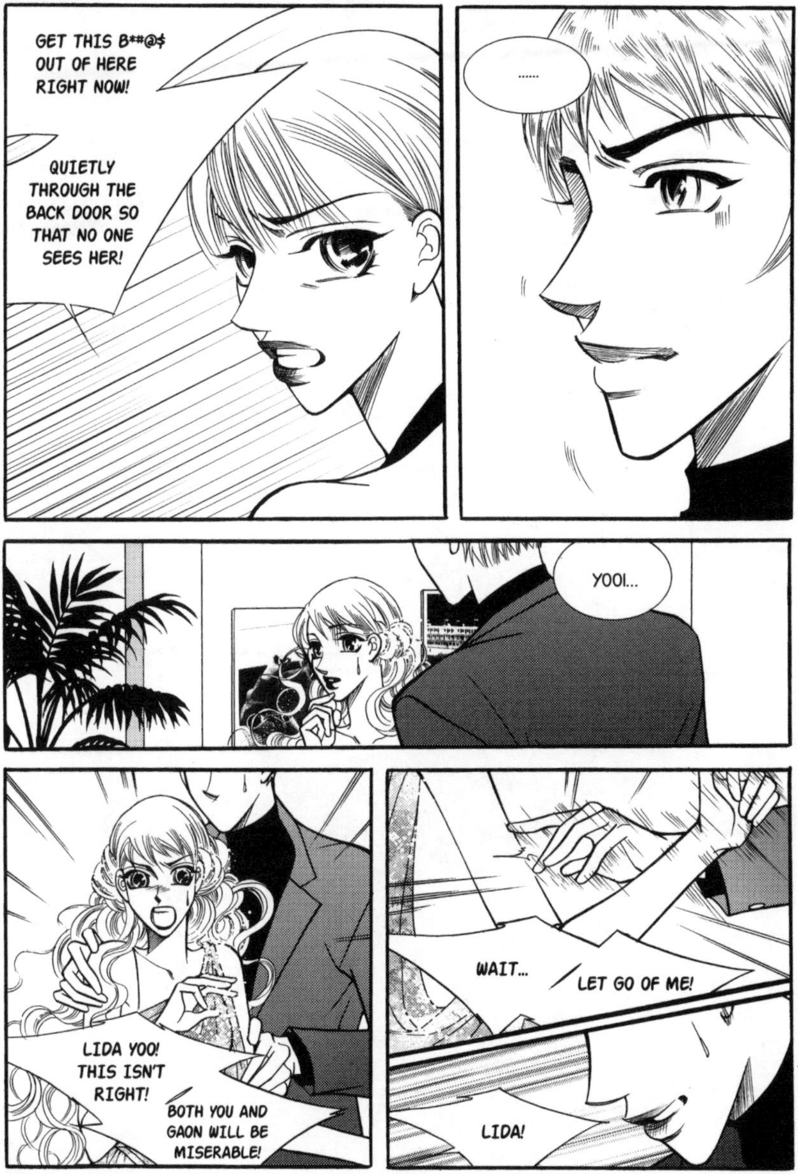
GET THIS B**@$ OUT OF HERE RIGHT NOW!
QUIETLY THROUGH THE BACK DOOR SO THAT NO ONE SEES HER!
......
YOOI...
LIDA YOO! THIS ISN'T RIGHT!
BOTH YOU AND GAON WILL BE MISERABLE!
WAIT...
LET GO OF ME!
LIDA!

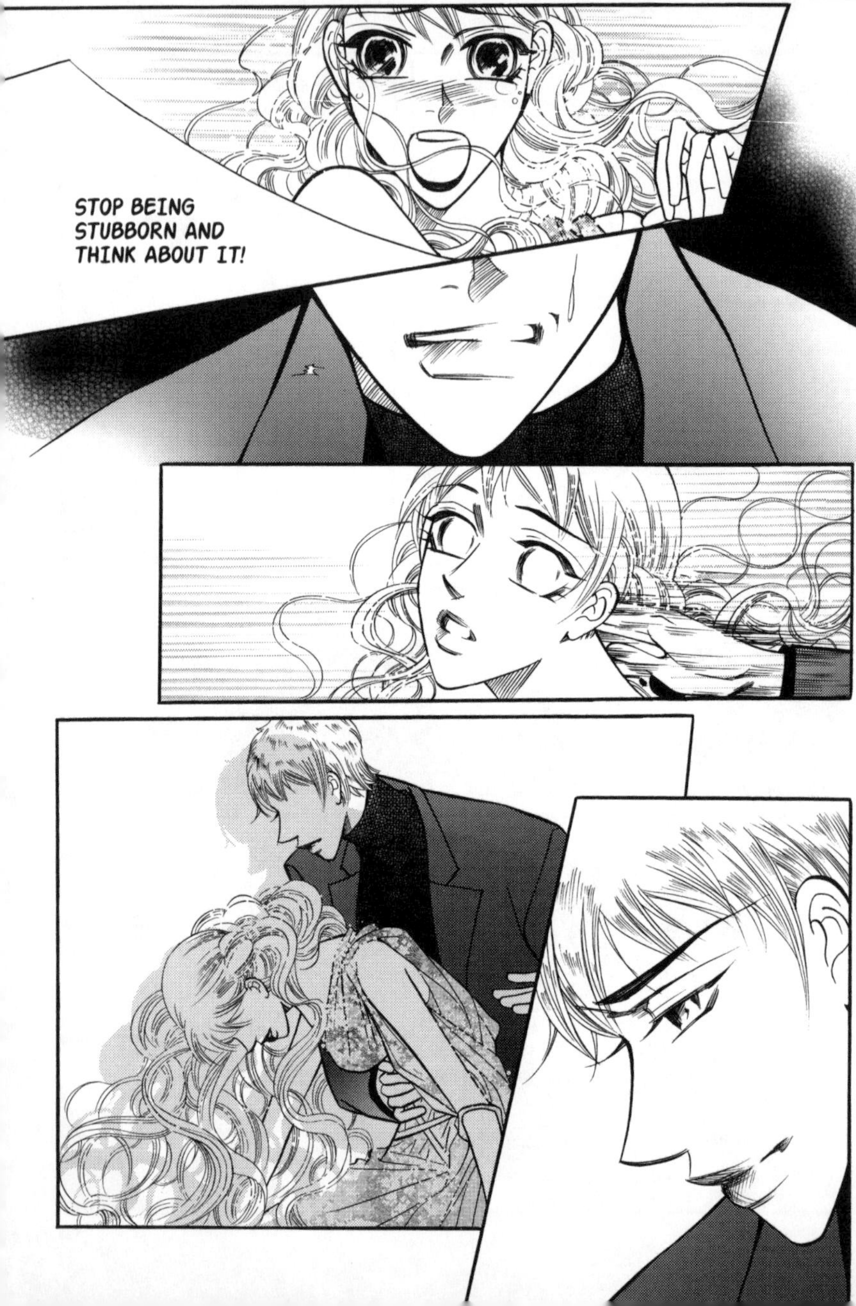
STOP BEING STUBBORN AND THINK ABOUT IT!

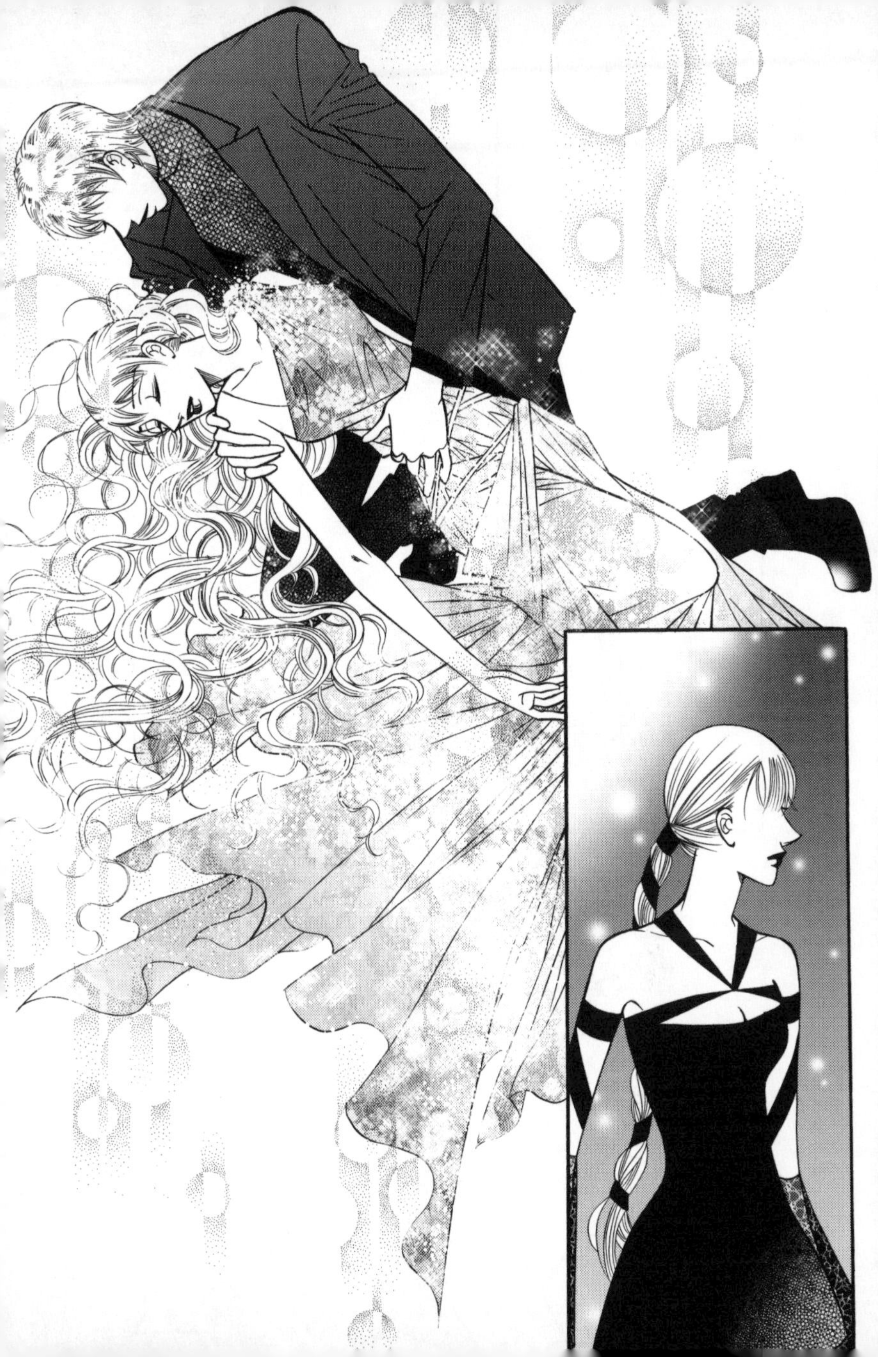

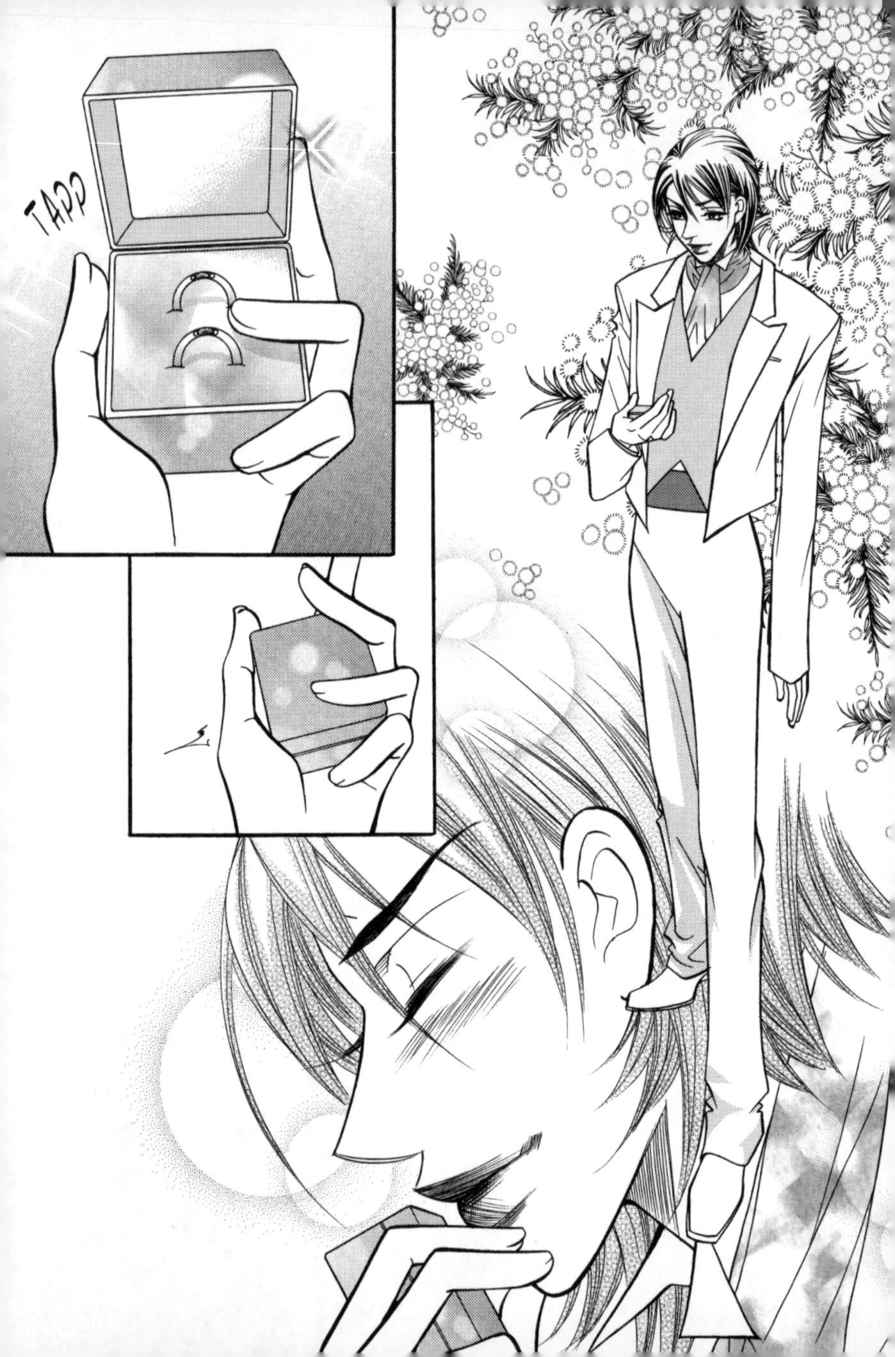
TAPP

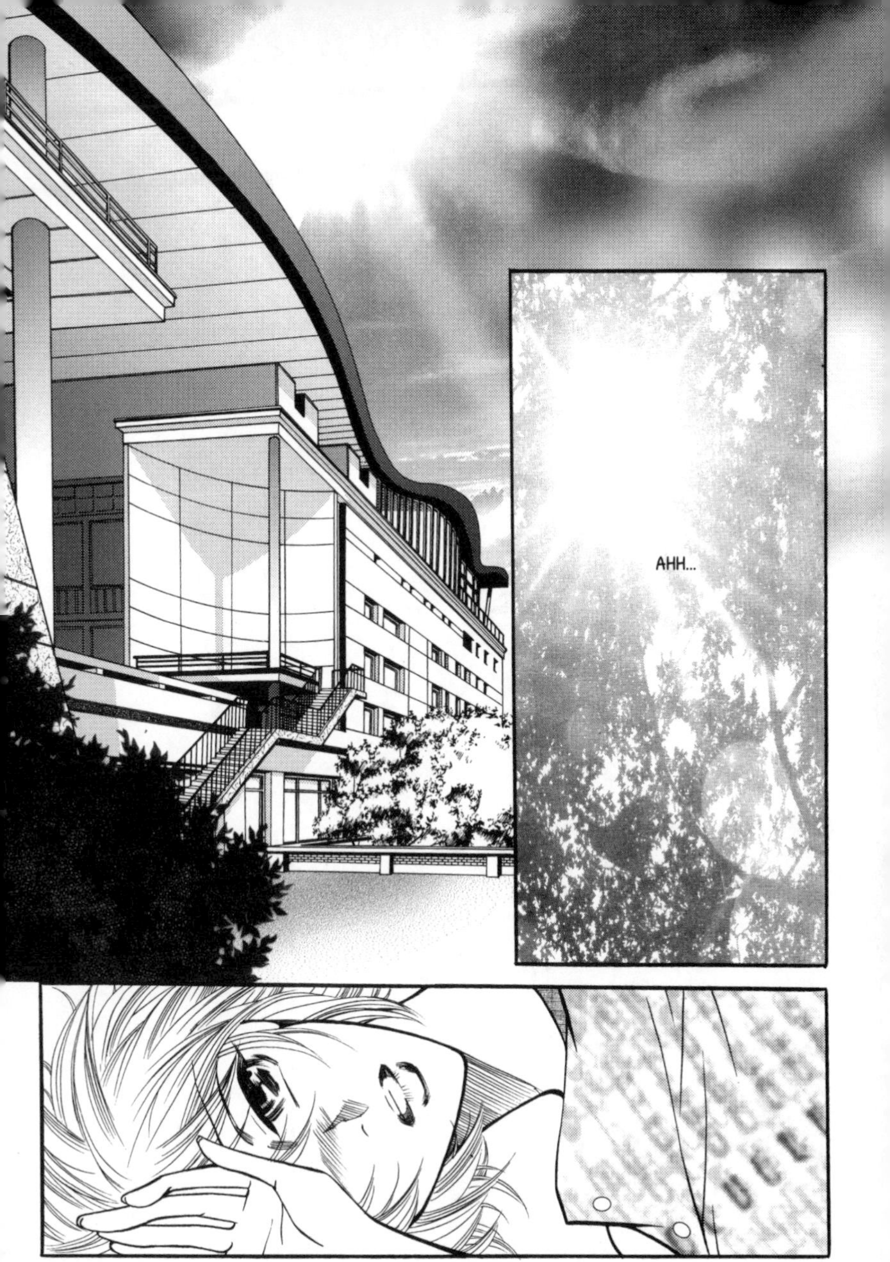
AHH...

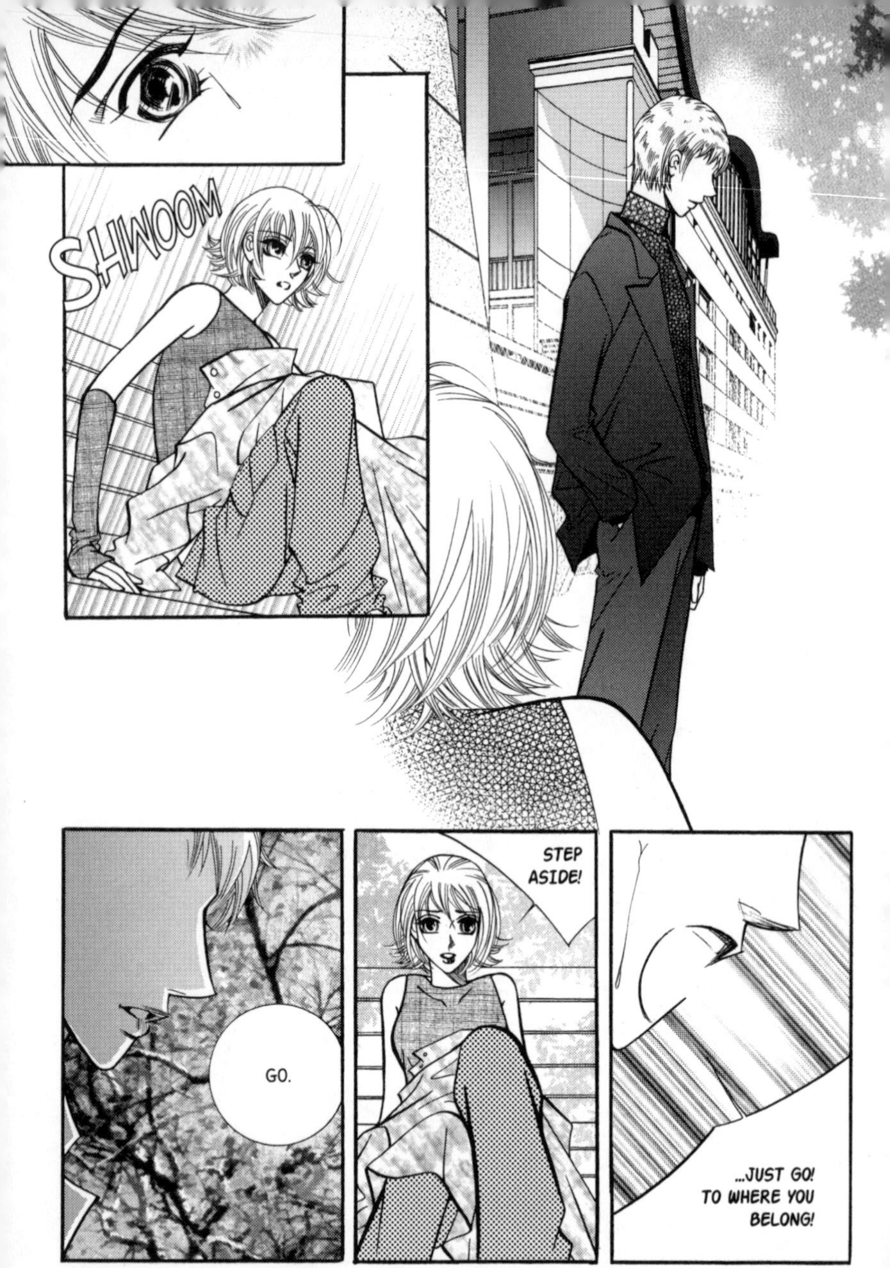
SHWOOM
GO.
STEP ASIDE!
...JUST GO! TO WHERE YOU BELONG!

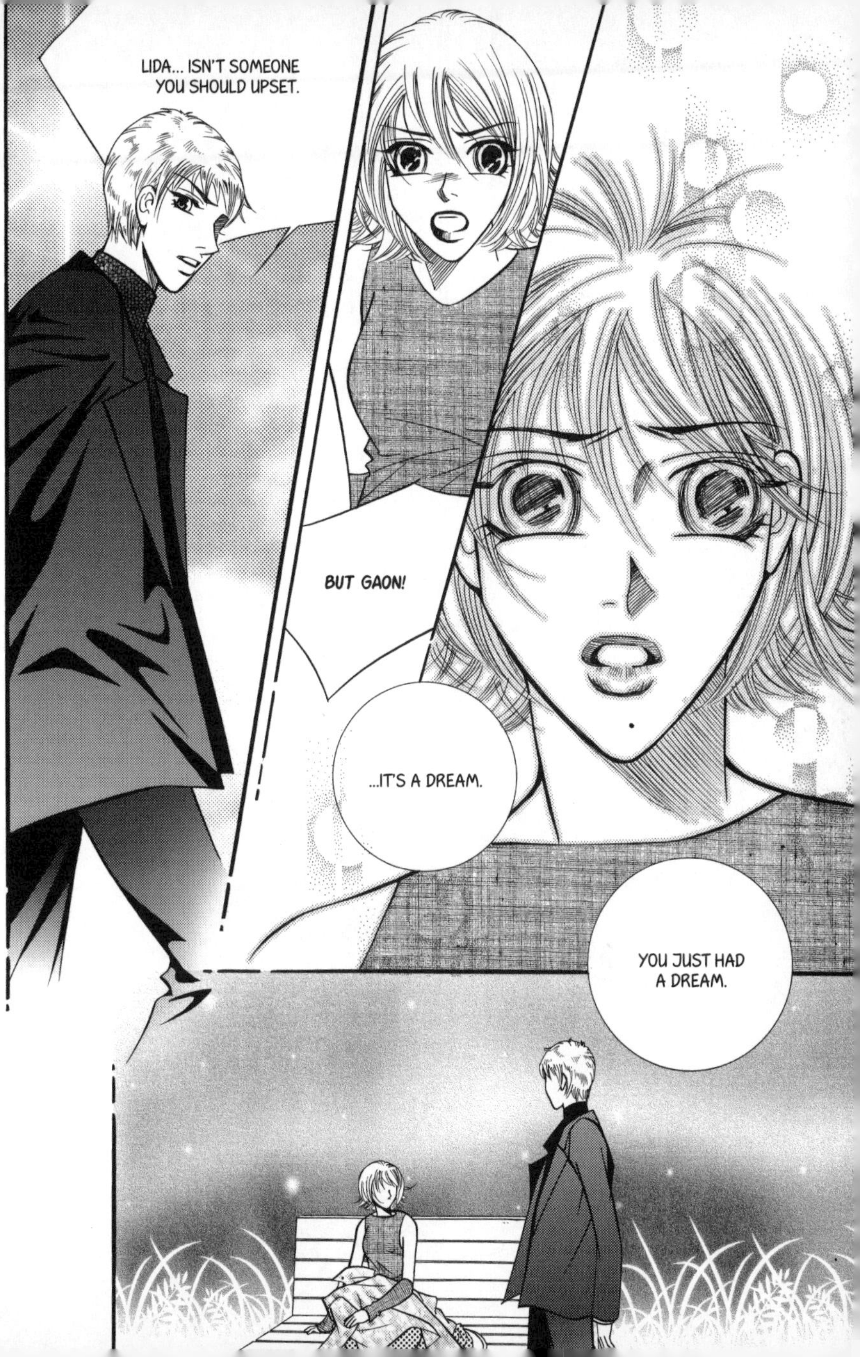
LIDA... ISN'T SOMEONE YOU SHOULD UPSET.
BUT GAON!
...IT'S A DREAM.
YOU JUST HAD A DREAM.

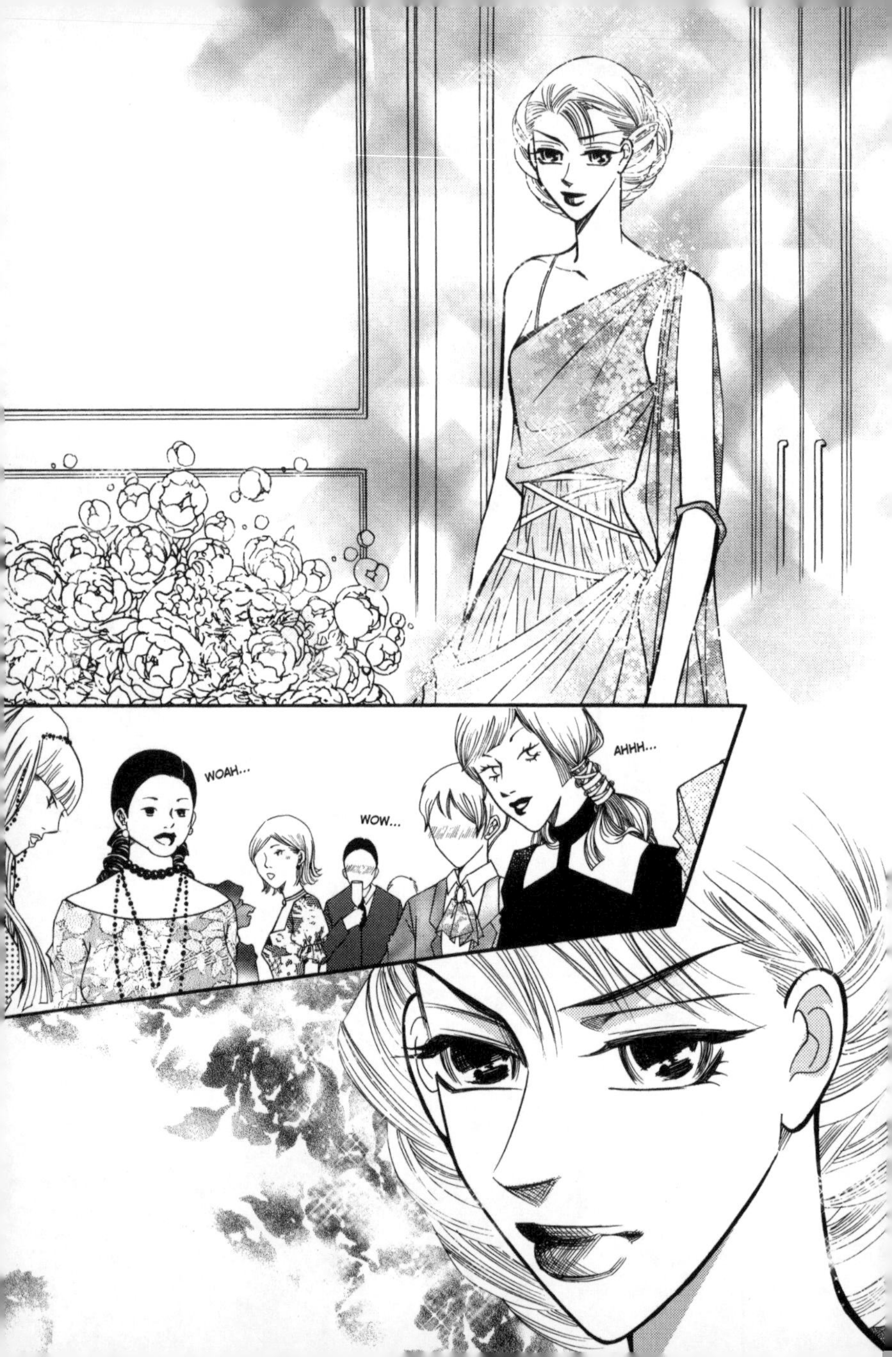
WOAH...
WOW...
AHHH...

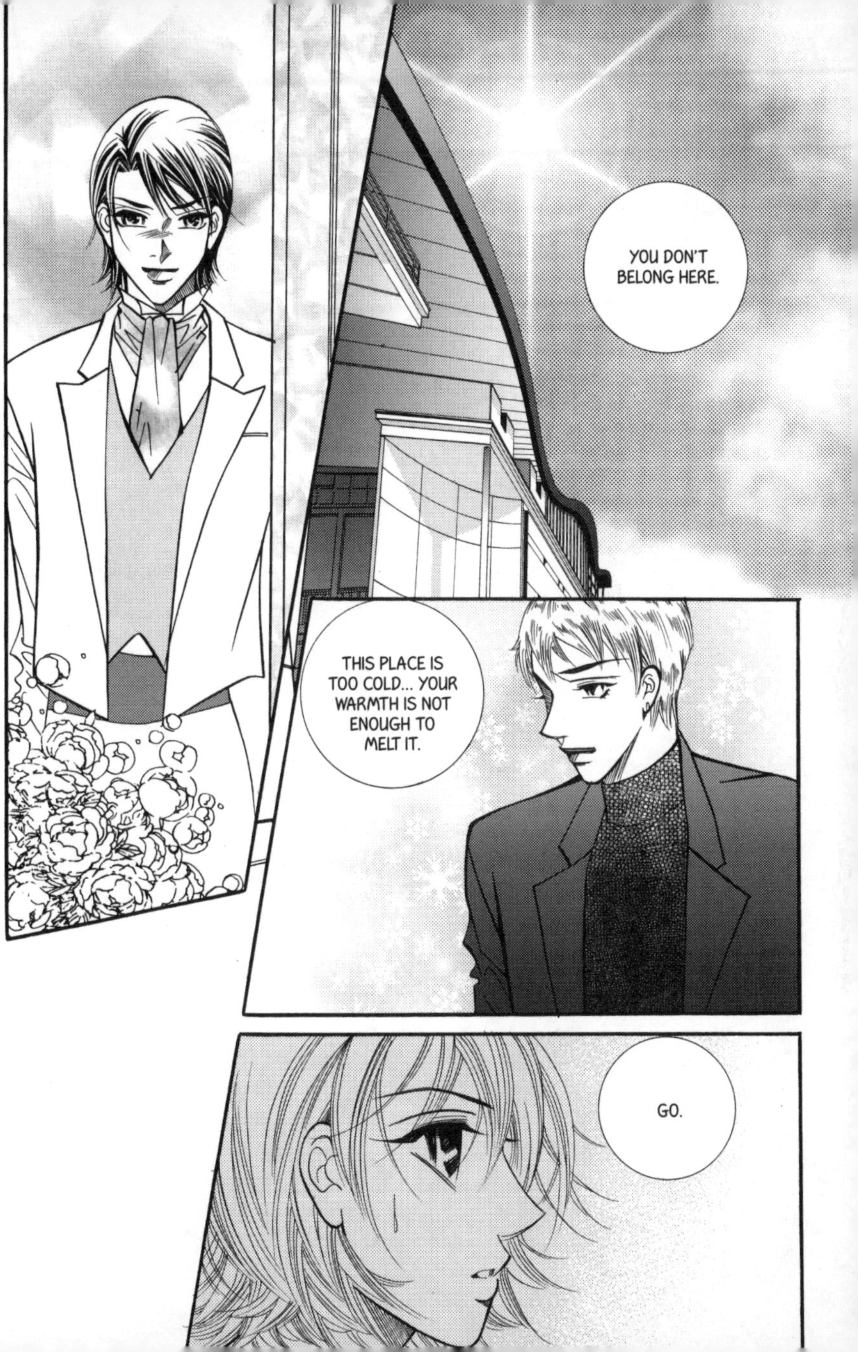
YOU DON'T BELONG HERE.
THIS PLACE IS TOO COLD... YOUR WARMTH IS NOT ENOUGH TO MELT IT.
GO.

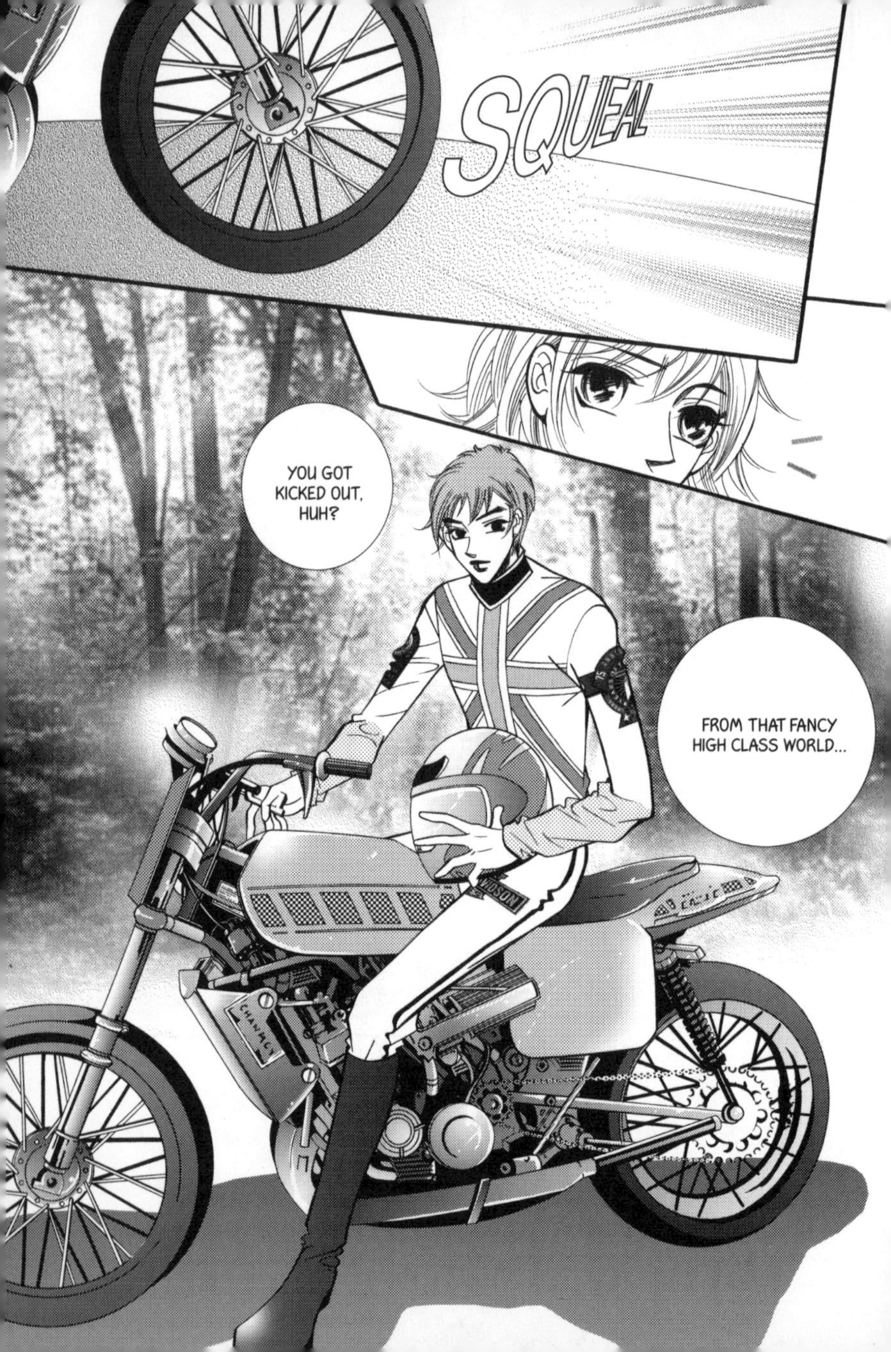
SQUEAL
YOU GOT KICKED OUT, HUH?
FROM THAT FANCY HIGH CLASS WORLD...

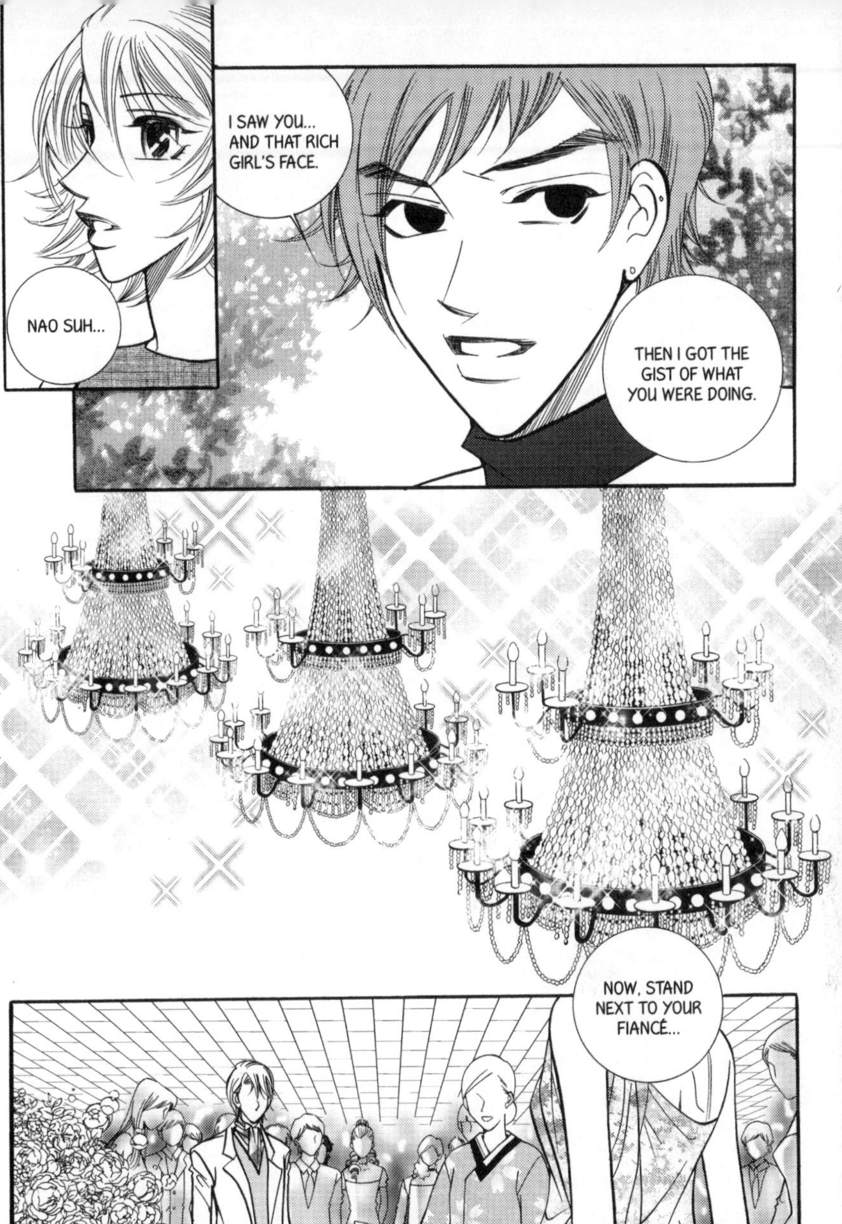
NAO SUH...
I SAW YOU... AND THAT RICH GIRL'S FACE.
THEN I GOT THE GIST OF WHAT YOU WERE DOING.
NOW, STAND NEXT TO YOUR FIANCÉ...

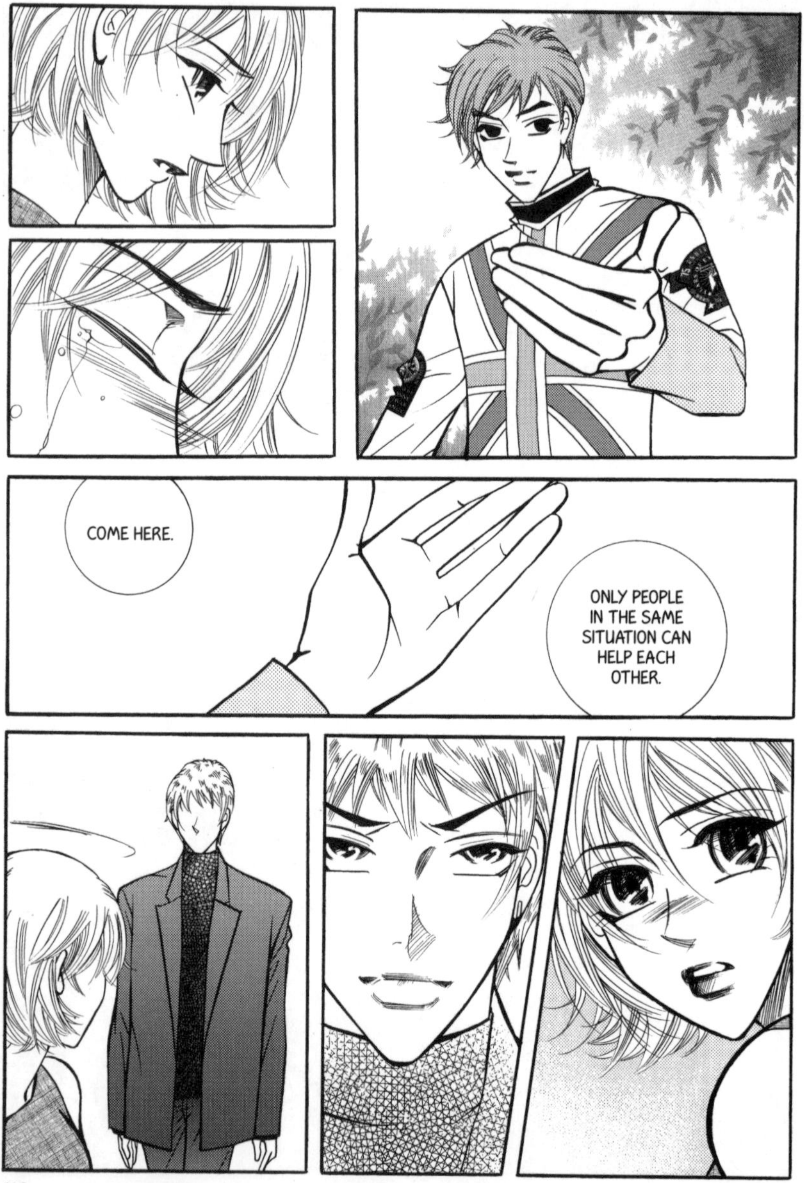
COME HERE.
ONLY PEOPLE IN THE SAME SITUATION CAN HELP EACH OTHER.

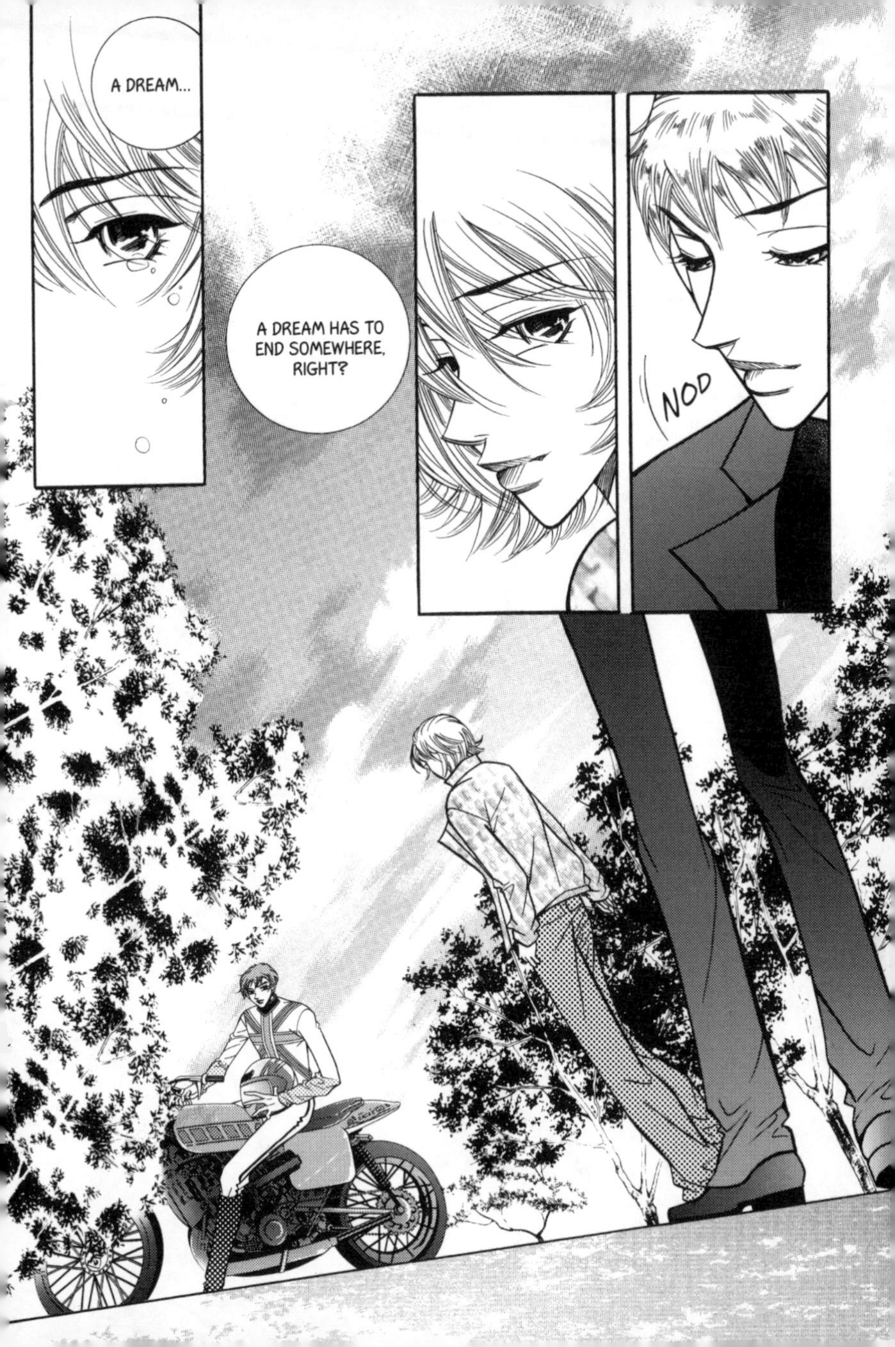
A DREAM...
A DREAM HAS TO END SOMEWHERE, RIGHT?
NOD

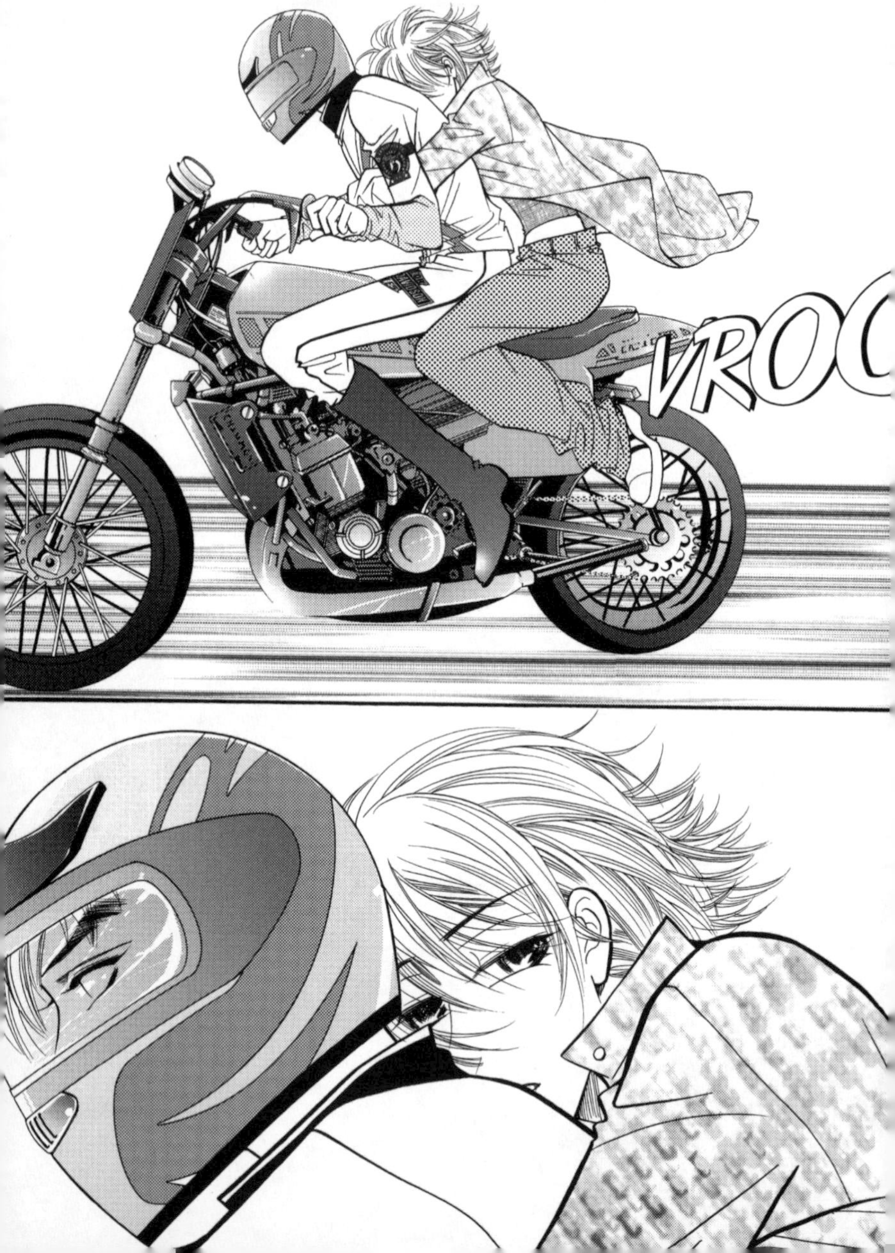
VROO

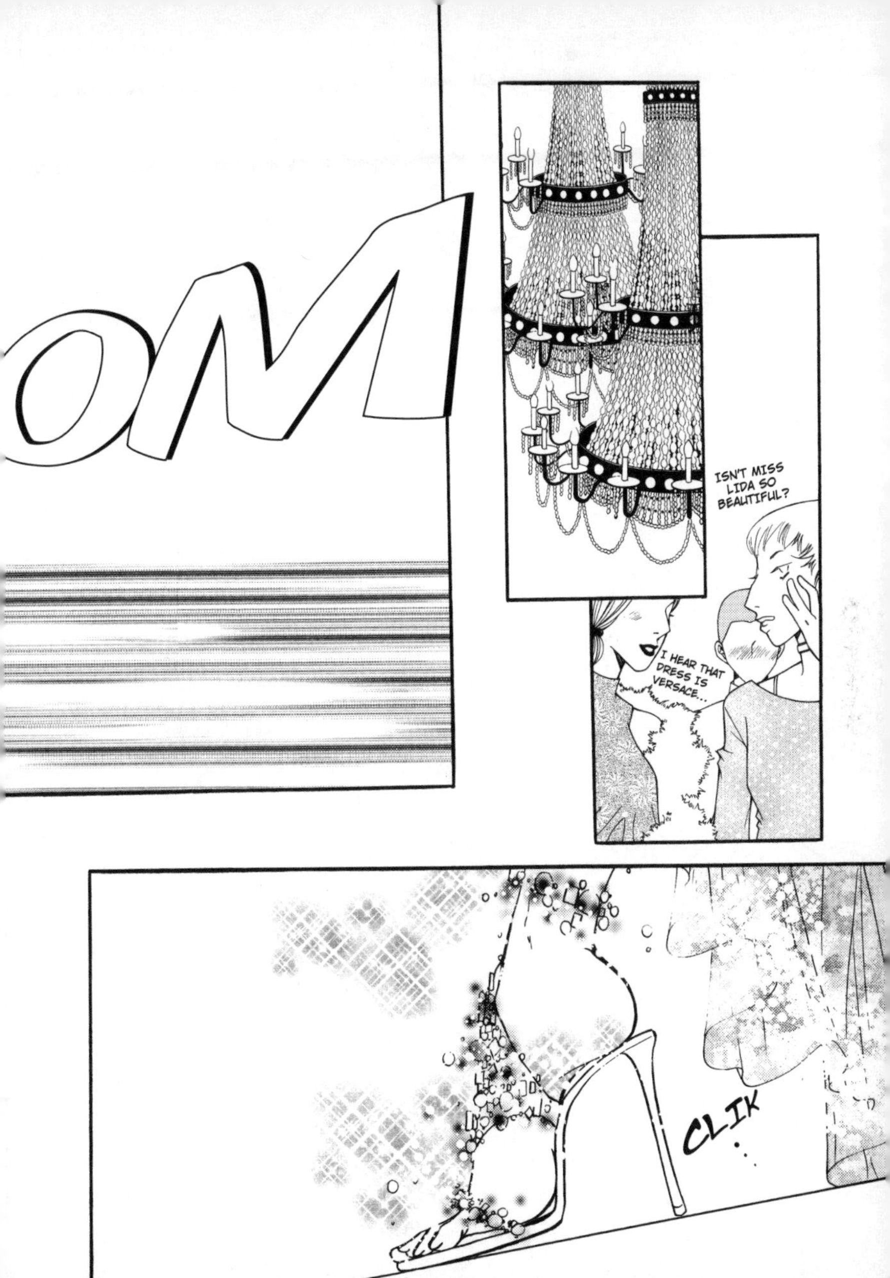
OM
ISN'T MISS LIDA SO BEAUTIFUL?
I HEAR THAT DRESS IS VERSACE...
CLIK...

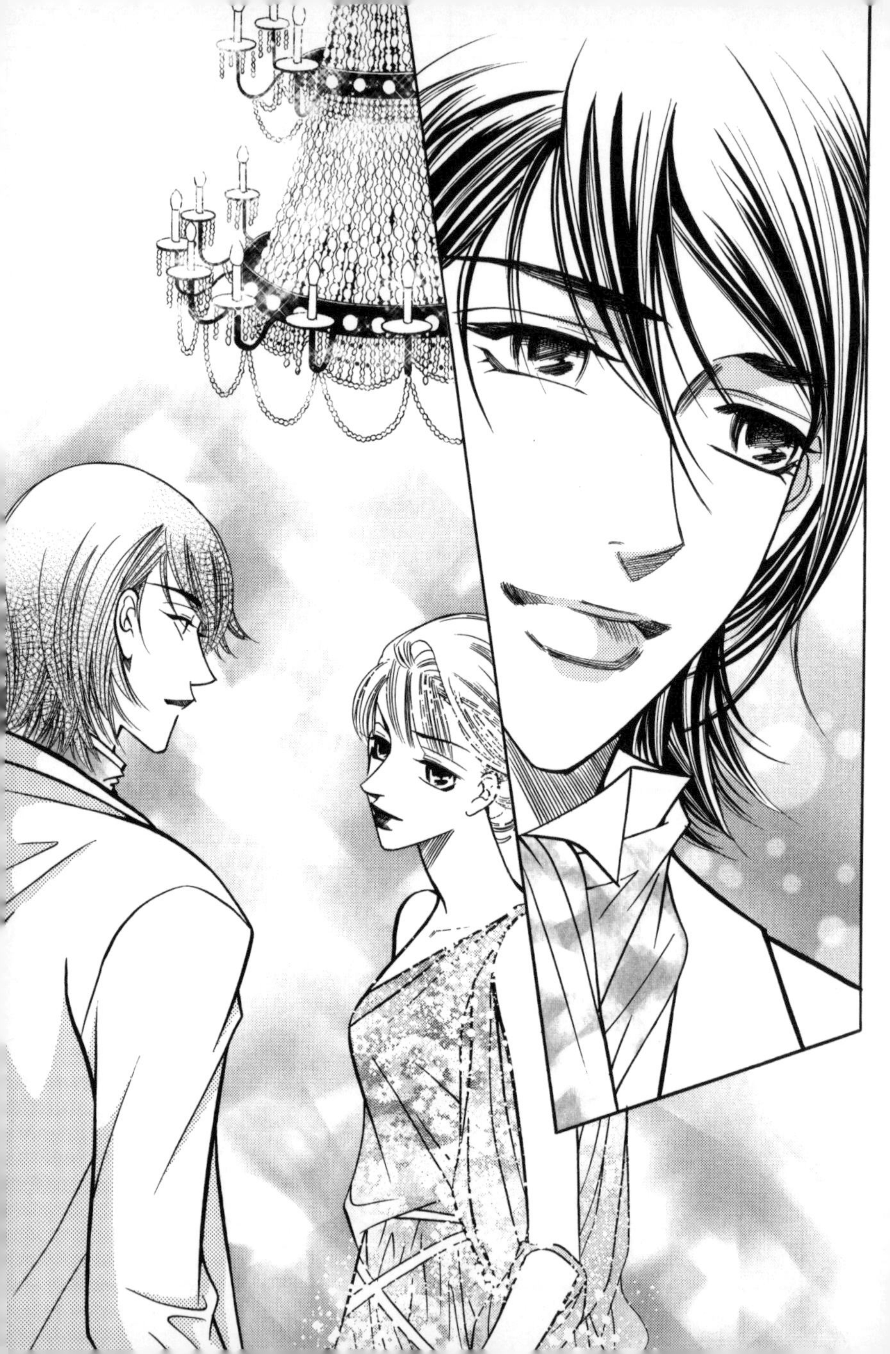

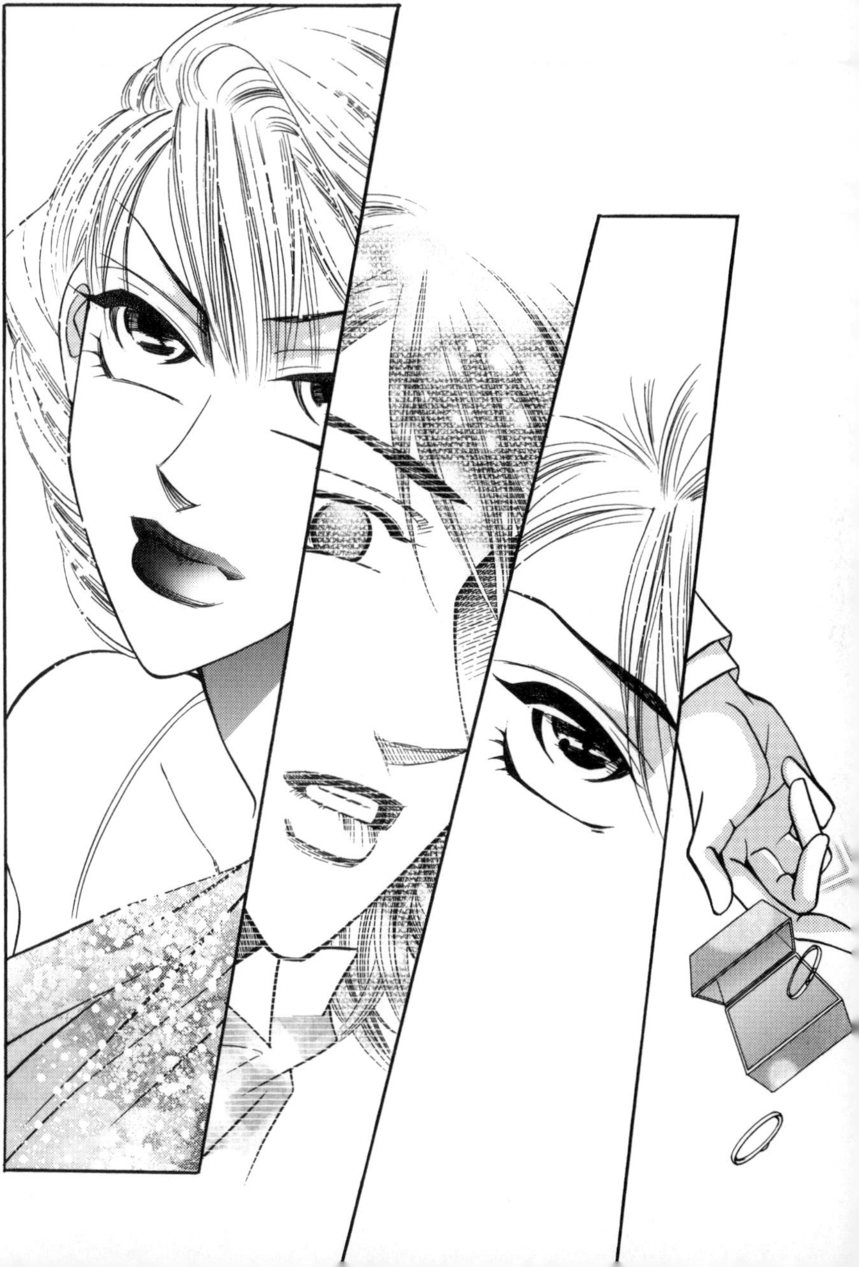

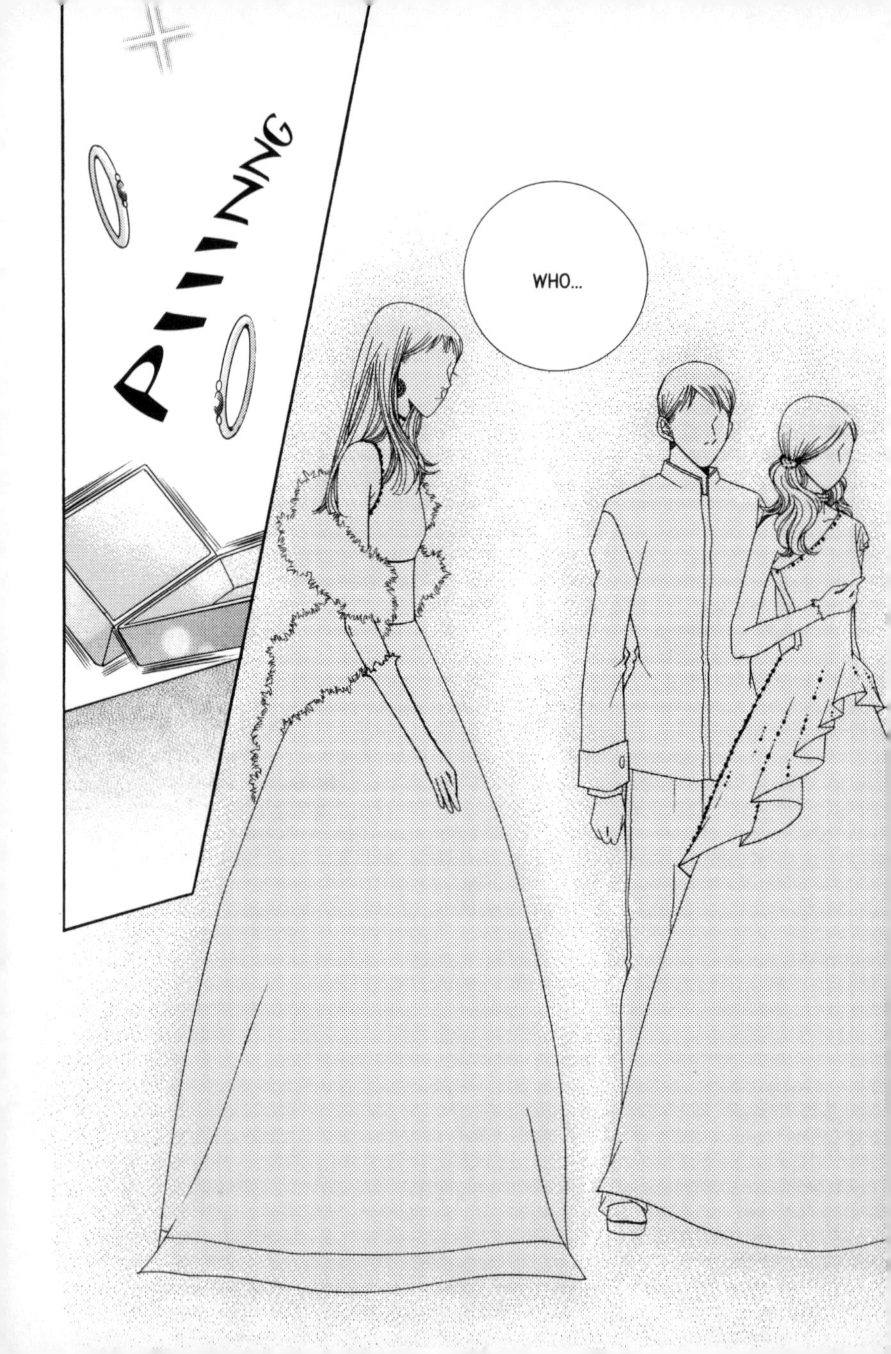
PIIIING
WHO...

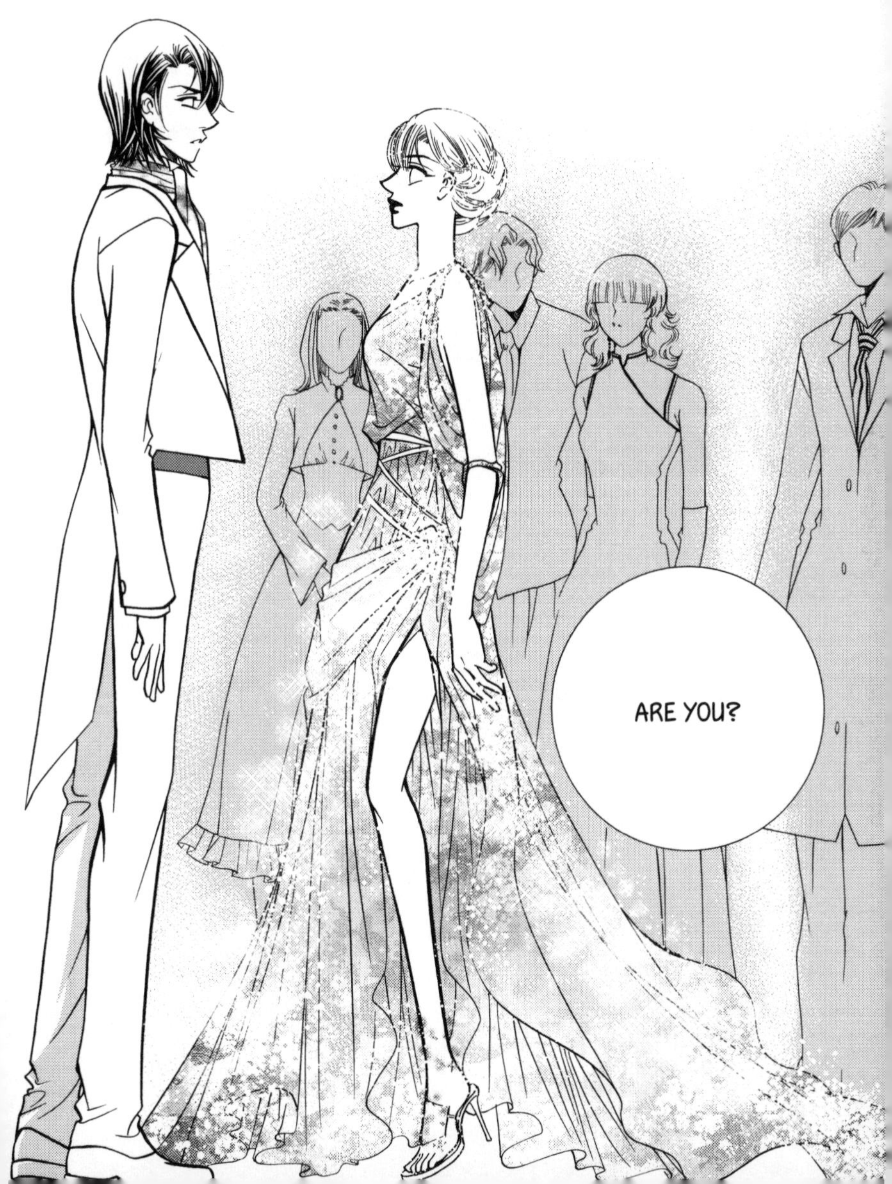
ARE YOU?

YOU CAME
FOR ME?

YOU'RE RIGHT.
I AM STUPID...

IT KEPT
BUGGING
ME.

YOU GOT NO ONE
TO HELP YOU.
AND YOU'RE
A STUPID GIRL
WITH NO SENSE OF
ADAPTABILITY.

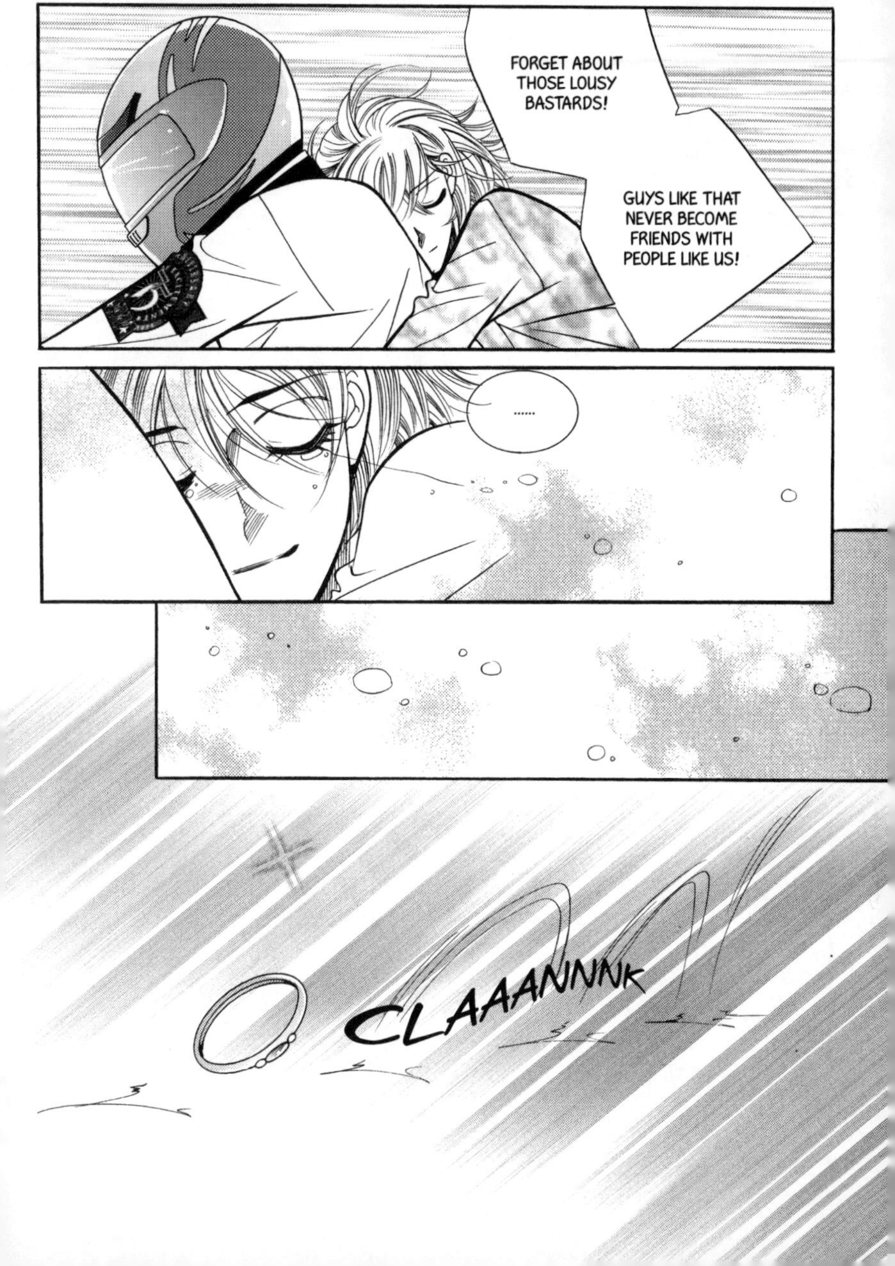
FORGET ABOUT THOSE LOUSY BASTARDS!
GUYS LIKE THAT NEVER BECOME FRIENDS WITH PEOPLE LIKE US!
......
CLAAANNNK

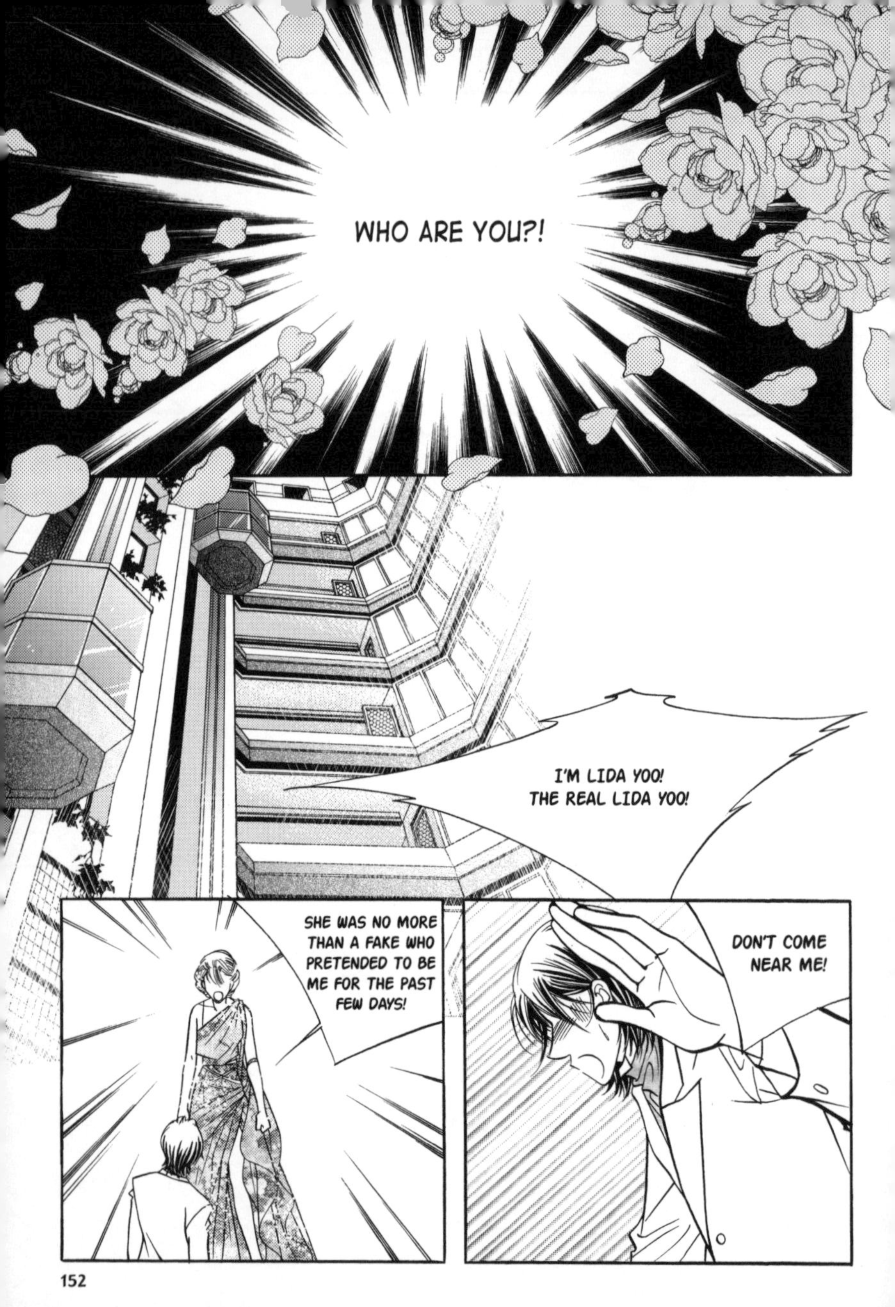
WHO ARE YOU?!
I'M LIDA YOO! THE REAL LIDA YOO!
SHE WAS NO MORE THAN A FAKE WHO PRETENDED TO BE ME FOR THE PAST FEW DAYS!
DON'T COME NEAR ME!

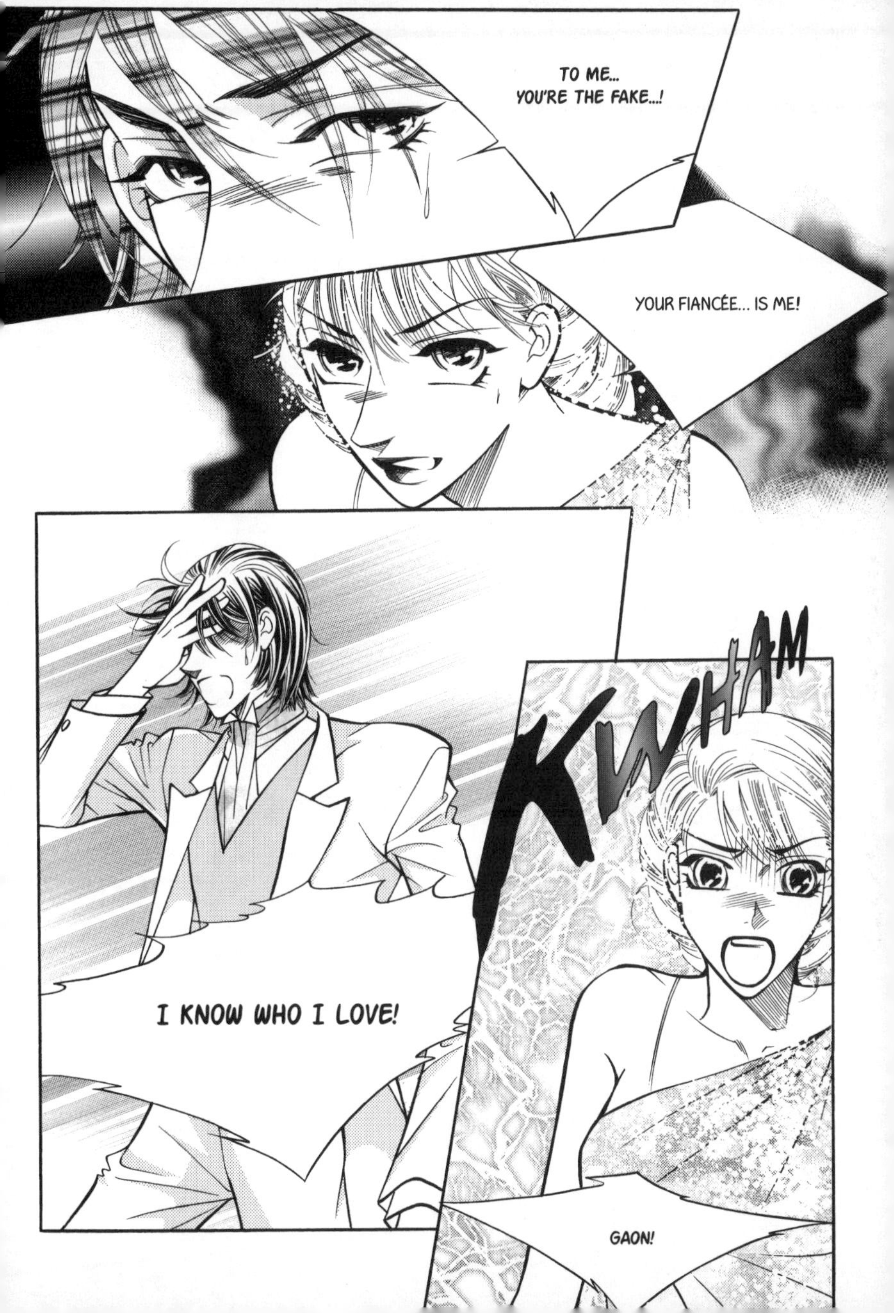
TO ME...
YOU'RE THE FAKE...!
YOUR FIANCÉE... IS ME!
I KNOW WHO I LOVE!
KWHAM
GAON!

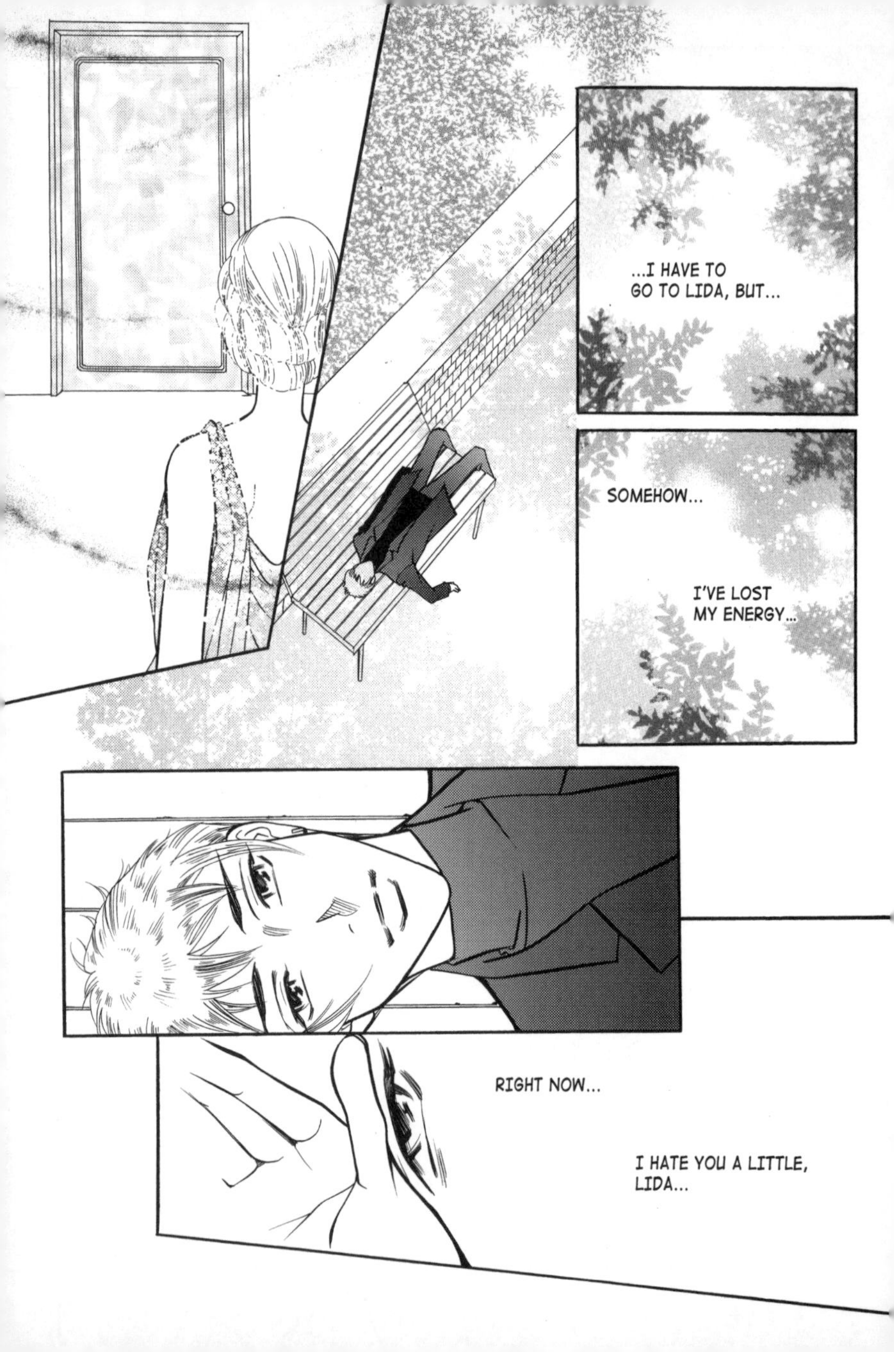
...I HAVE TO GO TO LIDA, BUT...
SOMEHOW...
I'VE LOST MY ENERGY...
RIGHT NOW...
I HATE YOU A LITTLE, LIDA...

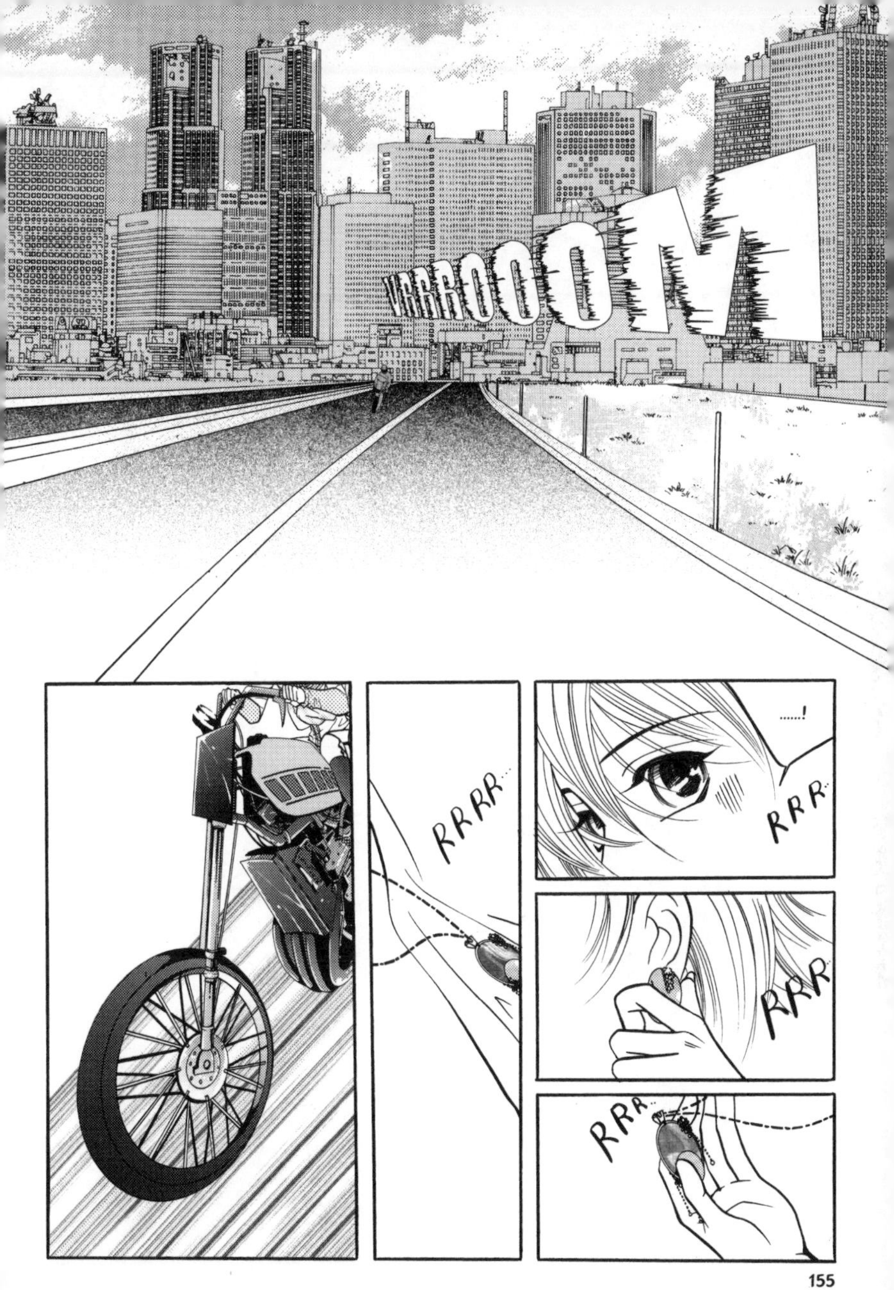
VRRROOOM
RRRR...
......!
RRR..
RRR
RRR..

WHERE... ARE YOU?!

I'M SORRY. I'M... NOT LIDA.

I'M SORRY I DIDN'T TELL YOU SOONER.

I DIDN'T MEAN TO DECEIVE YOU.

WHERE ARE YOU RIGHT NOW...?!!

I SAID, WHERE ARE YOU?!

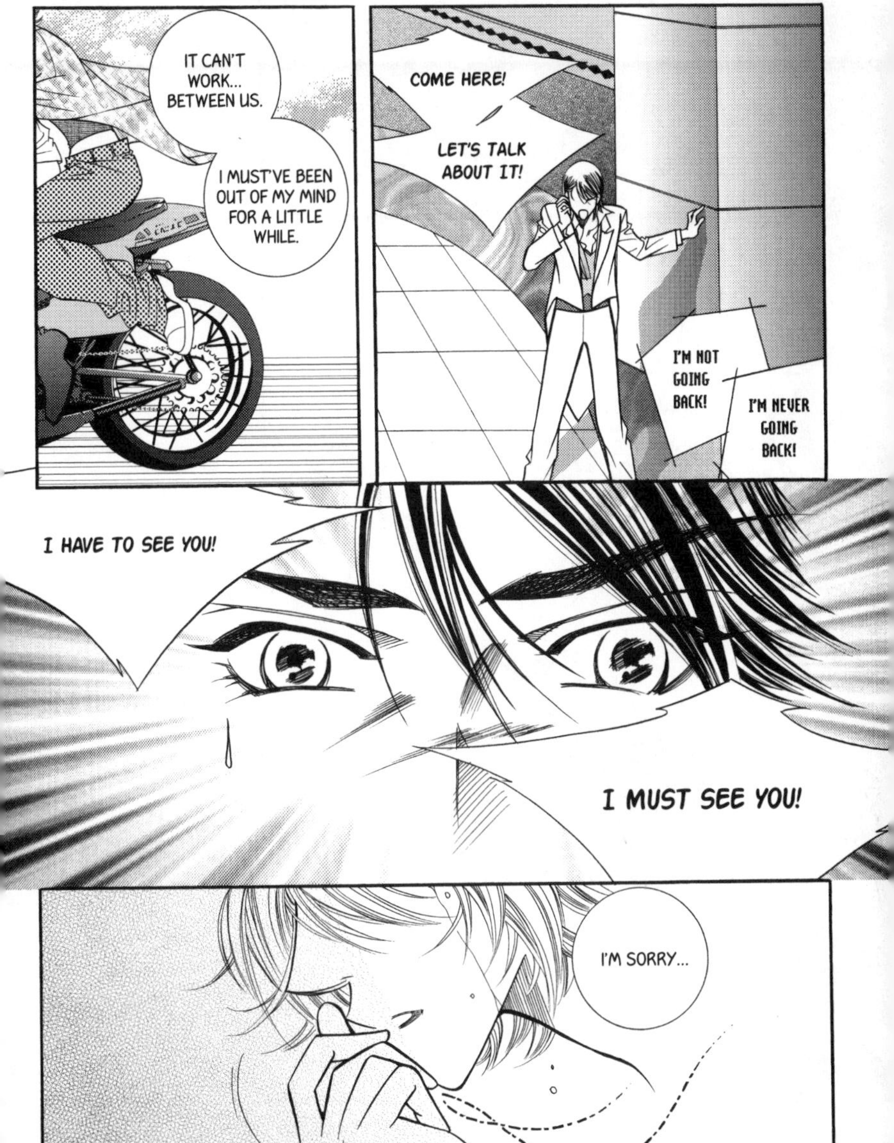
IT CAN'T WORK... BETWEEN US.
I MUST'VE BEEN OUT OF MY MIND FOR A LITTLE WHILE.
COME HERE!
LET'S TALK ABOUT IT!
I'M NOT GOING BACK!
I'M NEVER GOING BACK!
I HAVE TO SEE YOU!
I MUST SEE YOU!
I'M SORRY...

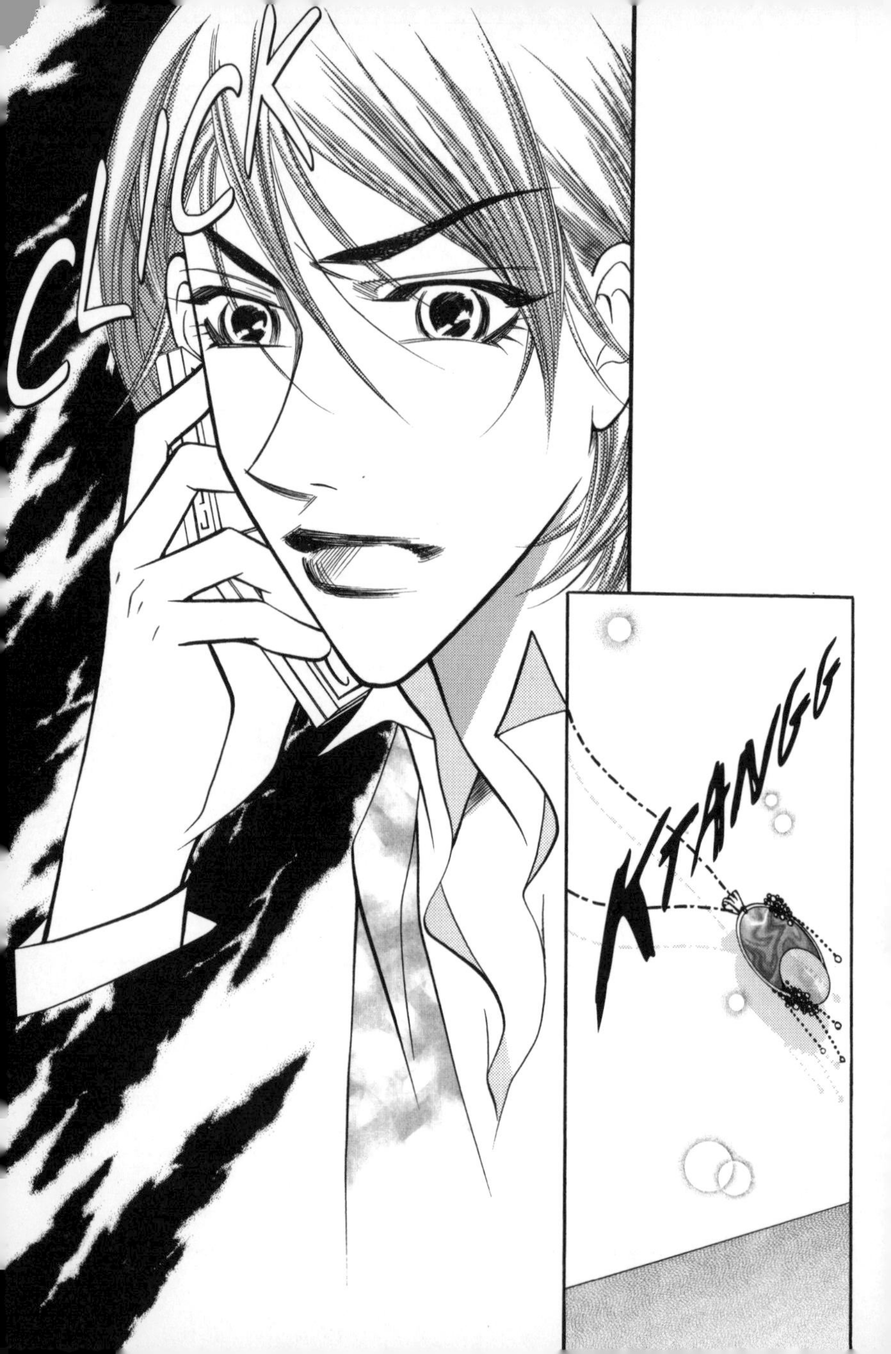
CLICK
KTANGG

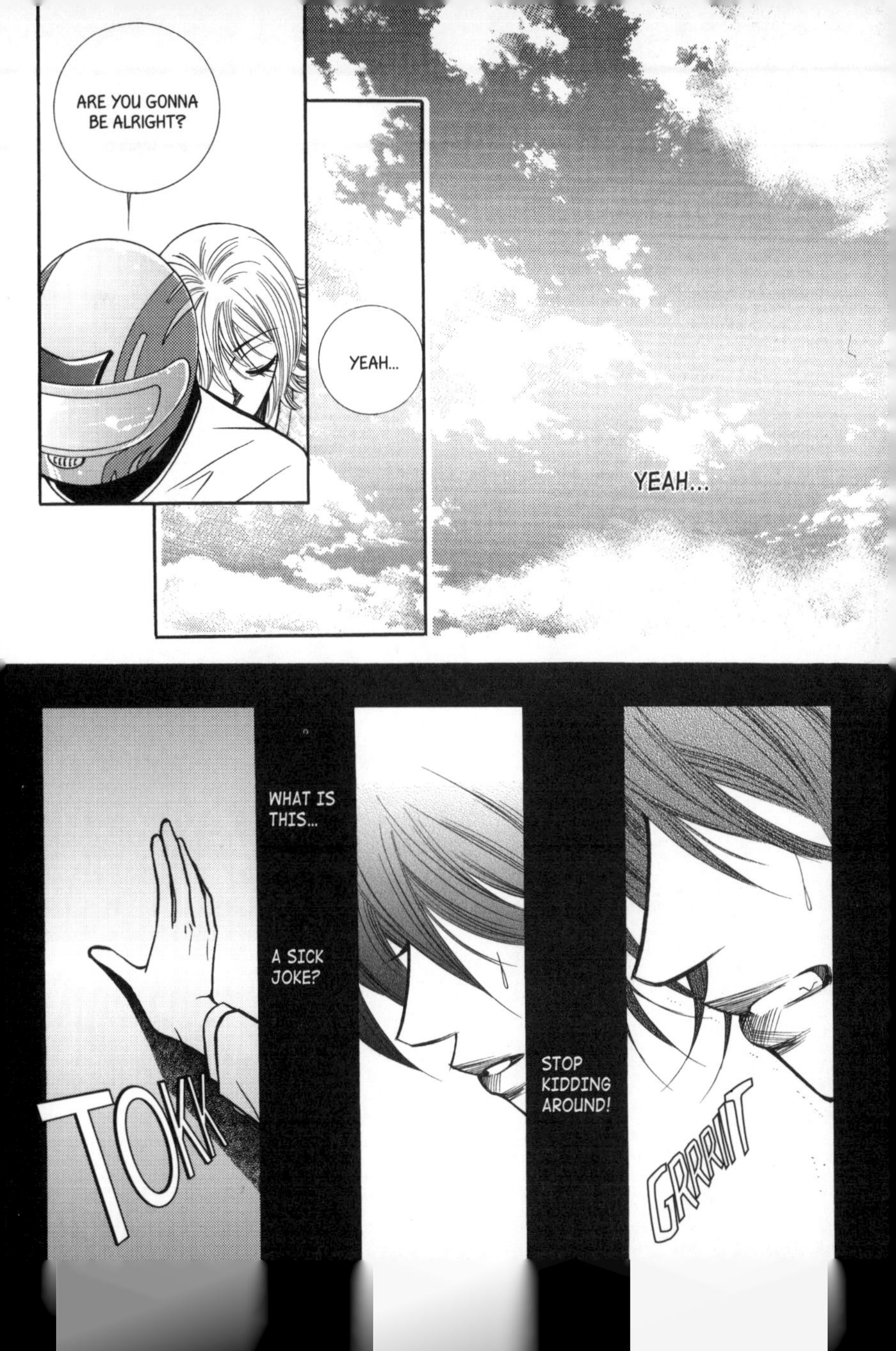
ARE YOU GONNA BE ALRIGHT?
YEAH...
YEAH...
WHAT IS THIS...
A SICK JOKE?
TOKK
STOP KIDDING AROUND!
GRRRIIT

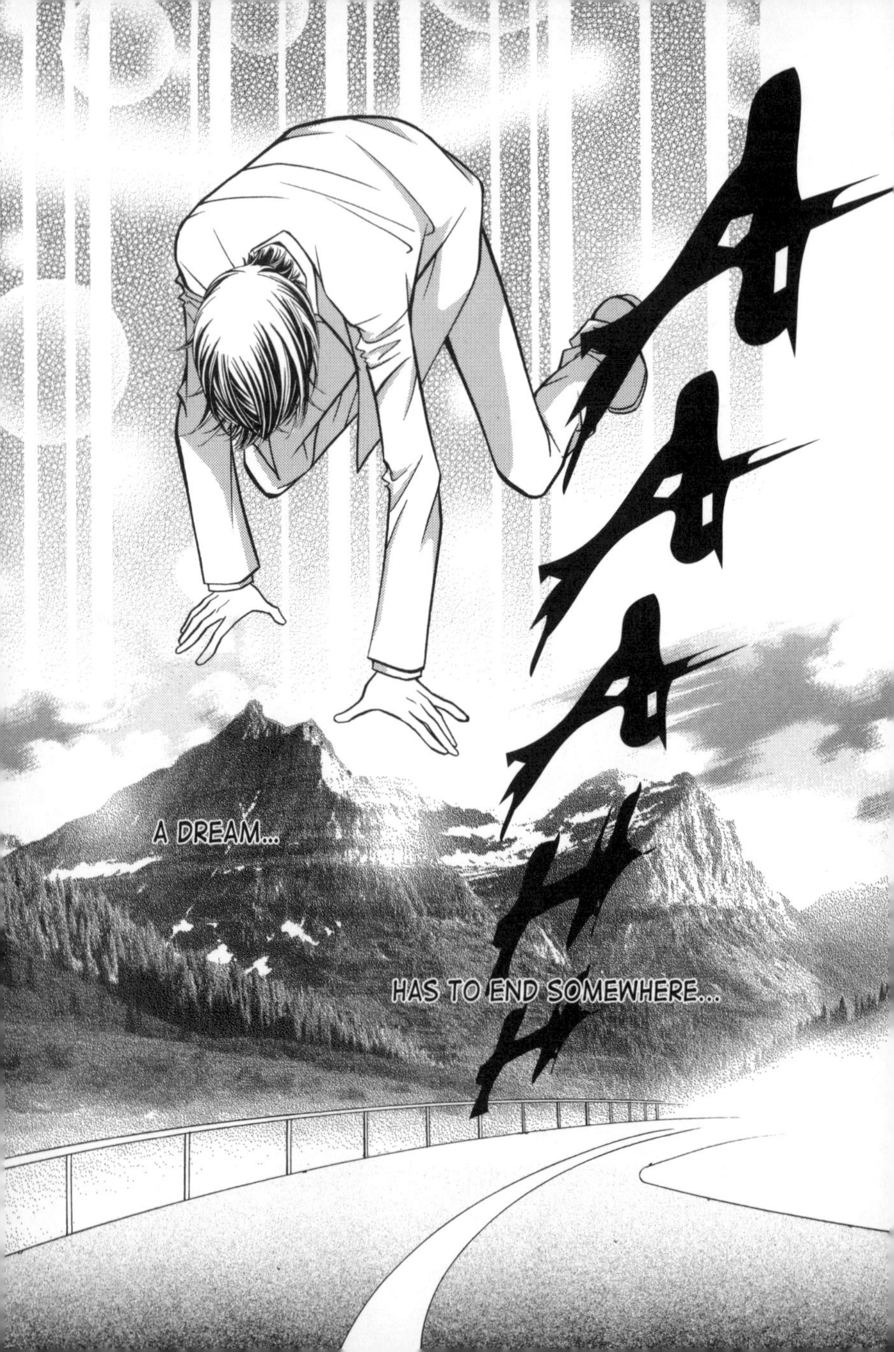
AAAHH
A DREAM...
HAS TO END SOMEWHERE...

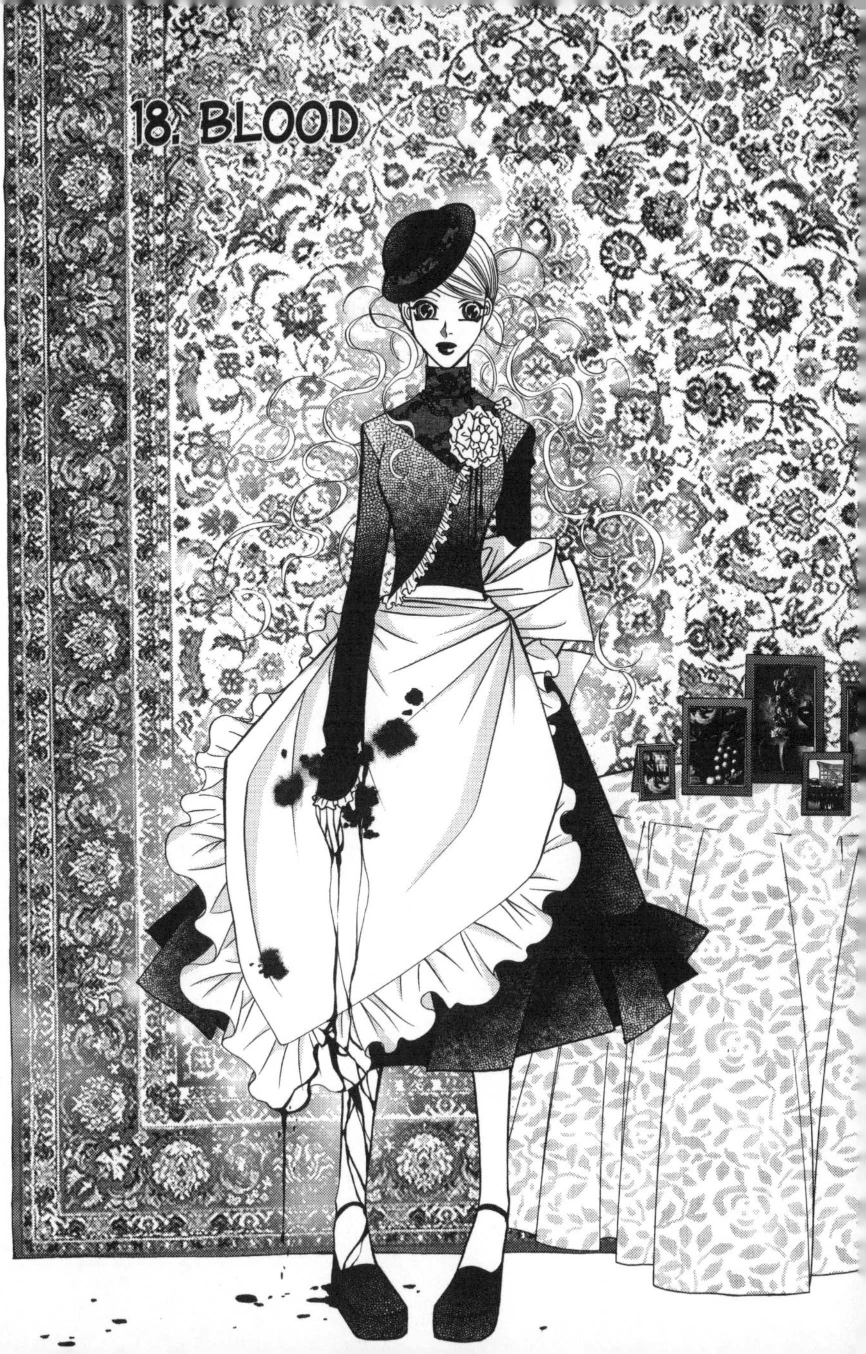
18. BLOOD

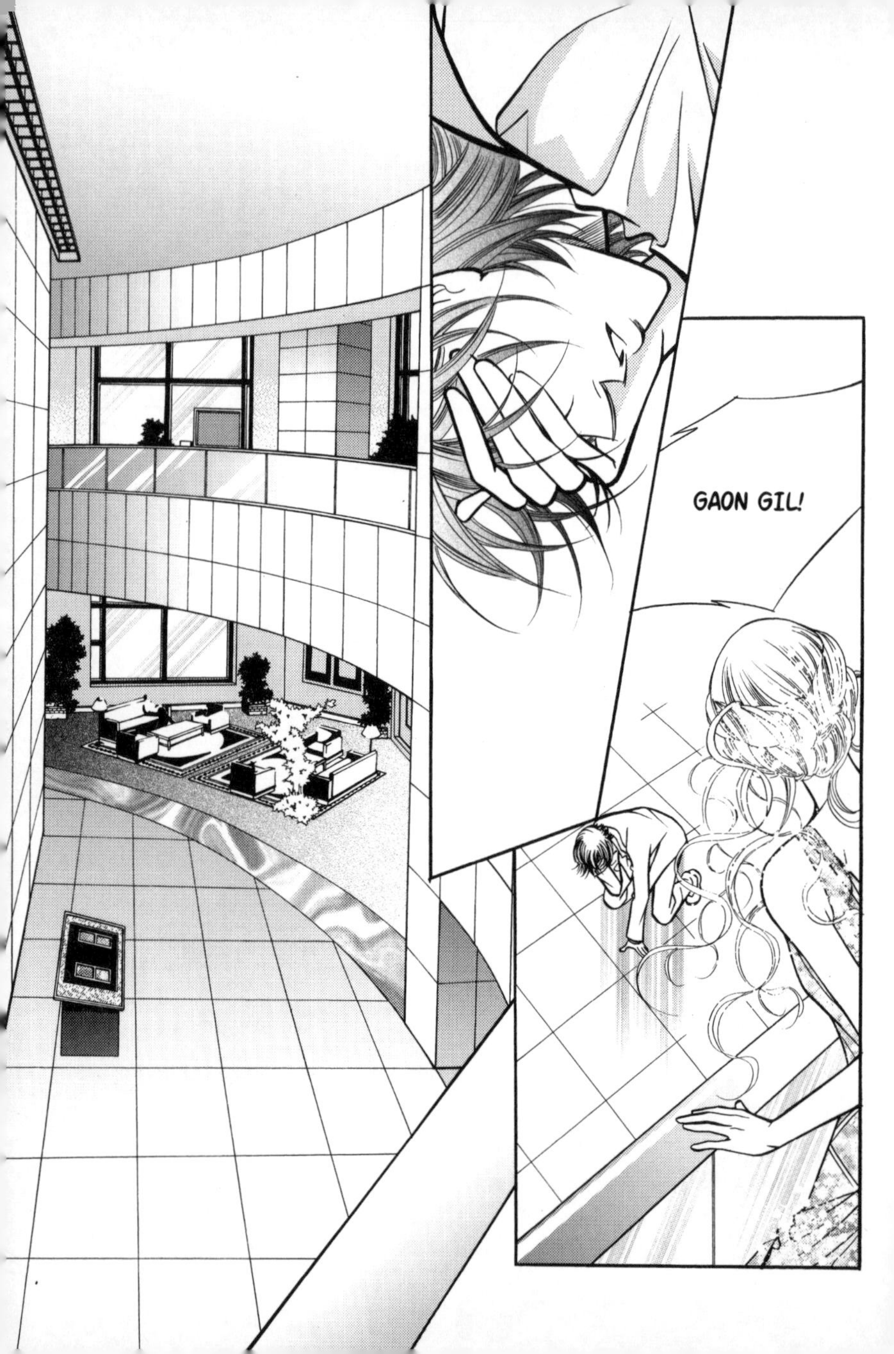
GAON GIL!

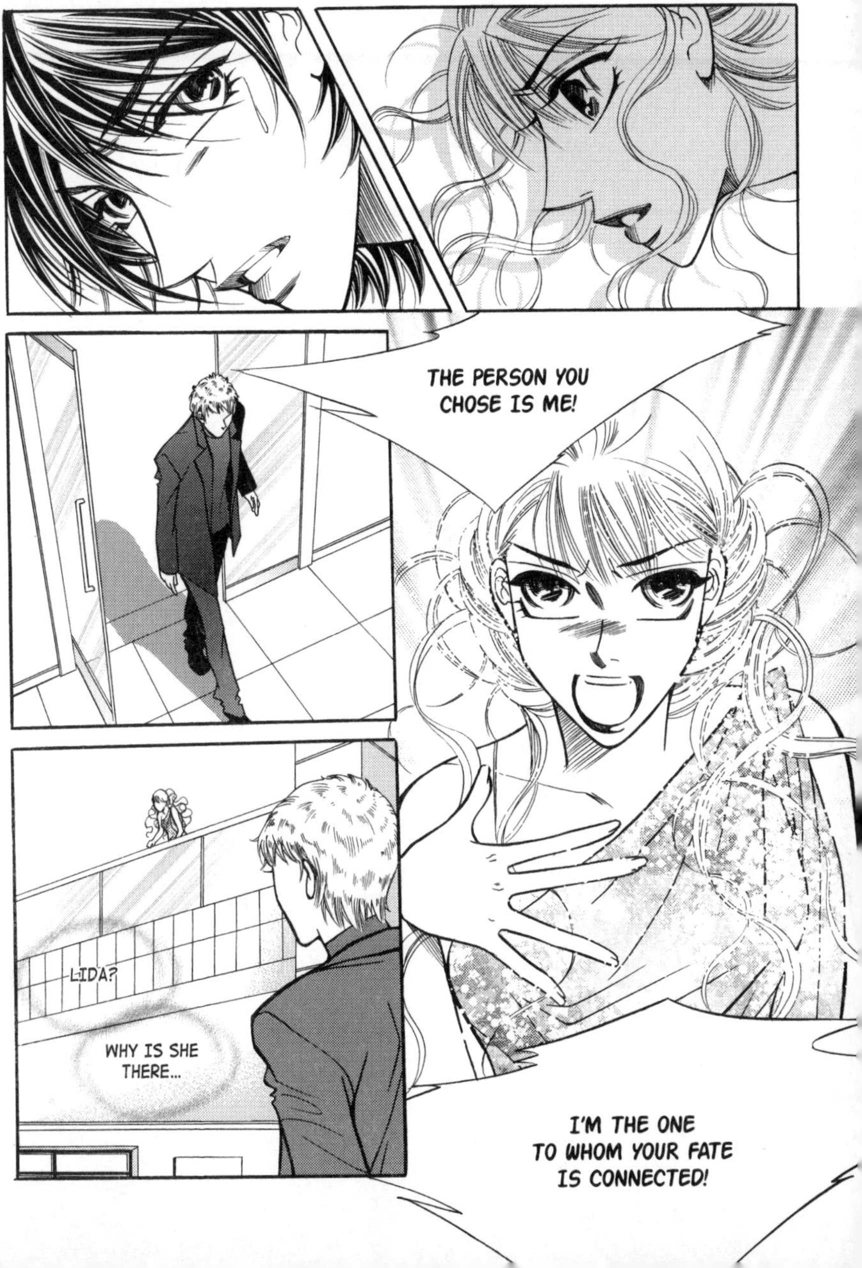
LIDA?
WHY IS SHE THERE...
THE PERSON YOU CHOSE IS ME!
I'M THE ONE TO WHOM YOUR FATE IS CONNECTED!

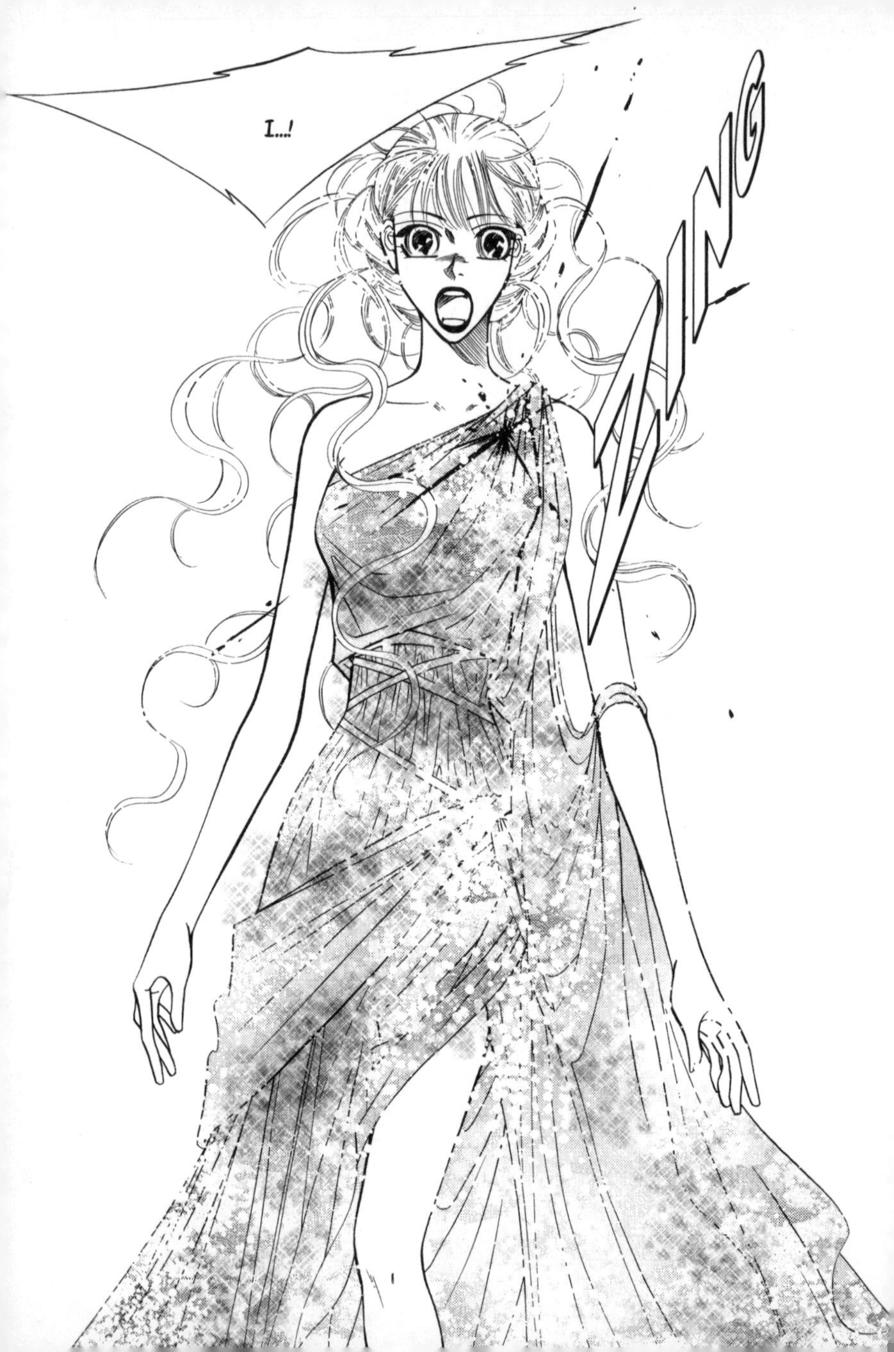
I...!
ZING

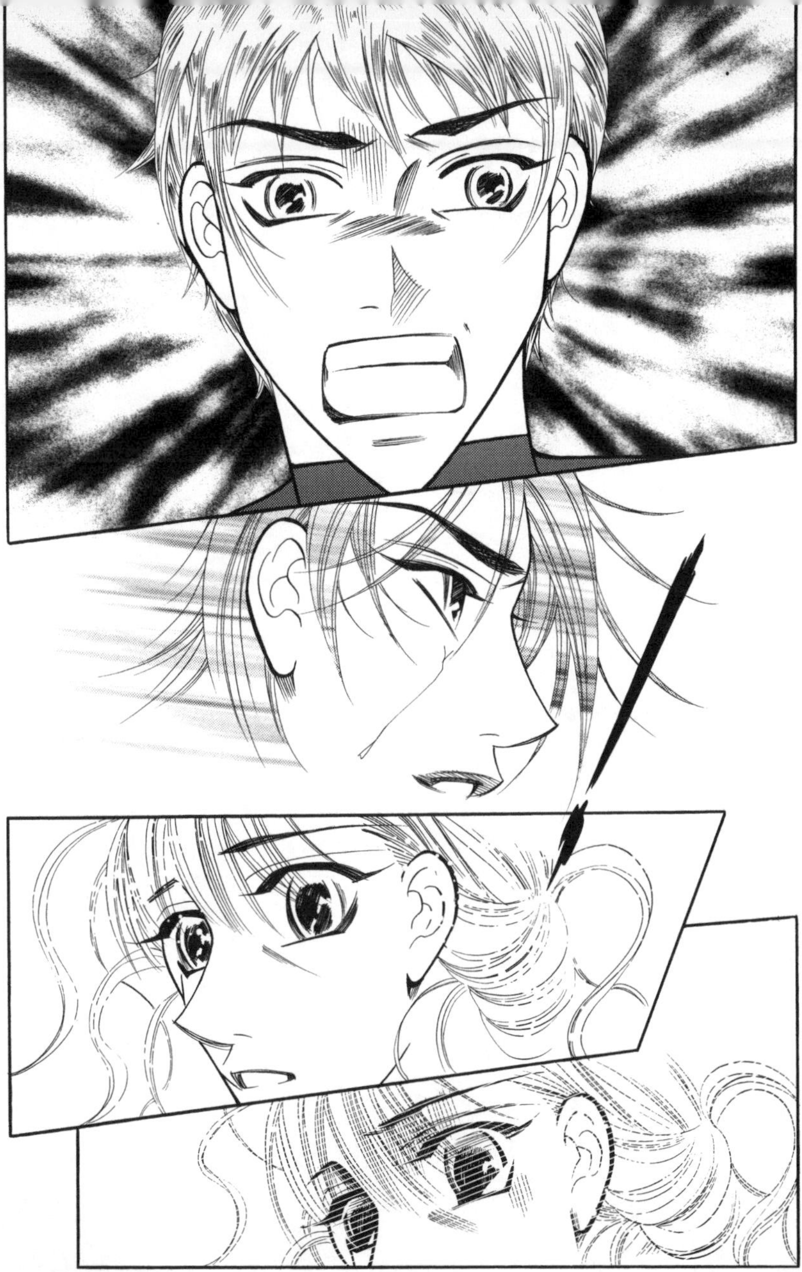

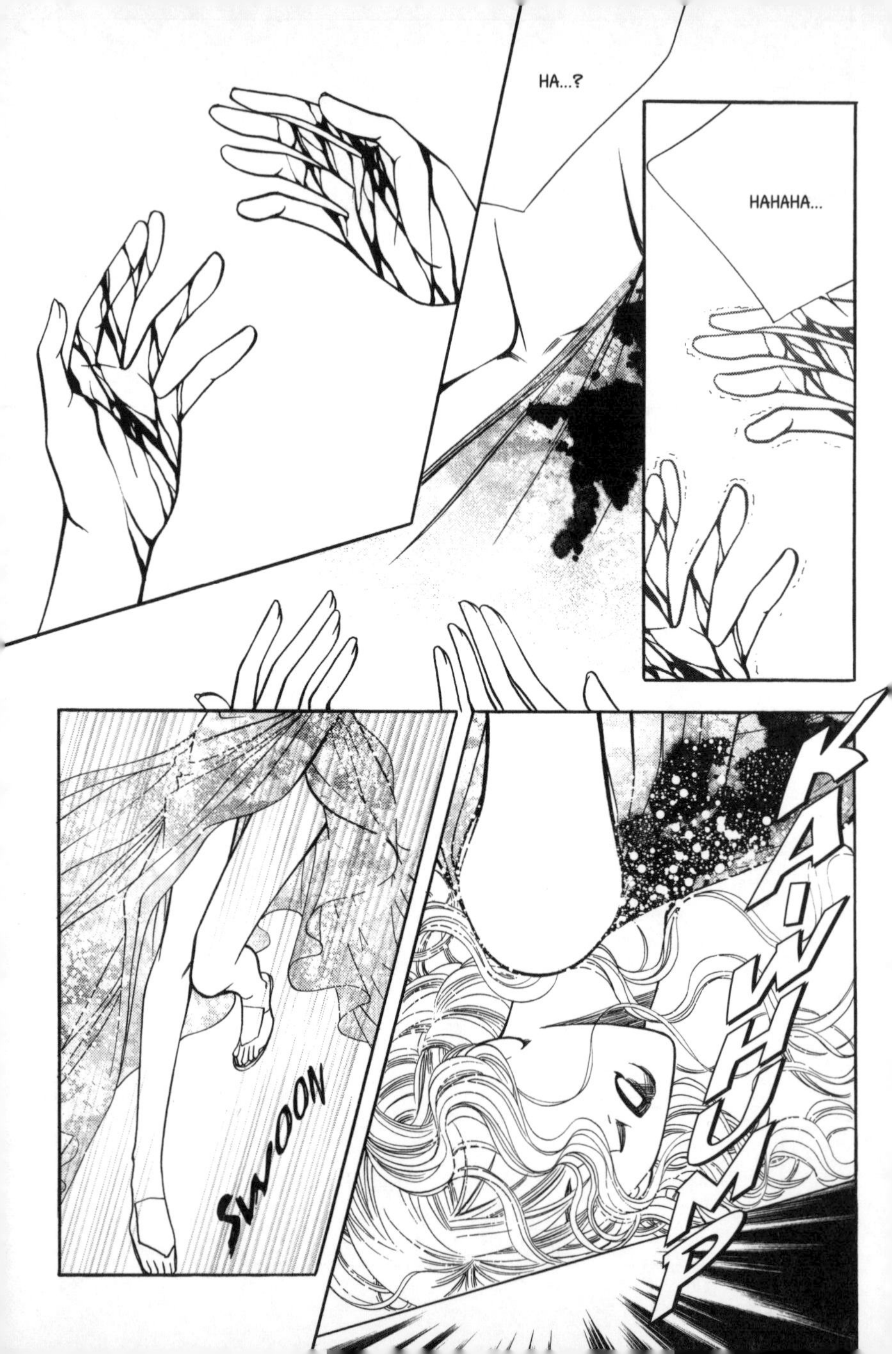
HA...?
HAHAHA...
SWOON
KA-THUMP

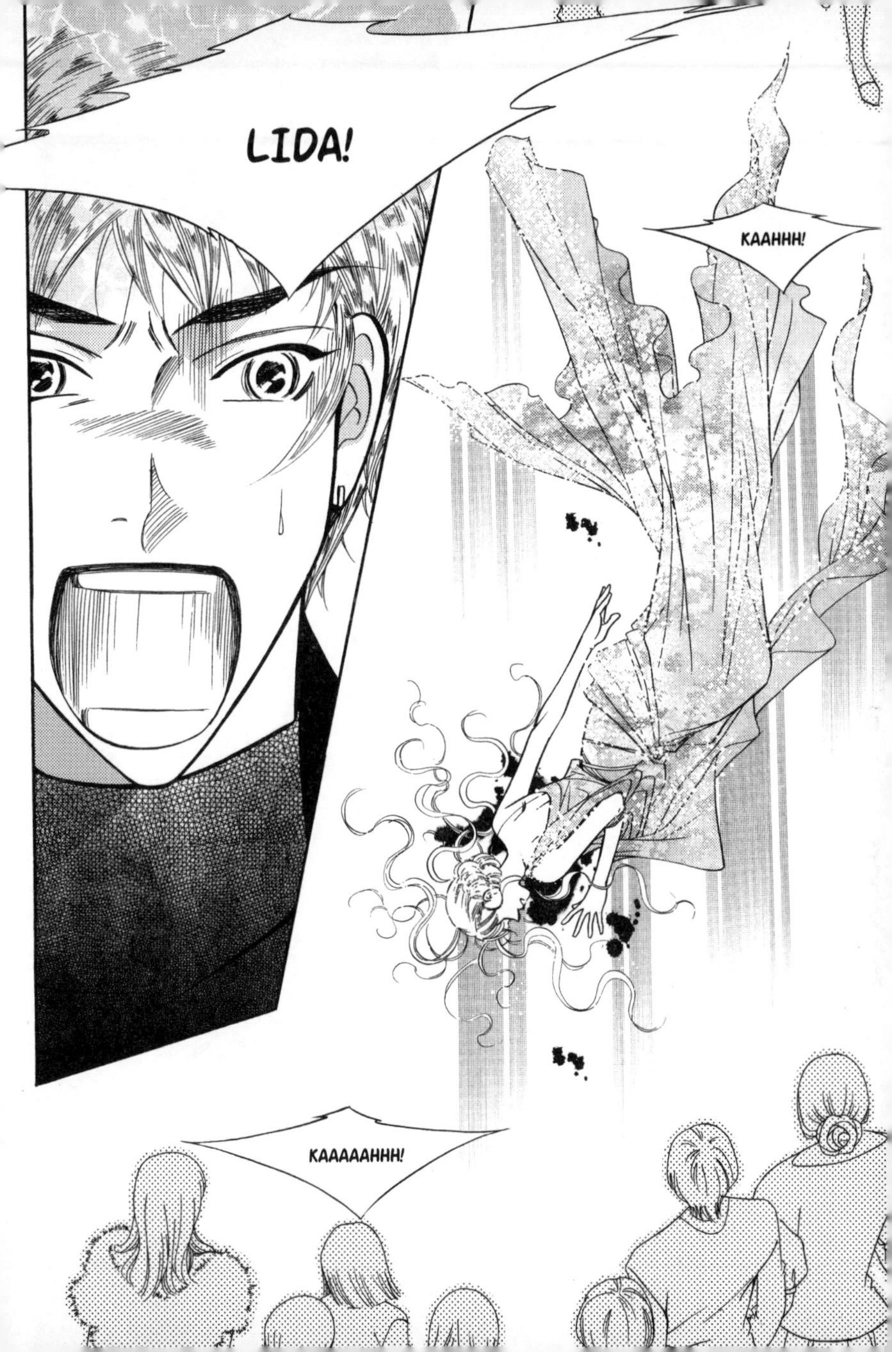
LIDA!
KAAHHH!
KAAAAAHHH!

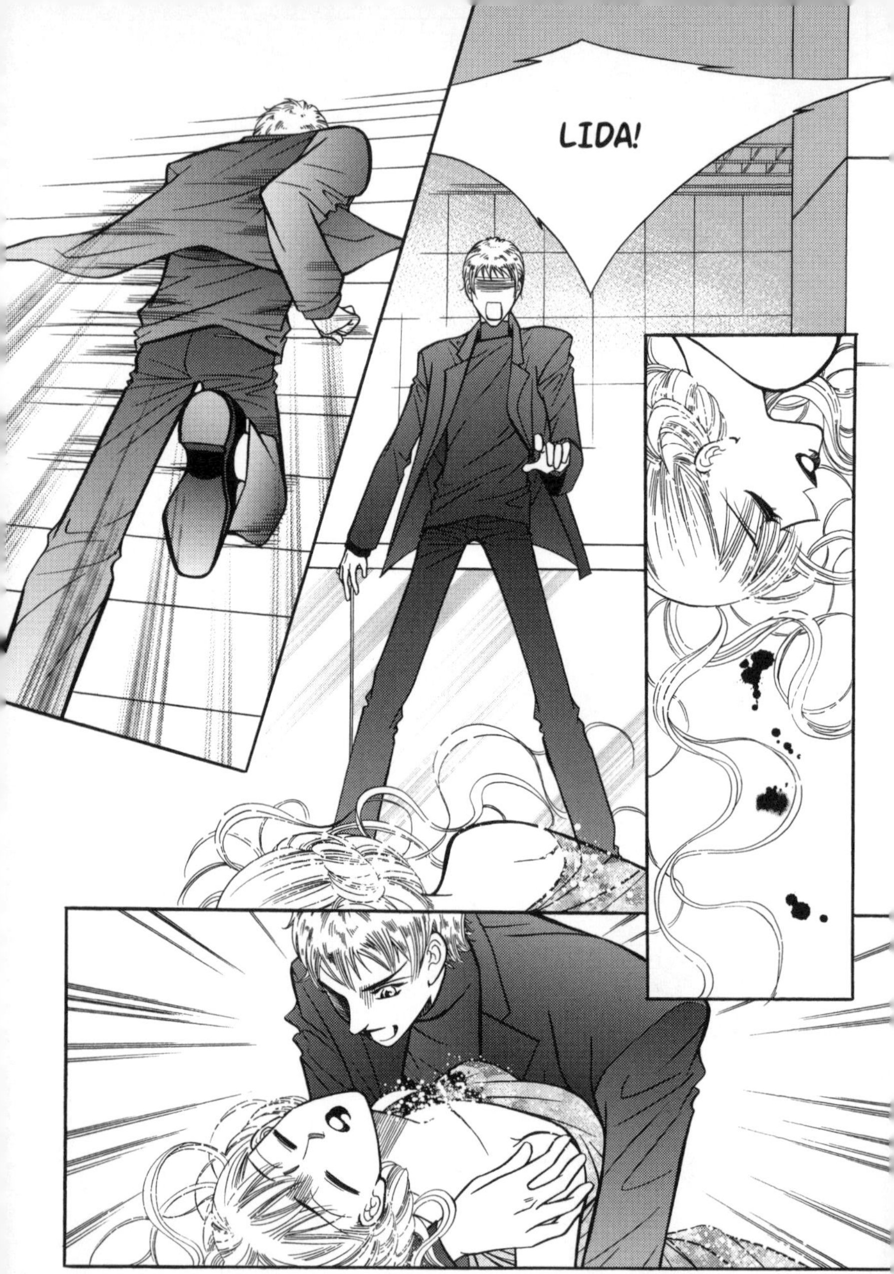
LIDA!

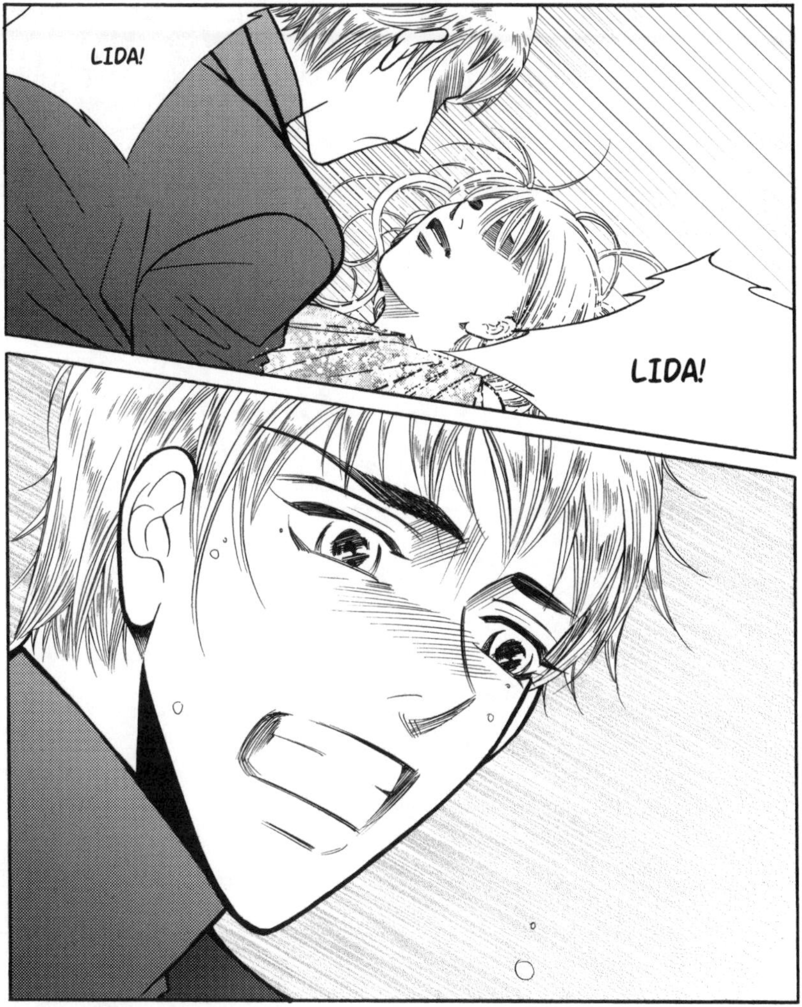
LIDA!
LIDA!

SHE'S STILL....

BREATHING...!

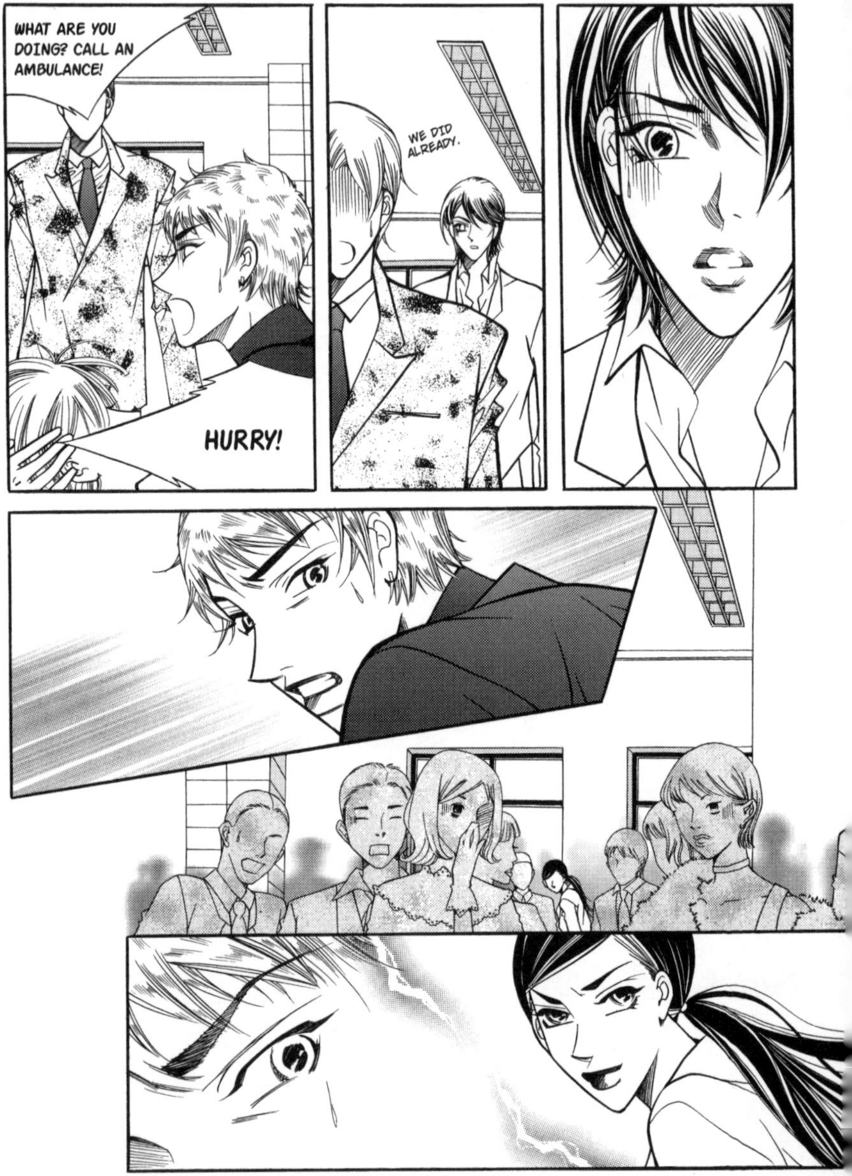
WHAT ARE YOU DOING? CALL AN AMBULANCE!
HURRY!
WE DID ALREADY.

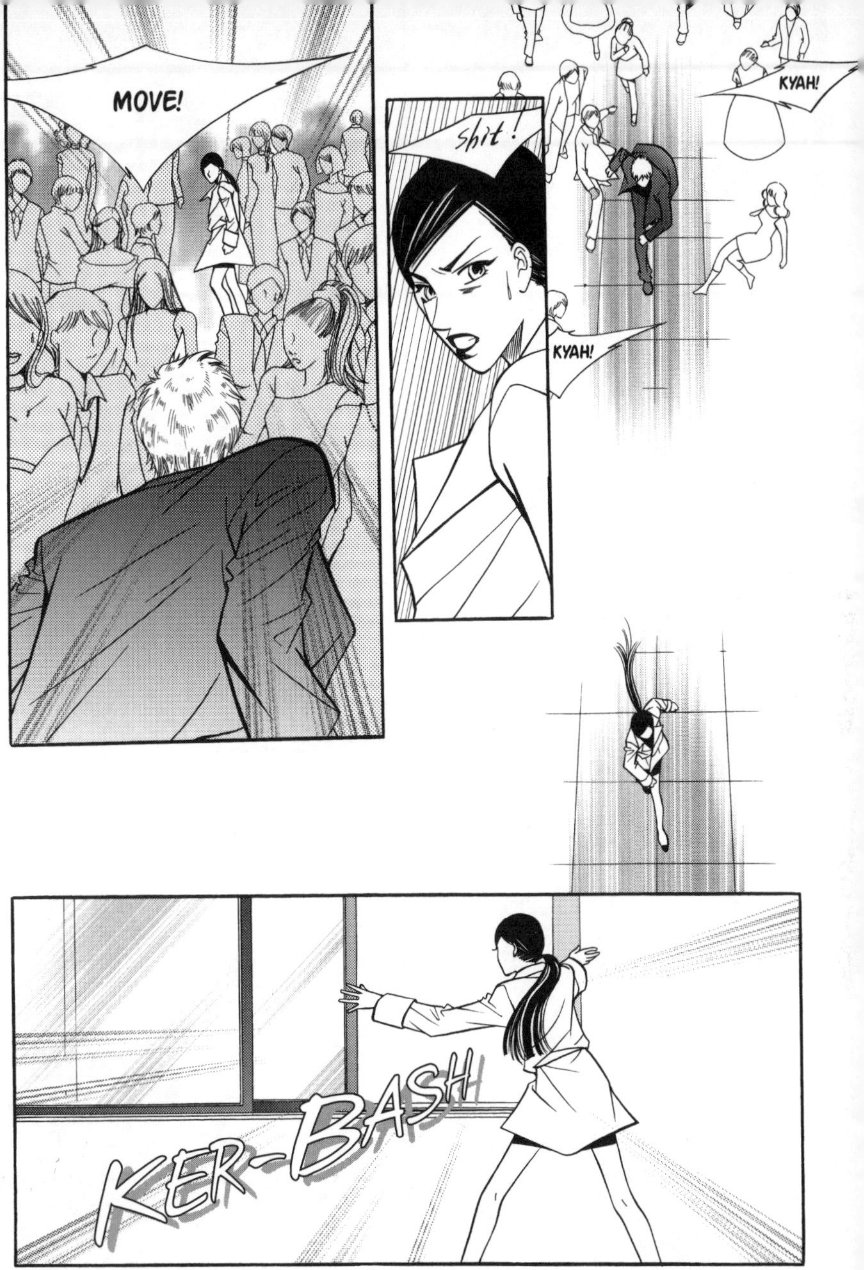
MOVE!
shit!
KYAH!
KYAH!
KER-BASH

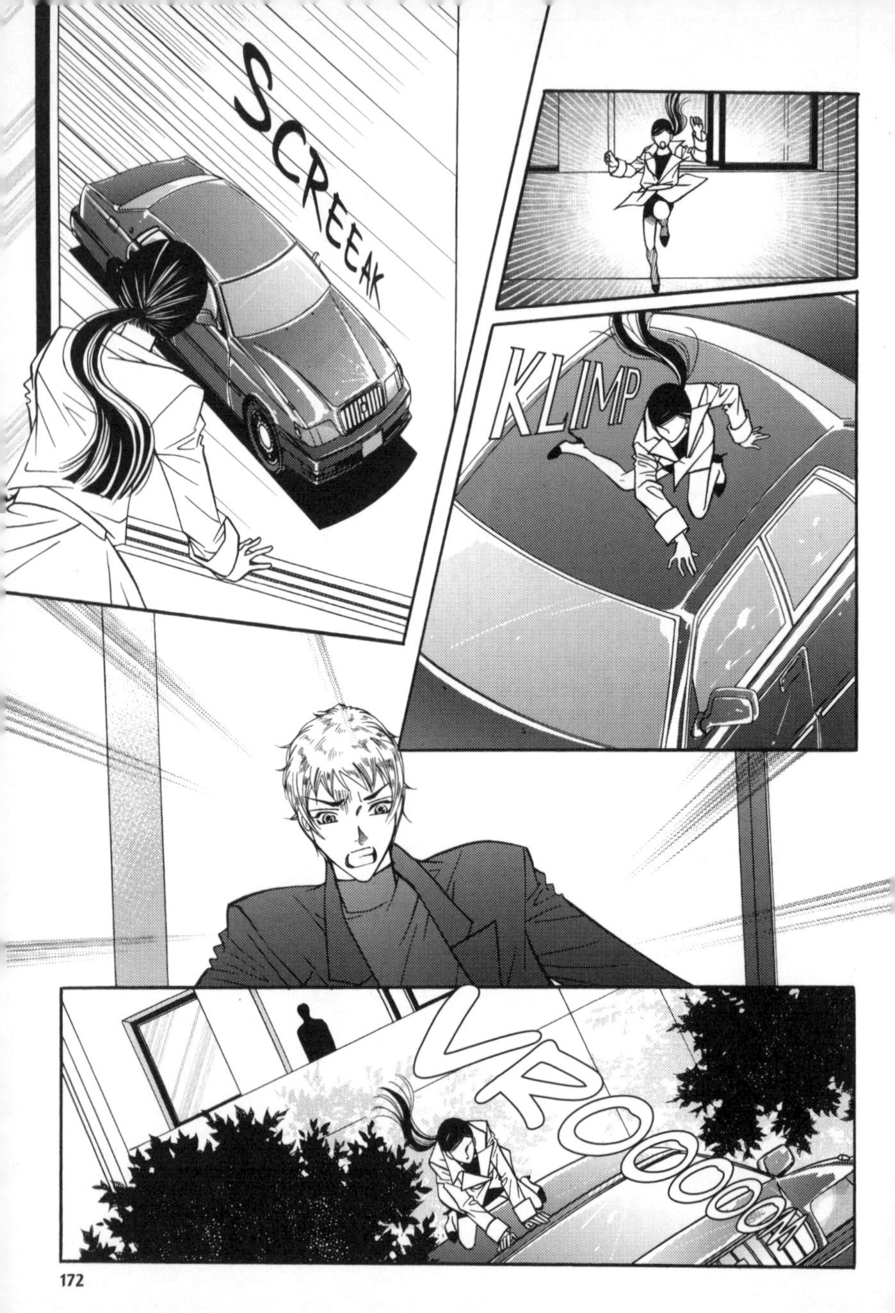
SCREEAK
KLIMP
VROOOOOOM

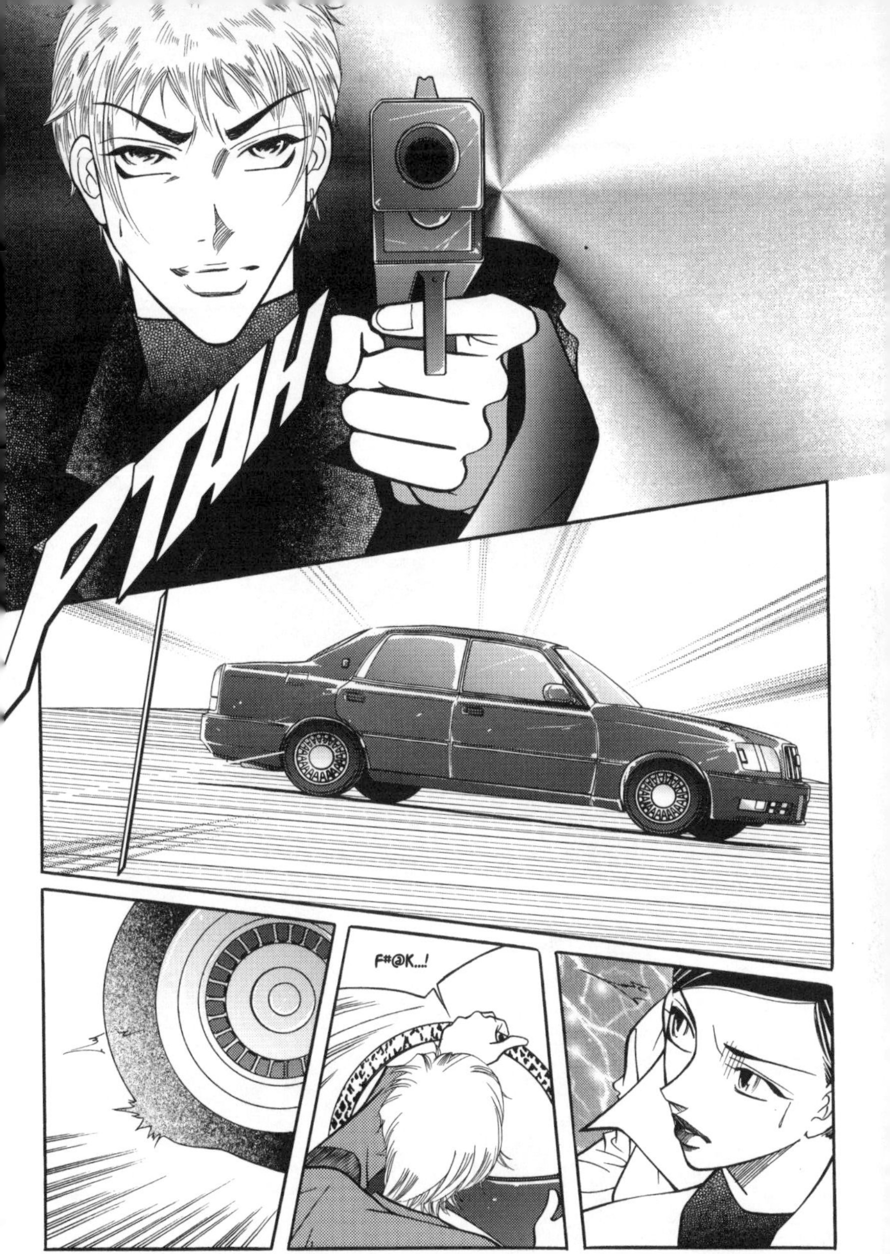
PTAH
F#@K...!

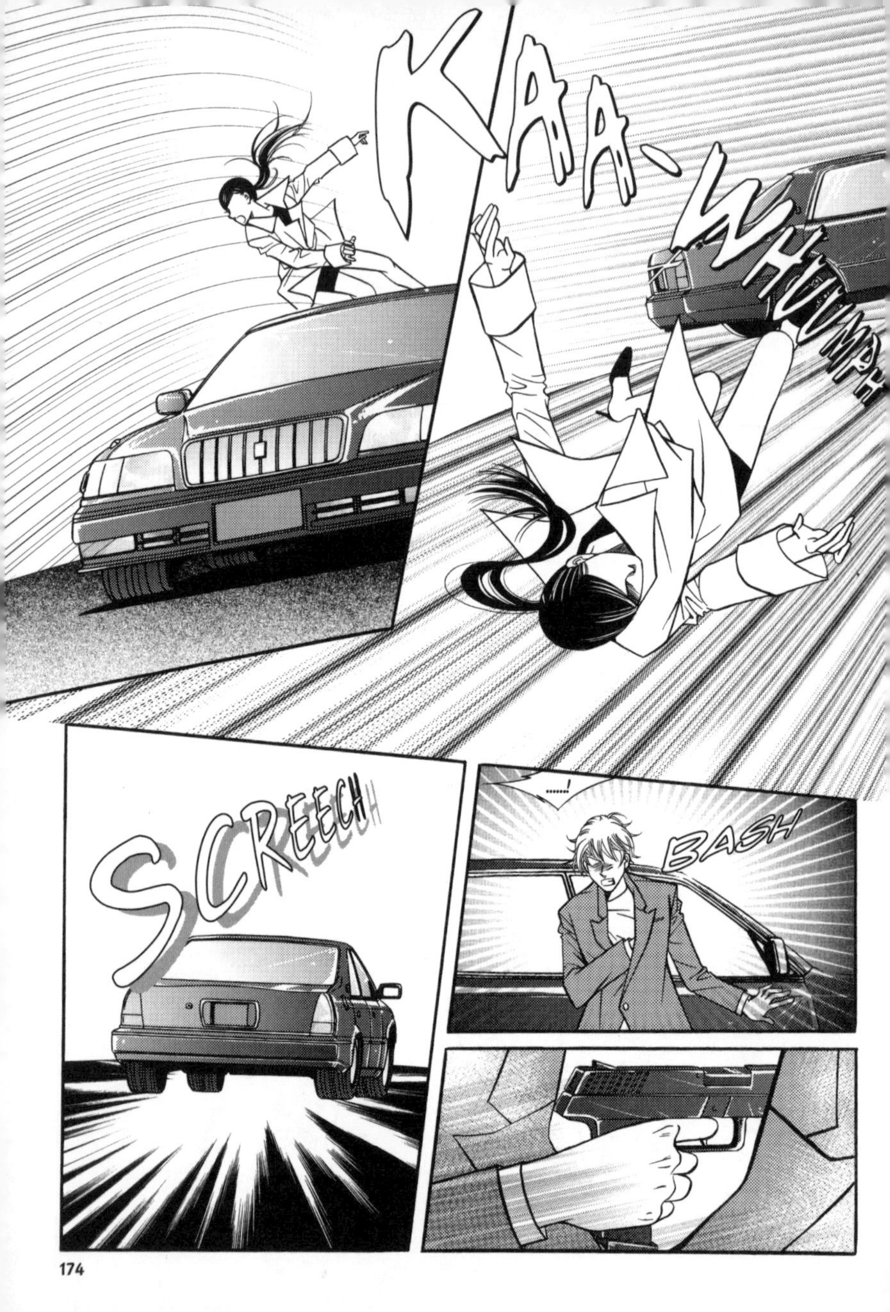
KAA-
WHUMPH
SCREECH
......!
BASH

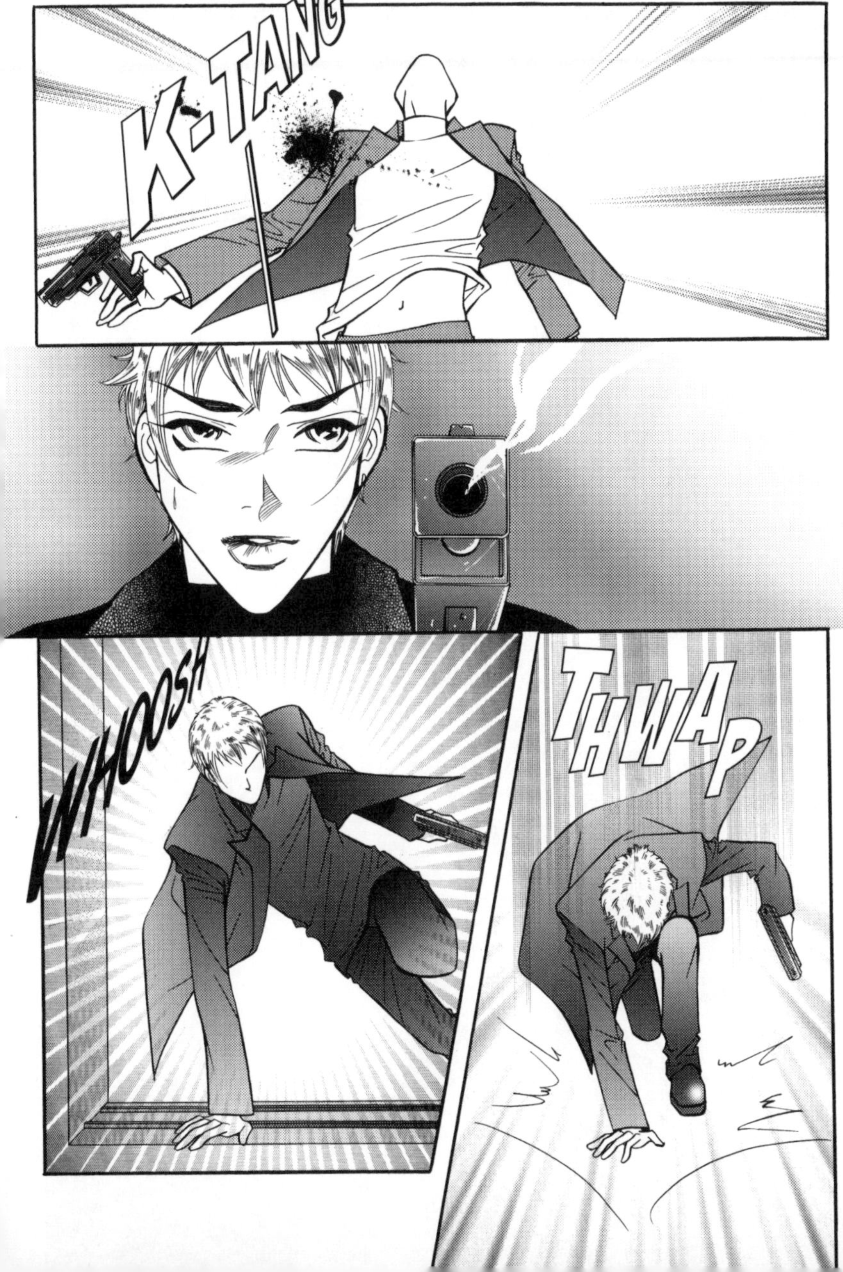
K-TANG
WHOOSH
THWAP

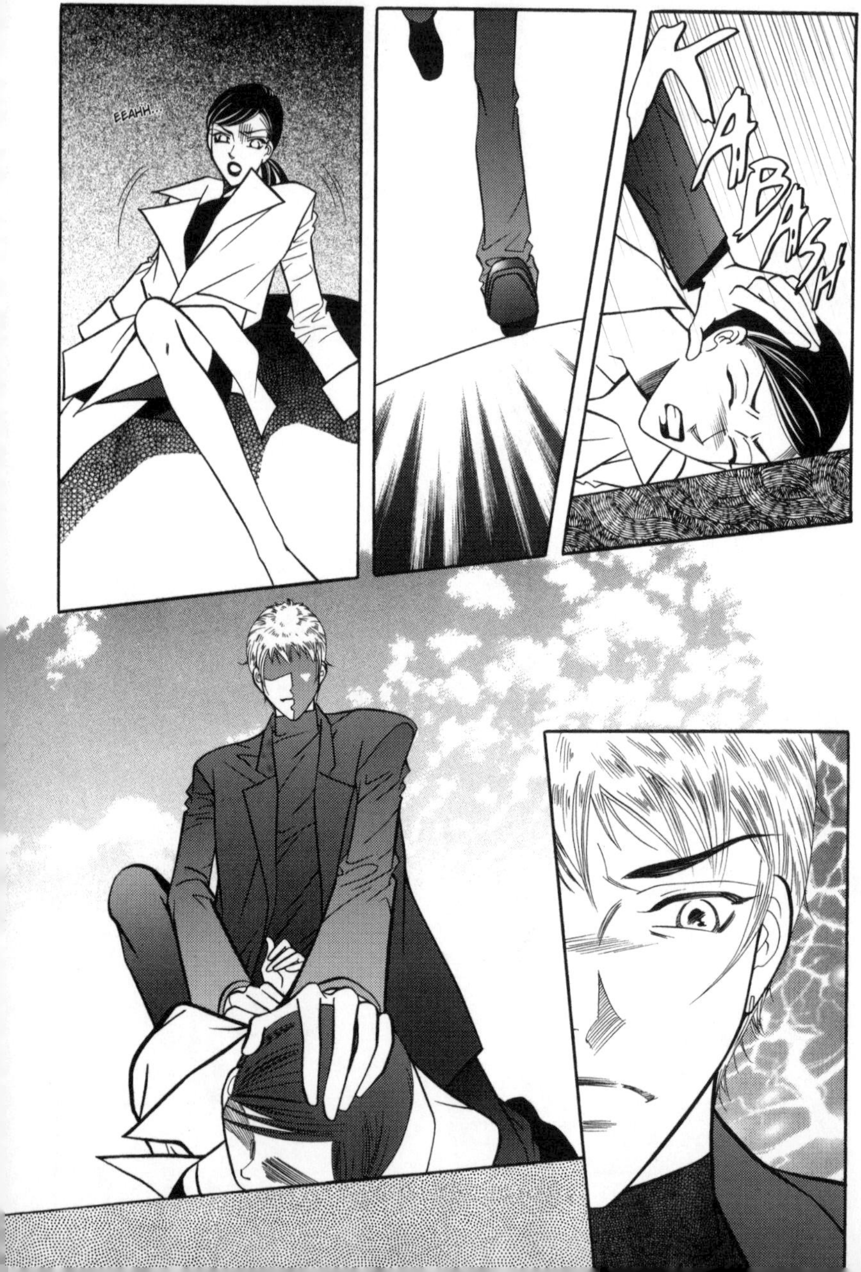
EEAHH...
BASH

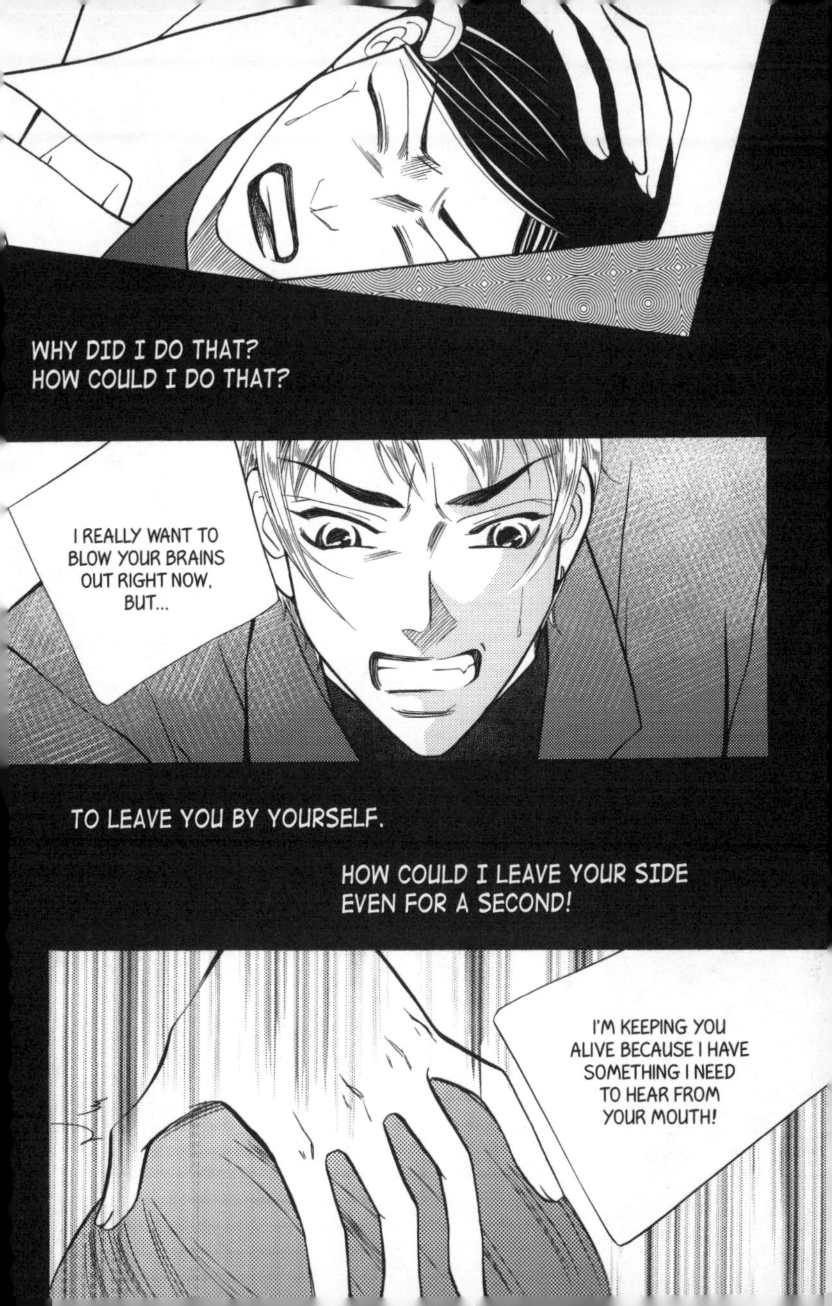
WHY DID I DO THAT?
HOW COULD I DO THAT?
I REALLY WANT TO BLOW YOUR BRAINS OUT RIGHT NOW, BUT...
TO LEAVE YOU BY YOURSELF.
HOW COULD I LEAVE YOUR SIDE EVEN FOR A SECOND!
I'M KEEPING YOU ALIVE BECAUSE I HAVE SOMETHING I NEED TO HEAR FROM YOUR MOUTH!

WE ARE GOING INTO SURGERY RIGHT AWAY!
THE BLEEDING IS SEVERE! PREPARE FOR BLOOD TRANSFUSION!

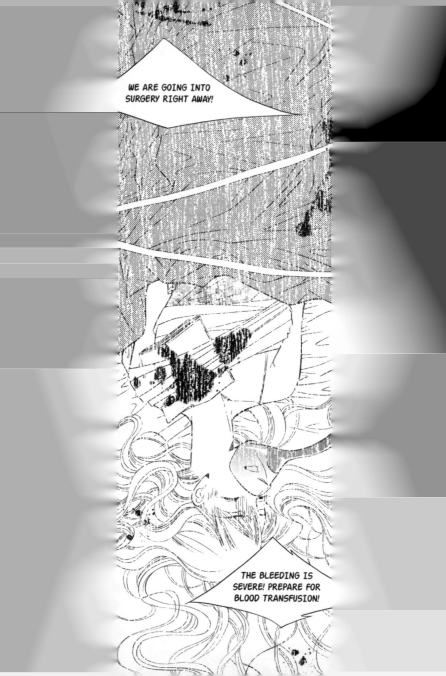

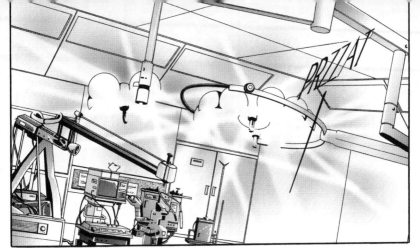

OPERATING ROOM

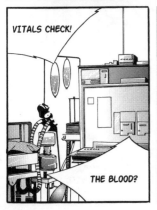

VITALS CHECK!

THE BLOOD?

DOC... DOCTOR, WE HAVE A BIG PROBLEM!

WHAT...?

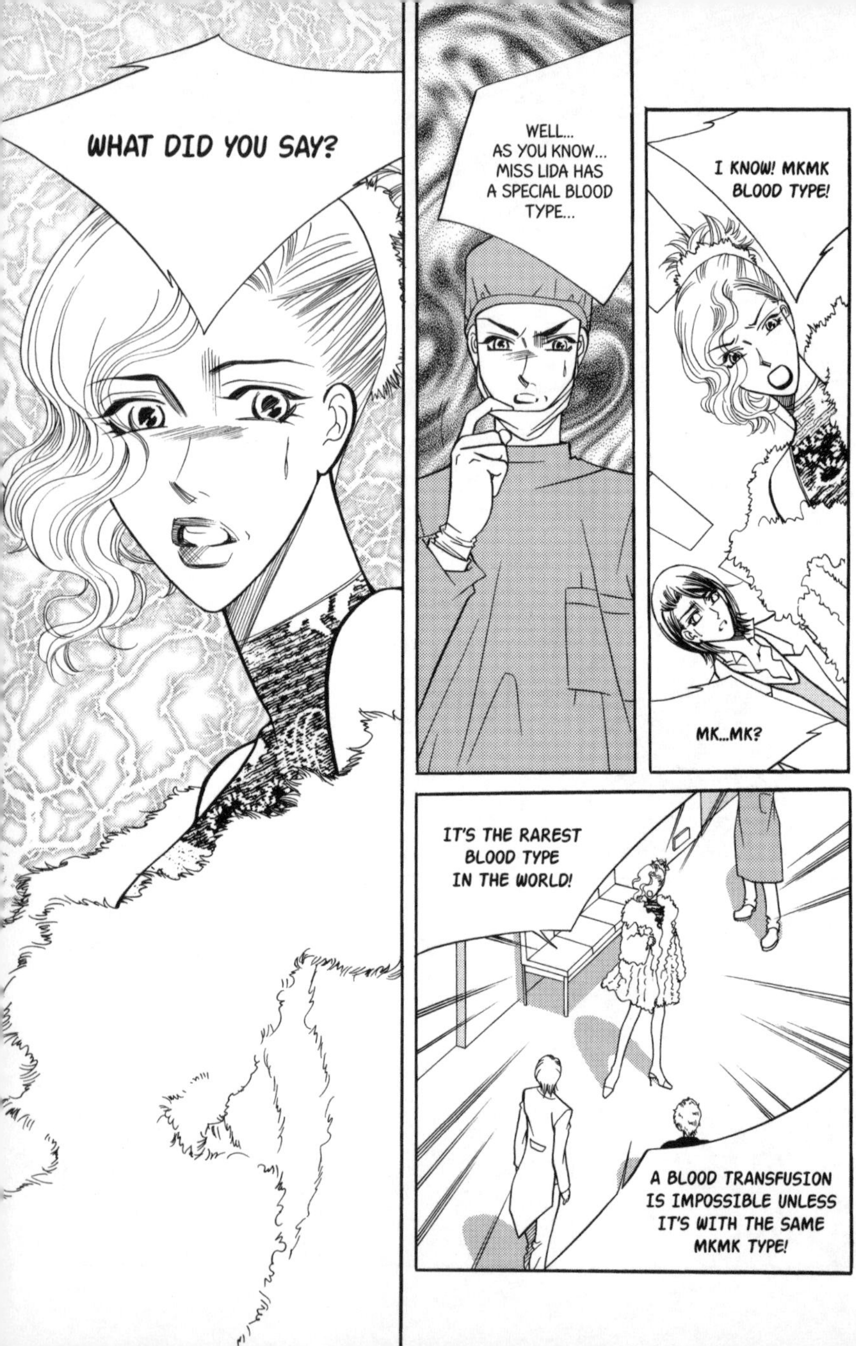
WHAT DID YOU SAY?
WELL... AS YOU KNOW... MISS LIDA HAS A SPECIAL BLOOD TYPE...
I KNOW! MKMK BLOOD TYPE!
MK...MK?
IT'S THE RAREST BLOOD TYPE IN THE WORLD!
A BLOOD TRANSFUSION IS IMPOSSIBLE UNLESS IT'S WITH THE SAME MKMK TYPE!

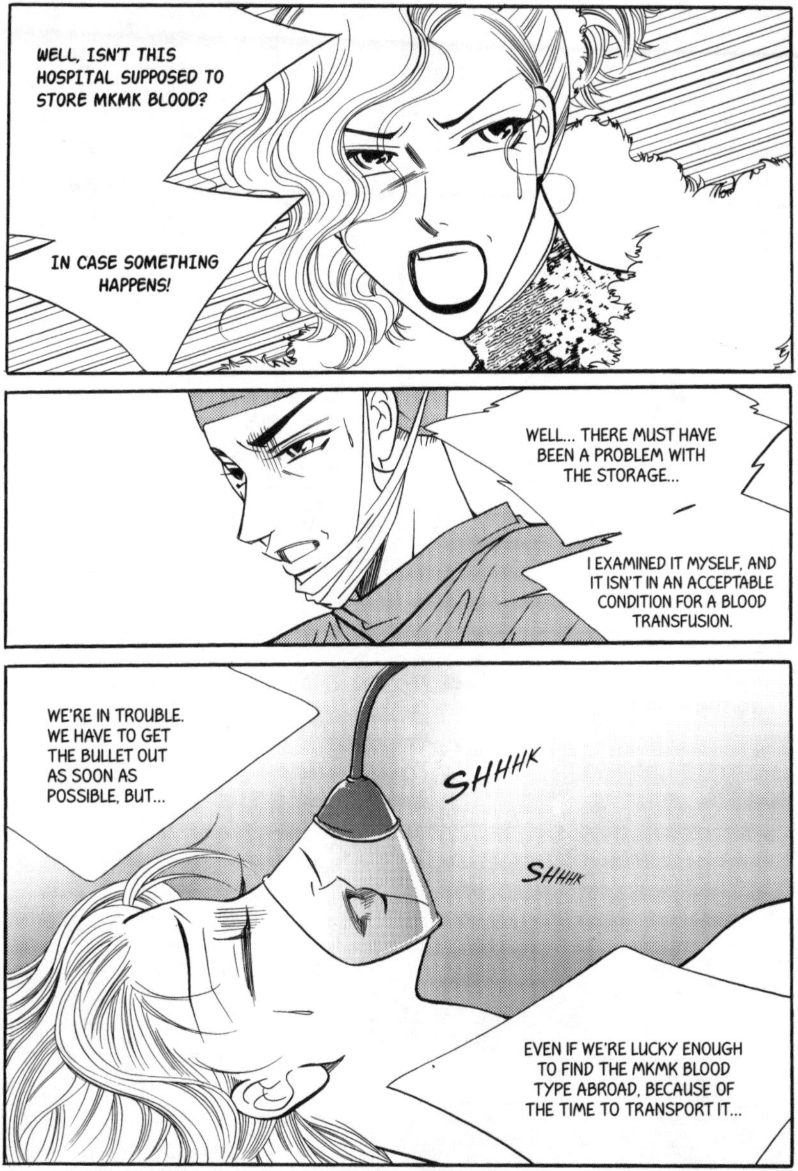
WELL, ISN'T THIS HOSPITAL SUPPOSED TO STORE MKMK BLOOD?
IN CASE SOMETHING HAPPENS!
WELL... THERE MUST HAVE BEEN A PROBLEM WITH THE STORAGE...
I EXAMINED IT MYSELF, AND IT ISN'T IN AN ACCEPTABLE CONDITION FOR A BLOOD TRANSFUSION.
WE'RE IN TROUBLE. WE HAVE TO GET THE BULLET OUT AS SOON AS POSSIBLE, BUT...
SHHHK
SHHHK
EVEN IF WE'RE LUCKY ENOUGH TO FIND THE MKMK BLOOD TYPE ABROAD, BECAUSE OF THE TIME TO TRANSPORT IT...

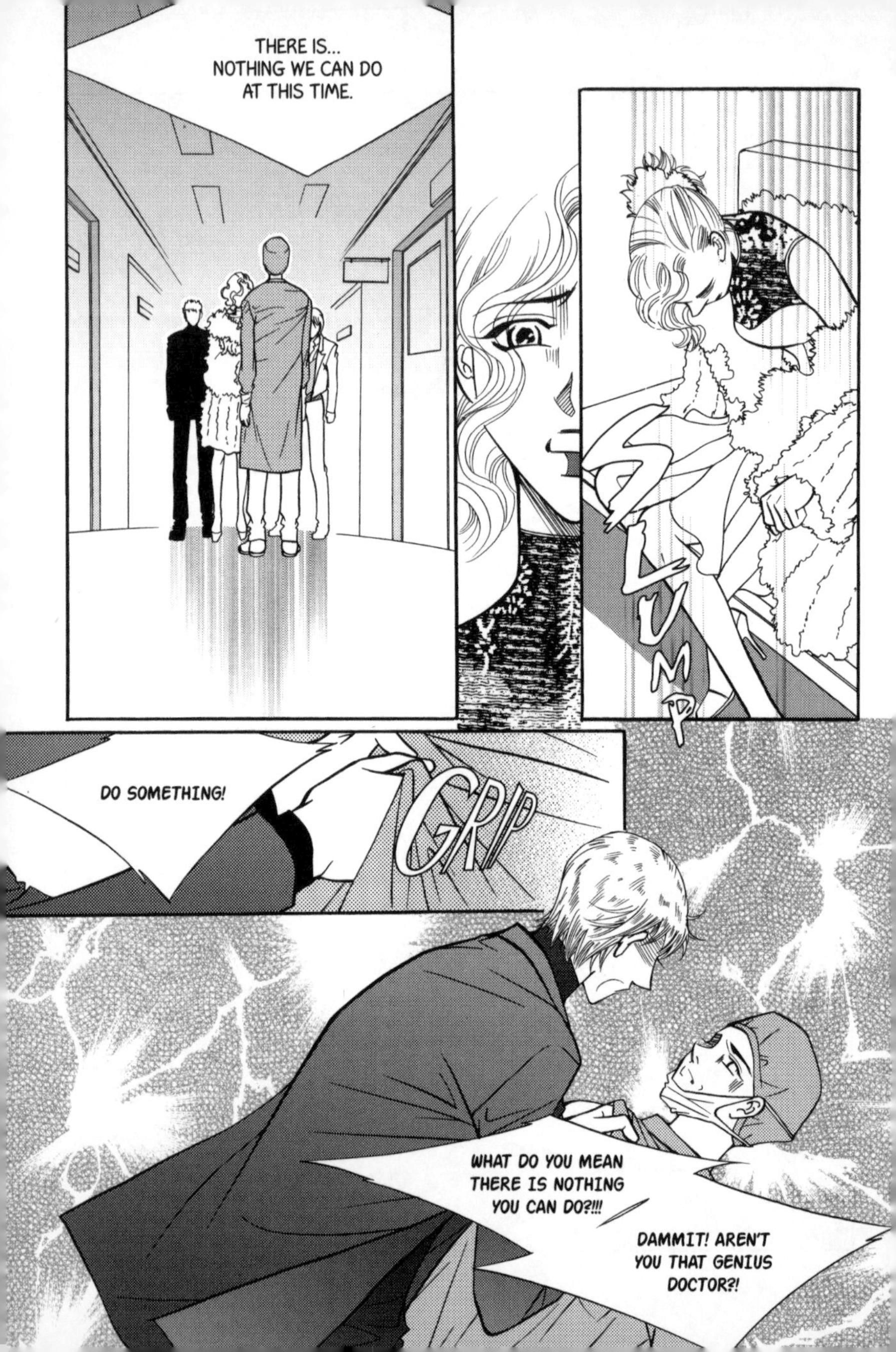
THERE IS... NOTHING WE CAN DO AT THIS TIME.
SLUMP
DO SOMETHING!
GRIP
WHAT DO YOU MEAN THERE IS NOTHING YOU CAN DO?!!!
DAMMIT! AREN'T YOU THAT GENIUS DOCTOR?!

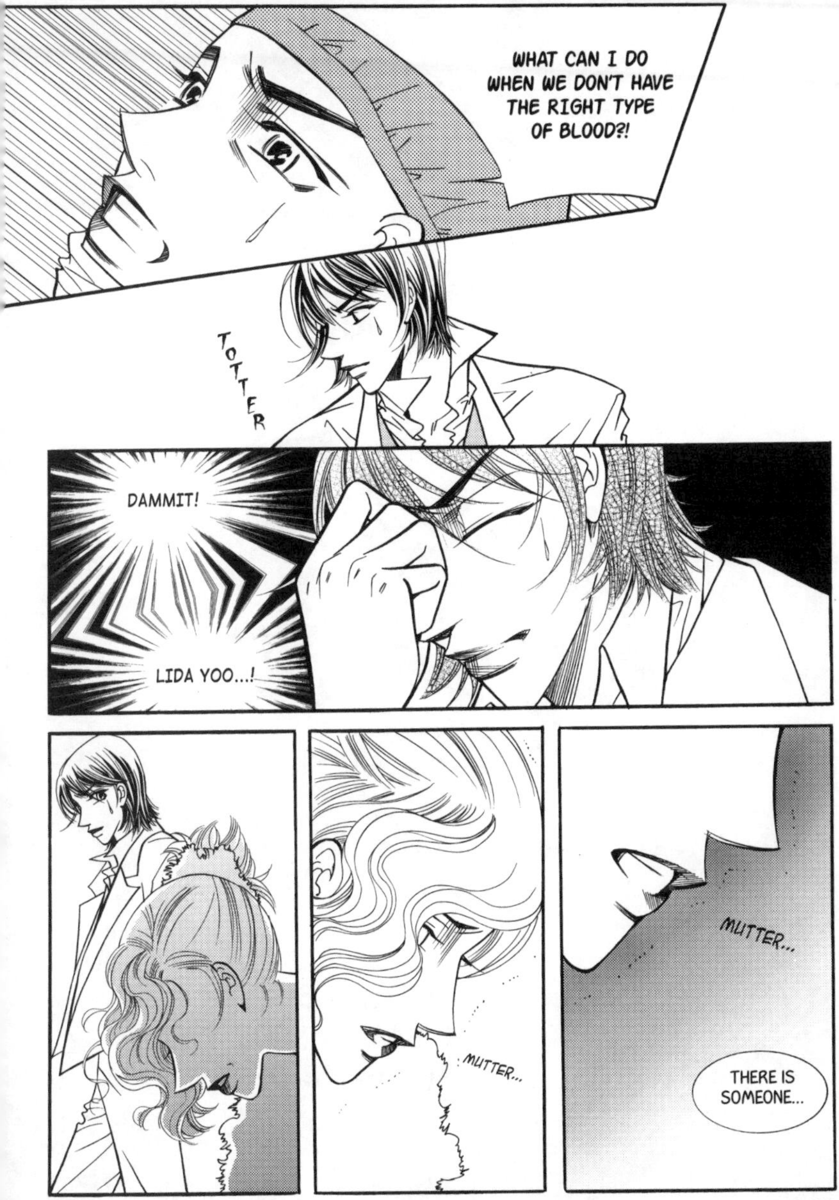
WHAT CAN I DO WHEN WE DON'T HAVE THE RIGHT TYPE OF BLOOD?!
TOTTER
DAMMIT!
LIDA YOO...!
MUTTER...
MUTTER...
THERE IS SOMEONE...

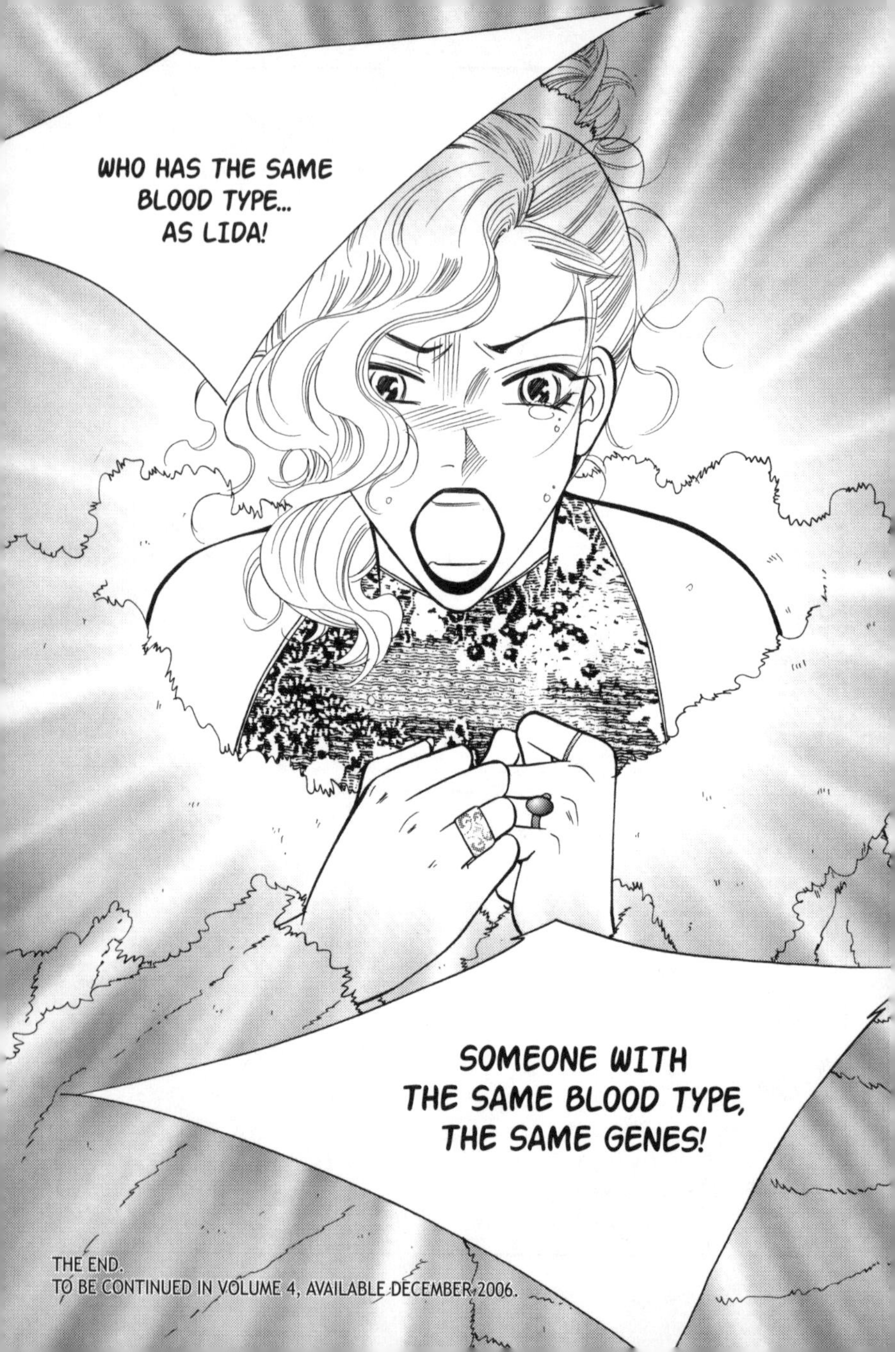
WHO HAS THE SAME BLOOD TYPE... AS LIDA!
SOMEONE WITH THE SAME BLOOD TYPE, THE SAME GENES!

THE END.
TO BE CONTINUED IN VOLUME 4, AVAILABLE DECEMBER 2006.

From Wanny's

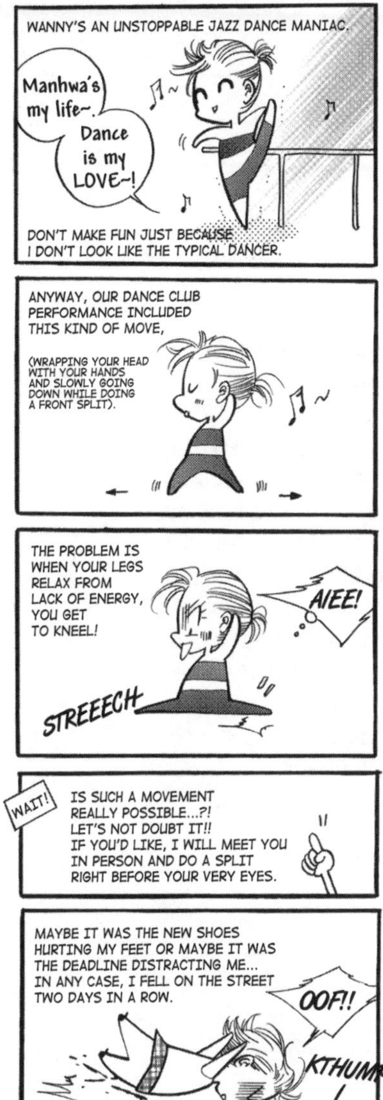
WANNY'S AN UNSTOPPABLE JAZZ DANCE MANIAC.
Manhwa's my life~.
Dance is my LOVE~!
DON'T MAKE FUN JUST BECAUSE I DON'T LOOK LIKE THE TYPICAL DANCER.
ANYWAY, OUR DANCE CLUB PERFORMANCE INCLUDED THIS KIND OF MOVE,
(WRAPPING YOUR HEAD WITH YOUR HANDS AND SLOWLY GOING DOWN WHILE DOING A FRONT SPLIT).
THE PROBLEM IS WHEN YOUR LEGS RELAX FROM LACK OF ENERGY, YOU GET TO KNEEL!
AIEE!
STREEECH
WAIT!
IS SUCH A MOVEMENT REALLY POSSIBLE...?! LET'S NOT DOUBT IT!! IF YOU'D LIKE, I WILL MEET YOU IN PERSON AND DO A SPLIT RIGHT BEFORE YOUR VERY EYES.
MAYBE IT WAS THE NEW SHOES HURTING MY FEET OR MAYBE IT WAS THE DEADLINE DISTRACTING ME... IN ANY CASE, I FELL ON THE STREET TWO DAYS IN A ROW.
OOF!!
KTHUMP!

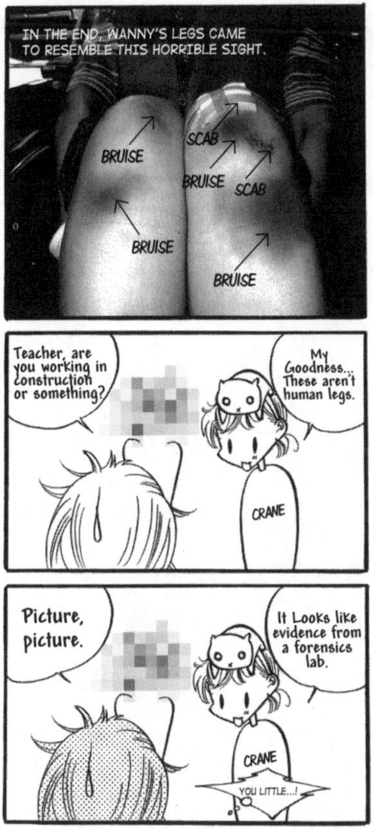
IN THE END, WANNY'S LEGS CAME TO RESEMBLE THIS HORRIBLE SIGHT.
SCAB
BRUISE
BRUISE
SCAB
BRUISE
BRUISE
Teacher, are you working in construction or something?
My Goodness... These aren't human legs.
CRANE
Picture, picture.
It Looks like evidence from a forensics lab.
CRANE
YOU LITTLE...!

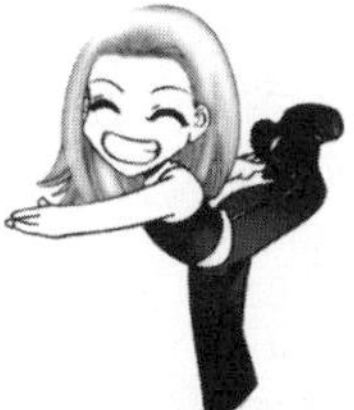

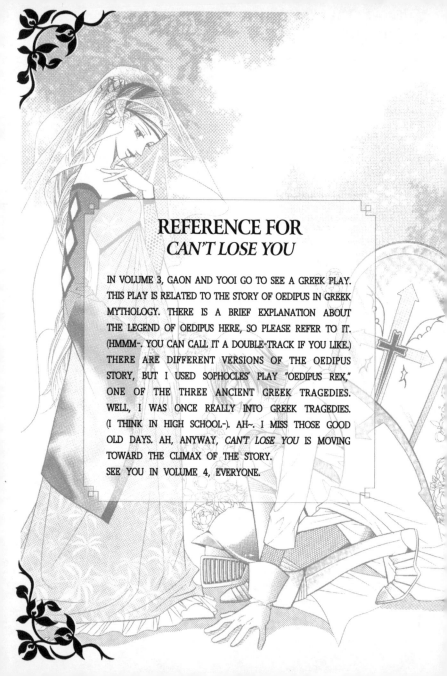

REFERENCE FOR
CAN'T LOSE YOU

IN VOLUME 3, GAON AND YOOI GO TO SEE A GREEK PLAY. THIS PLAY IS RELATED TO THE STORY OF OEDIPUS IN GREEK MYTHOLOGY. THERE IS A BRIEF EXPLANATION ABOUT THE LEGEND OF OEDIPUS HERE, SO PLEASE REFER TO IT. (HMMM~. YOU CAN CALL IT A DOUBLE-TRACK IF YOU LIKE.) THERE ARE DIFFERENT VERSIONS OF THE OEDIPUS STORY, BUT I USED SOPHOCLES' PLAY "OEDIPUS REX," ONE OF THE THREE ANCIENT GREEK TRAGEDIES. WELL, I WAS ONCE REALLY INTO GREEK TRAGEDIES. (I THINK IN HIGH SCHOOL~). AH~. I MISS THOSE GOOD OLD DAYS. AH, ANYWAY, *CAN'T LOSE YOU* IS MOVING TOWARD THE CLIMAX OF THE STORY.
SEE YOU IN VOLUME 4, EVERYONE.

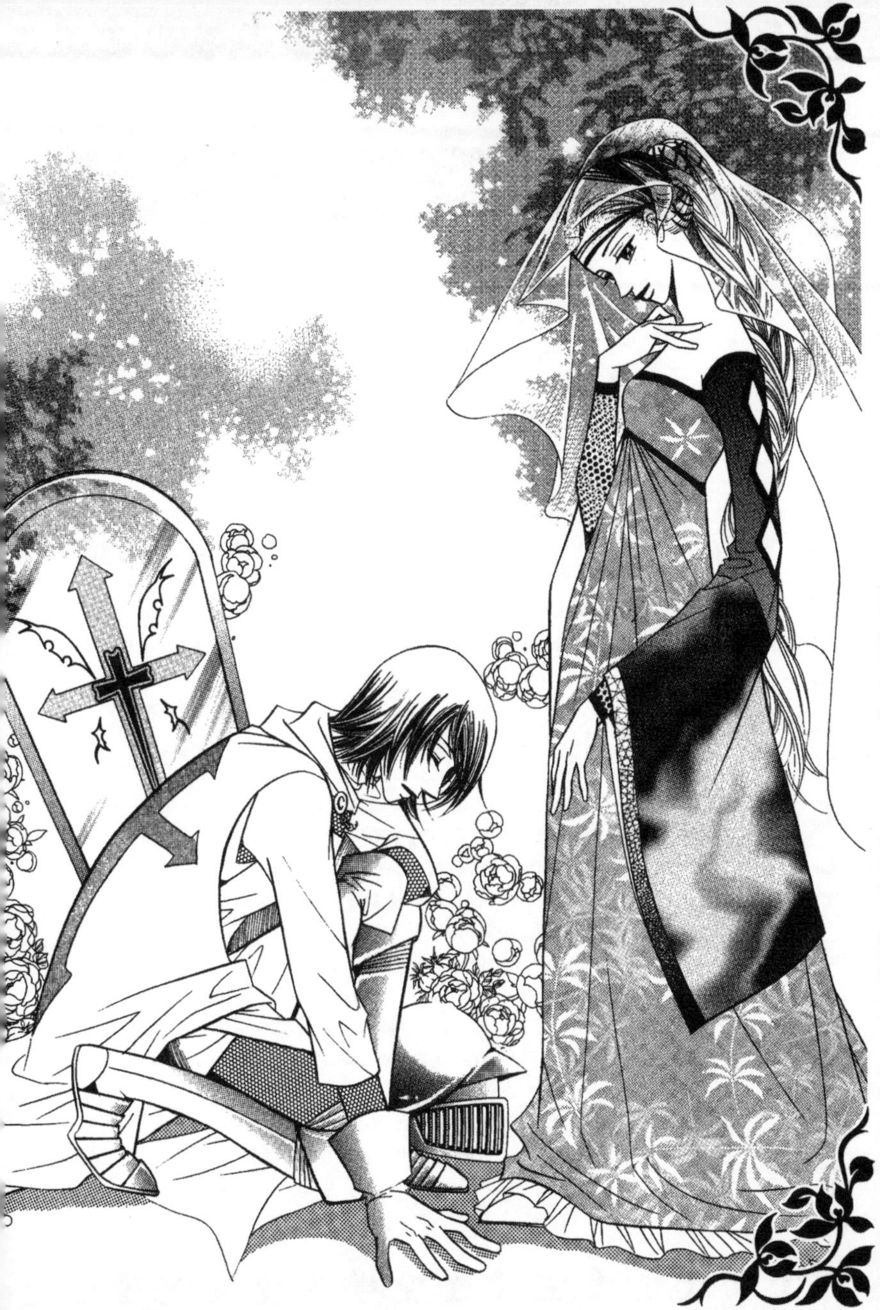

INFORMATION REGARDING THE LEGEND OF OEDIPUS

THE LEGEND OF OEDIPUS

OEDIPUS WAS BORN TO THE KING OF THEBES, KING LAIUS AND QUEEN JOCASTA. KING LAIUS HEARD A PROPHESY THAT THE CHILD BORN FROM HIS WIFE WOULD KILL HIS FATHER AND MARRY HIS MOTHER. WHEN A SON WAS BORN, THE KING PIERCED HIS BABY'S ANKLES WITH SPIKES AND HAD HIM ABANDONED IN MOUNT CITHAERON. BUT THE THEBIAN SHEPHERD WHO WAS ORDERED TO ABANDON THE BABY GAVE HIM INSTEAD TO A SHEPHERD IN CORINTH. THE SHEPHERD AND HIS WIFE TOOK THE BABY TO THE KING OF CORINTH, KING POLYBUS. THE KING AND QUEEN WERE CHILDLESS, SO THEY ADOPTED THE BABY AND NAMED HIM OEDIPUS. WHEN OEDIPUS BECAME AN ADULT AND ATTENDED A MEETING, HE HEARD THAT HE WAS NOT THE REAL SON OF KING POLYBUS. HE WENT TO INQUIRE THE ORACLE OF DELPHI IN ORDER TO FIND OUT THE TRUTH OF HIS BIRTH. THERE, HE LEARNED THAT HE WAS DESTINED TO KILL HIS FATHER AND TO MARRY HIS MOTHER. THE PRIESTS OF DELPHI CHASED HIM AWAY IN FEAR. STILL BELIEVING HIMSELF TO BE THE SON OF KING POLYBUS AND QUEEN PERIBOEA, OEDIPUS SWORE NEVER TO RETURN TO CORINTH UNTIL THEIR DEATHS AND CHOSE THE PATH TO BOEOTIA.

ON A CROSSROAD, OEDIPUS MET A STRANGER ON A CHARIOT. (IT WAS HIS BIRTH FATHER, KING LAIUS, BUT OEDIPUS DIDN'T RECOGNIZE HIM.) THE KING'S HERALD TOLD OEDIPUS TO GIVE WAY, BUT OEDIPUS DIDN'T LISTEN. THE HERALD URGED THE HORSES ON, AND A WHEEL FELL ON OEDIPUS' FOOT AND DROVE OVER IT. MOREOVER, THE STRANGER HIT OEDIPUS WITH HIS WHIP AS HE PASSED BY. IN HIS RAGE, OEDIPUS KILLED EVERYONE IN THAT GROUP EXCEPT FOR ONE SERVANT WHO RAN AWAY.

OEDIPUS CONTINUED HIS JOURNEY AND ARRIVED AT THEBES.

AT THE TIME, THEBES WAS IN FEAR OF THE MONSTER SPHINX AND WAS MOURNING FOR THEIR KING WHO HAD LEFT FOR THE ORACLE OF DELPHI AND HAD BEEN KILLED DURING HIS JOURNEY. THE QUEEN OF THEBES ANNOUNCED THAT SHE WOULD MARRY THE MAN WHO DEFEATED THE SPHINX AND WOULD GIVE HIM THE THRONE. OEDIPUS WENT TO DEFEAT THE SPHINX.

IT WAS A MONSTER WITH THE FACE OF A WOMAN, THE BODY OF A LION, AND THE WINGS OF AN EAGLE. THE SPHINX GUARDED THE ROAD AND GAVE A RIDDLE TO SOLVE TO THE PASSERSBY. IF THEY COULDN'T SOLVE THE RIDDLE, THE SPHINX WOULD DEVOUR THEM. THE SPHINX'S RIDDLE WAS: "WHAT CREATURE HAS FOUR LEGS IN THE MORNING, TWO IN THE DAY, AND THREE IN THE EVENING?" THE ANSWER WAS "MAN." WHEN OEDIPUS SOLVED THE RIDDLE, THE SPHINX THREW ITSELF INTO THE SEA AND DIED.

AFTER DEFEATING THE SPHINX, OEDIPUS MARRIED THE QUEEN AND BECAME THE KING OF THEBES.

AFTER OEDIPUS BECAME KING, FAMINE AND EPIDEMIC FELL UPON HIS PEOPLE, AND HE SOUGHT THE ORACLE OF DELPHI AGAIN. FINALLY, THE SECRET OF HIS BIRTH AND HIS PAST ACTS WERE REVEALED. THE QUEEN KILLED HERSELF AND OEDIPUS WENT MAD, DUG OUT HIS EYES, AND LEFT THEBES TO WANDER IN THE WILDERNESS. EVERYONE FEARED AND ABANDONED HIM, BUT HIS DAUGHTER FAITHFULLY CARED FOR HIM. OEDIPUS FINALLY DIED AFTER MISERABLY WANDERING FOR A LONG TIME.

ONE MORE NOTE

MKMK IS A RARE BLOOD TYPE THAT REALLY EXISTS.
BUT IT WASN'T ACTUALLY DISCOVERED IN KOREA…
A SEARCH MUST BE MADE THROUGHOUT THE WORLD FOR A BLOOD TRANSFUSION.

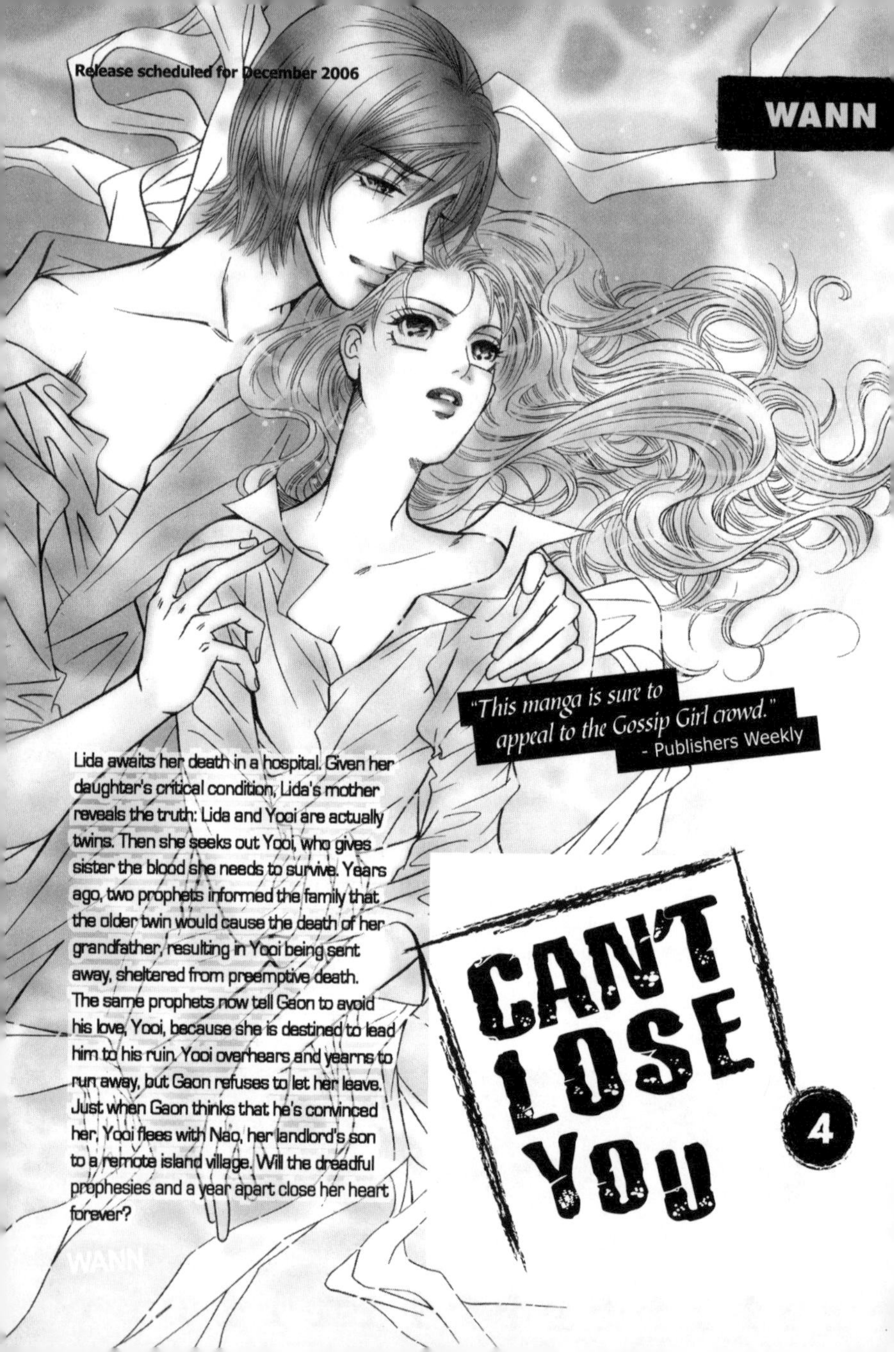
Release scheduled for December 2006
WANN
"This manga is sure to appeal to the Gossip Girl crowd."
- Publishers Weekly
Lida awaits her death in a hospital. Given her daughter's critical condition, Lida's mother reveals the truth: Lida and Yooi are actually twins. Then she seeks out Yooi, who gives sister the blood she needs to survive. Years ago, two prophets informed the family that the older twin would cause the death of her grandfather, resulting in Yooi being sent away, sheltered from preemptive death. The same prophets now tell Gaon to avoid his love, Yooi, because she is destined to lead him to his ruin. Yooi overhears and yearns to run away, but Gaon refuses to let her leave. Just when Gaon thinks that he's convinced her, Yooi flees with Nao, her landlord's son to a remote island village. Will the dreadful prophesies and a year apart close her heart forever?
CAN'T LOSE YOU
4
WANN

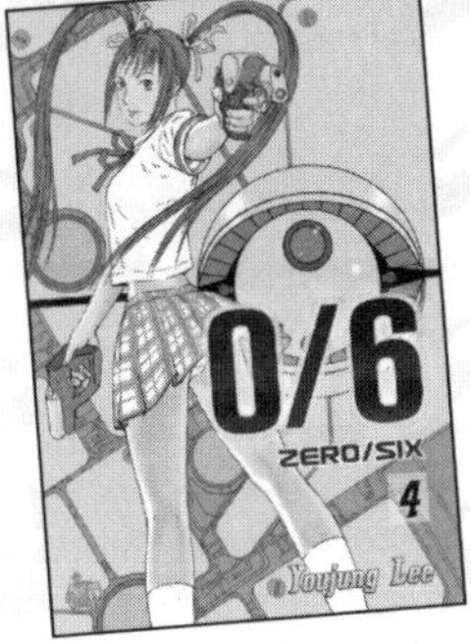
0/6
ZERO/SIX
4
Youjung Lee

0/6 (Zero/Six)

by Youjung Lee

Vol. 4

Kanghee is gone forever and her loss ripples through the school. Moolchi flees deep into the city. His aging accelerates beyond control. Meanwhile, his father returns to Korea seeking the fate of his son and determined to rescue Jong-E. Allies and enemies reveal themselves in the most unsuspecting people and places, setting the stage for Moolchi's final challenge.

Boy Princess

by Seyoung Kim

Vol. 4

Despite his tender, pleading cries, Nicole returns to his kingdom without a promise or even a sign of confidence from Jed. Nicole goes over to Jed's kingdom to change places with Elena. Meanwhile, Prince Derek and his mother conspire against Jed with dark and vicious political intrigues. Find out as the surprises of Volume 4 of *Boy Princess* unfurl!.

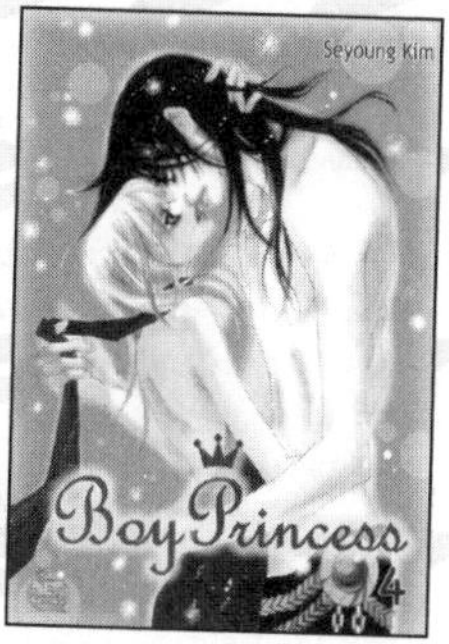
Seyoung Kim
Boy Princess
4

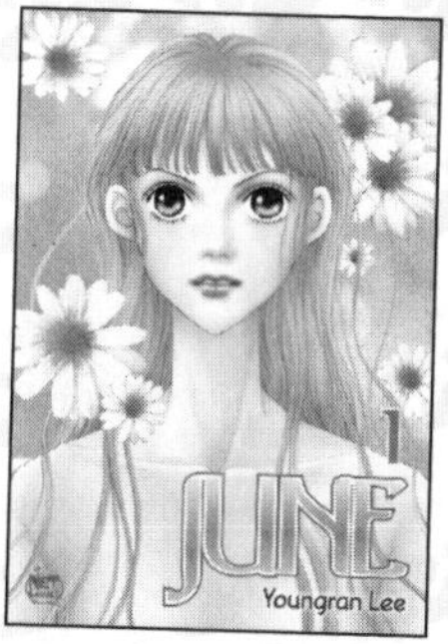
1
JUNE
Youngran Lee

June

by Youngran Lee

Vol. 1

While living a double life as a college research professor, Dr. Lee secretly participates in a human cloning project run by Dr. Suh. Through numerous trials and errors, a few clones are born. Although their methods improve, the two doctors give birth to another sub-quality clone, but this one is of Dr. Lee's wife, Jaehee. But one day, his wife gets brutally murdered and the story takes a different turn...

Releases scheduled for October 2006.
Read them online at www.NETCOMICS.com!

Let Dai

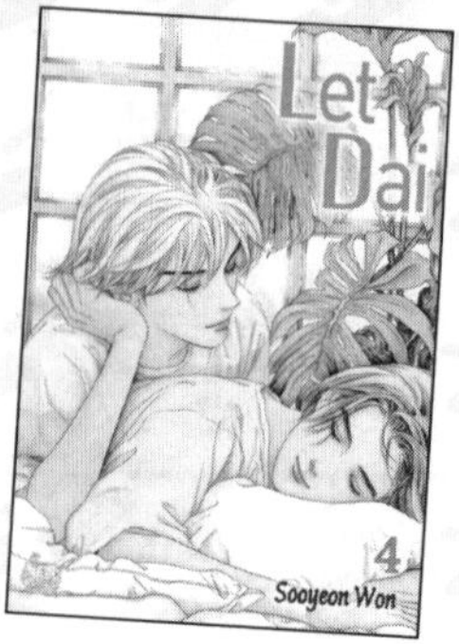
Let Dai
4
Sooyeon Won

by Sooyeon Won **Vol. 4**

To be closer to his beloved, Dai transfers to Jaehee's school, where he meets Jaehee's friend Naru. Jaehee reveals the whirlwind of anxiety Dai has brought into his life. Dai professes his love and promises never to betray Jaehee again. Meanwhile, Eunhyung can't escape her painful memories and Yooneun seeks out Jaehee again. Naru's heart finds its way to Yooneun, but the fate of their love becomes more callous when he discovers that Jaehee and Yooneun are not strangers.

Narration of Love at 17

by Kyungok Kang **Vol. 2**

Seyoung lands a minor part in a TV drama where her archrival Hyemi stars in the leading role. One evening, she finds herself at the door of Hyunwoo's house for no apparent reason, only to discover him returning home with Hyemi. Meanwhile, Yunho harbors secret feelings for Seyoung. Can Yunho, the sensitive captain of the drama club, make her forget her childhood love? And will Seyoung ever let herself move on?

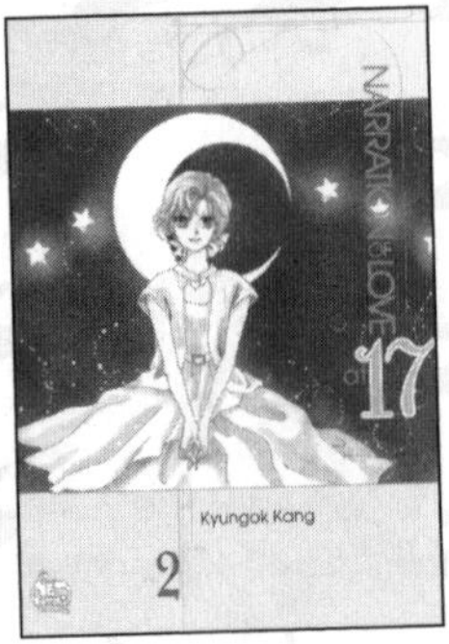
17
Kyungok Kang
2

X Diary

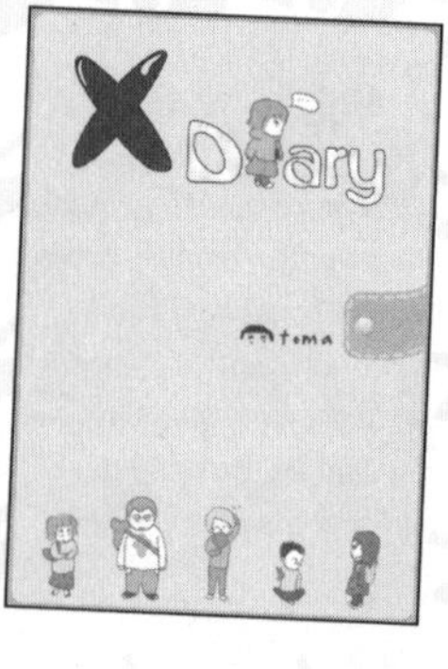
X Diary
toma

by Toma

Mingo is a cartoonist who breaks up with her easygoing musician boyfriend Jerry. They decide to stay friends, though they still have feelings for each other. Along for the ride are Mingo's younger sister Sam who has never dated, and Mingo's romantic idealist co-worker Jinjin. X Diary is a slice-of-life portrayal of two lovers who take a step back from love, and begin to look at each other once again and learn.

Releases scheduled for October 2006.
Read them online at www.NETCOMICS.com!